Oct. 7, 2008

teach®
yourself

french

D1362025

teach yourself®

french

gaëlle graham
advisory editor:
paul coggle

For over 60 years, more than 50 million people have learnt over 750 subjects the **teach yourself** way, with impressive results.

be where you want to be

For UK order enquiries: please contact Bookpoint Ltd, 130 Milton Park, Abingdon, Oxon, OX14 4SB. Telephone: +44 (0) 1235 827720. Fax: +44 (0) 1235 400454. Lines are open 09.00–17.00, Monday to Saturday, with a 24-hour message answering service. Details about our titles and how to order are available at www.teachyourself.co.uk

For USA order enquiries: please contact McGraw-Hill Customer Services, PO Box 545, Blacklick, OH 43004-0545, USA. Telephone: 1-800-722-4726. Fax: 1-614-755-5645.

For Canada order enquiries: please contact McGraw-Hill Ryerson Ltd, 300 Water St, Whitby, Ontario, L1N 9B6, Canada. Telephone: 905 430 5000. Fax: 905 430 5020.

Long renowned as the authoritative source for self-guided learning – with more than 50 million copies sold worldwide – the **teach yourself** series includes over 500 titles in the fields of languages, crafts, hobbies, business, computing and education.

British Library Cataloguing in Publication Data: a catalogue record for this title is available from the British Library.

Library of Congress Catalog Card Number: on file.

First published in UK 1998 by Hodder Education, 338 Euston Road, London, NW1 3BH.

First published in US 1998 by The McGraw-Hill Companies, Inc.

This edition published 2007.

The **teach yourself** name is a registered trade mark of Hodder Headline.

Copyright © 1998, 2003, 2007 Gaëlle Graham

Advisory Editor: Paul Coggle, University of Kent at Canterbury

Typeset by Transet Limited, Coventry, England.
Printed in Great Britain for Hodder Education, part of Hachette Livre UK, 338 Euston Road, London, NW1 3BH, by Cox & Wyman Ltd, Reading, Berkshire.

The publisher has used its best endeavours to ensure that the URLs for external websites referred to in this book are correct and active at the time of going to press. However, the publisher and the author have no responsibility for the websites and can make no guarantee that a site will remain live or that the content will remain relevant, decent or appropriate.

Hachette Livre UK's policy is to use papers that are natural, renewable and recyclable products and made from wood grown in sustainable forests. The logging and manufacturing processes are expected to conform to the environmental regulations of the country of origin.

Impression number   10 9 8 7 6 5 4 3 2
Year   2012 2011 2010 2009 2008

contents

introduction

Welcome to *Teach Yourself French!*

The aim of this book

If you are an adult learner with no previous knowledge of French and studying on your own, then this is the course for you. Perhaps you are taking up French again after a break from it, or you are intending to learn with the support of a class? Again, you will find this course very well suited to your purposes.

The language you will learn is introduced through everyday situations. The emphasis is first and foremost on using French, but we also aim to give you an idea of how the language works, so that you can create sentences of your own.

The course covers all four of the basic skills – listening and speaking, reading and writing. If you are working on your own, the recording will be all the more important, as it will provide you with the essential opportunity to listen to French and to speak it within a controlled framework. You should therefore try to get a copy of the recording if you haven't already got one.

The structure of the course

The course book contains 25 course units plus a reference section at the back. There is also an accompanying recording which you must have if you are going to get maximum benefit from the course.

Each course unit contains most or all of the following:

Statement of aims

At the beginning of each unit there is a list of what you can expect to learn by the end of that unit.

Presentation of new language

This is usually in the form of dialogues, on the recording ▶ and in the book or in reading passages. Some assistance with vocabulary is also given in the vocabulary boxes. The language is presented in manageable chunks, building carefully on what you have learned in earlier units.

Exercises

Exercises are graded so that activities which require mainly recognition come first. As you grow confident, in manipulating the language forms you will be encouraged to write and speak the language yourself.

Grammar

In these sections you will learn how to construct your own sentences correctly.

Pronunciation

The best way to acquire good pronunciation and intonation is to listen to the native speakers on the recording and to try to imitate them. However, as certain sounds in French are very unfamiliar we include specific advice on pronunciation within the course units.

Information on French-speaking countries ℹ️

Here you will find information on various aspects of everyday life such as the level of formality that is appropriate when you talk to strangers, and how the health service works if you should fall ill.

You will find a **Self-assessment test (unité de révision)** at the end of the book. This provides an opportunity for you to test yourself and judge whether you have successfully mastered the language in the book.

The **reference** section contains: a glossary of grammar terms, a key to the activities, transcripts of the recordings, a French–English glossary and an English–French glossary.

Study tips

Language learning is a bit like jogging – you need to do it regularly for it to do any good! Ideally, you should find a 'Study

Buddy' to work through the course with you. This way you will have someone to try out your French on. And when the going gets tough, you will have someone to chivvy you until you reach your target.

At the beginning of each course unit make sure that you are clear about what you can expect to learn. Read any background information that is provided, then listen to the first dialogue on the recording. Try to get the gist of what is being said before you look at the printed text in the book. Refer to the printed text and the vocabulary box in order to study the dialogues in more detail.

Don't fall into the trap of thinking that you have 'done that' when you have listened to the recording a couple of times and worked through the dialogues in the book. You may recognize what you have heard or read, but you almost certainly still have some way to go before you can produce the language of the dialogues correctly and fluently. This is why we recommend that you keep listening to the recording at every opportunity – sitting on the tube or bus, waiting at the dentist's or stuck in a traffic jam in the car – using what would otherwise be 'dead' time. Of course, you must also be internalizing what you hear and making sense of it – just playing it in the background without really paying attention is not enough!

Some of the recordings are listening-only exercises. The temptation may be to go straight to the transcriptions at the back of the book, but try not to do this. The whole point of listening exercises is to improve your listening skills. You will not do this by reading first. The transcriptions are there to help you if you get stuck.

As you work your way through the exercises, check your answers carefully in the back of the book. It is easy to overlook your own mistakes. If you have a study buddy it's a good idea to check each other's answers. Most of the exercises have fixed answers, but some are a bit more open-ended, especially when we are asking you to talk about yourself. Then, in most cases, we give you model answers which you can adapt for your own purposes.

We have tried to make the grammar explanations as user-friendly as possible, since we recognize that many people find grammar daunting. But in the end, it is up to you just how much time you spend on studying and sorting out the grammar points. Some people find that they can do better by getting an ear for what sounds right, others need to know in detail how the language is put together.

Before you move on to a new unit always check that you know all the new words and phrases in the current unit. Trying to recall the context in which words and phrases were used may help you learn them better.

We hope that you enjoy working your way through **Teach Yourself French**. Don't get discouraged. Mastering a new language does take time and perseverance and sometimes things can seem just too difficult. But then you'll come back another day and things will begin to make more sense again.

Beyond the course book

Where can I find real language?

Don't expect to be able to understand everything you hear or read straight away. If you watch French-speaking programmes on TV or buy a French magazine you should not get discouraged when you realize how quickly native-speakers speak and how much vocabulary there is still to learn. Just concentrate on a small extract – either a podcast, a video/audio clip or a short article – and work through it till you have mastered it. In this way, you will find that your command of French increases steadily.

Sources of real French

- Newspapers (*Le Monde*, *Libération*, *Le Figaro* – the weekend issue is particularly interesting)
- Magazines (*Le Nouvel Observateur*, *Cosmopolitan*, *Elle*, *Marie-Claire*, *Les Cahiers du Cinéma*, *Première*)
- Satellite TV channels (For films: Ciné Cinéma, Paris Première. For news: CNN and Euronews)
- Radio stations on long wave (France Inter 162, RTL, Europe Un). You may wish to the use the internet to download a radio programme, where possible, and listen to it again at leisure. For instance *Radio France* (which covers *France Inter*, *France Info*, *France Culture* and *France Musique*) keeps all the programmes archived for a week.
- World Wide Web: you can "google" almost anything in French and you will get directly to a French website. Each unit has a list of websites relating to the topics, which may be used, and also some short web extensions exercises, which, in most cases, can be done without internet access.

- Google *TV5* to access a whole range of francophone news programmes from all over the world.
- You may wish to use an online only daily free magazine, *France Gazette*, http://www.francegazette.com, which is specifically designed for those studying French. It gives readers access to up-to-date information on a wide range of topics, from political news to new films and to town twinning. It has a direct link *to Métro, a* free daily newspaper distributed in Paris and other main towns (Marseille, Lyon, Bordeaux, Nice, Cannes) as well as *Planetantilles*, a site with information on French overseas connections. Also *Francophonie* is a standard feature which covers cultural information, sports, political events etc. For those interested in a more in-depth use of *France Gazette* there is an archive section available on subscription.
- In London you can get information and activities at l'Institut Français, 17 Queensberry Place, London SW7 2DT (telephone 020 7073 1350 or visit www.institut.ambafrance. org.uk)

French in the modern world

Outside France, French is the first language for large communities in Belgium, Luxembourg and Switzerland. France also has four overseas **départements** which come under French administration and are part of the French Republic: Guadeloupe, Martinique, Réunion and Guyane. There are two territorial collectivities: Mayotte and St Pierre et Miquelon and other overseas territories which include Polynésie Française, Nouvelle Calédonie, Wallis-et-Futuna, terres Australes et Antarctiques (terre Adélie, Kerguelen, Crozet, St Paul).

French is also spoken in countries which have been under French rule in the past. In North Africa, French is the second language after Arabic in Tunisia, Algeria and Morocco. The same applies to many central African countries such as Senegal. There is still an ageing population which speaks and understands French in Vietnam. In North America, Louisiana still has some vestiges of the French language. In Canada, in the province of Quebec, French is spoken by many people as their first language. French in Quebec has developed differently from the French spoken in France. The accent and the intonations are very different and it has more or less become a language in its own right although its speakers can understand and communicate with French people without difficulty.

If you are able to access the website http://www.tlfq.ulaval.ca/AXL/francophonie/dom-tom.htm you can get an interactive map of the world and a detailed list showing the four French overseas **départements** and other French regions, formerly called DOM/TOM and now known as **DROM** «Départements et Régions d'Outre-Mer».

Les DOM-TOM français

01

salutations

greetings

In this unit you will learn
- how to say hello
- greetings for different times of the day
- greetings for special occasions
- a few places in the town
- food and drinks
- about gender and number

▶1 Simple greetings ✓

You may be starting to learn French because you would like to be able to communicate with people you meet for business or leisure when you travel to France or other parts of the world where French is spoken. It might be because you have French acquaintances visiting you or because your children are learning French at school. Communicating starts with very few words or, indeed, without words at all, for example shaking hands with someone, which French people do whether they are meeting friends or meeting people for the first time. It is usual to give close acquaintances two, three or even four kisses on the cheeks. If you watch young people at the terrace of a café, for example, you will see how spontaneous and communicative it all is!

The first few words are very important but also very simple. You will feel a great sense of satisfaction and achievement when you greet someone as if you have been speaking French all your life.

If you have the recording, listen to the following people saying *hello* and *goodbye*. It is day time:

Bonjour!	*Hello!*
Bonjour monsieur!	*Hello! (to a man)*
Bonjour Madame Martin!	*Hello! (to a woman – Mrs Martin)*
Salut Dominique!	*Hi!/Hello! (to a friend or acquaintance – Dominique)*
Au revoir mademoiselle!	*Goodbye (to a young, unmarried woman)*
À bientôt! À tout à l'heure!	*See you soon!*

Note that if you know someone's name, for example a neighbour, you greet them with their full name. Otherwise you greet them as **madame, monsieur** or **mademoiselle**. You usually use first names for family and close friends.

In addition, you need to know the correct greeting for each time of day:

Bonjour!	*Hello (any time in daytime)!*
Bon après-midi!	*Good afternoon!*
Bonsoir!	*Good evening!*
Bonne nuit!	*Good night!*

▶ **Exercise 1 Bonjour!**

Say the appropriate greeting to the following people:

a *Hello* to Madame Corre
b *Goodbye* to Marie-Claire
c *Good night* to Paul
d *Good afternoon* to a young woman at the cash desk in the supermarket
e *See you soon* to Monsieur Jarre

Raise your voice slightly at the end of each word or expression and make the last syllable linger a little. Now listen to the recording to check whether you have got it right. If you do not have the recording just look up the answer at the back of the book.

▶ **2 Comment ça va?** *How are you?*

Listen to the conversation between two neighbours and see whether you can tell who is feeling fine and who is feeling 'so so!'.

Madame Lebrun	Bonjour Monsieur Blanchard, comment ça va?
Monsieur Blanchard	Ça va bien merci et vous Madame Lebrun?
Madame Lebrun	Oh, comme ci, comme ça! Allez! Au revoir Monsieur Blanchard.

ℹ️ When asking somebody **Comment ça va?** it is not intended that the other person should give a full health bulletin in reply. Most of the time people reply **Ça va, ça va!** or **Ça va bien merci!** If someone replies **Comme ci, comme ça!** it indicates that all is not well, things could be better, but the person is unlikely to disclose more unless they are asked further questions.

When you listen to French people talking you are very likely to hear **Allez!** which comes from **Aller** *to go.*

It is almost impossible to translate **Allez!** but you are likely to hear it said before greetings, especially (but not always) when people want to indicate that they wish to terminate the conversation. It roughly means *Well then* I'll leave you to your food or to your fishing, or to whatever the other person is doing or about to do:

Allez, à bientôt!
Allez, bon appétit! (to someone eating or about to start a meal)
Allez, bonne pêche! (to someone fishing or collecting shellfish on the beach)

▶ **Exercise 2   Cherchez la bonne phrase** *Find the right expression*

Listen to some more greetings on the recording. Try to match them to the correct English expressions.

1 Allez, bon voyage!	**a** Have a good weekend!
2 Bon week-end!	**b** Happy birthday!
3 Allez, bonne route!	**c** Have a good journey!
4 Bonnes vacances!	**d** Happy New Year!
5 Bonne Année!	**e** Have a safe journey!
6 Bon anniversaire!	**f** Have a good holiday!

Check your answers at the back of the book.

▶3 À votre santé! *To your good health!*

French people always find a good reason to drink a toast. You will hear:

À votre santé! *To your (good) health!*	⎫ These are said to all those assembled, or individually to someone you would address formally.
À la vôtre! *To yours!*	
À ta santé! *To your (good) health!*	⎫ These are said to one person you know well.
À la tienne! *To yours!*	
Santé! *Good health! Cheers!*	

▶ Exercise 3 Quelle est la fête? *What's the celebration?*

Listen to the recording. You will hear three very short scenes. You have to decide what is being celebrated in each of of them:

Dialogue 1

– Bonne Année!
– À votre santé!
– Santé!
– À la vôtre!

A la vôtre!

Are they celebrating:

a a good holiday?   **b** a wedding?   **c** New Year?

Dialogue 2

– Bon Anniversaire Françoise!
– À la santé de Françoise!
– À la tienne Françoise!
– À la vôtre!

Are they celebrating:

a a good journey?   **b** a birthday?   **c** a good holiday?

Dialogue 3

– À la santé des mariés!
– À la santé d'Estelle et Paul!
– À la vôtre!

Are they celebrating:

a a wedding?   b an anniversary?   c New Year?

Vivent les mariés!

Vivent les mariés!	*Long live the bride and groom!*
Vive le marié!	*Long live the groom!*
Vive la mariée!	*Long live the bride!*

🛈 Le PACS (PActe Civil de Solidarité): a new law voted on 15 November 1999 gives the same rights to married and unmarried couples.

There are more and more French couples who do not get married. For example Ségolène Royal, the 2007 socialist presidential candidate and her partner François Hollande, Secretary of the French Socialist Party are not married and have four children. Some people now enter into a contract, which gives couples the same civil rights and responsibilities as married couples. It can also apply to same sex couples.

4 Buying and paying

All you need to know is the name of what you would like to buy and how to ask for the price. Saying *please* and *thank you* will help you feel confident that you can express yourself, even if you are only using a few words.

S'il vous plaît (S.V.P.)	please
Merci	thank you
Merci bien	thanks a lot
C'est combien?	How much is it?
L'addition s'il vous plaît!	The bill please!

Un sandwich et un coca s'il vous plaît!

▶ Exercise 4 Où sont-ils? *Where are they?*

Look at the illustrations and listen to the three short dialogues.

Dialogue 1
Are the people **a** at home? **b** at a grocery shop? **c** in the street?

Dialogue 2
Are the people **a** in church? **b** in a café? **c** at a grocery shop?

Dialogue 3
Are the people **a** at the station? **b** in the street? **c** at a grocery shop?

Now check your answers by reading the dialogues you have just heard.

Dialogue 1

– Taxi! Taxi! La gare du Nord s'il vous plaît!
– Oui madame!

Dialogue 2

– Un café, une bière et un sandwich au fromage s'il vous plaît.
– Oui monsieur.
– L'addition s'il vous plaît.

Dialogue 3

– Une baguette, un camembert et un kilo de pommes s'il vous plaît.
– Oui mademoiselle!
– Merci bien. C'est combien?
– Cinq euros mademoiselle.

Exercise 5

Look again at the three dialogues above and find the French expressions for the following:

a a kilo of apples
b five euros
c a cheese sandwich
d a beer
e the station

Now check your answers at the back of the book.

5 Dans la rue *In the street*

You want to find out where some places are in the village. The important thing is to know what to ask for, then people will point you in the right direction.

Pardon madame, la boulangerie s'il vous plaît?	*Excuse me, where is the baker's please?*

Try to guess which places are mentioned in the following examples.

a Pardon monsieur, la poste s'il vous plaît?
b Pardon mademoiselle, l'office du tourisme s'il vous plaît?
c Pardon madame, le supermarché s'il vous plaît?
d Pardon madame, le garage Citroën s'il vous plaît?

Grammar

So far you may have noticed three different ways of spelling the word for *good*:

Bon voyage!
Bonne année!
Bonnes vacances!

This is because in French, nouns (words which represent objects, people or ideas) have a gender; they can be either feminine or masculine. **Un voyage** *a journey* is masculine, **une année** *a year* is feminine, **des vacances** *holidays* is feminine but also plural.

The gender of nouns does not follow any logical pattern so you will need to be aware of the gender of every noun you learn.

Bon, bonne and **bons, bonnes** are four forms of the same adjective (a word which describes a noun) and they have the same gender as the nouns they describe, so we have masculine and feminine adjectives which can both be singular or plural.

French adjectives are spelt differently according to their genders. Generally (but not always) an -e at the end of an adjective is for feminine, an -s is for plural.

More examples:

If we take two other nouns **un raisin** *grape* (masc.) and **une pomme** *apple* (fem.) we have four spellings for **bon**:

un **bon** raisin *a good grape*   une **bonne** pomme *a good apple*
des **bons** raisins *good grapes*   des **bonnes** pommes *good apples*

des = *some/more than one*

▶ Pronunciation

- **Ça va** – C with a cedilla (ç) sounds like an **s**. It is only used in front of **a**, **o** and **u**: ça [sa], ço [so] and çu [su].
  Note that there is no cedilla in **merci** and that in **comme ci, comme ça** – only **ça** needs a cedilla.
- **Comment** – the -t at the end is silent and -en- is pronounced in a nasal fashion.
- **Année, santé, enchanté, présente, appétit** all have an e with an acute accent. It changes the neutral e sound into one close to the first sound in *ready*.

• Bon appétit – the two words are pronounced as if they were one. Because the second word starts with a vowel the -n of **bon** is linked to the a- of **appétit,** making **bon** sound like **bonne.** The same happens with **bon après-midi.**

Exercise 6 La liste de provisions *The shopping list*
Make your own shopping list using all the words for food and drinks in the unit.

1 kilo de pommes

▶ 6 Say it! *Dites-le!*

Explication: dites comes from the verb **dire** (*to say*)

e.g. Dites-le avec des fleurs (*say it with flowers*)
          des chocolats
          un livre
          une carte

Grandmother (**Grand-mère**) is telling the children (**les enfants**) what to say. Please respond as if you were the children

| **Grand-mère** | Dites bonjour à Elise. |
| **Les enfants** | Bonjour Elise! |

| **Grand-mère** | Dites au revoir à Papa. |
| **Les enfants** | Au revoir Papa! |

| **Grand-mère** | Dites bon anniversaire à Maman. |
| **Les enfants** | Bon anniversaire Maman! |

| **Grand-mère** | Dites bonnes vacances à Mademoiselle Lapierre. |
| **Les enfants** | Bonnes vacances Mademoiselle Lapierre! |

| **Grand-mère** | Dites bonne fête à Catherine. |
| **Les enfants** | Bonne fête Catherine! |

Surfez sur le web

- To send your best wishes in French you can find cards with greetings on the internet: http://carte.dromadaire.com/fr/

- **Entraînez-vous sur le web**
  Find the card category: **A fêter** *(to celebrate)* and click on the type of card you may use to celebrate 1. a wedding 2. a friend's name day 3. Bastille Day.

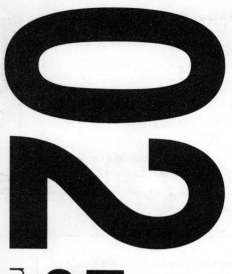

02

premiers contacts
meeting people

In this unit you will learn
- how to give and understand information about marital status, family links, age and profession
- numbers up to sixty-nine
- four verbs: être *to be*, parler *to speak*, s'appeler *to be called*, avoir *to have*

▶ 1 Enchanté de faire votre connaissance *Pleased to meet you*

There is a wedding in the family. People have travelled from all over the place. At the dinner table two people who have never met before find out each other's names and where they come from.

Listen to the recording.

a What is the man's name?

Now read the dialogue:

Homme Bonjour, je m'appelle Alain. Et vous, comment vous appelez-vous?
Femme Je m'appelle Claire.
Homme Enchanté de faire votre connaissance, Claire! Vous êtes d'où?
Femme Je suis de Paris. Et vous?
Homme Moi, je suis de Marseille.

b What is the woman's name?
c Where is Claire from?
d Where is Alain from?

un homme	*a man*
une femme	*a woman*
Comment vous appelez-vous?	*What is your name?*
Je m'appelle ...	*My name is ...*
Vous êtes d'où?	*Where are you from?*
moi	*me*

Find the French for:

e I am from Paris.
f Pleased to meet you.

To say where you are from you can name a town or a country:

Je suis de Bordeaux   Je suis de New York
Je suis de Londres   Je suis du Canada
Je suis du Pays de Galles   *I am from Wales*
Je suis des États-Unis   *I am from the United States*

▶ Exercise 1 D'où êtes-vous? *Where are you from?*

You are François or Françoise, a guest at the wedding. You are from Boulogne. Fill in your part of the dialogue.

Lucien	Bonjour, je m'appelle Lucien. Et vous, comment vous appelez-vous?
Vous	**a** *Give your name.*
Lucien	Enchanté de faire votre connaissance. D'où êtes-vous?
Vous	**b** *Say where you are from. Say 'And you?' to ask where Lucien is from.*
Lucien	Je suis de Bruxelles.

Now do the exercise again, using your own identity.

Grammar

▶ 1 Des nombres et des chiffres
Numbers and figures

The following table should allow you to work out numbers from 0 to 69.

0	zéro	10	dix	21	vingt et un
1	un	11	onze	22	vingt-deux
2	deux	12	douze	23	vingt-trois
3	trois	13	treize	30	trente
4	quatre	14	quatorze	31	trente et un
5	cinq	15	quinze	32	trente-deux
6	six	16	seize	40	quarante
7	sept	17	dix-sept	50	cinquante
8	huit	18	dix-huit	60	soixante
9	neuf	19	dix-neuf	61	soixante et un
		20	vingt	69	soixante-neuf

Look at the numbers above, listen to how they sound, and repeat after the speaker.

▶ Exercise 2 Le Loto
Look at the KENO® grid on the next page and answer the questions which follow:

a For each grid how many numbers can you tick?

b How many winning numbers are drawn every day?

c How much does it cost if you have two draws? If you have one draw?

d Listen to the recording. Write down all the numbers you hear and find out if you have any of the winning numbers.

ℹ Did you know that the French National Lottery started in 1918 to fund the war widows' pensions, soldiers' disability pensions and the upkeep and education of the First World War orphans?

In 1933 it officially became **la Loterie Nationale** and it existed as such until 1990. The lottery is now run by a body called **La Française des Jeux.**

▶ 2 Je suis la mère d'Isabelle
I am Isabelle's mother

Isabelle Lejeune and David Miller are getting married in Rouen in Normandy. David is English but works in France. Isabelle is French. At the wedding there are lots of people from both families. Listen to one of the conversations where people introduce themselves.

Listen for the first time to the recording.

a Who is Hélène Lejeune?
b Whose aunt is Anne Thompson?

Listen once more.

c Is Anne Thompson English?
d What is her husband's name?

Listen a final time.

e Where does she live?

Madame Lejeune	Bonjour Madame, je m'appelle Hélène Lejeune. Je suis la mère d'Isabelle. Et vous comment vous appelez-vous?

Anne Thompson	Enchantée de faire votre connaissance. Je m'appelle Anne Thompson, je suis la tante de David.
Madame Lejeune	Ah, vous êtes anglaise?
Anne Thompson	Non, non, je suis française. Je suis mariée à Mark Thompson, l'oncle de David. J'habite en Angleterre.
Madame Lejeune	Ah très bien! Enchantée!
Anne Thompson	Voici mon fils Raphaël et voilà ma fille Sophie. Raphaël, Sophie, je vous présente Madame Lejeune, la maman d'Isabelle.
Raphaël	Bonjour Madame.
Sophie	Bonjour.

Now read the written dialogue and try to find out how to say the following in French:

f I live in England   **i** My son
g David's aunt   **j** My daughter
h Let me introduce you to Madame ...

Check your answers at the back of the book.

Grammar

2 Voici/voilà *This is/that is*

Voici is used when introducing a first person, standing next to you.
Voilà is for introducing a second person, possibly standing further away from you.

More generally:

Voici is for pointing out someone or something close by.
Voilà is for pointing out someone or something slightly further away from you.

3 La famille *The family*

      1   2   3   4   5

1 Voici Jacques, le frère de Monsieur Norbert.
2 Voici Gaétan, le fils des Norbert.
3 Voici Madame Norbert.
4 Voici Monsieur Norbert.
5 Et voilà Joëlle, la fille des Norbert.

Voici la famille Charcot et **voilà la famille Bastide**

▶3 Tu as quel âge? *How old are you?*

The children at the wedding are getting to know one another.

Read what they say.

Camille Bonjour, je m'appelle Camille ... et toi comment tu t'appelles?
Sophie Moi, je m'appelle Sophie. Et mon frère s'appelle Raphaël.
Camille Moi je suis la sœur d'Isabelle. Je n'ai pas de frère.
Sophie Tu as quel âge?
Camille J'ai douze ans.
Sophie Ah moi aussi j'ai douze ans! Mon frère, il a quatorze ans.

la sœur	*the sister*	**ma soeur**	*my sister*
le frère	*the brother*	**mon frère**	*my brother*
moi	*me*	**toi**	*you*

Note that to say *my* in French you must use **ma** in front of a feminine word and **mon** in front of a masculine word.

Find the French for the following:

a I am twelve years old.
b My brother, he is fourteen.
c I don't have a brother.
d Me too!
e How old are you?

▶ Pronunciation

In French, words tend to be linked together, particularly when the second of two words starts with a vowel. When saying her age Camille says **J'ai douze ans**. These four short words are heard as two groups of sounds: [*jai douzan*].

Sophie says of her brother **Il a quatorze ans** which, again, is heard as two sets of sounds: [*ila quatorzan*].

It is important to know how the numbers are spelt because the last letter of the number is always linked with **an(s)** *year*. Here are some more examples:

Isabelle? Elle a vingt-cinq ans. [*ella vintcincan*]
Danielle? Elle a trente ans. [*ella trentan*]

Note that the **e** at the end of **trente, quarante**, etc. is not heard.

Arnaud? Il a neuf ans. [*ila neuvan*]

(an **f** sounds like a **v** when linking two words)

▶ Exercise 3 Quel âge avez-vous?

Try saying the following in French:

a I am twenty-one years old.
b He is thirty-eight.
c She is sixty-nine.
d He is forty.

Now listen to the recording to hear the answers.

▶ 4 Vous parlez français?
Do you speak French?

Still at the wedding, Hélène and Anne discuss which language is spoken in the Thompson household.

Listen to the recording a few times and see whether you can answer the following questions.

a Which two languages are mentioned?
b Does she speak English or French with Mark, her husband?
c What does Mark teach?

Hélène Lejeune	Vous parlez français avec les enfants?
Anne Thompson	Oui, je parle français à la maison. Les enfants parlent couramment les deux langues.
Hélène Lejeune	Et avec Mark?
Anne Thompson	Avec mon mari je parle français ou anglais, cela dépend. Il parle bien le français, il est professeur de français.

avec	*with*	**couramment**	*fluently*
à la maison	*at home*	**mon mari**	*my husband*
les enfants	*the children*	**professeur**	*teacher*

Find the French for the following in the dialogue.

d He is a French teacher.
e It depends.
f I speak French or English.
g I speak French at home.
h The children speak both languages fluently.
i He speaks French well.

Grammar

4 Verbs

In this unit you have already come across four important verbs. (A verb is the part of the language used to indicate an action or state of things.) Here is what you have learnt so far:

Être *to be*

Je **suis** française.	*I am French.*
Je **suis** mariée.	*I am married.*
Il **est** anglais.	*He is English.*
Il **est** professeur.	*He is a teacher.*
Vous **êtes** anglaise?	*Are you English?*

Être indicates a state of things.

Avoir *to have*

J'**ai** trente ans.	*I am (have) thirty (years).*
Il **a** dix ans.	*He is ten.*

Elle a vingt-cinq ans.   *She is twenty-five.*
Je n'ai pas de frère.   *I don't have a brother.*

S'appeler *to be called*

This a reflexive verb, that is, the subject and the object of the verb are one and the same. Word for word **s'appeler** means *to call oneself.*

Comment **vous appelez-vous?** *What's your name?* (lit. *How do you call yourself?*)

Je m'appelle Anne.   *I am called Anne.*
Comment **tu t'appelles?**   *What's your name?* (when speaking to a child or someone you know well)

Parler *to speak*

Je parle français.   *I speak French.*
Je parle anglais.   *I speak English.*
Vous parlez français?   *Do you speak French?*
Ils parlent français.   *They speak French.* (the **nt** in **ils parlent** is not pronounced)

▶ Exercise 4 Cherchez la bonne phrase

Listen to these French expressions. Link them to their English equivalents.

1 I am not married.
2 What's his name?
3 He has a brother and a sister.
4 I don't have a sister.
5 I don't speak English.

a Je n'ai pas de sœur.
b Je ne parle pas anglais.
c Je ne suis pas mariée.
d Il a un frère et une sœur.
e Comment il s'appelle?

Exercise 5 Qui est-ce?

Who is it? Read the explanations below and say what the family link is likely to be:

Your father? Your cousin? Your aunt? Your brother? Your grandmother?

a C'est la mère de mon père.
b C'est le mari de ma mère.
c C'est la sœur de mon père.
d C'est la fille du frère de ma mère.
e C'est le fils de mes parents.

Listen and say which of the following people from my family is the odd one out.

▶ Exercise 6 Trouvez l'intrus (literally *find the intruder*)

1 Annie, mon amie
2 ma mère
3 ma sœur
4 ma tante
5 mon oncle
6 ma cousine

Surfez sur le web

- Google "origine des noms et prénoms" or go to http://www.lexilogos.com/noms_prenoms.htm
- Research the origin and popularity, in France, of four of the first names used in this unit: Anne, Hélène, David and Raphaël.
- You may find other sites and try your luck with your own first name and surname.

BONNE CHANCE!

03

on fait connaissance

getting to know someone

In this unit you will learn
- how to introduce yourself fully
- how to understand what other people say about themselves
- how to talk and ask about professions, employment and unemployment, leisure activities, like and dislikes
- how to talk further about marital status and families

1 **En stage** *On a training course*

A group of people of all ages and backgrounds are on a weekend course (**un stage**) in Paris preparing for an amateur photography expedition to Vietnam. The first thing they do is a self-introduction exercise to get to know one another.

The course participants (**les stagiaires**) have been asked to say the following things about themselves:

- Name
- Age
- Town/area where they live
- Marital status + family details
- Profession
- Languages spoken
- Likes (leisure, hobbies)
- Dislikes

They all give the information in different ways, so listen for the expressions they use to say their name, their profession and what they like or dislike.

Listen to what the first person says and then stop the recording. You may need to listen more than once to understand what is being said.

▶ 2 Natalie Le Hénaff

J'aime faire de la photographie.

Je n'aime pas faire le ménage.

Without looking at the text below can you answer the following questions about Natalie?

a How old is she?
b Is she married?
c How many children does she have?
d Does she speak English?
e Can you tell at least one thing she likes doing?

Listen to the recording again but this time you may look at the text.

"Bonjour! Je m'appelle Natalie Le Hénaff. J'ai trente-six ans.
J'habite à Vannes en Bretagne.
Je suis mariée. J'ai deux enfants, un garçon et une fille.
Je suis professeur d'histoire dans un collège.
Je parle français, anglais et espagnol.
J'aime aller au cinéma, voyager, lire et faire de la photographie.
Je n'aime pas faire le ménage."

From the text above can you tell which French expressions Natalie uses to say the following things?

f I am a history teacher.
g I love travelling.
h I live in Vannes in Britanny.
i I love going to the cinema.
j I don't like doing the housework.

Grammar

1 Saying what your job is

In French there is no indefinite article (*a* or *an* in English) in front of the name of a profession.

Natalie says she is a history teacher in a secondary school:

Je suis professeur d'histoire dans un collège.

The next person, Antoine Durand (see page 26), says he is a sound engineer for a French TV channel, France 3:

Je suis ingénieur du son à France 3.

The omission of the indefinite article also applies when Antoine says he is a bachelor:

Je suis célibataire.

(**Célibataire** is used for both unmarried men and women.)

2 How to express likes

- **J'aime** *(I like/love)*
- **J'aime bien** *(I like / I quite like)*
- **J'aime beaucoup...** *(I like ... a lot)*
- **J'adore** *(I adore/love)*

Je becomes **j'** in front of **aime** because **aime** starts with a vowel. The same rule applies with **adore** and with all other verbs starting with a vowel. **e** is the only letter which can be replaced by an apostrophe in front of a vowel.

3 ... and dislikes

- **Je n'aime pas**

To make a verb negative (the equivalent of adding *not* in English), use **ne ... pas** (**ne** + verb + **pas**). Here **ne** becomes **n'** before a vowel (**aime**):

Je n'aime pas faire le ménage. *I don't like doing the housework.*

You can also use expressions such as:

Je déteste or **J'ai horreur de...** *I really don't like / I hate...*

▶ Pronunciation

Look back at what Natalie says and find all the apostrophes. In each case, an apostrophe replaces an -e because the word that follows begins with a vowel or an **h**:

There is also one example of **de** losing its **e** in front of a vowel sound: **professeur d'histoire**. Here and in **j'habite**, the **h** is silent.

All these expressions are pronounced as if they were one word:

je **ma**ppelle / **j**ai / **j**abite / **j**aime / je **nai**me pas / professeur **d**istoire.

▶ 3 Antoine Durand

Try to answer the following questions about Antoine after listening to the next part of the recording a few times:

a How old is he?
b Where does he live? *Paris*
c What foreign language does he speak? *German & French*
d What does he like doing best?

Now look at the text: *29*

"Alors moi, mon nom c'est Antoine Durand. J'ai vingt-neuf ans.
Je demeure à Paris.
Je suis célibataire.
Je suis ingénieur du son à France 3.
Je parle français et allemand.
J'aime bien regarder des films et le sport à la télé. J'adore la photographie et les voyages.
J'ai horreur des voitures, alors je vais au travail à vélo."

Using the text above find out the following expressions:

e I live in Paris.
f I like watching films on TV.
g I hate cars.
h I go to work by bike.

Grammar

4 Alors

As soon as you hear French people talking amongst themselves you will hear **alors** or **bon, alors** or **oui, alors**. It loosely means **then** or **so**, similar to someone saying *well / so then...* in English. It is used to fill a gap in the conversation. It also means *therefore*.

Task: Find two different uses of **alors** in what Antoine Durand says.

▶ 4 Monique Duval

Listen to the next part of the recording and answer the following questions about Monique:

a How old is she?
b Who is Pierre?
c Where does she work?
d Does she speak English?
e How does she feel about football on TV?

Now read the text below:

"Bonjour, je m'appelle Monique Duval. J'ai quarante-cinq ans. Je suis de Dijon.
Je suis mariée à Pierre mais je n'ai pas d'enfants. Pierre a un fils d'un premier mariage. Il s'appelle Guillaume, il a vingt-cinq ans mais il ne travaille pas, il est au chômage.
Je travaille à la poste.
Je parle un peu l'anglais et j'apprends le vietnamien.
J'aime beaucoup le sport, les voyages et la photographie.
Je déteste le football à la télévision."

Using the text above find out the following expressions:

f I work at the post office.
g I speak a little bit of English.
h I don't have any children.
i I am learning Vietnamese.
j He is unemployed.

▶ 5 Pierre Duval

Listen to Pierre speaking on the recording and answer the following questions:

a How old is Pierre?
b What is his wife's name?
c Where does he work?
d Where does he live?

Now read the text of what Pierre said:

"Alors je me présente: je m'appelle Duval Pierre.
J'ai cinquante-deux ans. J'habite à Dijon.
Je suis marié à Monique.
Ma mère est veuve et elle habite chez nous.
Je travaille chez Renault.
Je comprends un peu l'anglais.
J'adore les voyages et la lecture.
Je n'aime pas la télé sauf les documentaires sur les voyages."

The following words help you to understand what Pierre is saying.

avec	with	**sauf**	except
chez	at	**veuve**	widow/widowed (woman)

Using the text above find out the following expressions:

e My mother is a widow.
f I work at Renault.
g She lives with us.
h I love travel and reading.
i I don't like TV except travel documentaries.
j I understand English a little.

Grammar

5 Le nom de famille

When French people are introducing themselves in a formal way they often mention their surname first and then their first name:

Note that Pierre Duval says: **Je m'appelle Duval Pierre.** This is also the way names are written on envelopes for administrative or commercial purposes:

Monsieur Duval Pierre
16 Avenue de la Gare
DIJON

6 Quelles questions?

There is always more than one way to ask a question. Here are standard questions and answers about personal details.

Topics	Questions	Answers
Name	Comment vous appelez-vous? Quel est votre nom?	Je m'appelle Nathalie. Mon nom c'est Josianne.
Age	Quel âge avez-vous? Vous avez quel âge?	J'ai trente-deux ans. J'ai cinquante ans.
Where living	Où habitez-vous? Où est-ce que vous habitez? Où est-ce que vous demeurez?	J'habite à Nantes. Je demeure à Bordeaux.
Marital status	Vous êtes marié(e)?	Oui, je suis marié(e). Non, je suis célibataire.
Profession	Quelle est votre profession? Quel est votre métier? Quel travail faites-vous? Où est-ce que vous travaillez?	Je suis dentiste. Je suis dans le commerce. Je travaille chez Renault.
Languages	Quelles langues parlez-vous? Vous parlez anglais?	Je parle français et anglais. Oui, un petit peu.
Likes	Vous aimez le cinéma? Vous aimez le football?	Oui, j'adore le cinéma. Non, j'ai horreur du football.

Exercise 1 Je m'appelle...

You are a participant on the Paris photography course. Try to make a statement giving the following information:

- Your name is Anne-Marie Pélerin
- You are 45
- You live in Boulogne
- You are a dentist
- You speak French, English and German
- You love football and photography

Exercise 2 Questions et réponses

You will need to look back at the statements made by the people on the photography course. In the box opposite enter the missing questions or the missing answers.

Names	Questions	Answers
Natalie	Comment vous appelez-vous?	
Antoine	Quel âge avez-vous?	
Natalie		Je suis professeur d'histoire
Monique	Où travaillez-vous?	
Pierre		J'habite à Dijon
Antoine		Je parle français et allemand
Monique		Oui, j'aime beaucoup le sport
Pierre	Vous êtes marié?	

Exercise 3 Vrai ou faux?

The following statements are not all accurate. Looking back at our four course participants say which statements are true (**vrai**) and which ones are false (**faux**):

a Monique apprend le chinois.
b Pierre et Monique ont deux enfants.
c Natalie aime aller au cinéma.
d Antoine est célibataire.
e Antoine habite à Paris.
f Pierre travaille chez Citroën.

▶ Exercise 4 Qui est l'aîné?

Listen to the recording and say who is the oldest. First you need to learn the following two words:

plus *more*	**moins** *less*

a Bernard a cinquante-trois ans.
b Sylvie a trente-neuf ans.
c Mona a cinq ans de moins que Sylvie.
d Marc a dix ans de plus que Mona.
e Etienne a trois ans de moins que Bernard.
f Martin a dix ans de plus qu'Etienne.

☑ Unemployment in France – le chômage en France

In April 2006 unemployment figures were 9.3% overall but 22% for the under 30s. The strikes and unrest were mainly due to the high level of unemployment amongst young people and a clumsy Government attempt to impose new rules for the **CNE**, **C**ontrat **N**ouvelles **E**mbauches (contracts for first time/new employees).

Surfez sur le web
- Google: chômage en France. Choisissez le site www.educnet. education.fr/insee/chomage/default.htm
- **Recherchez** les statistiques sur le chômage en France
- **Cliquez** sur **Qui?** Et **suivez le lien** (*follow the link*)
- **Répondez aux questions par Vrai ou Faux** (*answer with True or False*)

(**L'Insee** is the French national institute for statistics and economic studies).

04

un voyage en bateau

a boat trip

In this unit you will learn

- how to ask where something is situated
- how to understand some directions
- how to ask if something you need is available
- how to ask most forms of questions
- how to say what you would like to do
- how to count to 101

Travelling to France on a cross-channel ferry you may find that most of the staff are French. Although they are likely to speak English, use the opportunity to try out your French!

▶ 1 Au pont cinq *On deck five*

Sarah Burgess is travelling to France with a French friend, Dominique Périer. They have left their car on the car deck (**le pont**) and now they are looking for their cabin.

Listen to the recording once through, then answer these questions:

a On which deck is their car? *5*
b On which deck is their cabin? *8*

Listen again.

bureau 7 d'information

c Where do they go to find out? On which deck is it?
d Is it morning or evening? *evening*
e Did you get the number of the cabin? *017*

Now read the dialogue.

Dominique	Bon, la voiture est au pont cinq. Maintenant allons à la cabine.
Sarah	Où se trouve notre cabine?
Dominique	Je ne sais pas. Allons au bureau d'information au pont sept.
Membre de l'équipage	Bonsoir madame.
Dominique	Bonsoir, j'ai réservé une cabine.
Membre de l'équipage	Oui, c'est à quel nom?
Dominique	Périer, Dominique Périer.
Membre de l'équipage	Oui, alors c'est la cabine 017 au pont huit. Prenez l'escalier à gauche.
Sarah	Allons-y.

la voiture	the car
je ne sais pas	I don't know
membre de l'équipage	a member of the crew
c'est à quel nom?	which name?
l'escalier	the staircase
à gauche	on the left
allons-y	let's go

You may be able to work out some words and expressions for yourself. Link the English phrases below to the equivalent French expressions:

1 Where is our cabin?
2 Let's go to the information desk.
3 Take the staircase on the left.
4 I have reserved a cabin.
5 The car is on deck five.

a Prenez l'escalier à gauche.
b J'ai réservé une cabine.
c La voiture est au pont cinq.
d Où est notre cabine?
e Allons au bureau d'information.

Grammar

1 Où se trouve...?/Où est...?

To ask where a place is use either **où se trouve...?** or **où est...?** These two expressions are totally interchangeable:

Où se trouve le bar?   *Where is the bar?* (lit. *where does the bar find itself?*)

Où est le bar?   *Where is the bar?*

Remember, if a noun is in the plural form, the verb will also be in the plural form:

Où se **trouvent** les toilettes? / Où **sont** les toilettes s'il vous plaît?

2 à, à la, au, aux

These are prepositions. They are used to indicate a direction (to, at, in...) and are placed immediately before a noun.

Although all four words mean the same, you use the one that matches the gender (feminine or masculine) and number (one: singular, more than one: plural) of the noun it precedes.

- **à** is generally used before the name of a place:
  Allons **à Paris**.   *Let's go to Paris.*

- **à la** is used in front of a feminine noun:
  Allons **à la cabine**.   *Let's go to the cabin.*

- **au** is used in front of a masculine noun. **au** is a contraction of **à + le**:
  La voiture est **au garage**.   *The car is in the garage.*

- **aux** is used in front of a plural noun, either feminine or masculine. It is a contraction of **à + les**:
  Allons **aux jeux vidéo**.   *Let's go to the video games.*

Exercise 1 Dans le bateau

Now it is your turn to ask questions about various locations on the boat. Look at the four diagrams of the boat below. The first one shows a plan of the boat; the others show various places on decks 7, 8 and 9.

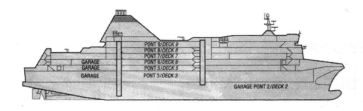

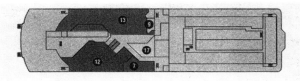

Pont 9

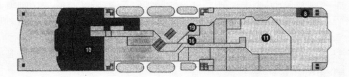

Pont 8

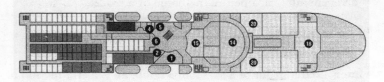

Pont 7

Here are some of the places that you can identify on the three decks.

1 Bureau d'information	PONT 7	**a** *Self-service restaurant*
2 Bureau de change	PONT 7	**b** *Baggage room*
4 Sièges inclinables	PONT 7	**c** *Children's playroom*
6 Local à bagages	PONT 7	**d** *Information desk*
7 Salle de jeux enfants	PONT 9	**e** *Shops*
11 Restaurant Self	PONT 8	**f** *Bureau de change*
12 Salon de thé	PONT 9	**g** *Reclining seats*
13 Le Bar «Le Derby»	PONT 9	**h** *Tea shop*
15 Les boutiques	PONT 7	**i** *Newsagent*
17 Le kiosque	PONT 9	**j** *'Le Derby' bar*

Match the French names of places on the boat with their English equivalents. The numbers in the first column correspond to numbers of the decks on the diagrams.

▶ Exercise 2 Répondez aux passagers
Answer the passengers' questions

Look at the plan of the boat and imagine that you are a member of the crew answering passengers' questions.

Exemple:
Passager Le restaurant self-service s'il vous plaît?
Membre de l'équipage C'est au pont huit, Monsieur.

Madame is used for a woman passenger (**passagère**), **monsieur** for a male passenger (**passager**).

How would you reply to these questions?

a Passager Pardon, les boutiques s'il vous plaît?
   Membre de l'équipage …
b Passagère Où est le salon de thé, s'il vous plaît?
   Membre de l'équipage …

c **Jeune garçon** S'il vous plaît madame, où sont les jeux pour les enfants?
Membre de l'équipage …
d **Passager** Le bar c'est à quel pont?
Membre de l'équipage …
e **Passagère** Il y a un bureau de change s'il vous plaît?
Membre de l'équipage …

Grammar

3 Un passager, une passagère

Nouns finishing with **-er** tend to change to **-ère** in the feminine form.

Other examples are:

masculine	feminine	
le boulanger	la boulangère	*the baker*
le fermier	la fermière	*the farmer*
le boucher	la bouchère	*the butcher*

▶2 Est-ce qu'il y a un cinéma?
Is there a cinema?

Sarah and Dominique are exploring the boat. What do they find?

Listen once to the recording and answer these questions:

a Is there a cinema on the boat?
b Are they going to see *Pirates of the Caribbean*?

Listen again.

c What film are they going to see?
d Is the film they are going to see at 21.00 or at 22.30?
e How much does it cost to get in?

Now look at the script:

Sarah	Est-ce qu'il y a un cinéma sur le bateau?
Dominique	Oui, ici au pont 6, il y a deux cinémas. On y va?
Sarah	Oui d'accord!
Dominique	Il y a deux films. À quelle heure?

Sarah	Alors, il y a *Pirates des Caraïbes* avec Johnny Depp à vingt et une heures et à vingt-deux heures trente il y a *Le Come-back* avec Hugh Grant, le fim s'appelle *Music and Lyrics* en anglais.
Dominique	Moi j'adore Hugh Grant, et toi?
Sarah	Moi aussi! Je voudrais voir *Le Come-Back*. C'est combien?
Dominique	C'est dix euros.

On y va?	*Let's go?* (**On** is frequently used in conversation to express a collective action)
Oui d'accord	*Yes O.K.*
Je voudrais + verb	*I would like to...*
Je voudrais voir	*I would like to see*
salon	*lounge*
salle	*room*
ici	*here*

Link these English phrases to the equivalent French expressions from the script:

1 What about you?
2 At 22.30 there is *Le Come-back*.
3 What would you like to see?
4 Me too.

a Qu'est-ce que tu voudrais voir?
b Moi aussi.
c Et toi?
d À vingt-deux heures trente il y a *Le Come-back*.

▶ Pronunciation

In French there is a tendency for groups of words to be pronounced as if all the letters were linked up. This applies to the following:

Il y a [ilia]   Y a t-il? [iatil]   Est-ce qu'il y a? [eskilia]

However it is not always possible to link up all words. Although **est une** can be linked [etune], **et une** cannot. The **t** of **et** cannot be linked with the following word **une** despite the fact that it starts with a vowel. Doing so would alter the sound of **et** *and* to **est** *is*.

So in **un homme et une femme** (*a man and a woman*) **et** and **une** must be pronounced quite separately to avoid the meaning *a man is a woman*!

Grammar

▶ 4 Des nombres et des chiffres de 70 à 101

Look, listen and repeat.

70	**soixante-dix** [60 + 10]	90	**quatre-vingt-dix**
71	**soixante et onze** [60 + 11]	91	**quatre-vingt-onze**
72	**soixante-douze**	92	**quatre-vingt-douze**
79	**soixante-dix-neuf**	99	**quatre-vingt-dix-neuf**
80	**quatre-vingts*** [4 × 20]	100	**cent**
81	**quatre-vingt-un**	101	**cent-un**
89	**quatre-vingt-neuf**		

*Only **quatre-vingts** is spelt with -s for plural (four twenties)

ℹ In some francophone countries 70, 80 and 90 are said differently:
70 is **septante** in Belgium, Switzerland and in the Democratic Republic of Congo
80 is **octante** in Belgium and Quebec
80 is **huitante** in Switzerland
90 is **nonante** in Belgium and Switzerland

▶ Exercise 3 C'est combien? *How much is it?*

Sarah and Dominique are at the shop. They are checking the price of drinks and cigarettes.

Listen to the recording and answer these questions:

a How much is the Cognac?
b How much is the whisky?
c How much are the cigarettes?
d How much is the gin?

Surfez sur le web
• Trouvez www.brittany-ferries.fr ou d'autres sites pour en savoir plus sur la traversée de la Manche (*the Channel*).

---

savoir	*to know*

05

on visite la vieille ville

visiting the old town

In this unit you will learn
- how to ask for various places in a town
- how to follow and give directions
- how to count from 102 to 10,500
- some adjectives
- the imperative

▶ 1 Pour aller à...? *How do I get to...?*

Some tourists have just arrived in St Malo after their crossing on the ferry. They visit the old town, **la Vieille Ville**, which in St Malo is normally referred to as **L'intra muros** (the Latin phrase for 'inside the walls').

In this dialogue the tourist is asking for the station but the passer-by is not sure whether she means the bus station (**la gare routière**) or the railway station (**la gare SNCF**).

ℹ **SNCF** stands for **S**ociété **N**ationale des **C**hemins de fer **F**rançais (*National Board of French Railways*).

First read the key directions:

C'est tout droit/Allez tout droit	*It is straight ahead/Go straight on*
C'est à droite/Tournez à droite	*It is on the right/Turn right*
C'est la première rue à gauche/Prenez la première rue à gauche	*It is the first road on the left/ Take the first road on the left*
C'est la deuxième rue à droite/ Prenez la deuxième rue à droite	*It is the second road on the right/Take the second road on the right*
C'est la troisième rue sur votre gauche/Prenez la troisième rue sur votre gauche	*It is the third road on your left/ Take the third road on your left*

Now listen to the recording and choose the correct answer.

a Can you tell whether the tourist is looking for:
  1 the bus station
  2 the railway station?

b Is it:
  1 the first street on the left and the next one on the right?
  2 the first one on the left and then straight ahead?

c How far away is it?
  1 one kilometre?
  2 one hundred metres?
  3 two hundred metres?
  4 more than two hundred metres?

Now listen to the recording again and read the dialogue.

Touriste	Pour aller à la gare s'il vous plaît madame?
Passante	La gare routière ou la gare SNCF?
Touriste	Euh, la gare SNCF...
Passante	Oui alors vous prenez la première rue à gauche et c'est tout droit.
Touriste	C'est loin?
Passante	Non c'est tout près. C'est à deux cents mètres, au maximum.
Touriste	Merci beaucoup madame.

Link the English phrases to the equivalent French expressions

1 at the most
2 Is it far?
3 It's two hundred metres away.
4 It's straight ahead.
5 Take the first street on the left.
6 It's very near.

a C'est à deux cents mètres.
b C'est tout près.
c C'est loin?
d Prenez la première rue à gauche.
e au maximum
f C'est tout droit.

Grammar

1 Feminine and masculine adjectives

You are already aware that there are feminine and masculine nouns in French. Similarly, adjectives describe the nouns they are linked up with and are feminine or masculine according to the gender of the nouns they accompany.

In French adjectives can be placed before or after nouns, although changing the position of an adjective can modify the meaning of the phrase. In many cases -e is added for the feminine form of the adjective and -s is added for the plural:

Masculine

un village	*a village*
un **joli** village	*a pretty village*
des **jolis petits** villages	*pretty little villages*
un **grand** château	*a big castle*
des **grands** châteaux	*big castles*

Feminine

une ville	*a town*
une **jolie** ville	*a pretty town*
des **jolies petites** villes	*pretty little towns*

| une **grande** maison | *a big house* |
| des **grandes** maisons | *big houses* |

But many adjectives change more radically from the masculine to the feminine:

| le **vieux** port | *the old port* | la **vieille** ville | *the old town* |
| le **premier** jour du mois | *the first day of the month* | la **première** rue à gauche | *the first street on the left* |

Masculine adjectives ending in **-e** remain the same in the feminine form:

| le bonnet **rouge** | *the red hat* | la fleur **rouge** | *the red flower* |
| le **deuxième** magasin | *the second shop* | la **deuxième** rue | *the second street* |

▶ 2 Some ordinal numbers

These are adjectives indicating a ranking position:

3rd	**troisième**	20th	**vingtième**
4th	**quatrième**	36th	**trente-sixième**
10th	**dixième**	100th	**centième**
15th	**quinzième**	1000th	**millième**

▶ 2 Vous tournez à gauche
You turn left

As Sarah and Dominique leave the port they decide to visit Saint Malo before continuing with their journey. They ask for directions.

Listen to the recording once through, and answer the questions.

a Who would like to visit the old town?
b Whom do they ask for directions?

Listen again.

c Is the old town far from the port?
d Are there problems with parking?

Now read the text.

Dominique   Je ne connais pas St Malo. Je voudrais bien visiter la Vieille Ville. Et toi, tu connais?

Sarah	Non je ne connais pas. On y va! Demande la direction au monsieur, là.
Dominique	Pardon monsieur. Pour aller à la Vieille Ville s'il vous plaît?
Un passant	Oh c'est tout près d'ici! Alors vous allez au rond point et là vous tournez à gauche. La Vieille Ville est à cinq cents mètres à gauche.
Sarah	Merci monsieur. Il y a un parking pas trop loin?
Passant	Pas de problèmes avec le stationnement à St Malo, il y a plusieurs grands parkings.
Dominique	C'est parfait! Merci monsieur!
Passant	De rien mesdemoiselles!

Link the English phrases to the equivalent French expressions.

1 there
2 at the roundabout
3 I don't know St Malo.
4 It's perfect!
5 Ask the way.
6 no problem with parking
7 several large car parks

a Je ne connais pas St Malo.
b C'est parfait!
c Demande la direction.
d pas de problème avec le stationnement
e plusieurs grands parkings.
f là
g au rond point

Grammar

3 Savoir *and* connaître

The verbs **savoir** and **connaître** both mean *to know*: **je sais** (*I know a fact*), **je connais** (*I know a place, something or someone*).

Je ne sais pas où c'est.   *I don't know where it is.*
Je ne connais pas la ville. *I don't know the town.*

4 Directions: the imperative

Here are some verbs used for directions: **aller** *to go*, **prendre** *to take*, **tourner** *to turn*, **continuer** *to carry on*.

When someone is giving directions or orders they use a verb form called the imperative (*Go…!, Take…!, Turn…!*). If the directions are given to a stranger or someone the speaker is not acquainted with, the form of the verb used is different from the form used for family or friends or children.

To an adult:

Allez jusqu'au château, **tournez** à gauche puis **prenez** la deuxième rue à droite.

To a child or to an adult you know well:

Va jusqu'au château, **tourne** à gauche puis **prends** la deuxième rue à droite.

jusqu'à/jusqu'au	*as far as*	**puis**	*then*

5 Vous *and* tu

There are two ways of addressing people in French:

Vous to individuals who are not friends or relatives, and to more than one person (**vouvoyer** is the verb which describes the action of addressing someone as **vous**).

Tu to a friend, relative or young child (**tutoyer** is the verb which describes the action of addressing someone as **tu**).

6 Directions: the present tense

It is also possible to use the present tense to give directions:

Vous allez jusqu'au château, **vous tournez** à gauche puis **vous prenez** la deuxième rue à droite. (*You go as far as the château, you turn left then you take the second road on the right.*)

Exercise 1 Vous tournez à gauche encore

Look back at the dialogue on pages 41–2.

a Can you find examples of people saying **tu** to one another?
b Can you find examples where someone gives directions using the present tense rather than the imperative?

Exercise 2 La piscine, s'il vous plaît?

Look at the diagram below (this is not an accurate map of St Malo). The ten places numbered on the diagram are listed in the key words box.

You are standing at the star, answering the questions of passers-by. Choose the correct reply.

INTRA-MUROS

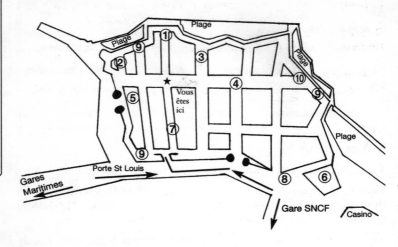

---

1 la piscine *the swimming pool*
2 le musée *the museum*
3 la cathédrale *the cathedral*
4 le marché aux poissons *the fish market*
5 le marché aux légumes *the vegetable market*

6 le château *the castle*
7 la Grand' Rue *the High Street*
8 l'Office du Tourisme *the Tourist Office*
9 les remparts *the ramparts*
10 le petit aquarium *the small aquarium*

Question 1	La piscine s'il vous plaît?
Réponse	**a** C'est sur votre gauche. **b** C'est à droite. **c** Continuez tout droit.
Question 2	La Grand' Rue SVP*?
Réponse	**a** C'est ici la Grand'Rue. **b** C'est à gauche. **c** Prenez la deuxième rue à droite.
Question 3	Pour aller au marché aux poissons SVP?
Réponse	**a** Vous prenez la deuxième rue à gauche. **b** Allez tout droit. **c** Vous tournez à droite et c'est la deuxième rue sur votre droite.

*SVP stands for *s'il vous plaît*.

Exercise 3 Quelle question?

This time you are still standing at the same spot but you are asking the questions.

Question 1	...
Réponse	Alors vous tournez à droite et vous continuez tout droit. C'est à deux cent cinquante mètres.
Question 2	...
Réponse	Oui, alors tournez à droite et c'est la première rue à gauche.
Question 3	...
Réponse	Tournez à gauche et prenez la deuxième rue à droite.

Grammar

▶ 7 Des nombres et des chiffres de 102 à 10500

102	cent deux	1000	mille
170	cent soixante-dix	1900	mille neuf cents/dix-neuf cents
200	deux cents	2000	deux mille
900	neuf cents	2020	deux mille vingt
926	neuf cent vingt-six	10500	dix mille cinq cents

Note that when there is more than one hundred, **cent** is spelt with an **s** but if another number follows, the **s** is dropped:

deux cents *200* but **deux cent cinq** *205*

❶ St Malo cité historique

St Malo was founded in the 6th century by the Welsh monk MacLow. It is the birth place of many sailors and discoverers. One of the most famous is Jacques Cartier who discovered Canada in the 16th century. There are still very strong links between St Malo and Canada, especially with Quebec. It is not unusual to see the Canadian flag flying in St Malo.

▶ Exercise 4 Répondez aux touristes

It is your turn to answer questions asked by tourists.

Listen to the recording and answer the questions you will hear.

You need to know that:

a the swimming pool is on the right
b the museum is 200 metres away
c the cathedral is very near
d the tourist office is straight ahead
e the castle is on the left

Surfez sur le web

- Google St Malo and you will have access to many sites referring you to hotels and places to visit.
- For the best site go to www.saint-malo.com/portailsites.asp?type=1&cat1=Divers/Pages+perso for many fascinating sites on St Malo and its region.
- For a virtual visit of the region go to **La vallée de la Rance maritime** Découverte de l'histoire et des plus beaux sites du littoral du Nord de la Bretagne. Use the key words: **Cartes** (maps), **Diapos** (for diapositives = slides) and **Index**.
- TV5 Monde: TV5 is a French language World TV channel. Try it out with a visit to the Québec website http://www.tv5.ca.

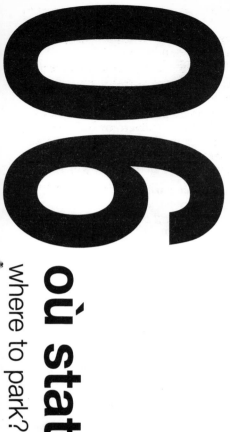

06

où stationner?

where to park?

In this unit you will learn
- how to understand instructions for car parking
- about using French money
- the time
- how to talk about daily routine

1 Où stationner? *Where to park?*

Dominique and Sarah are trying to find a car park space. They have a guide to all the parking zones in St Malo which they got from the Tourist Office: **l'Office de Tourisme** or **le Syndicat d'Initiative** (the name varies from town to town but they are interchangeable).

You are likely to hear a lot of French people refer to a car park as **un parking** but in an effort by various governments to remove the English and American influence on the French language you will notice that the official name for a car park is **une zone de stationnement**. On parking notices and tickets you will see:

Stationnement gratuit	*free parking*
Stationnement payant	*pay-parking*
Stationnement interdit	*Parking forbidden/No parking*
Stationnement autorisé	*Parking allowed*

Look at the information provided on the car parking leaflet and answer the following question:

What is the maximum amount of time you can stay in the short-stay car park?

STATIONNEMENT EN FONCTION DE VOS BESOINS.

compagnie
Générale de
Stationnement

INFORMATIONS ET CONTACTS
• Service du Stationnement.
Horaires d'ouverture:
du lundi au samedi de
9 H à 19 H.

Stationnement payant de courte durée, <u>2 H 30</u> maximum.
Tarifs: -1h = 1 €
-2h = 2 €
-2h30 = 2,50 €

NOTA:
Stationnement gratuit de 19h. à 9h

■ Stationnement interdit.
■ Stationnement libre et gratuit. Plusieurs centaines de places.

Stationnement payant de longue durée, <u>24 H</u> maximum.
Tarifs: -1h = 1 €
-2h = 2 € 3h = 3 €
-4h = 4 €= -8h = 8 €
-10h = 10 €

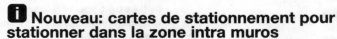

ℹ️ Nouveau: cartes de stationnement pour stationner dans la zone intra muros

You can buy a card which you can use as a pay as you go system. This is a new system which most towns are now adopting. In St Malo the machine (**horodateur**) also allows for coins (**pièces de monnaie**) to be used – please note that parking tariffs increase regularly. You can also leave you car outside the town and use the park and ride system (**Navette bus**) to visit St Malo.

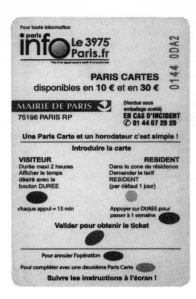

1 With this Paris parking card what is the maximum time a visitor may park when using the card with **un horodateur**?
2 Do residents pay the same rate?
3 What do you get if you press the **Valider** button?

▶2 Tu as de la monnaie?
Do you have any change?

Listen to the recording and then answer these questions.

1 Which type of car park did Sarah and Dominique use?
   a long stay   **b** short stay   **c** free
2 How long did they plan to stay?
3 How much did they pay?
4 How did they pay?
   Tick the coins they used and say how many of each type they used:
   a 50 centimes   **b** 1€   **c** 2€
   d 20 centimes   **e** 10 centimes

Now read the text.

Dominique	Il y des horodateurs comme à Paris mais ici on peut aussi utiliser des pièces de monnaie. A Paris, il faut des cartes de stationnement sauf pour le mois d'août. Au mois d'août à Paris le parking, c'est gratuit!
Sarah	Tiens! Il y a des places au parking là-bas sur le quai.

Dominique	D'accord. C'est une zone de stationnement payant de longue durée. Tu as de la monnaie?
Sarah	Oui un peu. Il faut combien?
Dominique	Je ne sais pas. On reste combien de temps?
Sarah	Trois ou quatre heures.
Dominique	Alors quatre heures, cela fait quatre euros. J'ai une pièce d'un euro, une de deux euros et une de cinquante centimes, c'est tout.
Sarah	Pas de problème, moi j'ai une pièce de dix centimes et deux de vingt centimes.
Dominique	Quelle heure est-il?
Sarah	Il est dix heures et quart, donc on a jusqu'à deux heures et quart.
Dominique	Voilà notre ticket. Fin de stationnement autorisé: quatorze heures quinze.

Tiens!	*Look!*	**donc**	*therefore*
là-bas	*over there*	**voilà**	*here is*
C'est tout!	*That's all!*		

Link the following English phrases to the correct French expressions.

1	Are there spaces on the quay?	**a** Quelle heure est-il?
2	How long will we stay?	**b** Fin de stationnement autorisé
3	How much do we need?	
4	What time is it?	**c** On a jusqu'à deux heures et quart.
5	We've got until a quarter past two.	**d** On reste combien de temps?
6	End of authorized parking	**e** Il y a des places sur le quai?
		f Il faut combien?

Grammar

1 More new verbs

- **Tiens!** is the imperative form for the verb **tenir** *to hold* but it is frequently used as an expression of surprise *Look!* or **Tiens! Tiens!** *Well! Well!*

- **Cela fait deux euros vingt-cinq.** *That makes it 2,25 €.* **Fait** is the verb **faire** *to do / to make* in the present tense.

- **Il faut combien?** literally means *How much is necessary/ required?* but it is best translated as *How much do we need?* The verb **falloir** means *to need / to have to.* It is only ever used with the pronoun **il** *it* in an impersonal form.

Il **faut** could also be translated as *one must*:

> **Il faut manger pour vivre**   *One must eat in order to live*
> **Il faut souffrir pour être**   *One must suffer to be*
>   **beau / belle!**   *beautiful!*

(**beau** is masculine, **belle** is feminine.)

- **On** is also an impersonal pronoun meaning *one*, but it is frequently used in conversation instead of **nous** *we*.

2 Formal and informal ways of asking questions

Most everyday conversations between people are informal. This is reflected in the way people ask questions.

In all cases the questioning is shown in the tone of voice which rises on the last syllables.

Formal	Informal
As-tu de la monnaie?	
Est-ce que tu as de la monnaie? }	Tu as de la monnaie?
Quelle heure est-il?	Il est quelle heure?
Combien faut-il?	Il faut combien?
Combien de temps reste-t-on?*	On reste combien de temps?

* see **On** above.

3 Des faux amis *False friends*

There are a few French words which are deceptively similar to English words although their meanings are quite different. There are two examples in the dialogue above:

- **rester** *to stay*
  On **reste** combien de temps? *How long are we staying?*
  (*to rest* is **se reposer** e.g. **je me repose** *I am resting*)

- **de la monnaie** *change*
  Tu as de la **monnaie**? *Have you got any change?*
  Une pièce de monnaie is *a coin* (although **pièce** is usually used on its own).
  Similarly **un billet** *a note* is short for **un billet de banque** *a bank note*.
  (*Money* is **de l'argent**. Note that **argent** is also the word for *silver*.)

Exercise 1 Remplissez les blancs

Choose some of the words from **Des faux amis** above to complete the following sentences.

a You are in a shop and you would like to get some change.
  J'ai un billet de 50 euros. Vous pouvez me faire la _____ SVP?

b Je suis fatiguée. Je _____ _____ cinq minutes.

c On _____ quatre heures ici.

d Oh le joli bracelet en _____!

e Oh là là! C'est cent cinquante euros. Je n'ai pas d'_____.

◖3 À l'heure française *On French time*

Two adults and two children have been asked three similar questions about their daily routine – **la routine quotidienne:**

1 *At what time do you get up in the morning?*
2 *At what time do you have lunch?*
3 *At what time do you go to bed?*

Questions aux adultes	**Questions aux enfants**
1 Vous vous levez à quelle heure le matin?	Tu te lèves à quelle heure?
2 Vous prenez votre déjeuner à quelle heure?	Tu prends ton déjeuner à quelle heure?
3 À quelle heure est-ce que vous vous couchez?	Tu te couches à quelle heure?

Before you listen to the recording, first check the French for the days of the week (page 58). Now look at the verbs in the three questions.

Se lever *to get up* and **se coucher** *to go to bed* are reflexive verbs. The first reflexive verb you came across in this book was **s'appeler** *to be called* (page 20). **Vous vous levez** literally means *you get yourself up*. The subject and the object of the action is the same person (**vous** *you*, in this case) in reflexive verbs.

Vous prenez / tu prends are the present tense of the verb **prendre** *to take*. To say you have a meal in French, you normally say **je prends…**

Look again at the three questions above.

a What are the two expressions used for saying *'your lunch'* (one to an adult and the other to a child)?

b Now listen to the recording and fill in this grid:

	Question 1	Question 2	Question 3
Femme	7.30	?	?
Homme	?	1.00–1.30	?
Fille	?	12.00	?
Garçon	6.45	?	?

c Who gets up between ten o'clock and half past ten on a Sunday morning?

d At what time does the boy claim he sometimes goes to bed at the weekend?

Grammar

4 L'heure *The time*

There is a general tendency to use the 24-hour clock in France. It is used for transport timetables (**les horaires**), TV programmes (**les programmes de télévision**), computers (**les ordinateurs**), the Internet (**l'Internet**), working hours (**les horaires de travail**), school timetables (**les emplois du temps scolaires**), etc.

Most people use a mixture of the more traditional way of telling the time and of the 24-hour clock:

4h00 il est quatre heures / il est seize heures

4h15 il est quatre heures et quart / il est seize heures quinze

4h30 il est quatre heures et demie / il est seize heures trente

4h45 il est cinq heures moins le quart / il est seize heures quarante-cinq

12h00 il est midi (*midday*) / il est minuit (*midnight*)

▶ Exercise 2 Quelle heure est-il?

Listen to the recording and write down the correct letter next to each of the following times:

1 1h20 ( )   **2** 23h45 ( )   **3** 17h05 ( )   **4** 12h30 ( )
5 8h56 ( )   **6** 11h15 ( )   **7** 3h00 ( )   **8** 6h45 ( )

▶ Exercise 3 Matin ou après-midi?

Il est quatre heures du matin ou quatre heures de l'après-midi?

The distinction a.m. and p.m. has never been used in French. Listen to the recording to hear what people say when there is a need to make a distinction between morning and afternoon/evening.

a What time is it for Jean-Pierre in Paris?
b What time is it for Martine in Sydney?

Exercise 4 À gagner!

Anyone watching the nature programme on **la Cinquième** can win a prize. Read the competition details and then answer the questions below.

a Which TV channel do you have to watch?
b Give the two dates and times when the programme is on.
c What is the 'Question of the Week'?

Exercise 5 Le manoir de Jacques Cartier

Un peu de lecture! Remember Jacques Cartier, the famous sailor from St Malo and discoverer of Canada?

You can visit le Manoir de Limœlou, his manor house, but when exactly? (Check with **Les jours de la semaine et les mois de l'année,** pages 58–9.)

Visite commentée du Manoir de Jacques Cartier

Musée ouvert toute l'année
Accès aux visites guidées
Tous les jours du 1er juillet au 31 août
sauf week-end du 1er septembre au 30 juin

Horaires des visites
du 1er juin au 30 septembre
de 10 heures à 11 h 30 et de 14 h 30 à 18 heures
du 1er octobre au 31 mai
à 10 heures et à 15 heures.

Prix réduit pour écoles
et groupes de 10 personnes minimum
(uniquement sur réservation)

Gratuit pour :
Enfants au-dessous de 5 ans.

---

a Between which dates is it open every day of the week?
b Could you have a guided tour the first weekend in September?
c In July what are the opening times?
d In May what time of day is it open?
e Who can get a reduction? Under what condition?
f How much does it cost for a child under the age of five to visit Jacques Cartier's Manor House?
g Find the French expressions for the following:

museum open all year round
every day from 1st July to 31st August

h Can you spot a difference between French and English in the way that days and months are written?

Grammar

5 Tout le, toute la, tous les, toutes les

In front of nouns these words are adjectives (respectively masculine, feminine, masculine plural and feminine plural according to the noun they are used with). They mean *all* or *every*:

Il faut visiter **toute** la ville   *We must visit the whole town*
    et **toutes** les vieilles rues.   *and all the old streets.*

J'adore **tout** le village et **tous**   *I love the whole village and*
    les monuments historiques.   *all the historic monuments.*

Look at your answers to **g** above: **toute** agrees with **l'année** (fem.) and **tous** agrees with **les jours** (masc. pl.).

Tous les jours ils arrivent en retard (*late*)

▶ 6 Les jours de la semaine et les mois de l'année

Les jours de la semaine			
lundi	*Monday*	vendredi	*Friday*
mardi	*Tuesday*	samedi	*Saturday*
mercredi	*Wednesday*	dimanche	*Sunday*
jeudi	*Thursday*		

Les saisons			
Le printemps	*Spring*	L'automne	*Autumn*
L'été	*Summer*	L'hiver	*Winter*

There is a saint for each day of the year. Until recently French children could only be given a name which appeared on this calendar. Many people celebrate their name day as well as their birthday.

JANVIER	FEVRIER	MARS	AVRIL	MAI	JUIN
1 J. DE L'AN	1 Ste Ella	1 Carème	1 St Hugues	1 F. DU TRAVAIL	1 St Justin
2 St Basile	2 Pres. Seign.	2 St Charles	2 Ste Sandrine	2 St Boris	2 Ste Blandine
3 Ste Geneviève	3 St Blaise	3 St Guénolé	3 St Richard	3 Sts Jacq./Philippe	3 St Kévin
4 Epiphanie	4 Ste Véronique	4 St Casimir	4 St Isidore	4 St Sylvian	4 Ste Clotilde
5 St Edouard	5 Ste Agathe	5 Ste Olive	5 Rameaux	5 Ste Judith	5 St Igor
6 St Mélanie	6 St Gaston	6 Ste Colette	6 St Marcellin	6 Ste Prudence	6 Norbert
7 St Raymond	7 Ste Eugenie	7 Ste Félicité	7 St J-B de la Salle	7 Ste Gisèle	7 Fête des Mères
8 St Lucien	8 Ste Jacqueline	8 St Jean de Dieu	8 Ste Julie	8 VICTOIRE	8 St Médard
9 Ste Alix	9 Ste Apolline	9 Ste Françoise	9 St Gautier	9 St Pacôme	9 Ste Diane
10 St Guillaume	10 St Arnaud	10 St Vivien	10 St Fubert	10 F. Jeanne d'Arc	10 St Landry
11 St Paulin	11 N-D Lourdes	11 Ste Rosine	11 St Stanislas	11 Ste Estelle	11 St Barnabé
12 Ste Tatiana	12 St Félix	12 Ste Justine	12 PAQUES	12 St Achille	12 St Guy
13 Ste Yvette	13 Ste Béatrice	13 St Rodrigue	13 Ste Ida	13 Ste Rolande	13 St Antoine
14 Ste Nina	14 St Valentin	14 Ste Matilde	14 St Maxime	14 St Matthias	14 Fête Dieu
15 St Rémi	15 St Claude	15 Ste Louise	15 St Paterne	15 Ste Denise	15 Ste Germaine
16 St Marcel	16 Ste Julienne	16 Ste Bénédicte	16 St Benoît Labre	16 St Honoré	16 St J.-F. Régis
17 St Roseane	17 St Alexis	17 St Patrice	17 St Anicet	17 St Pascal	17 St Hervé
18 Ste Prisca	18 Ste Bernadette	18 St Cyrille	18 St Parfait	18 St Eric	18 St Léonce
19 St Marius	19 St Gabin	19 St Joseph	19 Ste Emma	19 St Yves	19 St Romuald
20 St Sébastien	20 Ste Aimée	20 PRINTEMPS	20 Ste Odette	20 St Bernardin	20 St Silvère
21 Ste Agnes	21 St Pierre Damien	21 Ste Clémence	21 St Anselme	21 ASCENSION	21 Fêtes des Pères/ETÉ
22 St Vincent	22 Ste Isabelle	22 Ste Léa	22 St Alexandre	22 St Émile	22 St Alban
23 St Barnard	23 St Lazare	23 St Victorien	23 JSt Georges	23 St Didier	23 Ste Audrey
24 St François Sales	24 Mardi-Gras	24 Ste Catherine	24 St Fidèle	24 St Donatien	24 St Jean-Baptiste
25 Conv. St Paul	25 Cendres	25 Annonciation	25 St Marc	25 Ste Sophie	25 St Prosper
26 Ste Paule	26 St Nestor	26 Ste Larissa	26 Jour du Souvenir	26 St Bérenger	26 St Anthelme
27 Ste Angèle	27 Ste Honorine	27 St Habib	27 Ste Zita	27 St Augustin de C.	27 St Fernand
28 St Thomas d'Aq.	28 St Romain	28 St Gontran	28 Ste Valérie	28 St Germain	28 St Irénée
29 St Gildas		29 Ste Gwladys	29 Ste Cather. de S.	29 St Aymar	29 Sts Pierre/Paul
30 Ste Martine		30 St Amédée	30 St Robert	30 St Ferdinand	30 St Martial
31 Ste Marcelle		31 St Benjamin		31 PENTECÔTE	

JUILLET	AOUT	SEPTEMBRE	OCTOBRE	NOVEMBRE	DECEMBRE
1 St Thierry	1 St Alphonse	1 St Gilles	1 Ste Thérése E.-J.	1 TOUSSAINT	1 Ste Florence
2 St Martinien	2 St Julien	2 Ste Ingrid	2 St Léger	2 Défunts	2 Ste Vivance
3 St Thomas	3 Ste Lydie	3 St Grégoire	3 St Gérard	3 St Hubert	3 St François-Xavier
4 St Florent	4 St J-M Vianney	4 Ste Rosalie	4 St François d'Ass.	4 St Charles Boi	4 Ste Barbara
5 St Antoine-Marie	5 St Aber	5 Ste Raïssa	5 St Fleur	5 Ste Sylvie	5 St Gérald
6 Ste Marietta	6 Transfiguration	6 St Bertrand	6 St Bruno	6 Ste Bertille	6 St Nicolas
7 St Raoul	7 St Gaëton	7 Ste Reine	7 St Serge	7 Ste Carine	7 St Ambroise
8 St Thibaut	8 St Dominique	8 Nativité de N.-D.	8 Ste Pélagie	8 St Geoffroy	8 Imm. Concept.
9 Ste Amandine	9 St Amour	9 St Alan	9 St Denis	9 St Théodore	9 St Pierre Fourier
10 St Ulrich	10 St Laurent	10 Ste Ines	10 St Ghislain	10 St Léon	10 St Romaric
11 St Benoît	11 Ste Claire	11 St Adalphe	11 St Firmin	11 ARMISTICE	11 St Daniel
12 St Olivier	12 Ste Clarisse	12 St Apolinaire	12 St Wilfried	12 St Christian	12 Ste J.-F. De Chantal
13 Sts Henri/Joel	13 St Hippolyte	13 St Aimé	13 St Géraud	13 St Brice	13 Ste Lucie
14 FETE NATION	14 St Evrard	14 Sainte Croix	14 St Juste	14 St Sidoine	14 Ste Odile
15 St Donald	15 ASSOMPTION	15 St Roland	15 Ste Thérése d'Av.	15 St Albert	15 Ste Ninon
16 N-D Mt Carmel	16 St Armel	16 Ste Édith	16 Ste Edwige	16 Ste Marguerite	16 Ste Alice
17 St Frédéric	17 St Hyacinthe	17 St Renaud	17 St Baudouin	17 Ste Elizabeth	17 St Judicael
18 St Arsene·	18 Ste Hélène	18 Ste Nadège	18 St Luc	18 Ste Aude	18 St Gatien
19 Ste Marina	19 St Jean Eudes	19 Ste Émilie	19 St René	19 St Tanguy	19 St Urbain
20 Ste Marguerite	20 St Bernard	20 St Davy	20 Ste Adeline	20 St Edmond	20 St Abraham
21 St Victor	21 St Christophe	21 St Matthieu	21 Ste Céline	21 Présentation	21 St Pierre Canis.
22 Ste Marie-Madel.	22 St Fabrice	22 St Maurice	22 Ste Salomé	22 Ste Cécile	22 HIVER
23 Ste Brigitte	23 Ste Rosa	23 St Constant	23 St Jean de C.	23 St Clément	23 St Armand
24 Ste Christine	24 St Barthélemy	24 Ste Thècle	24 St Florentin	24 Ste Flora	24 Ste Adèle
25 St Jacques le M.	25 St Louis	25 St Hermann	25 St Crépin	25 Ste Catherine L.	25 NOËL
26 Ste Anne/Joachim	26 Ste Natacha	26 Sts Côme/Damien	26 St Dimitri	26 Ste Delphine	26 St Etienne
27 Ste Nathalie	27 Ste Monique	27 St Vincent de Paul	27 Ste Emeline	27 St Séverin	27 St Jean l'Apôtre
28 St Samson	28 St Augustin	28 St Vencaslas	28 Sts Simon/Jude	28 St Jacques M.	28 Sts Innocents
29 Ste Marthe	29 Ste Sabine	29 Sts Michel/Gap	29 St Narcisse	29 Avent	29 St David
30 Ste Juliette	30 St Fiacre	30 St Jérôme	30 Ste Bienvenue	30 St André	30 St Roger
31 St Ignace	31 St Aristide		31 St Quentin		31 St Sylvestre

Surfez sur le web
- Tout sur St Malo: http://www.ville-saint-malo.fr//guide/

Web extension exercise

Choose from the following menu:

- Se repérer *to find one's way around*
- Se loger *where to stay*
- Se restaurer *where to eat*
- Y circuler *traffic information* (including parking information)
- Y venir *how to get there* *
- Archives
- Multimédia
- Météo – weather forecast
- Adresses et numéros utiles

Go to **Y circuler** for the latest updates on parking arrangements

Go to **se loger** to check the campsites. Have you discovered how many camps sites there are in St Malo?

1 How many altogether?
2 How many are municipal (run by the council)?
3 How many are private ones?
4 How many have four stars?

* there (**y** replaces the name of a place e.g **venir à Saint Malo** = **y venir** (*to get here /there*)

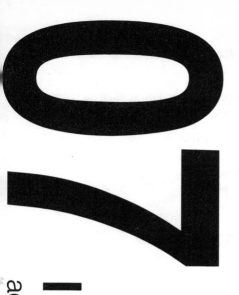

07

l'hébergement
accommodation

In this unit you will learn
- how to find a hotel
- how to book a hotel room
- how to ask for various facilities

ℹ️ À l'office de tourisme

Most French towns have **un Office de Tourisme**. The tourist office is an ideal place for you to get information and advice, **renseignements et conseils** whether you are on holiday or on a business trip, **en vacances ou en voyage d'affaires**. It can help you find somewhere to stay, somewhere to eat and also something interesting to do. Some offices will do the booking for you but if not they will give you all the information you need. As a general principle they deal with:

Hébergement	**Restauration**	**Loisirs**
Where to stay	*Where to eat*	*What to do – leisure*

1 Choisir un hôtel *Choosing a hotel*

You need to know which facilities you are looking for in order to choose somewhere to stay.

Match the following French and English expressions.

1 Une chambre simple
2 Une chambre double
3 Une chambre familiale (avec un grand lit + un lit pour enfant)
4 Une chambre pour personne handicapée
5 Pension (petit déjeuner + dîner)
6 Demi-pension (petit déjeuner)

a Full board (breakfast + dinner)
b A room for a disabled person
c A single room
d Half-board (breakfast)
e A double room
f A family room (with a double bed + a bed for a child)

Now match the symbols below and the French explanations to their English equivalents.

1 Facilités pour handicapés / pour voyageurs à mobilité réduite	a Main credit cards accepted
2 Ouvert toute l'année	b Bath & toilets
3 Catégorie (une /deux/ trois/quatre étoiles)	c Garage / private car park
4 Douches et wc	d Sea view
5 Salle de bains et wc	e Swimming pool
6 Garage / parking privé	f Children's games
7 Restaurant	g Lift
8 Principales cartes de crédit acceptées	h Facilities for disabled visitors
9 TV en chambres	i TV in rooms
10 Vue sur la mer	j Open all year round
11 Piscine	k Category (1/2/3/4 stars)
12 Ascenseur	l Pets welcomed
13 Jeux pour enfants	m Showers & toilets
14 Animaux acceptés	n Restaurant

▶2 Quelques renseignements
Some information

At the tourist office four tourists are requesting special facilities.

Listen to the recording, then answer these questions.

1 First tourist requires _____ 2 Second tourist requires_____
3 Third tourist requires _____ 4 Fourth tourist requires _____

Premier touriste	Je voudrais une chambre pour deux personnes pour une nuit dans un hôtel trois étoiles, avec vue sur la mer.
Deuxième touriste	J'ai un petit chien alors je cherche un hôtel où l'on accepte les animaux.
Troisième touriste	Je voudrais une chambre pour une personne dans un hôtel pas trop cher, avec restaurant et piscine.
Quatrième touriste	Ma fille est handicapée et elle a un fauteuil roulant. Nous voudrions une grande chambre pour trois personnes dans un hôtel avec ascenseur.

Grammar

1 Des verbes

There are three groups of verbs

Group 1: verbs ending with -**er**. They very nearly all follow a regular pattern (**aller** is an exception).

Group 2: verbs ending with -**ir**. Some of them follow a regular pattern.

Group 3: mostly verbs ending with -**re/-oir**. They are mostly irregular verbs.

Vouloir *to want*

This is a very useful verb to express a wish / something you would like. As in English, it is more polite to use the conditional tense, rather than the present tense: *I would like* rather than *I want*.

Compare:

Je veux une glace!   *I want an ice cream!*

and....

Je voudrais une chambre à deux lits.   *I would like a room with two beds.*

Nous voudrions louer des vélos.   *We would like to hire bikes.*

Chercher *to look for*
This is an easy verb to use. It is an **-er** verb because its infinitive (basic form) ends with **-er**. It is also a regular verb which means that it should provide you with a good example of how all regular **-er** verbs function.

Look carefully at the table below. It will provide you with some necessary information about French verbs in the present tense:

je cherche	Lit. *I look for* but best translated as *I am looking for*
tu cherches	*you are looking for* (see **tutoyer** page 45)
elle/il cherche	*she/he/it is looking for*
on cherche	Lit. *one is looking for* but best translated as *we are looking for*
nous cherchons	*we are looking for*
vous cherchez	*you are looking for* (see **vouvoyer** page 45)
ils/elles cherchent	*they are looking for* (It is pronounced the same way as **il/elle cherche**)

Exercise 1 Je voudrais une chambre double
Say what accommodation you require :

a I am looking for a single room in a hotel with sea view.
b I would like a double room in a hotel.
c We are looking for a hotel with a swimming pool. (use **nous**)
d We would like a hotel room for the weekend. (use **on**)

3 Quel mode d'hébergement choisir?
Which kind of accommodation should you choose?

i Tourism and business tourism **(le tourisme d'affaires)** are booming in France and there are now lots of places to stay to choose from. Apart from the traditional range of hotels in towns there are also much cheaper and sometimes more convenient ranges of accommodation in out-of-town hotels, often in commercial estates **(zones commerciales)** or close to motorways **(les autoroutes).** **Hôtels Formule 1, Etap Hôtels, Hôtels Première Classe, Hôtels Campanile** are mushrooming all over France and Europe.

Camping is still very popular in the summer and for young people there are youth hostels **(auberges de jeunesse – centres de rencontres internationales)** but the fastest growing area for accommodation is the equivalent of the English bed and breakfast **(chambres d'hôtes)** with the cost of breakfast included **(nuit + petit déjeuner)**. Many of them are located in genuine farmhouses and are registered with Gîtes de France.

Chambre d'Hôtes à la ferme

HEBERGEMENT

Chambre d'Hôtes à la Ferme

La chambre d'hôtes à la ferme, c'est le "bed and breakfast" à la française chez des agriculteurs. Que ce soit pour une ou plusieurs nuits, vous serez reçus "à la ferme". Le matin, vos hôtes serviront un petit déjeuner campagnard. Dans certains cas, il vous sera même possible de prendre vos repas chez l'habitant (table d'hôtes). La chambre labellisée "gîtes de France", c'est l'assurance de bénéficier d'un accueil de qualité dans un cadre chaleureux.

Read the text above and find the French words or phrases for:

a at farmers' homes
b either for one or several nights

c a country breakfast
d your hosts will serve you

Services 'plus' *Extras*

Now read the leaflet opposite from Campanile and make your own vocabulary list. Find the French words for the following objects:

a toothpaste
b baby bottle warmer
c hair dryer

d toothbrush
e shaving cream
f a fax*

* This is a new French expression for 'fax', again created in an effort to move away from English and American influence on the French language. However **un fax** is still used most of the time.

Services "Plus" • Service "Extras"

• Dans la plupart de nos hôtels, possibilité de prendre une chambre 24h/24 grâce à notre système de paiement par carte bancaire

• In most of our hotels, possibility to take a room 24 hours a day thanks to our automatic payment system operating by credit card.

• Renseignements - réservation de votre prochaine étape chez Campanile

• Information - Booking your next stopover at Campanile

• Envoi d'une télécopie

• Sending a fax

• Vente de boissons (non alcoolisées)

• (Non alcoholic) beverages on sale

• La boutique Campanile : rasoir, crème à raser, dentifrice, nécessaire à couture, brosse à dents...

• The Campanile boutique : razor, shaving cream, toothpaste, sewing kits, toothbrush...

• Prêt d'un fer à repasser, sèche-cheveux, oreillers synthétiques, chauffe-biberon

• At your disposal : an iron, hair dryer, synthetic pillows, baby bottle warmer

▶4 Un petit hôtel *A small hotel*

Having spent half a day in St Malo, Sarah and Dominique have decided that they want to see more of the town and the area around it (**la ville et ses environs/ses alentours**). They decide to stay for a few days (**quelques jours**) but are not sure about what to do and where to stay. At the tourist office they find that there is a lot of choice:

Listen to the recording and answer these questions.

a Are the two women likely to find something not too expensive for a few nights?
b Would they like a hotel with a restaurant?

Listen again.

c Do most hotels offer breakfast?
d Can they arrange hotel bookings for customers at the Tourist Office?

Now read the dialogue.

Dominique	Pardon monsieur, pouvez-vous nous renseigner? Nous passons quelques jours dans la région et nous cherchons un petit hôtel pas trop cher.
Employé	Oui, alors cela devrait être possible. Il y a beaucoup de petits hôtels deux étoiles qui sont très bien. Voici notre brochure… Vous voulez un hôtel avec ou sans restaurant?
Sarah	Sans restaurant. Il y a beaucoup de restaurants à St Malo.
Employé	Oh oui et la plupart des hôtels servent le petit déjeuner de toute façon.
Dominique	Vous vous chargez des réservations?
Employé	Non, je suis désolé madame! Nous ne nous chargeons pas des réservations, mais si vous voulez je peux téléphoner à l'hôtel de votre choix pour vérifier qu'il y a des chambres disponibles.

sans	*without*	**disponible(s)**	*available*
la plupart	*most*	**vérifier**	*to check*
de toute façon	*in any case*		

Find the French expressions for the following:

e It must be possible.
f Could you give us some information?
g Do you take care of reservations?
h No, I am afraid not (madame)!
i We are spending a few days in the area.

Grammar

2 Encore des verbes

There are several new verbs or new verb forms in the dialogue.

Vouloir *to want/to like to* (see page 64)

It is used with **vous** here:

Vous voulez un hôtel?   *Would you like a hotel?*
Voulez-vous une chambre? *Would you like a room?*

Devoir *ought to/must*

• In the present tense it mainly means *must*:
    Je dois partir.   *I must go.*

- Just as **je voudrais** is a conditional form of **vouloir**, so **je devrais** *I ought to* is a conditional form of **devoir**:

  Je devrais téléphoner à   *I ought to phone my mother.*
  ma mère.

- In the dialogue **devoir** is used with **cela** *that / it* (often shortened to **ça** as in **ça va?** See page 9):

  Cela/ça devrait être bon.   *It ought to be good.*

Servir *to serve*

There are two examples of **servir** in this unit:

- The first is in the dialogue:

  Les hôtels servent le   *Hotels serve breakfast.*
  petit déjeuner.

  Note that **-ent** at the end is the plural form and you cannot hear it. The singular form would be:

  L'hôtel sert le petit   *The hotel serves breakfast*
  déjeuner à partir de   *from 8.00 a.m.*
  huit heures.

- The other is in **Chambre d'hôtes à la ferme** (page 64):

  Vos hôtes vous **serviront**   *Your hosts will serve you a*
  un petit déjeuner   *country breakfast.*
  campagnard.

  Ils serviront *they will serve* is the future tense of the verb **servir**.

Se charger de *to take responsibility for something*

Je me charge de tout! *I'll take care of everything!* This is a reflexive verb:

L'Office de Tourisme de St Malo ne se charge pas des réservations. This is best translated as *St Malo's Tourist Office does not deal with reservations.*

Exercise 2 Chargez-vous de vos réservations avec l'Internet!

Take care of your own bookings with the Internet. If you have access to the Internet you can use **Yahoo France** as a server. Go to **Tourisme** and then **Hébergement,** and choose the region of France you want to visit.

Here is the information provided by the Hôtel du Palais at St Malo:

HÔTEL ✱ ✱
DU
PALAIS

Hôtel situé dans la partie haute de la vieille ville: l'Intra Muros.
Proche des remparts et de la plage, ainsi que des rues commerçantes
très animées tout en restant dans un environnement dégagé et calme.
Accès aisé en voiture en toutes saisons.

***

CHAMBRES

18 Chambres – Toilettes, WC – Douche ou bain – Ascenseur
Télévision, Chaînes françaises et anglaises – Petit déjeuner

Prix de base: Chambre double (2 personnes) 45 € à 79 €

a Where is l'Hôtel du Palais situated?

b How many rooms have they got?

c Would you be able to watch EastEnders?

d What other facilities do they offer?

e What is their basic price for a double room?

Surfez sur le web

- Où se loger? A l'hôtel? Au camping? Dans un gîte rural? Pour chercher une chambre d'hôte sur le web visitez http://www.chambre-d-hote.com. Pour louer des vélos (*rent bicycles*) visitez http://www.bretagnelocations.com/velos35s.php

louer	*to hire/to rent*
location	*hiring/renting*

08

à l'hôtel
at the hotel

In this unit you will learn
- how to express a preference and make some comparisons
- how to book a hotel, indicate requirements, understand instructions
- the alphabet, how to use accents and spell names
- **du, de la, des**
- the pronouns **le, la, les**
- **vouloir, pouvoir, prendre**

▶ 1 Quel hôtel choisir?
Which hotel should you choose?

Monsieur and Madame Olivier have some difficulties choosing a hotel. The choice is between:

L'HÔTEL DE LA GARE **	(*Station Hotel*)
L'HÔTEL DE L'ÉGLISE *	(*Church Hotel*)
L'HÔTEL DU CENTRE ****	(*Centre Hotel*)
L'HÔTEL DES VOYAGEURS ***	(*Travellers' Hotel*)

Listen once to the recording, then answer these questions:

a Which hotel does Monsieur Olivier suggest in the first place?
b He gives three reasons for his choice. Name one of them.

Listen to the recording again.

c Where is l'Hôtel des Voyageurs situated?
d Who makes the final choice?
e What reason is given for the choice?

Now read the dialogue:

Madame Olivier	Alors quel hôtel choisis-tu?
Monsieur Olivier	Pas de problèmes, descendons à l'Hôtel de la Gare. C'est tout près de la gare. C'est plus pratique, c'est plus facile avec les bagages et c'est l'hôtel le moins cher!
Madame Olivier	Oui d'accord mais il y a aussi l'Hôtel des Voyageurs. C'est aussi tout près de la gare!
Monsieur Olivier	Oh je te laisse choisir, c'est plus simple!
Madame Olivier	Dans ce cas je choisis l'Hôtel du Centre. C'est plus loin de la gare mais c'est certainement plus confortable!

Link the following English phrases to the equivalent French expressions:

1 It's further from the station.   a Oui, d'accord mais…
2 Yes OK but…   b C'est plus pratique.
3 It's the cheapest.   c C'est plus loin de la gare.
4 It's certainly more comfortable.   d Je te laisse choisir.
5 It's more convenient.   e C'est certainement plus confortable.
6 It's easier.   f C'est le moins cher.
7 I'll let you choose.   h C'est plus facile.

Grammar

1 Du, de la, de l', des

The names of the four hotels on the previous page have been used to show that there are four different ways to say *of the*.

Notice the word order in French: *Hotel of the station* rather than *Station hotel*.

You use **du, de la, de l'** or **des** according to the gender and number of the noun which follows. This can be illustrated with the following names of streets (**rues**) or town squares (**places**):

De + feminine noun = **de la**   **Rue de la Cité**
De + masculine noun = **du**   **Rue du Port**
De + singular noun beginning
    with a vowel or mute h = **de l'**   **Rue de l'Europe**
De + plural noun (fem. or masc.) = **des**   **Place des Québécois**

2 Choisir *to choose*

In Unit 7 (page 65) you met the verb **chercher** [to find], an -er verb with a regular pattern. Similarly **choisir** which belongs to the second group of verbs (those regular verbs ending in -**ir**) is a useful model for other -**ir** verbs. (Unfortunately quite a few verbs ending in -**ir** are irregular and belong to the third group of verbs.) The letters underlined in bold below show the pattern.

Choisir *in the present tense*

je chois**is**	*I choose/I am choosing*	nous choisiss**ons**	*we choose*
tu chois**is**	*you choose*	vous choisis**sez**	*you choose*
il/elle chois**it**	*he/she/it chooses*	ils/elles choisi**ssent**	*they choose*

3 Plus *more* and moins *less*

In order to make a comparison you need at least two comparable things: **C'est plus pratique** effectively means that the Station Hotel is more convenient in terms of location than the other three hotels. **C'est plus pratique** is therefore a short cut for: L'Hôtel de la Gare est **plus** pratique **que** l'Hôtel du Centre, etc. (*more convenient than...*).

- In more formal speech the sentence would start with **Il est...** Il est plus pratique de descendre* à l'Hôtel de la Gare que de descendre à l'Hôtel du Centre.

  * **Descendre** usually means *to go down, to alight* but here it means *to put up at a hotel*. In the dialogue **Descendons à l'Hôtel de la Gare** simply means *Let's go to ...*

- **C'est moins cher** is a short cut for: L'Hôtel de la Gare est **moins** cher **que** l'Hôtel du Centre (*less expensive than... / cheaper than ...*)

- **C'est le moins cher** (*it's the least expensive / it's the cheapest*)

Exercise 1 À qui sont les valises?

Three suitcases have been left in the corridor. Whose are they?

Look at the people and at the three suitcases and say whether the following statements are true or false (**vrai ou faux**).

a C'est la valise de la mère.   F
b C'est la valise du père.
c C'est la valise des enfants.

⟨Exercise 2 Nommez les cafés!

Choose the correct words to complete the name of each café.

EUROPE   **VIEILLE VILLE**   **PORT**   **AMIS** (*friends*)

a Café des ____   **c** Café de la ____
b Café du ____   **d** Café de l'____

Exercise 3 Jeu du café mystère

The name of a café, the name of a hotel and a name for the part of a town are hidden in the grid. Can you find them?

Mots cachés *hidden words*

```
C Q A D H B G T I C R V
H A P D E O U Y T N H I
S Q F X G L T W T T Y E
H O T E L D U P O R T I
R E G T D F M E D A W L
T G H W A E F P F M F L
A N G L A I S V I L L E
A M G L B I S Q C R U P
B C V N F T H W A Q S F
```

▶2 À l'hôtel de la Plage★★
At the Beach Hotel

Monsieur and Madame Landré are at the reception desk (**au bureau de réception**) of the Beach Hotel.

Listen once to the recording and answer these questions:

a Have Monsieur and Madame Landré reserved a room?
b How long do they intend to stay ?

Listen to the recording again.

c On which floor is their room?
d What is their room number?

Listen one more time.

e At what time is breakfast?
f At what time does the hotel door close?

Now read the dialogue:

Réceptionniste	Bonsoir monsieur-dame. Vous désirez?
Madame Landré	Nous avons réservé une chambre pour deux personnes, pour deux nuits.
Réceptionniste	Bien, c'est à quel nom?
Madame Landré	Landré, Jacques et Martine Landré.
Réceptionniste	Cela s'épelle comment?
Monsieur Landré	L-a-n-d-r-e accent aigu.
Réceptionniste	Ah oui, voilà. Une chambre double pour deux nuits. Alors vous avez la chambre vingt-cinq au troisième étage. L'ascenseur èst au bout du couloir. Voici votre clef. Vous prendrez le petit déjeuner?
Madame Landré	Euh oui! C'est à quelle heure?
Réceptionniste	Alors le petit déjeuner est servi dans la salle à manger de huit heures à dix heures mais vous pouvez le prendre dans votre chambre si vous voulez.
Monsieur Landré	Nous le prendrons dans la salle à manger, merci.
Réceptionniste	Très bien. Si vous avez besoin de quoi que ce soit, n'hésitez pas à m'appeler. Si vous sortez, gardez votre clef avec vous parce que la porte de l'hôtel ferme à vingt-trois heures. Bon séjour à l'Hôtel de la Plage, Monsieur et Madame Landré!
M. et Mme Landré	Merci bien Mademoiselle. A propos Mademoiselle, nous avons un petit problème. Nous avons un petit chien…
Réceptionniste	Pas de problèmes, ici les animaux sont acceptés.
M. et Mme Landré	Excellent! Merci Mademoiselle.

Vous désirez?	*What can I do for you?* (désirer *to wish/desire*)
Cela s'épelle comment?	*How do you spell it / how is it spelt?*
au bout du couloir	*at the end of the corridor*
la salle à manger	*the dining room*
avoir besoin de…	*to need…*
quoi que ce soit	*whatever it is*
parce que	*because**

*Another word for *because* is **car** but it is more formal and it is used less frequently in speech and more often in formal written French.

Link the following English phrases to the equivalent French expressions:

1 on the third floor   a si vous sortez
2 Do not hesitate to call me. b Nous avons réservé une
3 if you go out   chambre.
4 Keep your key.   c La porte de l'hôtel ferme à...
5 Have a good stay!   d N'hésitez pas à m'appeler.
6 The hotel door closes at... e au troisième étage
7 We have reserved a room. f Gardez votre clef.
                              g Bon séjour!

▶ Pronunciation

Monsieur Landré was asked how to spell his name (**Cela s'épelle comment?**). If you need to spell your name, you will need to know the French alphabet – listen to it on the recording and repeat it:

A, B, C, D, E, F, G, H, I, J, K, L, M, N, O, P, Q, R, S, T, U, V, W (double V), X, Y (I grec), Z

In addition to spelling the letters you also need to spell accents and other signs. Listen to them and repeat them:

é = e accent aigu
è = e accent grave
ê = e accent circonflexe (also â, î, ô, û - often in place of **s** in earlier language e.g. **h**ostel has become hôtel, **p**aste – **pâte**, hospital – hôpital)
ë = e tréma (used to keep two vowel sounds separate e.g. **Noël**)
ç = cédille
Examples of double letters: deux c, deux f, deux m, deux s, etc.

▶ Exercise 4 Écoutez et écrivez

Listen to the way people spell their names and write down what you hear:

1 Sylvie _____
2 _____ _____
3 _____ _____
4 Now can you spell your name in French?

Grammar

4 Pronouns: *le, la, les*

The receptionist says:

Vous pouvez le prendre dans votre chambre... *You can take it in your room...*

Le refers to **le petit déjeuner** *breakfast*. **Le** here is a pronoun, a word which stands in for a noun, although not necessarily in the same position. At a later stage you will learn how to use a whole range of pronouns but for the moment it is important to understand the difference between the articles **le, la,** and **les** which mean *the* and come in front of nouns, and the pronouns **le, la** and **les** which replace nouns altogether:

Vous prendrez le **petit déjeuner**?	
Oui nous **le** prendrons.	*Yes we will have it.*
Vous gardez **la clef**?	
Oui je **la** garde.	*Yes I am keeping it.*
Tu gardes **les clefs**?	
Oui je **les** garde.	*Yes I am keeping them.*

5 *Vouloir, pouvoir, prendre, dire*

These four verbs belong to the third group of verbs (mostly irregular which means that they do not all have the same spelling pattern). Here they are in the present tense.

Vouloir *to want*

je veux	*I want*	nous voulons	*we want*
tu veux	*you want*	vous voulez	*you want*
il/elle/on veut	*he/she/one wants*	ils /elles veulent	*they want*

Pouvoir *to be able to*

je peux	*I can*	nous pouvons	*we can*
tu peux	*you can*	vous pouvez	*you can*
il/elle/on peut	*he/she/one can*	ils/elles peuvent	*they can*

Prendre *to take*

je prends	*I take*	nous prenons	*we take*
tu prends	*you take*	vous prenez	*you take*
il/elle/on prend	*he/she/one takes*	ils/elles prennent	*they take*

Dire *to say*

je dis	*I say*	nous dis**ons**	*we say*
tu dis	*you say*	nous di**tes**	*you say*
il/elle/on dit	*he/she/one says*	ils/elles dis**ent**	*they say*

Useful expression: **C'est à dire** *That is to say*

You now know enough about verbs to look them up in the Verb table appendix (see page 337). However you do not have to check endings every time you want to use a verb. For instance you know that when you use **vous** in the present tense the ending of the verb is likely to be **-ez**, and with **nous** the ending is **-ons**.

08

6 Verb + infinitive

Vous pouvez prendre le petit   *You can have breakfast in*
déjeuner dans votre chambre.   *your room.*

In this sentence **prendre** is in the infinitive (the basic form of the verb). That is simply because when one verb follows another, the second one remains in the infinitive, except after **avoir** *to have* and **être** *to be*.

Exercise 5 Pouvoir et prendre

a It is your turn to find the correct endings for the verb **pouvoir** *can* and for the verb **prendre** *to take*.

The first column is a list of the pronouns *I, you*, etc. (referred to as subject pronouns). Link each pronoun to the correct part of the verb listed in the second column (each pronoun can be linked to more than one verb form). Try to do this without referring back to **Grammar 5**, to see if you have learnt them.

Je	pouvez
Tu	prends
Il	prennent
Elle	prend
On	peuvent
Nous	peux
Vous	prenons
Ils	prenez
Elles	peut

b In the dialogue on page 76 there are two examples of **prendre** in the future tense (*I will take* etc.). Can you identify them?

c Un proverbe! A proverb! Here are two versions of the same French proverb:

Quand on veut on peut.
Vouloir c'est pouvoir.

Can you find an equivalent English proverb?

Un entretien avec Sylvie Lécaille, toiletteuse

French people are very fond of animals, especially small dogs. This is something which has progressively developed in the last 20 years and with it a whole commerce related to animal care such as dog grooming salons.

Gaëlle Graham Sylvie, vous travaillez avec les animaux. Qu'est-ce que vous faites exactement?

Sylvie Lécaille Je suis toiletteuse, c'est à dire que je prends soin de l'hygiène des animaux de compagnie.

Gaëlle Graham Tous les animaux?

Sylvie Lécaille Non, je m'occupe en particulier du toilettage canin et également de l'hygiène des chats et des lapins.

Gaëlle Graham Vous aimez votre travail?

Sylvie Lécaille Oui, c'est une passion d'enfance que j'ai réalisée récemment.

Gaëlle Graham Il faut des diplômes pour exercer ce métier?

Sylvie Lécaille Non, ce n'est pas obligatoire mais dans mon cas j'ai obtenu le brevet de toiletteur canin et donc c'est un avantage au niveau technique.

Gaëlle Graham Du point de vue professionel, quel est le meilleur moment de la journée?

Sylvie Lécaille C'est le moment où le client voit son toutou* transformé après le toilettage et sort de chez moi tout fier de son chien.

Gaëlle Graham Vous avez beaucoup de travail?

Sylvie Lécaille Oui parce que les Français ont de plus en plus d'animaux de compagnie.

Gaëlle Graham Alors bonne chance Sylvie

Sylvie Lécaille Merci beaucoup

1 Sylvie grooms pets, which ones does she mention?
2 Is Sylvie qualified to do this particular job?
3 What makes her day?

* un toutou = slang name for a pet dog.

Recherchez des informations et entraînez-vous sur le web

Web extension

Go to http://www.tourisme.fr.

Click on **préparer son voyage** at the top of the home page then on Informations pratiques → Animaux de compagnie → Voyager avec des animaux

Find out all you need to know about travelling in France with a pet.

Surfez sur le web
- Trouvez votre bon heur avec www.tourisme.fr, www.tourisme.gouv.fr
- Si vous connaissez *Le Guide du Routard* (French equivalent to the *Rough Guides)*, allez voir www.routard.com

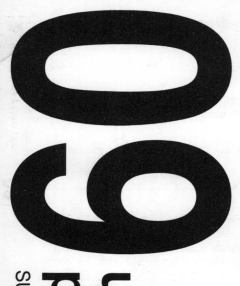

09

une si jolie petite ville!

such a pretty little town!

In this unit you will learn
- places in a town and their location
- more about the time
- to plan for the near future
- parts of the day

▶1 C'est à côté du commissariat
It's next to the police station

Dominique and Sarah visit the old town. They each go their own way.

Listen to the recording once, then answer these questions:

a What is Sarah going to do?
b Can it be found on the map of the town?

Listen to the recording again.

c What is Dominique going to do?
d When will they meet again? In:

   1 two hours' time   **2** an hour's time   **3** half an hour's time

Now read the dialogue:

Sarah	Je vais poster quelques cartes postales. Je vais essayer de trouver un bureau de poste.
Dominique	Regarde, la poste est indiquée sur le plan de la ville, là, PTT. C'est Place des Frères Lamennais. Tiens, regarde, c'est à côté du commissariat de police, en face de la cathédrale.
Sarah	Parfait, j'y vais! Et toi qu'est-ce que tu vas faire?
Dominique	Oh je ne sais pas, je vais peut-être faire un tour des remparts. On se retrouve dans une heure?
Sarah	OK! Où ça?
Dominique	Euh, au bout de la Grand' Rue, derrière la cathédrale, au coin de la rue Porcon de la Barbinais.
Sarah	Au revoir! Bonne promenade!
Dominique	Salut! A tout à l'heure!

à côté de	*next to*	**chacun/chacune**	*each one*
en face	*opposite*	**de l'autre côté***	*on the other side*
derrière	*behind*	**devant***	*in front of...*
entre*	*in between*		
au coin de...	*at the corner of / round the corner from*		(*not in the text)

Link the following English phrases (**1–8**) to the equivalent French expressions (**a–h**).

1 the police station

2 The post office is marked on the map.

a La poste est indiquée sur le plan.
b Où ça?
c Bonne promenade!

3 look
4 I may go round the ramparts
5 What are you going to do?
6 Have a good walk!
7 Let's meet again in an hour's time.
8 Whereabouts?

d On se retrouve dans une heure.
e le commissariat de police
f regarde
g Qu'est-ce que tu vas faire?
h Je vais peut-être faire un tour des remparts.

Vrai ou faux? Say whether the following statements are true or false.

a Le commissariat de police est derrière la cathédrale. F
b La poste est indiquée sur le plan. T
c Sarah cherche la cathédrale.
d Dominique va à la poste.
e Elles (les deux femmes) se retrouvent dans deux heures.

Grammar

1 Aller

The verb **aller** *to go* appears several times in the dialogue. In Unit 7 (page 64), you learnt that **aller** is the only verb ending in -er which does not follow the usual pattern. Here it is:

Aller *in the present tense*

je vais	*I go / I am going*	nous all**ons**	*we go / are going*
tu vas	*you go / are going*	vous all**ez**	*you go / are going*
il/elle/on va	*he/she/one goes / is going*	ils /elles vo**nt**	*they go / are going*

Aller + *a second verb in the infinitive*

This is used to indicate that an action will take place in the very near future:

Je **vais poster** quelques cartes postales.	*I am going to post a few postcards.*
Je **vais essayer** de **trouver** un bureau de poste.	*I am going to try and find a post office.*

In fact in this last example there are two verbs following **aller**, both of them in the infinitive.

Qu'est-ce que tu **vas faire**?	*What are you going to do?*
Je **vais** peut-être **faire** un tour des remparts	*Perhaps I'll take a walk around the ramparts.*

Je **vais faire** une promenade. *I am going to go for a walk.*

J'y vais *I am going (there)*

Y is a pronoun standing in place of a phrase beginning with **à**. When Sarah says **J'y vais** in the dialogue it is short for **Je vais à la poste**.

2 Trouver – se retrouver *to find – to meet again*

re- at the beginning of a verb indicates that the action is being done again e.g. **faire** *to do* and **refaire** *to redo/do again*.

Se retrouver is like a reflexive verb but here it involves two people. The action is reciprocal (Sarah is going to find Dominique again and Dominique is going to find Sarah).

S'embrasser *to kiss one another* is another example of a reciprocal action:

Les amants **s'embrassent**. *The lovers kiss.*

Exercise 1 Faites des phrases

What are all the people whose names appear in column A going to do? For each sentence columns A and D remain the same. Columns B and C are jumbled. You have to find the right items from these two columns to complete each sentence. Can you find eight correct sentences? Can you say what they mean?

A	B	C	D
1 M & Mme Olivier	allons	visiter	des cartes postales
2 Tu	va	téléphoner	à ton frère
3 Sarah Burgess	vas	choisir	le petit déjeuner au lit
4 Vous	vont	chercher	la vieille ville
5 Je	vont	faire	à St Malo
6 On	allez	rester	du travail
7 Les enfants	va	voir (*to see*)	une promenade
8 Nous	vais	prendre	le dernier film de Spielberg

i Les PTT ou La Poste

La Poste is no longer just a post office, it has changed its character to adapt to the needs of its customers. It has been privatized and is now also a bank and an organization which offers many of its services, including financial services, on the internet. For more information see the website for Le Groupe la Poste www.laposte.fr.

2 Une si jolie petite ville!
Such a pretty little town!

Spend a few minutes studying the diagram overleaf. There is a multitude of small French towns where you can find all the buildings, shops and institutions pictured in it. You have already learnt some of the names and therefore you only need to concentrate on the new ones.

Look at the names of all the places in the town and say which of them are referred to in the second column.

Lieu Place	C'est où? Where is it?
1 la Place de la République	a C'est entre la mairie et la boucherie.
2 le Bar-Tabac du Centre (bureau de tabac) *bar-tobacconist's*	b C'est derrière la poste, entre la banque et le bar-tabac.
3 l'église *the church*	
4 la pharmacie *the chemist's*	c C'est entre le Café de la Poste et l'Office de Tourisme.
5 le Commissariat de Police	
6 la Mairie *the Town Hall* (l'Hôtel de Ville in larger towns)	d C'est devant la bibliothèque et à côté de l'Office de Tourisme.
7 la bibliothèque municipale *the public library*	
8 la boucherie *the butcher's*	e C'est rue François Mitterand, derrière l'alimentation.
9 l'Office de Tourisme	
10 la Maison de la Presse *the newsagent's + bookshop*	f C'est à côté de l'église, près du Commissariat de Police.
11 le Café de la Poste	
12 l'Hôtel-Restaurant St Jacques	
13 l'alimentation (l'épicerie) *general food store*	g C'est derrière le bar-tabac et à côté du camping municipal.
14 la poste	
15 la boulangerie–pâtisserie *baker's/cake shop*	
16 la banque *the bank*	
17 la charcuterie *the delicatessen*	
18 le camping municipal *the municipal campsite*	

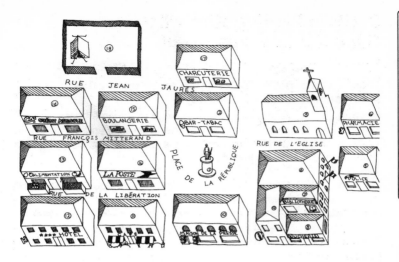

You are in **la Place de la République** when a passer-by stops you and asks you two questions. Complete the dialogue.

Passant   Excusez-moi Monsieur/Madame/Mademoiselle. Pour aller au _____ s'il vous plaît?

Vous   Le _____, c'est derrière la boulangerie et en face de la _____ .

Passant   Merci bien! Et où est la _____ s'il vous plaît?

Vous   C'est à côté de la _____municipale et en face du Commissariat de Police.

▶3 Qu'est-ce qu'on va faire aujourd'hui? *What shall we do today?*

A family is staying in St Malo for the weekend. They are planning what they are going to do.

Listen once to the recording and answer these questions:

a Who would like to go either to the beach or for a boat trip down the river?

b Who would like to go to Mont Saint Michel?

Listen again.

c What would the boy like to do?
d Who puts a stop to the discussion?
e At the end of the discussion what does the boy want to know?

C'est samedi matin [discussion entre deux ados (adolescents) et leurs parents]

Maman	Alors, soit on va à la plage et à marée basse on peut aller visiter la tombe de Chateaubriand sur le Grand Bé, ou bien on fait une excursion en bateau sur la Rance jusqu'à Dinan…
Jeune fille	Moi je voudrais aller au Mont Saint Michel!
Maman	Non, il y a beaucoup trop de monde au Mont Saint Michel le week-end!
Jeune garçon	Moi je veux prendre le petit train pour visiter St Malo. C'est moins fatigant et plus amusant!
Maman	Quel paresseux!
Papa	Bon, moi aussi j'ai une idée, on va visiter le barrage de la Rance. Plus de discussion!
Jeune garçon	Dis Papa et demain qu'est-ce qu'on va faire?

la marée basse	*low tide*
soit… ou bien	*either… or*
beaucoup trop de monde	*far too many people*
aujourd'hui	*today*
demain	*tomorrow*
la marée haute*	*high tide*
	(*not in the text)

Link the following English phrases to the equivalent French expressions:

1 We go to the beach.
2 I'd like to go on the little train.
3 What a lazy boy!
4 a boat trip
5 It's not so tiring.
6 It's more fun.

a Quel paresseux!
b une excursion en bateau
c C'est plus amusant!
d On va à la plage.
e Je voudrais prendre le petit train.
f C'est moins fatigant.

Grammar

3 The immediate future: aller + infinitive

You have already met (page 84) an easy way to talk about the future. You can use **aller** followed by another verb to refer to what will happen soon, for example in the next second, minute, hour or day, or even in the next few years in some cases:

Tu vas tomber!	*You are going to fall over!*
Il va pleuvoir.	*It's going to rain.*
Nous allons faire une promenade à vélo.	*We are going to go for a bike ride.*
Avec le nouveau gouvernement tout ça va changer!	*With the new government all that is going to change!*

In most cases the time scale is implicit but to be more precise use **aujourd'hui** *today*, **demain** *tomorrow*, **après-demain** *the day after tomorrow*, **bientôt** *soon*:

Qu'est-ce qu'**on va faire** aujourd'hui?	*What are we going to do today?*
Qu'est-ce qu'**on va faire** demain?	*What are we going to do tomorrow?*

4 The immediate future: present tense

You can also use the present tense to express the immediate future:

Qu'est ce que **tu fais** cet après-midi?	*What are you doing this afternoon?*
Qu'est-ce que **vous faites** ce soir?	*What are you doing this evening?*
Ce midi **nous allons** au restaurant.	*This lunch time we are going to the restaurant.*
Cette année **nous allons** en vacances en Irlande.	*This year we are going on holiday to Ireland.*

5 Amusant *amusing/funny*, fatigant *tiring*

-ant in French is equivalent to *-ing* in English:

Marcher toute la journée, c'est très fatigant.	*Walking all day is very tiring.*

| C'est un homme vraiment amusant. | *He's a really funny man.* |

Amuser means *to amuse/to entertain* and the reflexive verb **s'amuser** means *to enjoy oneself*:

| Les enfants s'amusent sur la plage. | *The children are enjoying themselves on the beach.* |

6 Dis Papa! / Dis Maman!

These are children's expressions generally used to attract the attention of adults. **Dis/dites** are the imperative forms of **dire** *to say*:

| Dis-moi la vérité. | *Tell me the truth.* |
| Dites-le au maire. | *Tell it to the mayor.* |

ⓘ Chateaubriand is a French Romantic author born in St Malo in 1768. His grave is on a tiny island or rock, **Le Grand Bé**, which can be reached from the beach at low tide.
Le Barrage de la Rance or **Usine marémotrice de la Rance** is a tidal dam across the river Rance which uses the tide as a means to create electricity.

Exercise 2 Le Petit Train de St Malo

Read the advert for the little train and answer the questions below.

LE PETIT TRAIN DE SAINT-MALO

Visite touristique et commentée de l'intra-muros et de ses alentours

Départ et arrivée : porte St-Vincent au pied du Château
NOCTURNE JUILLET/AOUT
Durée du trajet : 30 minutes

INFORMATIONS RESERVATIONS GROUPES
Tel. 02 99 40 49 49 - Fax 02 99 40 44 62
BP 173 35408 SAINT-MALO

ENGLISH GUIDED TOUR

a What could you expect to see if you took the little train?
b What happens at Porte St Vincent?
c Could you take a night ride all year round?

▶ Exercise 3 J'ai besoin de.../Je voudrais...

Advise people where to go when you hear what they need (**avoir besoin de...**) or want. Listen to the recording and respond appropriately.

Exemple: J'ai besoin d'argent.
               Vous: Allez à la banque.

1 Je voudrais du jambon et du pâté.
2 J'ai besoin de médicaments.
3 Je voudrais acheter des journaux.
4 Je voudrais des timbres poste.
5 Je voudrais du pain et des gâteaux.
6 J'ai besoin d'un plan de la ville.

Recherchez des informations et entraînez-vous sur le web

Web extension

1 Log on the Saint Malo official site http://www.saint-malo.fr/guide/index.html find **Guide Pratique** and click on **se repérer** (*finding out where you are*). You should see a map of St Malo and its area. You are invited to indicate your departure point. Please choose Dinard and then in the box below choose the type of itinary: **Itineraire Bis**, which is usually a tourist route, using secondary roads. Then click on **Calculer l'itinéraire** which will lead you to a box indicating the roads, the walking time (**itinéraire piéton**) and the distance. You can then click on **Modifier les options** and choose to go by car instead. Have fun calculating the distance, the time and how much you will spend on petrol, according to which type of car you drive and the petrol you use.

2 Log on **le site du Petit Train de Saint Malo** www.lepetittrain-saintmalo.com. L'accueil (*home page*) describes the advantages of visiting St Malo with **le Petit Train**. Which are they? You are then invited to choose a category. Please choose **Circuits**. You will be presented with the train route and pictures of St Malo. You can also listen to a commentary **écouter les commentaires** while watching the panoramic views **visualiser les vues panoramiques**. You can also read the commentary on each site. If you click on **Accès** you can read the following text and find information about distances between St Malo and other localities.

Porte Saint-Vincent, …est à 50 mètres de l'office du tourisme, au pied des remparts et du château. Saint-Malo, c'est aussi à : 10 km de Dinard, 32 km de Dinan, 15 km de Cancale, 56 km du Mont St-Michel et à 1 heure environ des îles Anglo-normandes (Jersey, Guernesey).

Say where exactly Porte St Vincent is.

10 choisir un restaurant

choosing a restaurant

In this unit you will learn
- about eating out
- how to express an opinion
- about the French and their attitude towards food

▶1 Où est-ce qu'on mange?
Where shall we eat?

Sarah and Dominique are enjoying their stay in St Malo. As well as places to visit they discuss the restaurants and other places where they can have meals.

Listen to the recording and answer these questions:

a What does Dominique suggest they do for lunch?
b Dominique sees a small restaurant. Where is it?
c How much would they have to pay for mussels, chips and a glass of wine?

Now read the dialogue:

Dominique Où est-ce qu'on mange ce midi? On fait un pique-nique?

Sarah Non! Il ne fait pas assez beau. En fait on dirait qu'il va pleuvoir.

Dominique Oui je pense que tu as raison. Alors qu'est-ce qu'on fait? On prend quelque chose de rapide dans une brasserie ou bien dans une crêperie? Qu'est-ce que tu en dis?

Sarah Euh... J'ai envie de manger des moules avec des frites.

Dominique Bonne idée! Tiens, regarde, il y a un petit restaurant de l'autre côté de la rue: repas express, moules-frites plus un verre de vin 10,50 € tout compris.

Sarah C'est parfait. On y va!

avoir envie de...	*to long for / to have a craving for/to feel like / to fancy...*
quelque chose	*something*
un verre de vin	*a glass of wine*
pleuvoir	*to rain*

Link the following English phrases to the equivalent French expressions:

1 In fact it looks as if it is going to rain.
2 What do you say to that?
3 The weather is not good enough.

a Il ne fait pas assez beau.
b On prend un petit repas rapide?
c J'ai envie de manger des moules avec des frites.

4 Where are we going to eat this lunch time?

5 Shall we have a quick meal?

6 Eight euros 50 centimes all included.

7 I think you are right.

8 I fancy eating mussels with chips.

d Je pense que tu as raison.

e Qu'est-ce que tu en dis?

f Où est-ce qu'on mange ce midi?

g En fait on dirait qu'il va pleuvoir.

h 10,50 € tout compris.

Grammar

1 Expressing an opinion and seeking an opinion from someone

To express an opinion you can use **penser** *to think* or **croire** *to believe*:

Je pense que / Je crois que	*I think / I believe that...*
Je pense que oui.	*I think so.*
Je crois qu'il est malade.	*I believe he's ill.*

To seek an opinion you can use **penser** and **dire** *to say*:

Qu'est-ce que tu en penses?	*What do you think (of it)?*
Qu'est ce que tu en dis?	*What do you say (about it)?*

En is a pronoun which replaces whatever has just been said or suggested. Addressing someone more formally you will use **vous**:

Qu'est-ce que vous en dites?

Qu'est-ce que vous en pensez?

Exercise 1 La cuisine française

The following statement contains new vocabulary which is essential for slightly more complex conversations. Use the keywords, learn them and then read the text.

En général les Français sont très chauvins, c'est-à-dire qu'ils font souvent preuve de chauvinisme, surtout lorsqu'il s'agit de ce qu'il y a de plus important: la cuisine française. Pour beaucoup de Français, c'est la meilleure cuisine du monde.

c'est-à-dire	*that is to say*
souvent	*often*
surtout	*above all*
lorsque/quand	*when*
partout	*everywhere*
faire preuve de	*to demonstrate / to show*
s'agir de	*to be a matter of*
la meilleure cuisine	*the best cooking*

Now answer the questions:

a What national trait is mentioned here?
b When is this particular trait mostly evident?

▶ Listen to the recording. What do they say? Three people are arguing about the best cooking in the world.

c How many think that French cooking is best?
d What is best about it?
e What other countries are mentioned as possible contenders?
f How many speakers think that the whole issue is a matter of taste?

ℹ There are different types of eating-out places in France, apart from traditional restaurants:

- **Une brasserie** is often a large café which sells mainly beer and serves all sorts of quick meals. They are generally very good value for money.

- **Une crêperie** is a type of restaurant specialising in the cooking of pancakes with various types of fillings. **Crêpes** *pancakes* are a speciality from Brittany but there are now **crêperies** all over France. **Crêpes** can have a savoury or a sweet filling and therefore it is possible to have a full meal eating a savoury pancake (or two) for the main course and a sweet one for dessert.

Brittany is also famous for its seafood and **plateaux de fruits de mer** (seafood platters with all sorts of shellfish which can be shared amongst several people).

Couscous, a North African dish, is often prepared and sold on certain days in campsites or supermarkets: **couscous à emporter** *couscous to take away*. There are also many North African restaurants, especially in Paris.

The latest trend is to eat at a farm house: **Une ferme auberge.** You can eat traditional French country cooking in traditional farm houses. Sometimes they are the same farms which offer **chambres d'hôtes.**

2 Les repas dans la vie des Français
Meals in the life of the French

Read this passage – you will understand it all!

> *Les Français aiment manger. Ils aiment la bonne nourriture* (good food) *et les bons repas* (good meals). *Toute occasion est bonne pour faire un repas de famille ou un repas entre amis: un baptême, une communion ou une confirmation, un mariage, un résultat d'examen, un anniversaire, et évidemment Noël et surtout le premier janvier.*

Did you understand it? Now answer these questions:

a What do French people like?
b Name at least six occasions which are particularly good pretexts for a family meal or a meal with friends.

Here is some more information:

Les heures des repas *meal times*

LES REPAS	LES MOMENTS DE LA JOURNÉE
Le petit déjeuner	*Le matin*
Le déjeuner	*À midi, entre midi et deux heures*
Le goûter	*L'après-midi (surtout pour les enfants)*
Le dîner	*Le soir, vers sept, huit heures*
Le souper	*Plus tard le soir (repas assez léger)*

Le midi les Français mangent à la cantine, à la cafétéria, au restaurant ou bien chez eux s'ils habitent près de leur lieu de travail.

le goûter	afternoon tea (nearest translation but not the same connotation)
goûter (as a verb)	to taste/to appreciate
assez léger	fairly light
chez eux	at (their) home (lit. at theirs)
leur lieu de travail	their place of work

Obviously everybody does not have all these meals every day but generally French people are fairly punctilious about when they eat their meals. You might find that roads are almost empty at meal times because nearly everybody eats at the same time. Also far fewer French people have snacks or sandwiches at lunchtime.

Here are some more questions:

c At what time are French people likely to have dinner in the evening?
d Who is **le goûter** mainly for?
e What is the difference between **le dîner** and **le souper**?
f Where do French people eat at midday?

Exercise 2 Où est-ce qu'on mange ce soir?

Look at the following adverts and say which eating places best fit your requirements. (You can have more than one for each question.)

De quoi est-ce que vous avez envie?

a You wish to eat seafood.
b You would like a meal to take away.
c You would like a Sunday lunch.
d You would like a pancake meal.
e You would like a restaurant with a sea view.
f You would like to take the children out for a meal.
g You are waiting for the boat to Ile de Sein.
h You would like a restaurant open every day until late in the summer.
i You would like a North African meal.
j You would like a seafood supper with mussels and chips.

① BAR - LOTO- PMU

4, place de la République - PONT-CROIX

Pizza à emporter

non stop, midi à 21 h 30

02 98 70 41 41

② ■ Pleuven :

Au Moulin-du-Pont, *crêperie « Chez Mimi »*, sur la route des plages Bénodet-Fouesnant. Crêpes traditionnelles, spécialités glaces. Ouverte tous les jours sauf dimanche midi. Recommandée par le Guide du routard. **Tél. 02.98.54.62.02 - fax 02.98.54.69.91**

③ *Crêperie de Pen al Lenn*
dans un vieux moulin
avec terrasse couverte côté jardin
sur la route de la Forêt-Fouesnant
Fouesnant - ☏ 02.98.56.08.80

OUVERTE
TOUS LES JOURS
en juillet-août
Service continu
de 11 h à 23 h

④ **RESTAURANT LE DORIS**
CHEZ EMMA
Port de Kérity, pointe de Penmarch
Prendre route côtière
phare d'Eckmühl - Le Guilvinec

Dégustation de crustacés, coquillages et poissons de la pêche côtière. Homards de notre vivier. Menu + carte, 7 jours sur 7. Vue sur mer. Repas de famille.
Tél. 02.98.58.60.92

⑤ **RESTAURANT**
"L'ESPADON"
Bourg de PLOBANNALEC
SOIRÉE COUSCOUS
et à emporter (sur réservation)
Tél. 02.98.82.22.52

⑥ PLOVAN

à partir de dix-neuf heures 30

15 AOÛT

SOUPER MARIN
Soupe de poissons
Moules
Frites
Dessert

Prix 10 €

Organisé par les Brochets de Plovan

⑦

Menus de 10 € à 20 €
Vue panoramique
RESTAURANT
LE SAINT-EVETTE
face à l'embarquadère de l'île de sein
Port de Ste.-Evette - ESQUIBIEN
Tél. 02 98 70 10 29

3 Le goûter à la ferme
Afternoon tea on the farm

This is an advert for a farm in the heart of Brittany – **La Ferme des Monts** – near an ancient site called **La Roche aux fées** (*Fairies' Rock*)

RESTAURATION

Goûter à la Ferme

ILLE-ET-VILAINE

Contact	Descriptif
Jacques RUPIN Les Monts 35150 PIRE SUR SEICHE Tél. 02 97 37 55 92	Au pays de la Roche aux fés, près d'l'axe Rennes-Angers, venez visiter les vergers de la ferme des Monts. Vous pourrez découvrir la fabrication traditionnelle du cidre, voir la cave et le matériel utilisé hier et aujourd'hui. Ensuite vous goûterez au jus de pomme, au cidre, aux crêpes et gâteaux maison accompagnés de confitures ou gelées. Vente directe sur place. Ouvert tous les après-midis sur réservation du 1/05 ou 15/09. Hors saison : ouvert sur RDV. Possibilité de recevoir des groupes.

You are not expected to understand every word in the advert but use the following keywords to answer the questions.

un verger	*an orchard*	**des confitures**	*jams*
la cave	*the cellar*	**des gelées**	*preserves*
hier	*yesterday/in the old days*		
	RDV=rendez-vous	*appointment*	

a Name two things you could see or visit at the farm.
b What could you drink?
c What could you eat with the home-made cakes?
d When is the farm open for **le goûter**?
e What would you need to do before going there?

▶ Exercise 3 Le souper marin

You and your friend Michel would like to go to the seafood supper at Plovan (see page 99). Listen to the recording and answer Michel's questions.

ℹ Moules-frites is the type of snack meal you can eat in a brasserie anywhere in France nowaday but it is primarily a Belgian speciality. **Jacques Brel** (8 April 1929 – 9 October 1978), the famous Belgian singer, referred to **frites, moules et bières** in some of his songs. The chain of restaurants, Léon de Bruxelles, which specializes in moules et frites, has expended to Paris and most other parts of France.

Exercise

Cochez les cases – tick the boxes where required to make a meaningful sentence

Les Belges ☐ les Suisses ☐ les Américains ☐ ne mangent pas ☐ n'aiment pas ☐ sont amateurs ☐ de beefburgers ☐ de moules-frites ☐ de couscous ☐ qu'ils mangent ☐ qu'ils boivent ☐ dans des restaurants ☐ dans des brasseries ☐ avec du vin rouge ☐ avec de la bière ☐ de la limonade ☐. Le chanteur et poète ☐ artiste peintre ☐ Jacques Brel ☐ a dénigré ☐ a célébré ☐ a refusé ☐ cette coutume natinale ☐ dans ses chansons ☐ dans son testament ☐.

Maintenant écrivez la phrase correcte.

Surfez sur le web

- Vous aimez les moules-frites? Amusez-vous en visitant le suite interactif de www.leon-de-bruxelles.fr.

Web extension exercise

Trouvez l'image du restaurant. Cliquez sur la première fenêtre à gauche de la porte d'entrée pour trouver des addresses. Cliquez sur la première fenêtre à droite de la porte pour des jeux (*games*) pour les enfants et pour les grands cliquez sur la porte.

---

la porte *the door*	**la fenêtre** *the window*
la porte-fenêtre *French windows*	

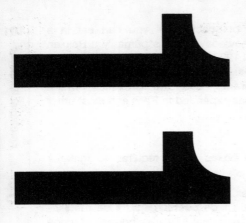

11 la pluie et le beau temps!

rain and shine!

In this unit you will learn
- how to talk about the weather
- how to listen to a radio bulletin and read the weather forecast in the newspaper
- about the regions of France
- to express the present and future

▶1 Il va faire de l'orage
It's going to be stormy

Sarah et Dominique sont dans leur voiture. Elles vont visiter Dinan, une cité médiévale sur la Rance. Elles parlent de la pluie et du beau temps...

Listen to the recording and answer these questions:

a When is it certainly going to rain?
b Why do they turn the radio on?

Listen again.

c The weather forecast mentions storms for at least three French regions. Can you name any of them?

Now read the dialogue.

Dominique	Tu as raison, le temps change...il fait lourd, il va faire de l'orage!
Sarah	Oui, le ciel est couvert. En tout cas il va certainement pleuvoir cet après-midi.
Dominique	Ah oui, voilà les première gouttes de pluie.
Sarah	Écoutons les prévisions météorologiques.

Elles écoutent France Inter

...et pour les jours suivants le temps lourd va persister. Il fera encore chaud et ensoleillé. L'évolution orageuse sera plus marquée sur les Pyrénées, les Alpes et sur la Corse. Dans l'ensemble de la France les températures resteront cinq degrés au-dessus des températures de saison. C'était notre bulletin météorologique de la mi-journée. Vous pourrez écouter notre prochain bulletin sur France Inter à seize heures cinquante-cinq. Et voici maintenant notre bulletin d'informations de treize heures...

Dominique	Alors c'est partout pareil en France.
Sarah	Qu'est-ce qu'on fait demain? On va dans le Finistère comme prévu?
Dominique	Oui d'accord et après cela on commencera à descendre vers Bordeaux en passant par chez moi à St Nazaire et chez mon copain à Nantes.

le temps	weather (in the text above) but also time
le temps est lourd	the weather is close/muggy
le ciel	the sky
une goutte de pluie	a raindrop
les prévisions météorologiques/la météo	weather forecast
la mi-journée	midday/lunchtime
au-dessus	above
au-dessous	below
pareil	the same
prévoir	to forecast/plan
comme prévu	as planned
mon copain	my friend/boyfriend
ma copine	my friend/girlfriend

Reread the dialogue and answer these questions:

d Will temperatures over France:
  1 go up   2 go down   3 be higher than the seasonal norm
  4 be very low

e The forecast is for:
  1 today only   2 tomorrow only   3 the weekend
  4 the next few days

f The weather bulletin was:
  1 at 6 a.m.   2 just before the 1 o'clock news   3 at 4.55 p.m.

g Tomorrow Dominique and Sarah:
  1 plan to stay in St Malo   2 move on to Finistère
  3 get to Bordeaux

h On their way to Bordeaux they will:
  1 visit Paris   2 stop on the way in St Nazaire
  3 stop to see Dominique's boyfriend

Grammar

French people tend to spend a lot of time talking about the weather. To discuss today's weather they use the present tense and the following structures:

1 Quel temps fait-il aujourd'hui?
What is the weather like today?

- **Il fait** ... best translated as: *It is...*
  Il fait beau (*nice*)/ chaud (*hot*) / froid (*cold*) /lourd (*muggy*)/ du soleil (*sunny*)/ du vent *(windy)*/ du brouillard (*foggy*) / de l'orage (*stormy*)
- **Le temps est....** *The weather is...*
  Le temps est ensoleillé (*sunny*) / nuageux (*cloudy*) / brumeux (*misty*) / pluvieux (*rainy*), orageux (*stormy*) / couvert (*overcast*)
- **Il y a...** *There is ...*
  Il y a du vent (*wind*)/des nuages *(clouds)*/de la pluie (*rain*)/de la neige (*snow*)
- **Il pleut** (*it's raining*) / **il neige** (*it's snowing*)

You can see how to read and understand most of the weather conditions on the map from the newspaper on pages 108–9.

2 Quel temps fera-t-il?

In conversational French you are likely to hear people using the immediate future: **il va** + infinitive:

- **Il va faire** beau / **il va pleuvoir** (*it's going to rain*) / **il va faire** de l'orage etc....

But in more formal situations (forecasts on the radio, TV or newspapers) the verbs are mainly in the future tense:

- Il **fera** beau (**faire** in the future tense)
- Le temps **sera** orageux (**être** in the future tense)
- Il y **aura**... (**avoir** in the future tense): Il y aura des **averses** (*showers*), des **éclaircies** (*bright periods*), de la **brume** (*mist*)
- Le vent **soufflera** (*the wind will blow*) (**souffler** in the future tense)
- Il **pleuvra** (*it will rain*)/il **neigera** (*it will snow*)

3 The future tense

Look at the text accompanying the map of France (see pages 104–5) and you will be able to find many more examples of verbs in the future tense.

Using verbs in the future tense is simple for most verbs ending with -er or -ir:

- When the subject is **il/elle** (*it*) use the verb (in the infinitive) + ending -a:
  Le soleil **brillera** *The sun will shine.* (**briller** + -a)
- When the subject is **ils /elles** (*they*) use the verb (in the infinitive) + ending -ont:
  Les températures **avoisineront** les 30 degrés *Temperatures will be close to 30 degrees.* (**avoisiner** + ont)
- Whatever the verb, the endings for verbs in the future are always the same:

je	-rai	nous	-rons
tu	-ras	vous	-rez
il	-ra	elles	-ront

⊕ Un peu de géographie

France is often referred to as **L'Hexagone** because of its shape (six sides).

Look at the map of France and the article above it (pages 108–9).

For weather forecast purposes France has been divided into seven broad areas, some representing a whole region and others several regions. The towns on the map can be used as markers for you to locate these regions.

Complete the following sentences either with the name of a town or with the name of a region of France:

1 Rennes est en B_____, Nantes est dans les Pays de Loire, Rouen et _____ sont en Normandie.
2 _____ et Amiens sont dans le Nord-Picardie, Paris est en Ile de France.
3 Metz et _____ sont dans le _____, Dijon est en Bourgogne et Besançon est en Franche-Comté.
4 Poitiers est dans le _____-_____, Orléans est dans le Centre et Limoge est dans le _____.
5 Toulouse est dans la région Midi-Pyrénées et _____ est dans l'Aquitaine.
6 Clermont-Ferrand est en A_____ et _____ est dans la région Rhône-Alpes.
7 Montpellier, _____ et _____ sont sur le Pourtour méditerranéen et Ajaccio est en _____.

Note that **Le Midi** is used as a generic name for the South of France.

Les points cardinaux:

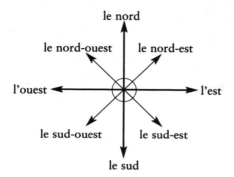

▶ Pronunciation

- **le sud:** you can hear the **d** at the end of the word but in **le nord** the **d** is dropped
- **le sud-est / le sud-ouest** : are both pronounced linking the two words and the **-t** at the end of **est** and **ouest** is also pronounced: [*le sudest/le sudouest*].
- **le nord-est / le nord-ouest:** are both pronounced linking the two words but dropping the **-d** at the end of **nord:** [*le norest / le norouest*]

Grammar

4 en, dans *and* sur

- **En** is usually used in front of the name of a region or province:
  en Bretagne *in Brittany*
- **Dans** is used in front of a geographical area:
  dans le nord-est *in the north-east*
- **Sur** is used in association with the name of a region mainly with reference to the weather:
  sur la Bretagne et la Normandie *over Brittany and Normandy*

▶ Exercise 1 Le temps aujourd'hui

Using the weather map and reading/listening to the text say where you can find the following weather conditions for the day (in some cases it applies to more than one area):

a Thunderstorms from midday onwards
b Sunny all day
c Muggy in the afternoon
d Morning mist
e A light north-east wind
f Temperatures ranging from 30° on the coast to 35° inland
g Temperatures 5° above the seasonal norm
h Cloudy (veiled) sky in the afternoon

LE TEMPS AUJOURD'HUI, RÉGION PAR RÉGION

Bretagne, Pays de la Loire, Normandie.
Sur la Bretagne et la Normandie, le soleil brillera largement toute la journée. Sur les Pays de la Loire, le soleil sera bien présent, mais le ciel se voilera dans l'après-midi. Il fera chaud, entre 24 et 30° du nord au sud.

Nord-Picardie, Ile-de-France. Après quelques brumes matinales, le soleil s'imposera largement. Un léger vent de nord-est soufflera. Le thermomètre indiquera entre 26 et 30° du nord au sud.

Nord-Est, Bourgogne, Franche-Comté.
Le temps sera chaud et bien ensoleillé. Les températures avoisineront les 30° soit 5 degrés au-dessus des températures de saison.

Poitou-Charentes, Centre, Limousin. La matinée sera bien ensoleillée mais le temps deviendra lourd et il y aura des ondées en Poitou-Charentes et sur le Limousin. Le thermomètre atteindra souvent les 30°.

Aquitaine, Midi-Pyrénées. Dans la matinée, le temps deviendra lourd. Des ondées orageuses se produiront l'après-midi et des orages éclateront sur les Pyrénées dès la mi-journée. Les températures seront comprises entre 27 et 31°.

Auvergne, Rhône-Alpes. En Auvergne, le temps deviendra lourd l'après-midi avec des risques d'ondées orageuses. Sur Rhône-Alpes, le temps sera ensoleillé. Des nuages se développeront sur les Alpes et quelques orages isolés éclateront. Le thermomètre indiquera entre 27 et 31°.

Pourtour méditerranéen, Corse. Sur le Languedoc-Roussillon, la matinée sera assez ensoleillée mais le temps deviendra lourd l'après-midi avec des ondées orageuses. Ailleurs, le soleil brillera largement. Il fera chaud entre 30° sur les côtes et 35° dans l'intérieur.

METEO

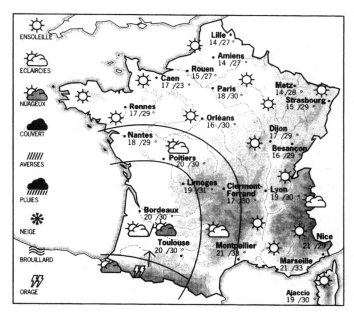

ENSOLEILLÉ

ÉCLAIRCIES

NUAGEUX

COUVERT

////// AVERSES

/////// PLUIES

❄ NEIGE

≋ BROUILLARD

⚡ ORAGE

Lille 14 /27°
Amiens 14 /27°
Rouen 15 /27°
Caen 17 /23°
Metz 14 /28°
Strasbourg 15 /29°
Paris 18 /30°
Rennes 17 /29°
Orléans 16 /30°
Dijon 17 /29°
Nantes 18 /29°
Besançon 16 /29°
Poitiers 20 /30°
Limoges 19 /31°
Clermont-Ferrand 17 /30°
Lyon 19 /30°
Bordeaux 20 /30°
Toulouse 20 /30°
Montpellier 21 /33°
Nice 21 /29°
Marseille 21 /33°
Ajaccio 19 /30°

▶ **Exercise 2 Où sont-ils en vacances?**
Where are they on holiday?

a Listen to the recording and look at the list of cities overleaf and their weather conditions. Then say where the following French people are spending their holidays.

Exemple: 'Bonjour, je m'appelle Étienne. La ville où je suis est ensoleillée et la température est entre 18 et 30 degrés.'

Réponse: Étienne est à Paris.

1 Fabienne est _____ .
2 Jérôme est _____ .
3 Stéphanie est _____ .
4 Alexandre est _____ .

b Say what the weather is like in the towns where you are holidaying.

1 Vous êtes à Varsovie. Quel temps fait-il?
2 Vous êtes à Berlin. Quel temps fait-il?

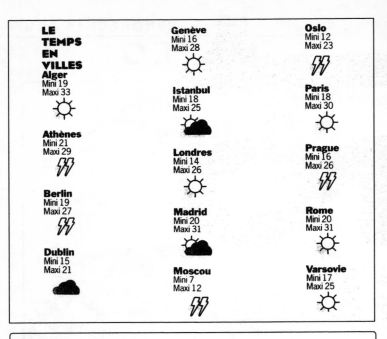

LE TEMPS EN VILLES

Alger
Mini 19
Maxi 33

Athènes
Mini 21
Maxi 29

Berlin
Mini 19
Maxi 27

Dublin
Mini 15
Maxi 21

Genève
Mini 16
Maxi 28

Istanbul
Mini 18
Maxi 25

Londres
Mini 14
Maxi 26

Madrid
Mini 20
Maxi 31

Moscou
Mini 7
Maxi 12

Oslo
Mini 12
Maxi 23

Paris
Mini 18
Maxi 30

Prague
Mini 16
Maxi 26

Rome
Mini 20
Maxi 31

Varsovie
Mini 17
Maxi 25

Surfez sur le web

- Vous pouvez voir une carte qui indique les prévisions météorologiques au jour le jour (*day by day*) sur le site de Météo France (www.meteofrance.com).
- Cliquez sur santé (*health*)/environnement pour accéder à des conseils sur la canicule (*heat wave*), les UVs et les pollens.

Web extension exercise

La canicule

La canicule tue chaque année à travers le monde, peut-être même plus encore que le froid...

Les ultraviolets

Qui n'a jamais souffert d'un coup de soleil?

Même si le soleil nous apporte bien-être et vitalité, il peut parfois se transformer en un terrible adversaire.

Les pollens

La pollinose, souvent appelée rhume des foins, est le nom donné à l'allergie au pollen des arbres, plantes, herbacées et graminées.

1 Throughout the world what meteorological phenomenon kills more than the cold?
2 Find the expression for sunburn.
3 Find the expression for hay fever.

12 au restaurant
at the restaurant

In this unit you will learn
- how to order a drink in a café
- how to read a menu in a restaurant and how to order a meal
- some information on **le Finistère**
- how to recognize the past tense and how to express the recent past

1 Un peu de lecture
A little bit of reading

Read the paragraph below.

C'est le mois de juillet. Nos deux amies, Dominique et Sarah, ont passé le week-end à Quimper pour les Fêtes de Cornouaille. Aujourd'hui elles viennent de visiter des chapelles dans le Pays Bigouden. Maintenant elles sont assises à la terrasse d'un café, Place de l'Église, à Plonéour-Lanvern. Il fait chaud et elles ont très soif.

Now answer these questions:

1 The month is:
a June b July c January

2 Our two friends have spent the weekend:
a in Cornwall b in St Malo c in Quimper

3 They have just visited:
a some chapels b some castles c some churches

4 They are now:
a in the church b in a restaurant c sitting at the terrace of a café

5 The weather is:
a muggy and they are tired b hot and they are very thirsty
c cold

Grammar

1 How to talk about events which have already happened

To say something has just happened use **venir** in the present tense + **de** + verb (in the infinitive):

Elles viennent de visiter des chapelles.	*They have just visited some chapels.*
Le bateau vient d'arriver au port.	*The boat has just arrived in the port.*
Tu viens de rencontrer le président.	*You've just met the president.*

Venir on its own means *to come* e.g. Venez-vous souvent ici? *Do you come here often?*

Venir de... indicates that something has just happened or has just been done.

Exercise 1 Faites des phrases
In the grid below, columns A and C remain the same. Columns B and D are jumbled.

Can you find the six correct sentences? Can you say what they mean?

A	B	C	D
1 Je	viennent	d'arriver	un bon film
2 Tu	venez	de finir	le gros lot au Loto
3 Jean-Paul	viens	de gagner	St Malo
4 Nous	vient	de visiter	à Paris
5 Vous	venons	de choisir	tes examens
6 Elles	viens	de voir	un menu

Il vient de gagner le gros lot au Loto!

Grammar

2 How to talk about events which happened recently

To say something or someone has recently completed an action use the perfect tense. The word *perfect* here means *complete* – something has been achieved or completed:

Elles **ont passé** le weekend à Quimper.	*They have spent the weekend in Quimper.*

How to form the perfect tense

- The perfect tense is formed with **avoir** or **être** (page 19) in the present tense + another verb: **j'ai choisi** *I chose.*

Avoir and **être** are called auxiliary verbs when they are used in this way. The verb which indicates the event or action which has been completed is in a form called a past participle. When Jean-Paul discovers that he has won the jackpot he says: J'ai **gagné** le gros lot. **Gagné** is the past participle of the verb **gagner** *to win.*

In this unit you will learn how to recognize and use the perfect tense with **avoir** which is the auxiliary verb used with the vast majority of verbs.

Verbs which end with **-er** and those which end with **-ir** are very easy to use:

All verbs ending with **-er** in their basic form (infinitive) have a past participle ending with **-é.**

All verbs ending with **-ir** have a past participle ending with **-i.**

visiter → visit**é**	finir → fin**i**
passer → pass**é**	choisir → chois**i**
gagner → gagn**é**	servir→ serv**i**
aller → all**é** (though **aller** is used with **être**)	

Exercise 2 Encore des phrases

Once again columns B and D have moved. Can you find six correct sentences in the box below and say what they mean?

A	B	C	D
1 J'	avons	écouté	des moules-frites
2 Tu	ont	fini	les infos à la radio
3 On	avez	mangé	vos cartes postales
4 Nous	a	choisi	ton travail
5 Vous	ai	posté	une cabine
6 Sarah et Dominique	as	réservé	un hôtel pas trop cher

ℹ️ Un peu de géographie et un peu de culture

France is divided administratively into 95 **départements**. **Le Finistère** is the furthest west, jutting into **l'Océan Atlantique**. It is one of Brittany's four **départements**. **Quimper** is the administrative capital of **Finistère** and at the heart of **la Cornouaille** (the French Cornwall).

Throughout the summer there are festivals all over Finistère and the other **départements bretons**. One of them is **les fêtes de Cornouaille** which celebrates Brittany's traditional costumes and Celtic music and always takes place the third weekend in July. Another well-known festival is **le Festival Inter-Celtique de Lorient** which takes place in Lorient (Morbihan) in the first two weeks of August each year and is dedicated to Celtic music from all Celtic areas of Europe.

ℹ️ Un peu d'histoire

The part of **Finistère**, south-west of Quimper, around the towns of **Pont-L'Abbé** and **Plonéour-Lanvern** is called **le Pays Bigouden**. There are still a few women, known as Bigoudènes, who wear an extremely high lace head dress some of the time. Although many parts of France have their own traditional costumes which often include a lace head dress, **les Bigoudènes** seem to have kept the tradition of wearing their **coiffes** even to go to the market.

The historical background for such a tradition appears to find its roots in events which took place a few years prior to the French Revolution when local peasants rioted against the local nobility. As a punishment the king ordered that the steeples of their churches and chapels be decapitated. In turn the local women are said to have decided to wear the high coiffes as a sign of defiance. From then onwards they have been wearing them higher and higher.

A *Bigoudène* riding her bicycle against the wind

▶2 Au Café de la Baie *At the Bay Café*

Sarah et Dominique sont à la terrasse d'un café.

Listen to the recording once and answer these questions:

a When the two women order their drinks do they both order the same thing?
b Does Sarah order anything else?
c Does Dominique sound very enthusiastic about it?

Listen again.

d Who asks for the bill?
e Who is going to pay? Why?

Listen for a third time.

f How much is the bill? Do they leave a tip?

Now read the dialogue.

Serveur	Bonjour mesdames, qu'est ce que je vous sers?
Sarah	Alors pour moi une bière pression...et toi Dominique?
Dominique	Euh … je conduis alors je vais prendre un panaché.
Serveur	Alors une bière pression et un panaché.
Sarah	Et nous allons prendre des glaces aussi?
Serveur	Tout de suite madame, je vous apporte la carte.

Quelques minutes plus tard

Sarah	Tu prends une glace Dominique?
Dominique	Non, je suis au régime!
Sarah	Eh bien prends un sorbet; il y a moins de calories.
Serveur	Vous avez choisi?
Sarah	Oui, alors une glace à la fraise et un sorbet au citron. Et l'addition s'il vous plaît.

Un peu plus tard

Dominique	C'est moi qui paie cette fois-ci, toi tu as payé la dernière fois! C'est combien l'addition?
Sarah	Ça fait neuf euros cinquante.
Dominique	Dix avec le pourboire.

une bière	*a beer*	**quelques minutes**	*a few minutes*
un panaché	*a shandy*	**plus tard**	*later*
une glace	*an ice-cream*	**être au régime**	*to be on a diet*
l'addition	*the bill*	**cette fois-ci**	*this time*
le pourboire	*the tip*	**tout de suite**	*right away*
conduire	*to drive*	**apporter**	*to bring*

Now read the dialogue and find the French equivalent for the following sentences:

g I'll bring you the menu.
h Have a sorbet; it's got fewer calories.
i A strawberry ice cream and a lemon sorbet.
j You paid last time.
k a few minutes later
l a short while later

There are also two examples of the perfect tense in the dialogue. Can you find them and say what they mean? Now find the verbs in the present and the immediate future.

Grammar

3 C'est moi

C'est moi qui paie cette fois-ci.   *It's me who is paying this time.*

In the dialogue, Dominique could have said **Je paie cette fois** *I am paying this time* but for emphasis she said **C'est moi qui paie**. In English we would probably use our voice for emphasis, stressing *I'm paying*.

Moi and other pronouns used in conversation to emphasize what is being said can be referred to as emphatic pronouns. In some cases (**elle, nous, vous, elles**) they are the same as subject pronouns, but the masculine singular pronoun is **lui** and the masculine plural pronoun is **eux**:

C'est **toi** qui as gagné?   *Is it **you** that won?*

C'est **lui** qui a choisi pas moi!   *He's the one that chose not **me**!*

C'est **elle** qui conduit!   *She's driving!*

C'est **nous** qui avons visité la Corse.   *We're the ones who've visited Corsica!*

Ce sont **elles** qui ont passé l'été en Bretagne.   *They're the ones who spent the summer in Britanny!* (fem. pl.)

C'est **vous** qui habitez à Marseille?   *Is it **you** that lives in Marseille?*

Ce sont **eux** qui arriveront les premiers.   *It's **them** who arrived first.* (masc. pl.)

ℹ Le tarif des consommations

There are some regulations about the price of drinks in France. These are guidelines and there are discrepancies between various places. Prices of drinks in cafés and restaurants are not in any way comparable with the price of drinks you buy in a supermarket or any other shop.

When you ask for **une bière pression** you can expect a 25 cl glass of draft lager. Labelled beers in bottles are more expensive. For English people tempted to ask for a pint of beer, there is obviously not such a concept in France so the best thing is to ask for **une grande bière** which means that you will probably get half a litre of beer.

**Et voilà, un coca et
un sandwich au fromage!**

▶ 3 Au restaurant *At the restaurant*

Didier et Véronique Morin et leurs deux enfants, Armelle et Fabien, passent la nuit à l'Hôtel des Voyageurs. Ils ont décidé de dîner au restaurant de l'hôtel.

Listen once to the recording, then answer the questions.

a What seating arrangement does the waitress offer the family?
b Do they wish to have an aperitive?

Listen to the recording again.

c Apart from fixed price menus, what kind of menu do they ask for?
d Would they like to see the wine list?

Listen once more.

e Véro asked for a 10 € menu. Why does the waitress say that she cannot serve it?

f What do they order?

Now read the dialogue.

Serveuse	Bonsoir Monsieur-dame. J'ai une table pour quatre près de la fenêtre, est-ce que cela vous convient?
Didier	Oui, très bien.
Serveuse	Vous désirez prendre un apéritif?
Didier	Non non, apportez-nous le menu s'il vous plaît.
Serveuse	Vous voulez le menu à la carte?
Didier	Non, nous prendrons des menus à prix fixes. Vous avez un menu pour enfants?
Serveuse	Oui monsieur. Je vous apporte la carte des vins?
Véro	Oui merci.

Quelques minutes plus tard

Serveuse	Monsieur-dame vous avez choisi?
Véro	Alors nous allons prendre un menu à 10 €, un menu à 20 €, deux menus pour enfants et une bouteille de Muscadet s'il vous plaît.
Serveuse	Je suis désolée madame mais le menu à 10 € est pour midi seulement.
Véro	Pas de problème, nous prendrons deux menus à 20 €.

la fenêtre	*the window*	**je suis désolée**	*I am sorry*
convenir	*to suit*	**cela vous convient?**	*does it*
une bouteille	*a bottle*		*suit you?*

ℹ The menu

Whether you order a meal **à la carte** or **un menu à prix fixe** the pattern of your meal is likely to be similar to the menu shown below:

une entrée / un hors d'œuvre (*a starter*)
un plat principal (*a main course*)
(either **de la viande** *meat* or **du poisson** *fish*)
du fromage (*cheese*)
un dessert

Unfortunately it is not easy to find restaurants with a vegetarian menu. If you are vegetarian (**Je suis végétarien/végétarienne**) you are likely to be offered:

---

une assiette de crudités
(*a plate of mixed salad*)
un plateau de fromages:
du camembert, du gruyère, du Roquefort (*a selection of cheeses*),
du fromage de chèvre (*goat's cheese*)
un dessert

When you order your meal check that the service is included in the price **Le service est compris?**

Restaurants are obliged to indicate on their menus if the prices quoted are net prices: **prix nets.**

▶ Exercise 3 Bon appétit!

Look at the four menus which follow and listen to the recording. You have to enter in the table below what Luc and Florence have ordered. You may have to listen to the recording several times.

The last row is for you. There are gaps on the recording for you to respond to the waitress with your order from the 25 € menu.

	Menus (prix)	First course	Second	Cheese	Dessert
Luc					
Florence					
Vous	25 €	6 oysters served hot with seaweed	Grilled scallop kebab	Cheese	Strawberry ice cream

MENU À 20 €

ASSIETTE DE FRUITS DE MER
PLATE OF SEAFOOD
OU
COQUILLE SAINT JACQUES À LA BRETONNE
SCALLOPS "À LA BRETONNE"
12 PALOURDES DES GLENAN FARCIES
12 STUFFED GLENAN CLAMS

BROCHETTE DE JOUE DE LOTTE À LA DIABLE
DEVIL MONKFISH KEBAB
OU
LE COQ AU VIN DU PATRON
COQ AU VIN SPECIAL
OU
CONTREFILET GRILLÉ MAÎTRE D'HÔTEL
GRILLED SIRLOIN STEAK MAîTRE D'HÔTEL

SALADE DE SAISON

PLATEAU DE FROMAGES OU CHOIX DE DESSERTS
CHEESE PLATTER OR CHOICE OF DESSERTS

MENU À 25 €

ASSIETTE DE FRUITS DE MER
PLATE OF SEAFOOD
OU
SALADE GOURMANDE AUX TROIS CANARDS
GOURMAND THREE DUCK SALAD
OU
6 HUITRES CHAUDES AU COCKTAIL D'ALGUES
6 OYSTERS SERVED HOT WITH SEAWEED COCKTAIL

BROCHETTE DE SAINT JACQUES AU BEURRE BLANC
GRILLED SCALLOP KEBAB IN BEURRE BLANC
OU
MAGRET DE CANARD AUX AIRELLES ET AU PORTO
MAGRET OF DUCK IN PORT AND BILBERRY
OU
CHÂTEAUBRIAND AUX CINQ POIVRES
STEAK CHÂTEAUBRIAND SEASONED WITH FIVE PEPPERS

PLATEAU DE FROMAGES
CHEESE PLATTER

CHOIX DE DESSERTS
CHOICE OF DESSERT

MENU À 35 €

PLATEAU DE FRUITS DE MER
SEAFOOD PLATTER

BROCHETTE DE SAINT JACQUES GRILLÉE, BEURRE BLANC
GRILLED SCALLOP KEBAB IN WHITE BUTTER

ROGNONS DE VEAU BEAUGE AUX MORILLES
VEAL KIDNEYS IN CREAM AND MORREL SAUCE

PLATEAU DE FROMAGES
CHEESE PLATTER

FRAISES MELBA
STRAWBERRY MELBA

MENU À 45 €

PLATEAU DE FRUITS DE MER
SEAFOOD PLATTER

HOMARD BRETON À NOTRE FAÇON
BRETON LOBSTER; CHEF'S SPECIAL

PLATEAU DE FROMAGES
CHEESE PLATTER

DESSERT
CHOICE OF DESSERT

Surfez sur le web

Vous aimez sortir au restaurant?
- Pour vos visites à Paris recherchez le restaurant de votre choix avec www.planresto.fr. Cliquez sur le chef et choisissez selon vos désirs: une envie (*a whim*), un budget, un lieu (*a place*), un nom.
- Pour choisir un bon vin www.cuisineetvinsdefrance.com est le site internet d'un magazine qui suggère le vin idéal pour toutes circonstances.

Web extension exercise

Le scénario

Vous êtes de passage à Paris. Vous avez invité un ami à manger au restaurant à midi, près de votre hôtel, dans le quatrième arrondissement, code postal 75004 (*4th district of Paris*). Votre budget est limité à 40 € maximum, pour vous deux. Vous visitez le site www.planresto.fr. Sélectionnez votre **budget: Indifférent? Prix le midi? Prix le soir?** C'est l'été, il fait chaud; à Paris, c'est la canicule. Vous sélectionnez un service supplémentaire pour pouvoir manger confortablement. Alors, vous choisissez un restaurant avec l'**air conditionné** ou bien **avec terrasse?**

C'est possible pour 40 €. Vrai ou Faux?

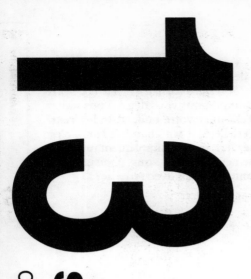

13

sur la route
on the road

In this unit you will learn
- about French roads and driving in France
- useful expressions to use in a service station
- some vocabulary
- pronouns y and en

La voiture de Dominique

▶1 Il y a une déviation
There is a diversion

Sarah et Dominique sont en route pour St Nazaire où habite Dominique. Elles sont sur la RN (route nationale) 175. C'est Sarah qui conduit.

> # TRAVAUX SUR RN 175
> # ROUTE BARRÉE À 500M
> # RALENTISSEZ!

Listen to the recording once, and answer these questions:

a What's happening on the road?
b What is the speed limit?

Listen again:

c Where are they going to stop next?
d Is the place they are stopping at on the left or on the right?

Now read the dialogue:

Dominique Ah zut alors! Tu as vu le panneau? La route est barrée à cinq cents mètres.

Sarah Oui il y a une déviation.

Dominique Il faut passer par Auray. Ralentis un peu. Sarah, regarde le panneau: 'Travaux'. La vitesse limite est de cinquante kilomètres à l'heure. En plus il y a souvent des gendarmes sur cette route!

Sarah De toute façon il faut qu'on s'arrête à la prochaine station service parce qu'il n'y a presque plus d'essence.

Dominique Tiens, il y en a une sur la droite, ici, tout de suite. On devrait aussi vérifier le niveau d'huile et la pression des pneus tant que nous y sommes. Prends la première pompe, là, 'sans plomb'.

Sarah On fait le plein?

Dominique Oui il vaut mieux.

Zut!	Drat! (mild expletive)
en plus	what's more
de toute façon	in any case
tout de suite	right here (immediately)
il vaut mieux	we'd better
il faut...	we must...
il faut qu'on...	it's necessary that we ...
il n'y a presque plus de ...	there is hardly any ...

Link the following English phrases to the equivalent French expressions:

1 There is a diversion.
2 Did you see the road sign?
3 The road is closed in 500 metres.
4 The speed limit is 50km/h.
5 We'll have to stop.
6 We ought to check the tyre pressure.
7 Shall we fill up?
8 Slow down a bit, Sarah!

a On devrait vérifier la pression des pneus.
b La vitesse limite est 50km à l'heure.
c On fait le plein?
d Ralentis un peu, Sarah!
e Il y a une déviation.
f Il va falloir s'arrêter.
g La route est barrée à 500 mètres.
h Tu as vu le panneau?

Grammar

1 Il faut / il faut que

The verb **falloir** *to be necessary* is only ever used in an impersonal form with subject pronoun **il**: **il faut**.

- **Il faut** + verb in the infinitive:

    Il faut conduire à droite. *You must drive on the right.*

    Il faut se reposer souvent quand on conduit sur de grandes distances. *You must rest often when driving long distances.*

- **Il faut que** + verb in a present form. As the second verb must be in the present subjunctive (see page 190) it is best to avoid this structure and use **il faut** + infinitive. However, for **-er** verbs the singular present subjunctive looks like the present tense you know:

    Il faut qu'on s'arrête à la prochaine station service. *We have to stop at the next petrol station.*

    Il faut que j'achète un litre d'huile. *I have to buy a litre of oil.*

2 Ne ... plus / ne ... pas / ne ... que

Il **n'**y a **plus** / il **ne** reste **plus** d'essence. *There is no petrol left.*
Il **n'**y a **presque plus** d'essence. *There is hardly any petrol left*
Il **n'**y a **pas** de station service sur cette route. *There is no service station on this road.*
Il **n'**y a pas assez d'huile. *There is not enough oil.*
Il **n'**y a **que** de l'essence super. *There is only high grade petrol.*
Il **ne** reste **qu'** un billet de vingt euros. *There is only a 20 € note left.*

Reminder:

Use **ne** in front of a consonant and **n'** in front of a vowel.

3 Pronouns y and en

- **Y** is used frequently in expressions like **il y a** (*there is* or *there are*):

    Tant que nous y sommes. *While we are about it.* (Lit. *here* y – *here / there*)

- **En** is used with expressions of quantity and replaces a word already mentioned:

Une station service? Il y en a une sur la droite. *A service station? There is one on the right.*

(en replaces **une station service**)

Il ne reste plus de bonbons, j'en achète? *There aren't any sweets left, shall I buy some?*

(en replaces **bonbons**)

- **Y** and **en** are used in negative sentences:

  – Il reste du pain? *Is there some bread left?*
  – Non, il n'y en a plus. *No, there isn't any (left).*

  – Tu as du lait? *Have you got some milk?*
  – Non, je n'en ai pas. *No, I haven't got any.*

▶ Pronunciation

- **Il n'y en a** may seem difficult to pronounce but all the sounds roll into one [*ilniena*].

  For **i** (like the *mi* and *ti* in English) your lips are straight but taut.

- **Zut!** Getting your **u** right is essential to sound at all French. You may need to practise in front of a mirror in order to get the correct position for your lips, which should be tightly rounded, as though you are going to whistle. Now try to say **ee** - the result will be a French **u**!

  Try saying **i** … **u** … **i** …**u** … **i** … **u** several times, alternately stretching your lips and then pursing them.

Exercise 1 Il manque toujours quelque chose!
There is always something missing!

Link the first part of each sentence to the correct ending from the second column. You need to use all the information contained in the **Grammar** section, opposite.

1 Il n'y a plus d'essence, il faut	**a** en remettre*.
2 Il ne reste que cinquante euros, il faut	**b** j'en achète.
3 Je n'ai plus d'argent, il faut que	**c** trouver une station service.
4 Il n'y a pas assez de café, il faut que	**d** je trouve du travail.
5 On n'a plus de fromage, il faut qu'	**e** trouver une banque.
6 Il n'y a plus d'huile dans le moteur, il faut	**f** on en achète.

Note that there are two possible ways of ending sentences 1 and 6.

* **mettre** *to put* and **remettre** *to put more / again*

Exercise 2 Qu'est ce qu'elles doivent faire?

Look back at the dialogue on page 126. What is the third thing that Sarah and Dominique must do when they get to the petrol station?

1 Faire le plein d'essence

2 Vérifier le niveau d'huile

3 …

▶ Exercise 3 À la station service

Choisissez la bonne pompe et le carburant qui convient à votre voiture.

Attention! Si vous avez un moteur diesel il faut mettre du gazole/diesel. La plupart des voitures modernes utilisent de l'essence sans plomb *(lead-free petrol)*.

Listen to the recording and say which car each person is driving: **A, B** or **C**.

A   **B**   **C**

1 La première personne conduit la voiture_____.
2 La deuxième personne conduit la voiture_____.
3 La troisième personne conduit la voiture_____.

Filling up

petrol	*essence*	**unleaded**	*sans plomb*
leaded 4 star	*essence super*	**diesel**	*gazole*
liquid petroleum gas GPL	*(gaz de pétrole liquéfié)*		

Listen to the recording again.

4 What do each of the three drivers ask for?

❚ Roulez à droite

The main thing not to forget if you are a British driver arriving in France is that you have to drive on the right-hand side. There are signs when coming out of the port or off the Shuttle.

ROULEZ À DROITE	CONDUISEZ À DROITE

TOURISTES BRITANNIQUES N'OUBLIEZ PAS DE ROULER À DROITE!

N'oubliez pas!

Don't forget!

❚ La priorité à droite

There is one particular rule to remember on French roads. It is known as **priorité à droite** (*priority to the right*). It means that cars have to let vehicles coming from the right go first. This does not apply if you are on a **route prioritaire** (*a main road*). Smaller roads intersecting with the main ones have signs telling drivers to stop at the white line. It is important to check for signs indicating on which kind of road you are driving.

In small towns, street intersections often have **priorité à droite** and most drivers use their rights mercilessly. Many road accidents are due to this particular rule.

On some roads you are told if you do not have priority:

ATTENTION!

VOUS N'AVEZ PAS LA PRIORITÉ

Les routes

There are several kinds of roads in France:

A: Autoroute (a motorway; many motorways have a toll: **route à péage**)

E: Route Européenne (the same road as **A** but with a different number: the motorway from Dunkerque to Lille is the **A25** and also the **E 42**)

N: Route Nationale (e.g. the **RN 175**, equivalent to a British 'A' road)

D: Route départementale (maintained by the Département)

C: Route communale (municipal road maintained by the locality; not shown on 1/200 000 road maps.)

Opération Bison Futé is the code name for a police and national safety exercise which takes place any time there are major holidays (14 July and 15 August). Drivers are given advice via the radio and more police are out on the roads.

Exercise 4 Quelle route?

Look at the map of the North of France.

Find the numbers for the following roads:

a The A road going from Boulogne towards Calais.
b The N road going from Calais towards Ardres.
c The D road from Boulogne to Calais via the coast.

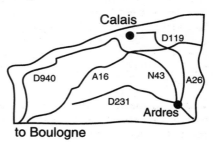

2 Les panneaux de la signalisation routière *Road signs*

The following table from **La prévention routière** shows the four kinds of road signs which are used on French roads.

La signalisation routière est une forme de langage très simple;

elle peut être comprise par tous.

Il suffit d'en connaître **les clefs**

- La **FORME** permet de reconnaître facilement un panneau.

- La **COULEUR** précise la nature exacte du panneau:

  ROUGE = interdiction, BLEU = obligation.

- Un **SYMBOLE** facilement identifiable lui donne un sens précis.

- Enfin, une **BARRE OBLIQUE** sur un panneau signifiera toujours la fin d'une interdiction, d'une obligation ou d'une indication.

Ces quelques clefs suffisent à comprendre la signification de la plupart des panneaux routiers.

les principales couleurs

blanc/blanche	*white*	*Words for colours can be nouns or adjectives. As adjectives they change according to the gender (unless they end with an -e) and number of the noun they are linked to.*
bleu/bleue	*blue*	
noir/noire	*black*	
vert/verte	*green*	
orange	*orange*	
rouge	*red*	
rose	*pink*	

obligation	*mandatory*
interdiction	*strictly forbidden*

Maintenant vous comprenez les panneaux! Répondez aux questions.

a What does it mean when there is a sign with an oblique line across?
b Which colour indicates that you have to do something?
c Which colour sign indicates that something is forbidden?
d Which colour and shape gives you some information?

Un peu de lecture

In the box below tick only those sentences which reflect what is written in the two paragraphs accompanying these two road signs.

ZONES A VITESSE LIMITÉE

De nombreuses agglomérations ont vu la création de zones de circulation à vitesse limitée, dites "Zones 30", à l'intérieur desquelles la vitesse des véhicules est réduite à 30 km/h. En l'absence de panneau, rappelez-vous qu'en agglomération, vous ne devez pas dépasser 50 km/h.

STATION DE GONFLAGE

Cette signalisation annonce une station de gonflage qui vous permettra de vérifier la pression de vos pneus (sans oublier la roue de secours!). Faites-le au moins une fois par mois et surtout avant un départ en vacances. Attention, la pression se vérifie sur un pneu froid ou ayant roulé moins de 15 km. En cas de mesure à chaud, il ne faut pas enlever de pression. N'oubliez pas que la profondeur des rainures ne doit pas être inférieure à 1,6 mm.

1 Don't forget to check the spare wheel.	
2 Most built-up areas do not have speed limit road signs.	
3 If there is no speed limit sign in a built-up area the maximum speed is 50 km per hour.	
4 Check your tyre pressure when your tyres are cold.	
5 Many built-up areas have ramps to slow down traffic.	
6 Check your tyre pressure before going on holidays.	
7 Check your tyres when you have driven less than 15 km.	
8 Ask someone to measure the grooves in your tyres.	
9 Check your tyres at least once a month.	
10 Many built-up areas have 30 km per hour speed limit signs.	

ℹ Quels embouteillages sur les routes!

Un autocar   **des voitures**   **un camion**

When travelling in France during the summer it is important to remember two dates which can mean chaos on the roads – 14 July and 15 August. These are both bank holidays and people tend to take a few days off around them. For example if 14 July is on a Thursday most people are likely to take the Friday off. This practice is known as **faire le pont** *to do the bridge.* Special traffic measures are put in place to prevent accidents and excessive traffic jams at busy times (see **Opération Bison Futé** page 131).

embouteillages	*bottle necks*
bouchons	*bottlenecks* (Lit. *corks*)

▶ 3 Les informations: un week-end meurtrier sur les routes françaises
The news: a murderous weekend on French roads

On the recording you will hear a news bulletin following a particularly bad weekend on French roads.

tué	*killed*	**meurtrier**	*murderous*
blessé	*hurt*		

You will need to listen to the recording several times in order to fill in the grid. Listen to all the news in the first place and then listen separately to each accident report.

Accidents	Type of vehicles involved in the accident	Place where accident occurred	Number of people killed	Number of people injured
1				
2				
3				

Once you have listened to the news you may read the article below, reporting one of the accidents mentioned on the radio. Use the information to help you fill in the grid.

FAITS DIVERS

**Accident mortel sur la Route Nationale 10
Un camion sort d'un chemin privé devant
un autocar bilan:
8 morts, 24 blessés**

Comment l'accident s'est-il produit?

Un accident grave a fait huit morts et vingt-quatre blessés dans la nuit de mardi à mercredi, sur une section dangereuse de la Route Nationale 10 au sud de Bordeaux. Un autocar portugais a percuté un camion qui sortait d'un chemin privé devant l'autocar. Les deux chauffeurs portugais ont été tués. Le chauffeur du camion a été blessé.

ℹ Informations supplémentaires

If you are not used to driving in France, you need to be able to read these signs in order to drive safely.

Signs on other cars

Conduite accompagnée is the equivalent of a red learner's L, compulsory when people are learning to drive under supervision in a private car.

A red **A** at the back of a car indicates that the driver has passed the driving test less than two years ago.
A stands for **apprentissage** *apprenticeship*.

And on the roads, especially on Routes Nationales and Autoroutes there is a constant dialogue between **La prévention routière** (*accident prevention department*) and drivers.

Exercise 5 Qu'est-ce que ça veut dire?

Use the words in the vocabulary box to work out what the signs below mean.

un créneau de dépassement	*overtaking lane*
le frein moteur	*engine brake*
le pied	*foot*
briser	*to break (an object)*
la vie	*life*

What do they mean?

1
Votre sécurité. Créneau de dépassement dans 3 minutes

2
La vie est fragile. Ne la brisez pas!

3
Trop Vite! 90 Levez le pied

4
Merci de votre prudence Bonne route!

5
Utilisez votre frein moteur

6
Merci de ralentir

7
Cédez le passage

Now match each of the signs above to its message below.

a	You are going too fast! The speed limit is 90 kilometres per hour so be sensible, take your foot off the accelerator.
b	You are not on a priority road so give way.
c	Thank you for slowing down.
d	Thank you for being careful. Have a good journey!
e	You are going down a steep road. Use a low gear to slow down.
f	Think about safety. Don't overtake now when in three minutes' time you can use the overtaking lane.
g	Life is fragile. Don't break it!

Surfez sur le web

Entraînez-vous sur le web

- http://www.code-route-facile.com leads to a driving test site where you can practice your knowledge of the French highway code: **le Code de la Route**. There are 20 topics and 7 slides for each topic.
- Consultez Bison Fûté www.bison-fute.equipment.gov.fr/ et vous voyagerez tranquille.

Web Extension

Visitez http://www.code-route-facile.com

Cliquez pour sélectionnez le panneau suivant: 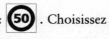 . Choisissez la réponse A ou B.

Réponse B:

Explications:

Ce panneau aux formes rondes et au bord rouge est un panneau d'interdiction. Il limite la vitesse à 70 km/h. Le pannonceau qui lui est associé indique que la limitation de vitesse s'appliquera à 150 mètres. A cette distance, je rencontrerai donc un autre panneau, sans pannonceau (*without a small sign*).

Visitez le site des urgences

http://www.lesannuaires.com/numero-urgence-renseignements.html

Les numéros d'urgences en France	
Pompiers – Incendies et urgences médicales (*fire brigade and medical emergencies*)	**18**
SAMU – Urgences médicales des grandes agglomérations (*ambulance*)	**15**
Police secours ou gendarmerie	**17**
Centre anti-poison	Paris: 01.40.37.04.04
SOS Médecin	0820.33.24.24 – Paris 01.47.07.77.77

En France, avec votre **téléphone mobile** faites le numéro **112** (**cent douze**). 112 will redirect you automatically to 15,17 and 18.

14

on cherche un appartement

looking for a flat

In this unit you will learn
- about housing in France
- about looking for a flat to rent
- how to enquire about a flat on the telephone
- more about pronouns
- adjectives ending with -al

▶ 1 L'appartement de Dominique
Dominique's flat

Porte d'entrée

Escaliers

| Bureau | Salle de bains | Toilettes | Cuisine |

Couloir

| Chambre | Salle de séjour | Coin salle à manger |

↑
Fenêtre

Balcon

L'appartement de Dominique

Dominique Périer
5 Avenue de la Vieille Ville
St NAZAIRE 44600

Look at the plan of Dominique's flat above and listen to the recording. Then answer these questions:

a On which floor is Dominique's flat?
b Is there a lift?
c Does she like her flat? Why or why not? (Give one reason)

Listen again.

d Why is Dominique out of breath?
e What does Sarah say is as good as aerobics?

Listen for a third time.

f Who decorated Dominique's flat?
g What can they just about see when leaning out of the window?

Now read the dialogue.

Dominique Je te préviens, mon appartement est au quatrième étage et il n'y a pas d'ascenseur dans l'immeuble.

Sarah Tu devrais déménager alors!

Dominique Non! Je l'adore, mon appartement! Je le loue pour presque rien, il y a une vue magnifique sur les anciens chantiers navals de St Nazaire, et puis mes voisins sont tranquilles. Ouf! Nous y sommes! Je suis à bout de souffle.

Sarah Ne te plains pas, ma vieille! Monter et descendre les escaliers c'est aussi bien que de faire de l'aérobic, tu sais!

Dominique Zut! Je ne trouve pas mes clefs. Ah si, les voilà!

Sarah Oh la, la, quel bel appartement! C'est toi qui l'a décoré?

Dominique Euh ... oui, plus ou moins, avec l'aide de mon copain.

Sarah Tu me fais visiter?

Dominique Allons-y pour le tour du propriétaire: voici la salle de séjour avec le coin salle à manger, sans oublier le balcon. Ici c'est la cuisine et au bout du couloir il y a ma chambre, et mon bureau: tu vas dormir là, sur le canapé. Ici à gauche il y a la salle de bains et les toilettes.

Sarah Il me plaît ton appartement. Bon, je m'installe!

Dominique Tiens, ouvre la fenêtre. Viens voir, en se penchant on aperçoit la mer! Tu la vois?

je te préviens	*I am warning you (**prévenir** to warn)*
déménager	*to move (house)*
louer	*to rent*
les voisins	*the neighbours*
à bout de souffle	*breathless*
un copain	*a friend/boyfriend*
une copine	*a friend/girlfriend*
le tour du propriétaire	*the tour of the property*
le propriétaire	*the owner*
la propriété	*the property*

Now link the following English phrases to the equivalent French expressions.

1	There is no lift in the building.	a	Ouvre la fenêtre.
2	I rent it for next to nothing.	b	la salle de séjour
3	going up and down stairs	c	Ici c'est la cuisine.
4	with my friend's help	d	Tu vas dormir sur le sofa.
5	the living room	e	Je le loue pour presque rien.
6	Here is the kitchen.	f	En se penchant on aperçoit la mer.
7	You are going to sleep on the sofa.	g	monter et descendre les escaliers
8	When you lean out you can just about see the sea	h	Il n'y a pas d'ascenseur dans l'immeuble.
9	Don't complain, old thing!	i	Viens voir.
10	Open the window.	j	Ne te plains pas, ma vieille.
11	Come and see.	k	avec l'aide de mon copain

Grammar

1 Les pronoms: l'/le/la/les

You already know these four pronouns, which are used to replace nouns.

In the dialogue on page 141 there are five examples of these pronouns. The first is:

Je l'adore mon appartement! *I love (it) my flat!*

l' replaces **appartement**. This is an example where the pronoun is used first, in anticipation of the noun which comes next. It is used in spoken French to emphasize a point.

Remember that with pronouns and articles the -e is dropped in front of a vowel: **J'adore mon appart!** (**appart** is short for **appartement**). When the pronoun **le** is placed directly in front of the verb, the -e of **je** is reinstated and the -e of **le** is dropped instead: **je l'adore**. The same process applies with pronoun **la**.

À vous de les reconnaître *Your turn to recognize them*

1 Can you find the four other pronouns used in the dialogue above?
2 Say which nouns they replace.

2 Les pronoms: me, te, lui, nous, vous, leur

At this point you need to be able to recognize these pronouns rather than use them yourself.

Tu **me** fais visiter?	*Can you show **me** round?*
Il **me** plaît ton appartement.	*I like **it**.* Lit. *It pleases me your flat.*

These pronouns are used in front of verbs. You have already met some of them in reflexive verbs but here their function is slightly different. They are used to target the recipient of an action, as for example in **faire visiter sa maison à quelqu'un** *to show one's home to somebody*:

Faire visiter à ...

tu **me** fais visiter	*you show **me** round*
je **te** fais visiter	*I show **you*** (to one person, familiar)
je **lui** fais visiter	*I show **him** or **her***
tu **nous** fais visiter	*you show **us***
je **vous** fais visiter	*I show **you*** (to more than one person or one person you address formally)
tu **leur** fais visiter	*you show **them***

A slightly different set of pronouns applies with a verb like **prévenir**. **Prévenir quelqu'un** means *to warn someone/to inform someone in advance of an event.*

If the verb is followed by à (**faire visiter à**) the above pronouns are used. However, if the verb is not followed by à (**prévenir**), **l'**, **le**, **la**, **les** are used for *him, her, it them.*

Compare the two examples:

Je préviens Sarah. *I warn Sarah.* Je **la** préviens.
Je fais visiter à Sarah. *I show Sarah round.* Je **lui** fais visiter.

Here are more examples of pronouns with **prévenir**:

Tu **me** préviens s'il pleut, n'est-ce pas? *You'll let me know if it rains, won't you?*
Je **la** préviens. *I am warning her.*
Je **le** préviens. *I am warning him.*
Je préviens **mes parents** de notre arrivée. Je **les** préviens. *I'm letting my parents know about our arrival. I'm letting them know.*

For more about these pronouns see the table on page 333.

3 Adjectives ending in -*al*

In the masculine form most adjectives ending in **-al** have a plural form ending in **-aux**:

un repas normal *a normal meal* des repas normaux *normal meals*

In the feminine form all adjectives ending in **-al** take an **-e**, with a plural form ending in **-ales**:

une vie normale *a normal life* des vies normales *normal lives*

But there are a few exceptions which you need to know about: in the dialogue above Dominique says that her flat has a fantastic view over the old shipyards:

Il y a une vue magnifique sur les anciens chantiers **navals**.

Naval is one of the extremely rare adjectives ending in **-al** which have a plural form with **-s**:

un chantier naval des chantiers navals

Another example:

un accident fatal des accidents fatals

▶ Pronunciation

When *c* becomes *ç*

The verb **apercevoir** (*to perceive/to catch a glimpse*) is one of the many verbs which changes **c** to **ç** in order to keep to an original [*s*] sound. This is necessary if the letter **c** is followed by **a/o/u** when it would normally have a [*k*] sound. To keep to the [*s*] sound the letter **c** becomes **ç**:

J'aperçois un ami là-bas. *I can see a friend over there.*
Nous **apercevons** les *We can see the mountains.*
  montagnes.
J'ai **aperçu** la Tour Eiffel. *I spotted the Eiffel Tower.*

With other verbs this change does not always occur for the same part of the verb:

Nous **commençons** à *We are beginning to learn*
  apprendre l'anglais. *English.*

Nous **recevons** des amis pour dîner.	*We are having friends for dinner.*
Il **reçoit** une récompense.	*He gets a reward.*

Exercise 1 Comment déménager sans soucis

Read the article below and the 20 questions on moving home:

Tick the correct answers only.

a *Why are you moving?*

1 You are moving because you have got a new job.
2 You are moving because your family needs more space.
3 You have found the house of your dreams.

b *How are you going to manage it?*

4 It is simpler to do the lot yourself, with the help of your children.
5 Your friends can help.
6 You have to hire a van.
7 You have to make sandwiches for your friends.
8 You need lots of milk cartons.
9 You need to collect lots of cardboard boxes.

COMMENT
déménager
SANS SOUCIS

Vous avez trouvé la maison de vos rêves ! Votre petite famille aspire à un peu plus d'espace ! Bref, vous devez déménager.

Pour déménager, la solution la plus simple reste de faire appel aux copains. On amasse les cartons, on loue une camionnette, on prépare des sandwichs et le tour est joué! Oui mais voilà, tout le monde n'a pas des amis disponibles. A fortiori quand on habite au dernier étage sans ascenseur ou quand le piano à queue pèse trois tonnes! Dans certaines situations, mieux vaut faire appel à des pros.

c *What problems are you likely to face?*

10 You have no friends available for the task.
11 Your friends are a little bit careless.
12 Your friends are not strong enough.
13 Your front door is too narrow.
14 You live on the top floor.
15 Your washing machine weighs a ton.
16 You have a grand piano.
17 There is no lift.

d *What should you do if in doubt?*

18 Decide not to move.
19 Leave the piano in your old flat.
20 Call a professional removal firm.

▶2 Où loger? *Where should I live?*

Corinne is about to start her first year at university in Paris. She is looking for somewhere to live.

Listen to the recording once and answer these questions:

a Who is Corinne speaking to?
b What did Corinne fail to get?

Listen a second time.

c What does Corinne want to do?
d She says that all she needs is a table, two chairs and a bed. How is she going to pay for it?

Now read the dialogue.

Corinne Allô Maman, c'est Corinne. Je téléphone pour te dire que je n'ai pas obtenu de chambre à la cité universitaire. Je crois que je vais chercher un studio à louer ou bien un appartement avec une ou deux copines.

Maman Un studio! Mais c'est beaucoup trop cher! Et puis il faudrait le meubler!

Corinne Bien sûr mais je vais travailler pendant les vacances pour acheter des meubles. J'ai besoin d'une table, deux chaises et un lit ou un sofa, c'est tout!

Maman Non, il n'en est pas question! Alors tu m'écoutes: il serait beaucoup plus simple de prendre une chambre meublée chez des particuliers, dans une famille. Cherche dans les petites annonces dans le journal demain.

Corinne OK! Je regarderai dans le journal, en cherchant bien j'arriverai à trouver un studio pas cher!

des meubles	*furniture*
meubler	*to furnish*
une chambre meublée	*a furnished room*

Link the following English phrases to their French equivalent:

1 I am going to look for a studio to rent.
2 I need a table, two chairs and a bed.
3 I am going to work.
4 It's out of the question.
5 I shall look in the newspaper.
6 by looking thoroughly

a Je vais travailler.
b en cherchant bien
c Je regarderai dans le journal.
d Je vais chercher un studio à louer.
e Il n'en est pas question.
f J'ai besoin d'une table, deux chaises et un lit.

Grammar

4 *En*

You already know about the present participle of a verb: **-ant** in French is equivalent to **-ing** in English (see page 89).

When used with **en** *when/while* it is a verb form referred to as a gerund in English:

En se penchant par la fenêtre on aperçoit la mer.
en cherchant bien

Leaning out of the window one can see the sea.
looking thoroughly

Sometimes present participle in French is not translated by a gerund in English:

Ils sifflent **en travaillant**.
Corinne fait ses devoirs **en écoutant** de la musique.

They whistle while they work.
Corinne does her homework whilst she listens to music.

ℹ L'immobilier

If you are looking for a flat or a house to rent you can search for it in any newspaper under **annonces immobilières** or you can go to an estate agent, **une agence immobilière**. **L'immobilier** literally refers to what cannot be moved as opposed to **le mobilier**, another word for furniture.

There are three indicators to give you an idea of the size of places to rent or buy, whether it is a flat or a house (**une maison**): The letter **T** followed by a number indicates the number of people the place is designed to accommodate: **T1/T2/T3/T4/T5**. Some adverts indicate the number of rooms (**le nombre de pièces: 2P/3P etc.**). The number of rooms indicated includes all types of rooms except the kitchen and the bathroom. Finally there is always a figure (25m², 50m², etc.) which relates to the measurements of the place in square metres and which will answer the question: **Il fait combien de mètres carrés?**

You also need to understand a vast number of abbreviations and vocabulary. The following table should help.

M°	métro *tube station* (this applies to Paris, Lyon and Marseille)
12è.	douzième arrondissement (Paris district number – 20 districts in all)
2è. étg/der. étg	deuxième étage/dernier étage
c.c./ch.comp	charges comprises *charges included*
sdb/wc	salle de bains/wc (pronounced *les double v c* or *wouataires*)
cuis.équip.	cuisine équipée
asc.	ascenseur
ch.perso.	chambre personnelle
10m² env.	10 m² environ *approximately*
ref.nf	refait neuf *newly decorated*
chauff.élec.	chauffage électrique
rép	répondeur automatique *answerphone*

3 Corinne cherche un studio à Paris
Corinne looks for a studio in Paris

Corinne a découpé des petites annonces dans des journaux. Elle n'a pas l'intention de prendre une chambre chez des particuliers. Elle cherche un petit appartement à partager avec une copine ou bien un petit studio pas cher. Elle a 450 € par mois pour payer son loyer.

Maisons & appartements

Particuliers

*46 € la parution
de 5 lignes
Tél.: 01.44.78.39.51*

Studios Location

a) 14è. M° PLAISANCE Studio
20m² Refait à neuf, 3è, étage
450 €ccJP2L01.43.35.15.40

b) ☐ 19è.CITE de la MUSIQUE
Studio meublé sympa
imm. très calme, pour 1 an
au moins, loyer 410 € cc.
Gilles 01.40.17.15.35

c) ☐ Paris 3è. Particulier loue
petit 2 P., 25m², wc, bains,
490 € cc. visite sur place lundi
1er septembre de 12h à 14h
4, RUE BLONDEL.
01.40.60.10.50

d) ☐ 18è.M° Marx-Dormoy
studio 18m², tbe. coin cuisine
s. de bains, 2è. et dern. étg.
clair, calme sur cour. Chauff.
élec. 350 € cc. 01.40.37.71.21

e) ☐ NATION - Studio 25m²
clair, calme, 1er. étg. sur cour,
salle de bains, wc, kitchenette,
480 € cc. Direct propriétaire
01.48.60.60.15

f) ☐ 20è. Pyrénées - Gd. studio
40m², 6è. étg. asc. beaucoup
de charme, poutres, ref. nf. cuis.
équip. vue dégagée, ds. imm.
PdT.620 €cc 01.43.61.49.37

g) ☐ 2è M° Strasbourg St-Denis
Studio 27m², séjour + vraie
cuis., sdb.libre le 1er octobre
460 € charges et chauffage
compris - 01.48.02.40.10

h) ☐ 3è. M° Fille du Calvaire
STUDIO MEUBLE
470 € ch. comprises
Tél.: 01.43.65.75.57

Partages

i) ☐ **20è. M° JOURDAIN**
100M² Meublé sympa, sdb. +
chambre perso. 550 € cc.
Tél.: 01.43.65.80.15

j) ☐ 9e. Place Clichy Part. grd
appart. 120m² Chbre. 400 €.
C.C. Tél.: 01.42.70.60.50

2 Pièces Location

k) ☐ M° LOUIS BLANC
2 Pièces 45m², cuisine équipée
nombreux rangements,
Libre tout de suite
Tél. 01.43.59.39.32

Look at the adverts Corinne has cut out from the newspaper and answer the following questions:

1 How many studios, flat shares or small flats are within her price range?
2 Which ad is about a furnished studio flat for rent for at least a year?
3 Which ads should she call if she wants to move in immediately or no later than 1 October?
4 How much could she pay for a room in a flat share?
5 Which studio flat is on the 3rd floor and has recently been decorated?

▶ Exercise 2 Un coup de téléphone

You want to rent a studio flat in Paris. You have decided to phone about advert **b** from page 149.

There are very few details about the studio so you need to ask a few questions.

The telephone conversation below is incomplete. The **propriétaire's** lines are in the correct place. Your lines have been jumbled up. You can find all your responses in the box.

Propriétaire	Allô, j'écoute!
1 Vous	…
Propriétaire	Oui, c'est bien cela.
2 Vous	…
Propriétaire	C'est au sixième.
3 Vous	…
Propriétaire	Euh, non mais monter et descendre les escaliers est excellent pour la santé!
4 Vous	…
Propriétaire	Non, le chauffage est électrique.
5 Vous	…
Propriétaire	Oui il y a une cuisine moderne toute équipée.
6 Vous	…
Propriétaire	C'est bien cela. Vous pouvez visiter aujourd'hui?
7 Vous	…

a Il y a un ascenseur?
b Je viendrais cet après-midi si vous êtes disponible.
c C'est bien 400 € toutes charges comprises?
d Il y a une cuisine?
e J'ai vu une annonce pour un studio dans *Libé*. C'est bien ici?
f Il y a le chauffage central?
g C'est à quel étage?

Now listen to the whole dialogue and check your answers.

Surfez sur le web

Si vous voulez acheter ou louer une maison ou un appartement, vous pouvez visiter de nombreux sites sur le web.

- www.acheter-louer.fr
  Sur acheter-louer.fr, vous pouvez :

  Rechercher un **appartement** ou une **maison** neufs à la vente ou à la location (*renting*)

  Rechercher un **appartement** ou une **maison** rénovés à la vente ou à la location

  Rechercher un **appartement** ou une **maison** de prestige à la vente ou à la location

  Rechercher tout type d'**appartements** ou de **maison** à la **vente** ou à la **location**

Pour rechercher un **appartement** ou une **maison,** venez visiter le portail immobilier acheter-louer.fr et **rechercher** en quelques secondes votre **appartement** ou votre **maison à vendre** ou à **louer.**

Cliquez sur « les annonces », choisissez vos critères, regardez le diaporama.

* www.maison.fr

Web extension exercise

Voici ce que vous offrent les agences immobilières (*estate agencies*). Vous devez indiquer le type de bien (*type of property*) que vous cherchez, le nombre de pièces (*number of rooms not including kitchen and bathroom*) et le nombre de mètres carrés (*number of square metres*). **Imaginez que vous avez beaucoup d'argent. Amusez-vous bien!**

Retrouvez nos annonces immobilieres en location en France:

types de bien (types of property)

- ☐ : Loft (penthouse)
- ☐ : Garage
- ☐ : Programme Neuf (new construction)
- ☐ : Propriété
- ☐ : Château Manoir (town mansion)
- ☐ : Immeuble (block of flats)
- ☐ : Parking
- ☐ : Hôtel Particulier
- ☐ : Haras (horse stables)
- ☐ : Ferme
- ☐ : Villa
- ☐ : Habitation légère
- ☐ : Autres
- ☐ : Chalet
- ☐ Commerces (shop/commercial property)

Infos prix et taille (price and size):

Prix min (en €): ☐   Prix max (en €): ☐

Pièces min: ☐   Surf. min (en m^2): ☐

Localisation (area):

Ville, cp: ☐   sur ☐▼ aux alentours (nearby)

Département: ☐   (*Essonne, 91*)

lancer la recherche

15

dans les grandes surfaces

at shopping centres

In this unit you will learn
- about shopping in hypermarkets
- about buying clothes
- how to make comparisons, say something is better or worse
- how to find a bargain
- demonstrative pronouns: **celui-ci, celui-là, etc.**

▶ 1 Rien dans le frigo
Nothing in the fridge

Dominique has come home to an empty fridge. The two friends decide to go shopping. They go to one of the many out-of-town supermarkets.

Listen once to the recording, then answer these questions:

a Name four items on Dominique's list.
b Who are the tins for?
c Who looks after him when Dominique is away?

Listen again.

d Name three items on Sarah's list.
e Who is the wine for?

Listen for a third time.

f Dominique noticed that there were sales in the clothes and shoes department. What attracted their attention?
g Do they buy anything?
h Which colour suits Dominique best?

Listen again for the last time.

i Which department do they go to?

Dominique	Je n'ai plus rien dans le frigo. Il faut que j'achète de tout.
Sarah	N'oublie pas que tu as fait une liste ce matin.
Dominique	Ah oui, ma liste ... je l'ai. Alors lait, fromage, yaourts, beurre, pain, poisson, fruits et légumes, liquide lave-vaisselle, sans oublier des boîtes pour Papaguéno!
Sarah	Pour qui?
Dominique	Papaguéno? C'est mon chat. Ma voisine s'en occupe quand je pars en voyage.
Sarah	Eh bien moi j'ai besoin d'une pellicule pour mon appareil photo, des piles pour ma torche et puis une bonne bouteille de vin blanc pour boire avec le poisson et un gâteau de pâtisserie pour le dessert.
Dominique	Tu as vu, il y a des soldes de vêtements et de chaussures.
Sarah	J'aime beaucoup beaucoup ces chaussures - il n'y en a qu'une paire. C'est quelle pointure?
Dominique	C'est du trente-huit.
Sarah	Dommage, je chausse du trente-neuf!

Dominique	Regarde, il n'est pas mal ce pull! Et celui-ci est encore mieux!
Sarah	Oui mais j'ai vu meilleure qualité! Et puis le vert te va mieux que le bleu ... Ah non pas le rouge, c'est encore pire!
Dominique	Oh la la, tu es agaçante, tu as toujours raison! Allez viens, on va au rayon poissonnerie acheter du poisson. J'espère qu'ils ne vendent pas de poisson rouge sinon on ne mangera rien ce soir!

le frigo short for **réfrigérateur**	*the fridge*
des boîtes short for **des boîtes de conserve**	*tins*
Une pellicule pour appareil photo	*a film for a camera*
des vêtements et des chaussures	*clothes and shoes*
le rayon poissonnerie	*the fish counter*
un pull short for **un pullover**	
la taille	*size (for clothes)*
la pointure	*size (for shoes)*
agaçante	*annoying*
un poisson rouge	*a goldfish*

Link the following English phrases to the equivalent French expressions.

1 I have nothing left in the fridge.

2 washing-up liquid

3 My neighbour looks after him.

4 to drink with the fish

5 There are sales on.

6 Pity, I take size 39.

7 Green suits you better than blue.

8 otherwise we won't eat anything tonight

a Dommage, je chausse du trente-neuf.

b pour boire avec le poisson

c Il y a des soldes.

d Le vert te va mieux que le bleu.

e Je n'ai plus rien dans le frigo.

f du liquide lave-vaisselle

g sinon on ne mangera rien ce soir

h Ma voisine s'en occupe.

Dominique plaisante. At the end of the dialogue Dominique makes a joke which would be meaningless in translation. Why is it a joke in French and not in English?

On va à quel rayon pour nos provisions? Look at the map opposite of the supermarket where Dominique and Sarah are now. Listen to the dialogue again and say which departments they go to (take their shopping lists into account). Tick the department numbers below.

1	2	3	4	5	6	7	8	9	10
11	12	13	14	15	16	17	18	19	20
21	22	23	24	25	26	27	28	29	30
31	32	33	34	35	36	37	38	39	40

Grammar

1 *En*

There is a further example of **en** in the dialogue:

C'est mon chat. Ma voisine
s'**en** occupe.

*It's my cat. My neighbour
looks after it.*

Here **en** replaces **de mon chat**. (Ma voisine s'occupe **de mon chat**.)

• **S'occuper de** *to mind/to look after/to take care of*:

Elle s'occupe **de ma maison**. Elle s'**en** occupe.

2 Making comparisons

Plus/plus ... que

You have already met **plus ... que** *more ... than* and **moins ... que** *less ... than*: You can use **plus ... que** with almost all adjectives:

C'est **plus cher qu'**à Continent.

*It's more expensive than at
Continent.*

Plus ... que can also be used with adverbs:

Tu marches **plus vite que** moi.

You walk faster than me.

Meilleur(e)(s)/mieux

Plus and **plus ... que** cannot be used with the adjectives **bon(s)/bonne(s)** *good* **meilleur(e)(s)** *better* is used instead:

Les glaces à la fraise sont
meilleures (que les glaces
à la vanille).

*Strawberry ice creams are
better (than vanilla
ice creams).*

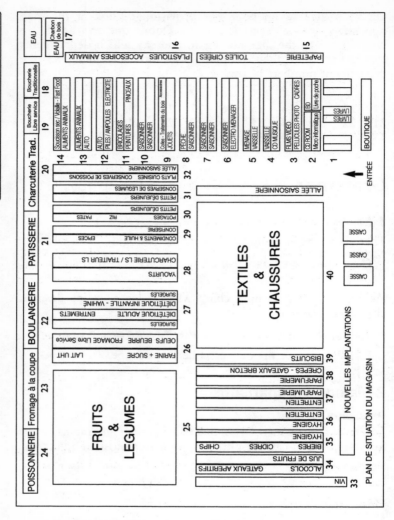

Le climat est **meilleur** dans le Midi de la France.	*The climate is better in the south of France.*

Meilleur can also be used as a superlative: *the best!*

– Les vins français sont **les meilleurs** vins du monde.	*– French wines are the best wines in the world.*
– Les vins allemands, les vins italiens ... sont bons aussi.	*– German wines, Italian wines ... are good too.*

– Oui mais les français sont **les meilleurs!**	*Yes but French ones are the best!*
La championne olympique de natation c'est **la meilleure** nageuse du monde.	*The Olympic swimming champion is the best swimmer in the world.*

Plus and **plus ... que** cannot be used with the adverb **bien** *good/well*. **Mieux** *better* is used instead:

Le bleu te va bien.	*Blue suits you (Lit. Blue goes well with you.)*
Le vert te va mieux (que le rouge).	*Green suits you better (than red).*

Plus mauvais(e)(s) (pire) *and* plus mal (pis)

Although **plus** and **plus ... que** can be used with the adjective **mauvais(e)(s)** *bad* and the adverb **mal** *badly*, you may come across their alternative forms: **pire** and **pis**. **Pis** is not commonly used in comparisons, but you will often hear the expression **Tant pis!** *Too bad!* (lit. *So much the worse!*)

Il est **mauvais** ce vin! Pouah!

Celui-ci est encore **plus mauvais!**	*This one is even worse!*
Celui-ci est encore **pire!**	
Marc conduit **plus mal** que son frère.	*Marc drives worse than his brother.*

3 Demonstrative pronouns

You can use demonstrative pronouns when you need to refer to something which is present at the time of the conversation:

(masc.sing.)	**Celui-ci**	*this one*	**Celui-là**	*that one*
(fem.sing.)	**Celle-ci**		**Celle-là**	
(fem.pl.)	**Celles-ci**	*these ones*	**Celles-là**	*those ones*
(masc.pl.)	**Ceux-ci**		**Ceux-là**	

Exercise 1 Trouvez les phrases correctes

Choose the correct ending for each of the sentences below.

1 Ce poisson a l'air frais	**a** mais celles-ci sont meilleures.
2 Cet artichaut est gros	**b** mais celui-ci sent encore meilleur.
3 Ces pommes sont bonnes	**c** mais celle-ci est meilleure.
4 Ce melon sent bon	**d** mais ceux-ci sont meilleurs.
5 Ces gâteaux sont bons	**e** mais celui-ci a l'air plus frais.
6 Cette bière est bonne	**f** mais celui-ci est encore plus gros.

ℹ Les grandes surfaces

All French towns have out-of-town shopping centres with a vast range of supermarkets and hypermarkets (Auchan, Carrefour, Continent, Géant, Leclerc, Mammouth, etc.). They are generally referred to as **grandes surfaces** because of the large space they occupy. Some have up to thirty checkouts (**caisses**) and have a policy of employing young people on roller skates to help with customer service. Most of them are located in large shopping arcades, with a whole range of smaller shops, boutiques of all sorts and restaurants. In addition to the permanent shopping area, they frequently have seasonal products at competitive prices under a large marquee (**Sous Chapiteau**): wines in the autumn, chrysanthemums for All Saints Day on 1 November, oysters for Christmas and the New Year, bedding and furniture in the spring and camping equipment in the summer.

They all compete with one another by having promotional offers (**Promotions**), sales (**Soldes**), the bargains of the day (**Affaire du jour**), special offers (**Offres spéciales**). Once or twice in the year all the shops in an area all have sales on at the same time (**Grande braderie** or **Foire aux soldes**). They all advertise in the local press and have slogans like: **Guerre sur les prix** (*War on Prices*), **Prix fous** (*Crazy prices*) or **Prix défi** (*Price challenge*).

All **grandes surfaces** have **Un Point / Espace environnement** for recycling glass and plastic bottles.

Exercise 2 Prix fous!

Look at the adverts from local papers where local shops have advertised their bargains.

PRIX FOUS ...

«**L'AFFAIRE DU JOUR!!**
A ne pas manquer.»

OFFRE VALABLE DU 1er AU 3 AOÛT
(le 3 août pour les magasins ouverts le dimanche matin)

NECTARINE BLANCHE

origine France
catégorie 1, calibre B

2,50 €

le kg

CHEZ STOC, UN CLIENT C'EST SACRÉ

stoc
SUPERMARCHÉ

FOUESNANT   MORLAIX
4, rue de Kerneveleck   Rue de Brest
CONCARNEAU   CARANTEC
17, quai Carnot   Kérougadenn
LE GUILVINEC   PLOUGUERNEAU
1, rue des Moulins   Douar Nevez

D

AUJOURD'HUI MERCREDI 6 AOÛT
DERNIER JOUR
FOIRE AUX SOLDES
à PONT-L'ABBÉ
C'est à côté
U.D.C.P.

A

SOLDES
DERNIERS JOURS

B

MEUBLES *L.Bilien*
15, rue du Général-De Gaulle
29750 LOCTUDY

PROMO LITERIE

SOUS CHAPITEAU

GRANDES MARQUES

monsieur meuble
nous sommes bien ensemble!

Route de Quimper
PONT-L'ABBÉ

E

C

AURAY · CENTRE-VILLE · MARDI 12 · MERCREDI 13 AOÛT

GRANDE BRADERIE

Organisation : Auray Préférence
et Rugby Auray Club

CRÉDIT AGRICOLE
DU MORBIHAN

OFFRE SPÉCIALE

**MOTEUR
135 CV 2L V6
MERCURY**
Prix catalogue :
12 600 €

Vendu
7800 €

F

BREST NAUTIC
Port du Moulin-Blanc - BREST
02 98 41 43 76

Answer these questions:

a What is the bargain of the day at STOC?

b How long will it last?

c What day of the week is 3 August?

d Where and when in Auray is the Grande Braderie taking place?

e What is 'Monsieur Meuble' selling **Sous Chapiteau**? (Clue: first three letters of LITERIE)

f How much would one save at Brest Nautic?

g When does **La Foire Aux Soldes** end in Pont-L'Abbé?

h What is in the sales at 15 rue du Général de Gaulle?

▶ 2 Au rayon charcuterie
At the delicatessen counter

Madame Rouzeau has a long list of delicatessen products she wants to buy: Bayonne ham, garlic sausage, farmhouse pâté, Greek mushrooms, scallops.

Listen to the dialogue as many times as necessary so you can identify everything on Madame Rouzeau's shopping list.

In the grid below fill in the quantity required for each item:

Bayonne ham	
Garlic sausage	
Farmhouse pâté	
Greek mushrooms	
Scallops	

Now read the dialogue and check your answers.

Vendeuse   Soixante-quinze? C'est à qui le tour?

Madame R   C'est à moi. Mettez-moi six tranches de jambon de Bayonne s'il vous plaît.

Vendeuse   Ça vous va comme cela?

Mme R   Oui, c'est bien.

Vendeuse   Et avec ça?

Mme R   Alors il me faut douze tranches de saucisson à l'ail, ... deux cent cinquante grammes de pâté de campagne, ... deux cents grammes de champignons à la grecque, ... et quatre coquilles St Jacques.

Vendeuse	Et avec cela?
Mme R	Ça sera tout merci!
Vendeuse	Voilà Madame, bonne journée.

Dans les paniers de Madame Rouzeau il y a des fruits et des légumes frais. Look in Madame Rouzeau's basket, and then try the puzzle overleaf.

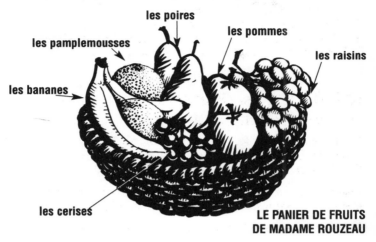

les poires

les pamplemousses

les pommes

les raisins

les bananes

les cerises

**LE PANIER DE FRUITS
DE MADAME ROUZEAU**

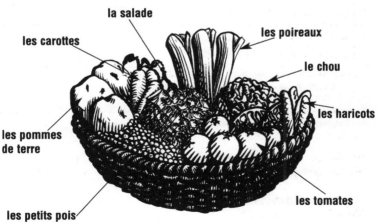

la salade

les carottes

les poireaux

le chou

les haricots

les pommes
de terre

les tomates

les petits pois

**LE PANIER DE LÉGUMES
DE MADAME ROUZEAU**

Find the names of fruit and vegetables hidden in the grid.

```
P  A  C  C  D  M  N  G  H  I  L  P  K
A  D  S  E  A  P  O  M  M  E  S  O  D
M  S  Q  R  D  S  A  T  E  E  G  M  H
P  E  T  I  T  S  P  O  I  S  K  M  K
L  R  G  S  F  T  Y  M  S  E  L  E  H
E  A  P  E  B  A  N  A  N  E  S  S  A
M  I  O  S  D  C  E  T  A  P  A  D  R
O  S  I  Z  A  H  R  E  T  O  L  E  I
U  I  R  C  V  O  B  S  M  I  A  T  C
S  N  E  R  H  U  S  G  D  R  D  E  O
S  C  A  R  O  T  T  E  S  E  E  R  T
E  T  U  Y  U  H  N  F  D  S  V  R  S
S  F  X  J  V  B  C  A  S  W  R  E  M
```

🔢 Les cartes de crédit

In France chip and PIN cards (**les cartes à puces**) have been in use for many years. If you are paying with a debit or credit card you will be asked to insert your card in the machine. The following instructions will then appear on the screen.

Insérez votre carte → Patientez → Composez votre code → Code bon → Retirez votre carte (*remove your card*)

However in many places the directions will automatically appear in the language associated with your card.

> *Tapez votre code à l'abri des regards indiscrets*

Surfez sur le web

Voulez-vous faire votre shopping sur le web? Alors visitez les sites suivants:

- Supermarchés Leclerc: http://fr.wikipedia.org/wiki/E.Leclerc **Leclerc** est une enseigne de supermarchés (*supermarket chain*) française. Elle regroupe des magasins indépendants respectant les exigences de l'organisation. Leclerc est le premier supermarché qui a eu l'idée de produire **un sac pour la vie** (*a bag for life*).
- Recherchez les faits et lisez un article de Wikipédia, l'encyclopédie libre, sur Leclerc et le sac plastique.
- www.supercasino.fr est un des plus grands hypermarchés français.

Web extension

Voici ce que vous pouvez lire dans l'article: le sac plastique ou sac de caisse est un sac offert, vendu ou prêté (*loaned*) par les **commerces** à leur **clients** pour faciliter le transport de leurs achats. Il est, à ce jour, composé essentiellement en **polyéthylène**.

- **1995** : Leclerc arrête de distribuer des **sacs plastiques** jetables

Maintenant visitez le site de supercasino et faite votre liste pour le petit déjeuner

www.supercasino.fr → Vive la vie facile → Allons-y → liste de courses → choix de rayons → petit déjeuner

Petit déjeuner

Café en grains `⊟ 1 ⊞`

Café soluble `⊟ 1 ⊞`

Pains suédois `⊟ 1 ⊞`

Thé `⊟ 1 ⊞`

Biscottes `⊟ 1 ⊞`

Café moulu (*ground coffee*) `⊟ 1 ⊞`

Céréales `⊟ 1 ⊞`

Chocolat en poudre `⊟ 1 ⊞`

Confitures (*jam*) `⊟ 1 ⊞`

Filtres à café `⊟ 1 ⊞`

Infusions `⊟ 1 ⊞`

Lait concentré `⊟ 1 ⊞`

Lait demi-écrémé (*semi skimmed milk*) `⊟ 1 ⊞`

Lait écrémé `⊟ 1 ⊞`

Lait entier `⊟ 1 ⊞`

Miel (*honey*) `⊟ 1 ⊞`

Maintenant essayez la même chose avec les légumes frais, les boissons, les alcools etc…

Bonnes courses!

16

à la maison du peuple
at the community centre

In this unit you will learn
- a little about multi-ethnic France
- about young people and out-of-school activities
- about tackling racism
- the perfect tense with **être**

▶ 1 Je suis animateur
I am a youth worker

As planned Dominique and Sarah are on their way to
Dominique's parents in Bordeaux but on the way they stop for
one night at Dominique's boyfriend's house in Nantes.

*Le copain de Dominique s'appelle Gildas Marrec. Il est
Directeur de la Maison du Peuple dans un quartier populaire
de Nantes.*

Listen to the recording once, then answer the questions:

1 Who is Djamel?
  a Gildas' brother **b** a colleague **c** a neighbour
2 Djamel works
  a with adults **b** in a college **c** with young people
3 What kind of activities does he supervise?

Listen to the recording again.

4 Where did Djamel and some young people travel to?
5 How long did they stay there?
6 How many young people and how many adults went on the
  journey?

Listen for the last time to the recording.

7 Where did some young people stay?
8 Who did they all meet?

Now read the dialogue.

Gildas	Salut! Vous avez fait un bon voyage?
Dominique	Oui, très bien. Gildas je te présente Sarah.
Sarah	Enchantée!
Gildas	Enchanté! Dominique m'a beaucoup parlé de vous. Je vous présente Djamel, un collègue de travail. Djamel, Dominique, ma copine, et Sarah, une amie à elle.
Sarah	(*à Djamel*) Vous travaillez avec des jeunes aussi?
Djamel	Oui, je suis animateur, c'est-à-dire que j'encadre des jeunes dans de nombreuses activités en dehors du collège.
Sarah	Quel genre d'activités?
Djamel	Oh un peu de tout: du sport, de la photo, de la musique et même des voyages. Nous avons beaucoup de jeunes maghrébins dans le quartier. Ils n'ont pas grand'chose à faire, à part regarder la télé. Là on vient de rentrer d'un voyage au Maroc.

Gildas	Djamel est formidable avec les gamins.
Dominique	Combien sont allés au Maroc?
Djamel	Dix-huit et on était trois animateurs. On est resté trois semaines. Certains ont logé dans leurs familles.
Sarah	Ils ont rencontré des jeunes marocains?
Djamel	Oui, bien sûr. Ils ont tous fait énormément de découvertes.

---

un animateur (une animatrice) *someone organizing activities, youth worker* (the full name for this profession is **animateur socio-culturel**)
encadrer *to provide a framework for activities* (**un cadre:** *a frame, support.* In a work context it also means *a manager*)
des jeunes maghrébins *young people with North African origins*
le quartier *the district / the area*

Link the following English phrases to the equivalent French expressions.

1 Dominique has told me lots of things about you
2 Do you work with young people too?
3 a bit of everything
4 There aren't many things for them to do.
5 Djamel is fantastic with kids.
6 We stayed three weeks.
7 Some stayed with their own family.
8 They met young Moroccans.

a Djamel est formidable avec les gamins.
b On est resté trois semaines.
c Ils ont rencontré des jeunes marocains.
d Certains sont restés avec leur famille.
e un peu de tout
f Vous travaillez avec des jeunes aussi?
g Ils n'ont pas grand'chose à faire.
h Dominique m'a beaucoup parlé de vous.

Grammar

1 The perfect tense with *être*

Look back at Unit 12 page 114 where you met the perfect tense with **avoir**. Since then you have come across many examples of verbs which are formed with **avoir** in the perfect tense.

There are fewer verbs which form the perfect tense with **être** and they function slightly differently from those with **avoir**. They are closer to adjectives and in fact the past participle varies according to the gender and number of the subject in the same way that some adjectives do:

Elle est fatiguée (adjective)   *She is tired*

fatiguée ends with an **-e** for feminine because it is she who is tired.

Elle est allée (past participle) en ville.   *She went to town.*

allée also ends with -e because it is she who went.

▶ The thirteen verbs with *être*

There are only thirteen frequently used verbs which form the perfect tense with **être**:

aller *to go*	**allé**	naître *to be born*	**né**
arriver *to arrive*	**arrivé**	partir *to leave*	**parti**
descendre *to go down*	**descendu**	rester *to stay*	**resté**
devenir *to become*	**devenu**	sortir *to go out*	**sorti**
entrer *to enter*	**entré**	tomber *to fall*	**tombé**
monter *to go up*	**monté**	venir *to come*	**venu**
mourir *to die*	**mort**		

Study carefully the examples below, paying particular attention to the spelling of the past participle:

* Je suis **allée** à la banque. (a woman speaking)
* Tu es **arrivé** en retard ce matin, Pierre! (someone speaking to a young boy)
* Sophie est **devenue** très sage. (*very well-behaved*)
* Mathieu est **entré** à l'université.
* Nous sommes **descendus** de voiture (m.pl. – more than one man or a man and a woman)
* Nous sommes **entrées** à la Samaritaine (f.pl. – more than one woman speaking)
* Vous êtes **né** à Paris, Maurice? (addressing one male only)
* Vous êtes **partis** sans moi les garçons! (m.pl.)
* Ils sont **morts** dans un accident de voiture (Dodi and Princess Diana)
* Elles sont **venues** à pied (f.pl.) (*They walked here.*)

How to remember the verbs with *être*

The following story is a mnemonic device which you can use to remember easily most of these: It is the story of Henri, who was born in Marseille, went to Paris, went up the Eiffel Tower, went up to the second floor stayed there half an hour, came down, came out, went to see la Seine, fell in it and died:

> Henri est **né** à Marseille. À l'âge de trente ans il est **venu** à Paris. Il est **allé** à la Tour Eiffel. Il est **entré**. Il est **monté** jusqu'au deuxième étage. Il est **resté** là une demi-heure. Il est **descendu**. Il est **sorti**. Il est **allé** au bord de la Seine. Malheureusement il est **tombé** et il est **mort**.

You may write the story of Henri's twin sister, Henriette: Henriette est **née** à Marseille…

If you want to write a different version with Henri and Henriette both involved, its starts: Henri et Henriette sont **nés** à Marseille … (One masculine + one feminine = masculine plural in French grammar rules).

Reflexive verbs with *être*

In addition to these specific thirteen verbs, all reflexive verbs form the perfect tense with **être**. When they are not reflexive they form the perfect tense with **avoir**.

Exemples: couper *to cut*, past participle **coupé**

- Caroline **a coupé** du pain avec un couteau. (perfect tense with **avoir**)
  she cut the bread with a knife BUT

- Caroline **s'est coupée** avec un couteau. (perfect tense with **être**)
  She cut herself with a knife. (Reflexive verb has extra -e on past participle because Caroline is feminine).

Exercise 1 Faites six phrases correctes

Find six correct sentences and say what they mean.

1 Djamel est l'animateur qui s'	**a** sont allés au Maroc.
2 Sarah et Dominique	**b** êtes parti avec un groupe de jeunes?
3 Je	**c** est occupé du voyage.
4 Les jeunes	**d** est resté trois semaines au Maroc.
5 Vous	**e** sont arrivées chez Gildas.
6 Le groupe	**f** suis monté(e) à la Tour Eiffel.

▶ **Exercise 2 À votre tour de poser des questions**

It's your turn to ask questions – you are being told what to say.

You are speaking to Adidja, Djamel's friend, who is also an **animatrice socio-culturelle**.

a Vous   *Ask her if she went to Morocco with the group.*
   Adidja   Oui, j'y suis allée.
b Vous   *Ask her how many young people went to Morocco.*
   Adidja   Dix-huit. Huit filles et dix garçons.
c Vous   *Ask her how long they stayed.*
   Adidja   Nous sommes restés trois semaines.
d Vous   *Ask her if they met young Moroccans.*
   Adidja   Oui beaucoup. C'était formidable.

If you are satisfied with your questions you can now listen to the recording.

ℹ All French towns have places such as **centres socio-culturels, Maisons des Jeunes, Maisons du Peuple** or **Maisons de Quartier.** These centres are normally run by **la municipalité** (*the Council*) and do not only cater for young people. There are usually cultural and leisure activities for various groups of people at various times of the day. They can vary in terms of the facilities they offer but most of them have their own premises, sports halls, art rooms, games rooms, etc. They do not normally share buildings or facilities with schools. The role of the **animateur socio-culturel** is to provide a place for leisure and social purposes and also for education but clearly distinct from the school system. With many French school children on a four day week* now, the role of **animateurs socio-culturels** is vital although attendance at these centres is not compulsory. Part of the task includes tackling racism in a constructive way.

In the dialogue (page 166) Djamel refers to **jeunes maghrébins**: young people from the **Maghreb**, the area of North Africa which covers **la Tunisie** *Tunisia*, **l'Algérie** *Algeria* and **le Maroc.** These countries were at one time French colonies. Most young people of Arabic origin were born in France but they live with a dual culture which is not always understood or accepted. Young Arabs are often pejoratively called **les beurs** or **les harkis** (born from North African parents – second generation people). In the 1980s young French people became aware of racial problems and under the leadership of a young black man called **Harlem Désir** started a movement called **SOS Racisme**, with a slogan **'Touche pas à mon pote!'** (*Don't touch my mate!*) and an open hand as a symbol.

* The reason why more and more French schools operate a four day week is that traditionally Wednesday is a day off school used for various activities or for private study. Saturday, from being a full school-day, has become over the years morning only. But under parental pressure many schools are no longer time-tabling lessons at all on Saturdays. French children are still having to work hard: each of their four days can be a nine-hour day in school, seven hours of lessons and a heavy homework programme.

▶2 Je suis né en France
I was born in France

Sarah continues the conversation with Djamel.

Listen to the recording and answer the questions.

a What question does Sarah ask Djamel?
b Where was he born?
c Who did he go to Morocco with?
d How many times have they been there?

Listen again.

e Which language does Djamel speak at home?
f How many languages can he speak?

Now read the dialogue.

Sarah	Et vous, c'est la première fois que vous êtes allé au Maroc?
Djamel	Non, non, je suis né en France mais avec mes parents et mes sœurs nous y sommes allés une dizaine de fois.
Sarah	Vous parlez l'arabe alors?
Djamel	Bien sûr, on parle l'arabe à la maison. Je pense que c'est enrichissant d'avoir une double culture. Je parle trois langues: le français, l'arabe et l'anglais. Je me sens ouvert et tolérant.

Exercise 3 Un sondage d'opinion

Lisez les résultats de l'enquête du *Nouvel Observateur*. Est-ce que la France mérite la réputation d'être le pays des droits de l'homme? *Does France deserve its reputation as the country of human rights?*

SONDAGE

«Le Nouvel Observateur» vient de publier une enquête sur la façon dont les Français d'origine étrangère jugent la France. Voici ce qu'ils répondent à deux des questions.

– Est-ce que vous avez été personnellement victime de propos ou de comportements racistes?

Oui	65%
Non	32%
Ne se prononcent pas	3%

– Pensez-vous que la réputation de la France comme pays d'accueil et pays des droits de l'homme est tout à fait justifiée, assez justifiée, peu justifiée, ou pas du tout justifiée?

Tout à fait et assez justifiée	50%
Peu et pas du tout justifiée	48%
Ne se prononcent pas	2%

une enquête	*an investigation*
étranger/étrangère	*foreign*
des propos	*remark/utterance*
des comportements	*attitudes*
accueil	*welcome*

Now link the English phrases to the French expressions.

1	No opinion	a	Tout à fait justifiée
2	Little justified	b	Assez justifiée
3	Fully justified	c	Ne se prononcent pas
4	Fairly justified	d	Pas du tout justifiée
5	Not at all justified	e	Peu justifiée

Exercise 4 Combien de Français?

Look at the results of the opinion poll (above) and answer the questions verbally only.

Reminder: **20% se dit 'vingt pour cent'**

Combien de Français d'origine étrangère :

a pensent que la réputation de la France est justifiée?
b pensent que la réputation de la France n'est pas justifiée?
c ont été victimes de racisme?
d n'ont pas été victimes de racisme?

Surfez sur le web

Trouvez des activités pour les jeunes.

- www.ufjt.org est le site de l'organisation Union des Foyers et des Services pour Jeunes Travailleurs
- http://fr.wikipedia.org/wiki/Lilian_Thuram

Web extension

Lisez le paragraphe ci-dessous sur le footballeur Lilian Thuram. Vous pourrez retrouver ce texte sur le site wikipédia http://fr.wikipedia.org/wiki/Lilian_Thuram.

Lilian Thuram (né le 1er janvier 1972 à Pointe-à-Pitre, Guadeloupe) est un **footballeur français,** qui évolue en défense. Au-delà de sa carrière sportive, il intervient dans la vie politique française, en particulier sur les questions d'intégration. Il est membre du **Haut conseil à l'intégration.**

Lilian Thuram, membre de l'équipe championne du monde de football en 1998, a surpris les médias le mardi 8 novembre 2005 par sa déclaration offensive*, "Moi aussi j'ai grandi en banlieue". Il a critiqué les propos du ministre de l'Intérieur, **Nicolas Sarkozy,** en expliquant que ces jeunes ne sont pas des **racailles****: "Avant de parler **d'insécurité,** il faut peut-être parler de **justice sociale.**" Le ministre a plus tard répliqué, affirmant que "Lilian Thuram ne vit plus en banlieue depuis longtemps".

*confrontational **scum.

Répondez aux questions:

1 Who is Lilian Thuram?
2 Where did he grow up?
3 Why was he critical of Nicolas Sarkozy's remarks?
4 What post did Sarkozy hold in November 2005?
5 What was his response to Thuram's statement?

17

on cherche du travail
looking for work

In this unit you will learn
- to talk about jobs and professions
- to look for jobs in the newspapers
- one more way to express the past: the imperfect tense

► 1 Mon père était professeur
My father was a teacher

Dominique et Sarah sont arrivées chez les parents de Dominique, Monsieur et Madame Périer, à Pessac, une ville près de Bordeaux.

Listen once to the recording and answer these questions:

a What does M. Périer think of Sarah's French?
b What does Dominique say about it?
c Who spoke French at home when Sarah was a child?

Listen again.

d What happened to Sarah's father?
e How long ago was that?
f How is Sarah's mother?

Listen one more time.

g Why does Mme Périer interrupt her husband?
h What is she going to show Sarah?
i How long ago did M. et Mme Périer retire?

Now read the dialogue.

M. Périer	Mais vous parlez bien le français Sarah.
Dominique	Sarah est bilingue, Papa!
Sarah	C'est-à-dire que ma mère est française et elle m'a appris le français dès toute petite et le français était la première langue à la maison.
M. Périer	Ah bon! Et qu'est-ce qu'ils font vos parents?
Sarah	Mes parents étaient tous les deux professeurs de langues. Mon père était professeur d'allemand mais il est mort d'un cancer il y a cinq ans. Il parlait couramment le français et l'allemand.
Mme Périer	Je suis désolée. Votre maman va bien?
Sarah	Oui, oui, elle enseigne toujours le français dans une école à Londres.
M. Périer	Et vous, qu'est-ce que vous faites comme profession?
Sarah	Je suis éditrice dans une maison d'édition.
M.Périer	Ah, c'est un métier très intéressant! Dites-moi...
Mme Périer	Voyons François, tu vas fatiguer Sarah avec toutes tes questions. Je vais vous montrer votre chambre.

Un peu plus tard

Sarah   Quelle belle maison! Qu'est-ce qu'ils font tes parents?

Dominique   Oh ils sont à la retraite depuis deux ans. Ma mère travaillait en tant que pharmacienne dans une grande pharmacie de Bordeaux et mon père était viticulteur.

apprendre	*to learn* but also *to teach someone something*
dès	*since*
dès que	*as soon as*
enseigner	*to teach (as a job)*
être à la retraite	*to be retired*
couramment	*fluently*
maison d'édition	*publishing company*

In the grid below only the first row is completed correctly. Place the correct profession by each name and also its correct translation. Tick the names of thoses who are still working.

Noms	profession/métier	profession/job
Dominique	Prof de Philo	*Philosophy teacher*
Sarah	Professeur de français	*Wine grower*
Mme Périer	Viticulteur	*French teacher*
M. Périer	Editrice	*Pharmacist*
Mr. Burgess	Pharmacienne	*German teacher*
Mrs. Burgess	Professeur d'allemand	*Editor*

Grammar

1 Talking about professions

On page 24 you learnt that there is no article in front of the name of a profession. This applies with the following structure only: subject + **être** + name of profession:

Elle était pharmacienne.   *She used to be a pharmacist*
Elle est Ministre de   *She is the Minister for*
l'Environnement.   *the Environment.*
Il est ingénieur.   *He is an engineer.*
Je suis professeur d'allemand.   *I am a German teacher.*

But in other structures the article is necessary:

J'avais horreur de **la** prof de maths.   *I couldn't stand the maths teacher.*

Professeur is always a masculine word, except in pupils' vocabulary at school when the abbreviation '**prof**' is commonly used. When among school pupils you are likely to hear : '**Chouette! On a la prof**' **d'anglais de l'année dernière**' or **Le prof de physique est vache avec nous!**

Chouette!	*Cool! Great! Brill!* (Lit. *owl*) (slang)
Vache	*nasty* (Lit. *cow*) (slang)

2 Apprendre et enseigner

- Enseigner: *to teach* (e.g. in a school):
  J'enseigne l'espagnol dans un lycée *I teach Spanish in an upper secondary school.*

- Apprendre *to learn*:
  J'apprends la musique. *I am learning music.*

- Apprendre quelque chose à quelqu'un *to teach someone something*:
  Mon professeur m'apprend à jouer du piano. *My teacher teaches me to play the piano.*
  Ma mère a appris à lire à tous ses enfants. *My mother taught all her children to read.*

3 One more way to express the past: the imperfect tense

The various past tenses of verbs offer a range of nuances for what happened in the past. The perfect and the imperfect are often used in the same sentence to express when one event occurred in relation to another event.

How to form the imperfect

To form the imperfect tense you need to learn the following endings. They apply to all verbs without exception:

je	**-ais**	nous	**-ions**
tu	**-ais**	vous	**-iez**
il/elle	**-ait**	ils/elles	**-aient**

The four verbs below should provide you with a pattern for all other verbs in the imperfect.

Subject pronouns	être	parler	finir	prendre
je/j'	étais	parlais	finissais	prenais
tu	étais	parlais	finissais	prenais
il/elle/on	était	parlait	finissait	prenait
nous	étions	parlions	finissions	prenions
vous	étiez	parliez	finissiez	preniez
ils/elles	étaient	parlaient	finissaient	prenaient

When to use the imperfect tense:

1 When an action which was continuous or relatively lengthy is interrupted by a shorter one expressed by the perfect:

J'étais aux Etats-Unis quand **j'ai appris** la mort de mon père. *I was in the US when I learnt of my father's death.* (both events took place in the past but being in the US is longer than the few seconds it took to hear the news)

Nous sommes arrivées au moment où **il prenait** sa douche. *We arrived just as he was taking his shower.* (taking a shower is relatively longer than the action of arriving somewhere)

Les jeunes filles travaillaient au café quand **la bombe a explosé.** *The girls were working in the café when the bomb went off.*

2 When reminiscing, talking about and describing how things used to be and referring to events which occurred repeatedly in the past.

Quand **j'étais** petite **je passais** toutes mes vacances en France. *When I was little I used to spend all my holiday in France.*

Nous allions chez notre grand-mère en Provence. *We used to go to my grandmother in Provence.*

Nos grand-parents s'occupaient bien de nous. *Our grandparents took good care of us.*

Nous travaillions dans les champs tous les étés. *We used to work in the fields every summer.*

Nous prenions le goûter tous les après-midi. **On mangeait** des confitures délicieuses. *We had tea every afternoon. We ate delicious jams.*

Exercise 1 Qu'est-ce que vous faisiez quand vous étiez jeune?

Answer with the verbs in the imperfect tense.

Start your answers with **Je/J':**

a danser

b skier

c faire du basket

d aller à la pêche

e faire de la planche à roulettes

f jouer du piano

▶ Pronunciation

In Unit 14 on page 144 you were given a few examples of verbs where **c** became **ç** in order to keep the same sound. A similar process takes place in the imperfect tense with verbs ending in -**cer** and verbs ending in -**ger**.

- **Commencer** *to begin*: **je commençais, elle commençait, ils commençaient**

  These are all pronounced the same way. With **nous commencions** and **vous commenciez** the cedilla disappears again because it is not required: **c** followed by **i** sounds [s].

- **Manger** *to eat*, **nager** *to swim*

  In order to keep the sound [*je*] verbs ending with -**ger** keep the **e** after the **g**:

  Je nageais, elle nageait, ils nageaient

  The -**e** disappears with **nous nagions** and **vous nagiez** because **g**+**i** has a [*je*] sound.

▶2 À l'A.N.P.E.
At the National Employment Agency

Three unemployed young people are outside the **Agence Nationale pour l'Emploi** (the National Employment Agency) known as **l'A.N.P.E** (pronounced by spelling out each of the letters of the acronym).

Listen to the recording once, then answer these questions:

a What kind of apprenticeship does Raphaël want to do?
b What does Youssef say about his brother?
c What does his brother do now?

Listen again.

d According to Youssef what can't his brother do any longer?
e At what time does he start work in the morning?
f Where does Lætitia say she would like to work?

Now read the dialogue.

Raphaël   Salut, vous venez avec moi?
Lætitia   Où ça? A l'A.N.P.E.? Qu'est-ce que tu vas faire?
Raphaël   Je voudrais des renseignements sur l'apprentissage.
Lætitia   Un apprentissage pour faire quoi?
Raphaël   Je ne sais pas moi, je vais demander ce qu'on peut faire.
Youssef   Mon frère Rashid, il était apprenti-boulanger.
Lætitia   Ah oui? Et maintenant qu'est-ce qu'il fait? Des croissants?
Raphaël   Arrête un moment Lætitia!
Youssef   Maintenant mon frère a un vrai boulot chez un boulanger. L'inconvénient, avant il aimait bien sortir en boîte et tout et maintenant il ne peut plus parce qu'il commence à travailler à cinq heures du matin.
Lætitia   Bon alors vous venez? On y va à l'A.N.P.E. mais pas pour devenir apprenti-boulanger! Moi j'aimerais bien travailler dans une pharmacie ou quelque chose comme ça. Alors tu viens Youssef, on va aider Raphaël à choisir son apprentissage.
Raphaël   Ah, non, elle me casse les pieds celle-là! Tu n'as qu'à en choisir un pour toi d'apprentissage!

Link the following English phrases to the equivalent French expressions:

1 Are you coming with me?
2 My brother used to be an apprentice.
3 He starts work at five in the morning.
4 What does he do now?
5 something like that
6 We are going to help Raphaël choose.

a Il commence à travailler à cinq heures du matin.
b quelque chose comme ça
c Et maintenant qu'est-ce qu'il fait?
d Vous venez avec moi?
e On va aider Raphaël à choisir.
f Mon frère était apprenti.

Surfez sur le web

Maintenant l'A.N.P.E a un site non seulement pour informer sur ses services mais on y trouve aussi plus de 100 000 offres d'emploi sur toute la France: www.anpe.fr

▶ Pronunciation

Because some words tend to be linked up together, you may frequently hear utterances which are not exactly grammatically correct but which are used in every day conversation:

> Tu n'as qu'à en choisir un pour toi ! *You'd better choose one.*
> Lit. *You only have to choose one for yourself.*

The structure is: **ne + avoir +que + à** but in every day language the **ne** disappears, even in public talk by most eminent people (on TV, radio etc.).

This is high on the list of language used to give advice, for making suggestions in all sorts of circumstances but especially when people suggest what the government should be doing:

Ils n'ont qu'à... *all they need to do...* becomes **ils ont qu'à...** [*isonka*]

Tu n'as qu'à ... *all you need to do...* becomes **t'as qu'à...** [*taka*]

Il n'y a qu'à... *all there is to do...* becomes **y a qu'à...** [*yaka*]

You may even see YACKA used as the name of bars or cafés, places where people put the world right!

BAR - TABAC
LE YACKA

ℹ L'emploi

Le chômage *unemployment* is still high in France. Over three million people are out of work (**au chômage**) and the trend is getting worse. **L'Agence Nationale pour l'Emploi** *the National Employment Agency* was created in 1967 and its work is needed more than ever. All sorts of measures have been put in place to get young people on to the work market.

Le Contrat d'apprentissage (*apprenticeship*) has been revised, following the March 2006 demonstrations and the unrest created by government plans for new legislation on young people's work contracts (**Contrat Première Embauche** – *Contract for First Job*). The Government was forced to backtrack and has now come up with a more versatile plan for apprenticeship. This includes **L'Apprentissage Junior**, which can apply, under certain circumstances, to young people from the age of 14. The apprentice's salary is based on the Minimum Wage, **le SMIC (Salaire Minimum Interprofessionnel de Croissance** 8,27 € per hour) and various percentages apply according to age and number of years of contract. For example anyone under the age of 18 and in their first year of apprenticeship will get 25% of the minimum wage, 37% in their second year and 53% in their third and final year.

3 Le contrat d'apprentissage
The apprentice's contract

The text opposite is an excerpt from an apprentice's contract.

Read it and then answer the questions. You are not expected to understand every word of the text.

1 How old do you have to be to sign the contract?
2 How long is the apprenticeship for ?
3 Can it be lengthened or shortened?
4 How long is the trial period?
5 What can happen during that time?
6 How many weeks' holiday does an apprentice have?
7 How much maternity leave does a young woman get?
8 How many days off do apprentices get:
   a to get married?
   b for the birth of a child?
9 What kind of course does the apprentice have to attend?
10 What proportion of the time has to be spent on a course?

l'employeur	employer	une période d'essai	trial period
en fonction	according	rompu	broken
du métier	to the job	pendant laquelle	during which
durée	duration		

183

on cherche du travail

17

LE CONTRAT D'APPRENTISSAGE

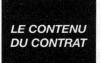
*LE CONTENU
DU CONTRAT*

Le contrat d'apprentissage est un contrat de travail de type particulier qui permet au jeune d'acquérir une qualification professionnelle sanctionnée par un diplôme technologique ou professionnel, ou un titre homologué. Ce type de contrat associe une formation en entreprise et des enseignements dans un Centre de Formation d'Apprentis (CFA).

SIGNATAIRES

Le contrat d'apprentissage est signé entre l'employeur, l'apprenti et le C.F.A. Il concerne tous les employeurs et tous les jeunes de 16 à moins de 26 ans.

DURÉE

La durée d'un contrat d'apprentissage est en général de 2 ans. Elle peut être portée à 3 ans ou réduite à 1 an en fonction du métier, de la qualification préparée et du niveau initial de l'apprenti.

PÉRIODE D'ESSAI

Les deux premiers mois constituent une période d'essai pendant laquelle le contrat peut être rompu.

CONGÉS

● L'apprenti bénéficie d'un congé annuel de 5 semaines.

● Au même titre que les autres salariées, l'apprentie peut bénéficier d'un congé maternité (6 semaines avant la date présumée de l'accouchement et 10 semaines après).

● Des congés pour événements familiaux sont également accordés, à savoir :

    4 jours pour le mariage de l'apprenti,
    3 jours pour la naissance de l'enfant de l'apprenti,
    2 jours pour le décès du conjoint ou d'un enfant de l'apprenti,
    1 jour pour le décès du père ou de la mère de l'apprenti.

*TEMPS DE
FORMATION*

Sur son temps de travail, le jeune suit une formation générale et technologique dans un centre de formation. La durée varie en fonction de la formation choisie (entre 1 à 2 semaines par mois).

▶ Exercise 2 À l'A.N.P.E.

You have decided to choose an apprenticeship. Tell the A.N.P.E. employee which category of work interests you.

Look at the list below, then listen to the recording to hear your questions.

Exemple:
Looking at the list, you think you are interested in the building trade:

Employé de l'A.N.P.E. Quel genre de métiers vous intéressent?
Vous   Je m'intéresse aux métiers du bâtiment.

a **Employé** Quel genre de métiers vous intéresse?
   Vous   *Say you are interested in the hotel industry.*
b **Employé** Qu'est-ce qui vous intéresse?
   Vous   *Say you are interested in photography.*
c **Employé** Vous vous intéressez à quoi?
   Vous   *Say you are interested in catering.*
d **Employé** Quel genre de métiers vous intéresse?
   Vous   *Say you are interested in jobs to do with health.*
e **Employé** À quoi vous intéressez-vous?
   Vous   *Say you are interested in the clothing industry.*

Métiers du bâtiment ....

Métiers de la chaudronnerie et de la métallerie ....

Métiers de l'hôtellerie et de la restauration.......................................

Métiers de la santé et des soins personnels ....

Métiers de l'hygiène et de l'environnement ....

Métiers de l'habillement ....

Métiers de la photographie et des industries graphiques................

Métiers du commerce et de la distribution.......................................

Métiers du secrétariat et de la comptabilité.....................................

Métiers du secteur agricole...

Métiers de la pierre ....

Exercise 3 Où chercher du travail? *Where to look for work?*

Look at the adverts below and answer questions **a–h** on page 186.

----

1 Internet

http://www.liberation.com

PROFILS NET

Toutes les annonces
d'offres d'emploi
parues dans Libération depuis
quinze jours. Dès aujourd'hui
vous pouvez y *répondre*
instantanément en laissant *votre CV.*

OPPORTUNITES

Des *formations,*
des *voyages,* des *services,*
des *produits*

----

2 Journaux

NOTRE OBJECTIF :

VOUS FORMER À L'INFORMATIQUE DE GESTION

Nous vous proposons une formation de 1200 heures à l'informatique, dans le cadre d'un contrat de qualification.

Dynamique, motivé, âgé de moins de 26 ans, vous êtes diplômé de mathématiques, physique, chimie, sciences économiques, gestion…, l'informatique vous intéresse et vous souhaitez en faire votre métier.

Alors n'hésitez plus, prenez contact avec nous, nous nous ferons un plaisir de vous présenter notre structure et nos projets de développement.

EMPLOIS OFFRES

COMMERCIAL VENTES

Sté LVG, vins de Bordeaux, recrute **2 VENDEURS** sur votre secteur, clientèle particuliers exclusivement, sur rendez-vous, profil, contact, convivialité, poste stable, débutants acceptés. Formation assurée. Tél. 02.99.51.66.51, pour rendez-vous, de 9 h à 17 h, sauf samedi.

EMPLOIS DU COMMERCE

Discothèque Finistère-Sud cherche **PORTIER.** Tél. 02.98.60.15.71

METIERS DE BOUCHE

Recherche **PATISSIER** sérieux, sachant travailler seul, Pont-de-Buis.
Tél. 02.98.79.01.17

HOTELLERIE RESTAURATION

SERVEUSE, 2 ans expérience, recherche emploi **RESTAURATION** traditionnelle ou gastronomique, région Brest ou Quimper. Tél. 02.38.61.07.10

APPRENTISSAGE

Recherche **APPRENTI(E) VENDEUR(SE) en charcuterie-traiteur.** Super U, Plestin-les-Greves. Tél. 02.96.51.19.21

GENS DE MAISON

LAVAL: recherche employée de maison, **temps plein**, logée, nourrie, pour s'occuper de deux enfants et entretien maison. 02.908.17.16.25

Recherche DAME pour contrat temps plein, dans appartement **centre QUIMPER**, garde bébé, ménage, repassage. Tél. 02.98.66.31.15

EMPLOIS DEMANDES

ADMINISTRATION COMPTABILITE

FEMME, 48 ans, avec expérience, cherche emploi temps partiel, **SECRETARIAT, COMPTABILITE** ou **COMMERCE**, secteur Quimperlé ou environs. Tél. 02.98.75.15.14

TECHNIQUE PRODUCTION

ELECTRICIEN possédant CAP électroménager, bon bricoleur, expérience homme d'entretien, cherche **EMPLOI**, pour toutes propositions, tél. 02.98.17.19.15

Sur internet

On the Internet, the national newspaper *Libération* has a site which you may wish to look up.

a What can you find on the Internet?
b What if the advert is one week old, can you still find it?
c How and when can you answer the job adverts?

Dans les journaux locaux

d Can you name three jobs which are advertised in the local paper?
e Can you give three types of jobs people are looking for?
f If you wanted to be trained in information technology for management purposes how old would you have to be?
g Which qualities would you have to demonstrate?
h Which background would you need?

Surfez sur le web

Surfez sur le web et trouvez un nouvel emploi.

- D'abord il vous faut un CV. Pour en savoir plus visitez: www.cvconseils.com

Si vous voulez trouver du travail, visitez les sites suivants:

- http://www.anpe.fr/
  Vous pouvez consulter, via la WebTV ANPE, les vidéos réalisées par l'Agence. Cliquez sur espace jeunes (jeunes de moins de 26 ans) pour des renseignements spécifiques aux jeunes.
- http://www.keljob.com
- http://www.cyber-emploi-centre.com
  Ouvrez le site, sur le troisième cadre, choisissez Echanges Européens → stages → Erasmus
- http://www.travail.gouv.fr et www.apprentissage.gouv.fr
  Sur ce site vous pouvez aussi voir des vidéos.

on prend le TGV

catching the high-speed train

In this unit you will learn
- about travelling by rail, and how to buy a ticket
- all about **la SNCF** and **le TGV**
- more verbs in the imperfect tense
- the subjunctive

◢ 1 Vous prenez le TGV? *Are you catching the TGV?*

Sarah has spent a week visiting Bordeaux and **Les Landes** (vast pine forests south of Bordeaux). She is now planning to travel back to London via Paris.

Listen to the recording once through and answer these questions.

a Why is Sarah leaving the Périers?
b Name two things, which according to Dominique, Sarah is starting to know well.
c What does Sarah think of the area?

Listen again.

d Where is Sarah going tomorrow?
e How is she getting there?
f How long will it take?

Listen for a third time.

g How long did it used to take when Monsieur Périer was a student?
h What could Sarah use the Minitel for?

Listen one more time.

i At what time is Sarah leaving tomorrow?
j Who is meeting Sarah on arrival?

Now read the dialogue.

M. Périer	Alors Sarah, vous nous quittez déjà?
Dominique	C'est vrai, la semaine est passée très vite! Sarah commence à bien connaître Bordeaux et les Landes, les vins de la région...
Sarah	Oui, j'adore votre région mais il faut que je rentre à Londres, je reprends le travail lundi et j'ai promis à ma sœur de passer quelques jours chez elle à Paris.
M. Périer	Vous prenez le TGV?
Sarah	Oui, c'est très rapide.
Mme Périer	Ça prend combien de temps maintenant pour monter à Paris?
Sarah	Ça dépend des trains mais en choisissant bien c'est faisable en trois heures.

M. Périer	Incroyable! On n'arrête pas le progrès! Savez-vous que lorsque j'étais jeune j'étais étudiant à Paris alors je prenais souvent le train pour rentrer. Cela prenait douze heures, sinon plus!
Dominique	Eh oui le progrès! Au fait Sarah, tu as réservé ta place dans le TGV? Tu pourrais le faire par Minitel.
Sarah	Non, je te remercie mais je préfère tout bonnement acheter mon billet à la gare. De toute façon on devait aller à Bordeaux cet après-midi, non?
Dominique	Oui bien sûr, c'est comme tu veux. À quelle heure tu pars demain?
Sarah	Je ne sais pas encore mais probablement entre quinze et seize heures: ma sœur viendra me chercher à Montparnasse après le travail, je pensais lui donner rendez-vous vers dix-neuf heures, dix-neuf heures quinze environ.

le TGV: Train à Grande Vitesse	*high-speed train*
tout bonnement/tout simplement	*very simply*
sinon plus	*if not more*
la gare	*the station*
lorsque	*when*

Link the following English phrases to the equivalent French expressions.

1 Well, then, Sarah, are you leaving us already?
2 Sarah is starting to know Bordeaux well.
3 I am going back to work on Monday.
4 Incredible! Progress never stops!
5 I used to be a student.
6 I often took the train to get home.
7 We were going to go to Bordeaux this afternoon, weren't we?
8 I thought I would arrange to meet her around 7 p.m.

a Je reprends le travail lundi.
b J'étais étudiant.
c Je prenais souvent le train pour rentrer.
d Alors Sarah, vous nous quittez déjà?
e Je pensais lui donner rendezvous vers 7h.
f Sarah commence à bien connaître Bordeaux.
g Incroyable! On n'arrête pas le progrès.
h On devait aller à Bordeaux cet après-midi, non?

Grammar

1 Prepositions + infinitive

You already know that when two verbs follow one another the second one is in the infinitive form:

On **devait aller** à Bordeaux.

Verbs following a preposition are also in the infinitive (prepositions are words which have a constant spelling, they are placed in front of nouns or pronouns or in front of verbs). The following prepositions are frequently used in front of verbs in the infinitive: **à** *at*, **de** *to, of,* **pour** *for / in order to,* **sans** *without*:

pour monter à Paris	*in order to get to Paris*
sans arrêter	*without stopping*
J'ai essayé **de ranger**.	*I tried to tidy up.*

2 The subjunctive

The subjunctive is a verb form which is commonly used in French. In fact you have already come across it on page 127 in sentences starting with **il faut que**. The subjunctive is a verb form which has its own range of past tenses although the present tense of the subjunctive is the most used of all. This course will only provide you with examples of the present subjunctive and a few examples of the past form with **avoir** and **être**, as you are not likely to meet other forms when you hear spoken French.

The subjunctive is usually preceded by a verb + **que**. However, there are many verbs with **que** which are not followed by the subjunctive. So this alone is not a guide to whether or not you should use the subjunctive. Instead, look at the meaning of the sentence. The subjunctive is mainly used to express necessity, possibility, doubt, regrets, wishes, fear. The subjunctive is automatically used after the following expressions:

- Necessity: **Il faut que** je rentre à Londres.
  It is necessary that I should go back to London.

- Possibility: **Il est possible que** je rentre à Londres la semaine prochaine.
  There is a possibility that I shall return to London next week.

- Doubt: **Je doute que** je rentre à Londres avant dimanche.
  I doubt that I shall be going back to London before Sunday.

- Regrets: **Je regrette qu**'elle rentre déjà à Londres.
  I am sorry that she is already going back to London.

- Wishes: **Je veux qu**'elle rentre à Londres immédiatement.
  I want her to go back to London immediately.

- Fear **J'ai peur qu**'elle rentre à Londres sans moi.
  I am afraid that she may return to London without me.

The ending pattern is similar for all verbs in the present subjunctive except for **avoir** and **être**.

Verb endings of the present subjunctive

je **–e**	nous **–ions** (**–yons** for **avoir** and **être**)
tu **–es**	vous **–iez** (**–yez** for **avoir** and **être**)
elle **–e**	ils **–ent**

Prendre *to take*

que je prenne	que nous prenions
que tu prennes	que vous preniez
qu'elle prenne	qu'ils prennent

Sometimes the subjunctive can be avoided by omitting **que** and using **de** + infinitive:

Il est possible **que je rentre** à Paris la semaine prochaine. (subjunctive)
Il est possible **de rentrer** à Paris la semaine prochaine. (infinitive after preposition **de**)

However the sense may be slightly changed.

When you feel ready to use the subjunctive you will find that your French has a slightly more authentic ring to it.

▶ Pronunciation

- C'est faisable. *It's feasible*

  Here, -ai- has a neutral sound similar to the **e** of **je** [*je*].

- **On n'arrête** pas le progrès. **On arrête** la voiture.

  There is no difference in sound between the two highlighted phrases. But the listener knows that the first example is a negative sentence because of **pas** after the verb.

Exercise 1 Quel temps? *Which tense?*

See whether you can identify which tenses are being used in the following examples. Match the sentence with the correct tense.

Examples found in first dialogue	tenses (jumbled)
1 tu as réservé ta place?	**a** present subjunctive
2 je te remercie	**b** perfect tense
3 je prenais souvent le train	**c** present indicative
4 il faut que je rentre à Londres	**d** imperfect
5 ma sœur viendra me chercher	**e** conditional
6 tu pourrais le faire par Minitel	**f** future

▶ Exercise 2 Ça prend combien de temps...?

The map opposite shows lengths of journeys from Paris to several destinations in France on the TGV. If you want more detailed information, look at the map on the TGV website: http://www.TGV.com (click on 'Découvrir le reseau Grande Vitesse'). How long does each journey from Paris take?

Look at the map, listen to the recording, and answer the four questions that you hear.

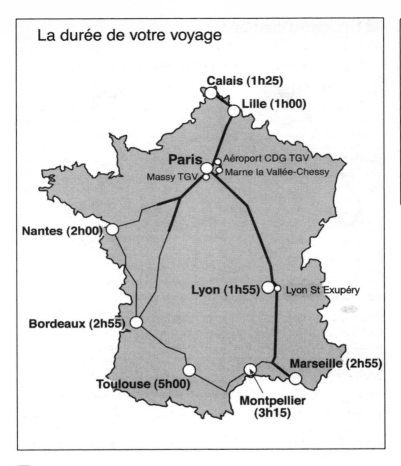

La durée de votre voyage

ℹ Le TGV (Train à Grande Vítesse) – speed record 575 km/hour on 04/04/07

The TGV links all major French towns to Paris. It normally travels at 300 kilometres per hour.

All seats have to be booked. Your ticket is issued to you for a specific journey at a specific time and a specific seat and your ticket cannot be used on a different train. When you buy your ticket the price includes the reservation. There is a buffet car in all TGVs.

ℹ️ Les gares de Paris

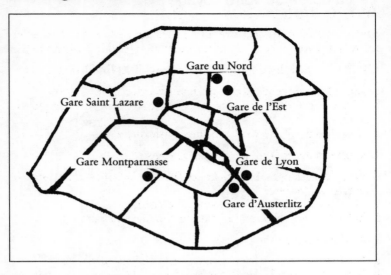

Starting or ending your journey in Paris? There are six main line stations which can take you to any corner of France. There are also links (**liaisons**) to airports and other major TGV stations around Paris. For instance if you are going to Disneyland your station is Marne la Vallée Chessy.

Look at the map of Paris above with the six main railway stations:

- From the **Gare Montparnasse** you can go west (Altlantic coast, Brittany, south-west France and Spain).
- From the **Gare St Lazare** you can get to Normandy.
- From the **Gare du Nord** you can get to the north of France and Belgium.
- From the **Gare de l'Est** you can reach the east of France and Germany.
- From the **Gare de Lyon** you can go to the south-east of France, the Mediterranean and Italy.
- From the **Gare d'Austerlitz** you can reach places in central France.

▶2 Au guichet de la gare
At the station ticket office

Sarah and Dominique are at the ticket office at Bordeaux railway station. There are other customers in front of them.

Listen to / read the dialogue, and answer these questions.

a How long does it take to go from Bordeaux to Poitiers?
b What kind of tickets do the old couple want? Single or return?
c Which day of the week do they wish to travel?

Listen/read again and answer these questions.

d One train leaves Bordeaux at 08.26. At what time does it arrive in Poitiers?
e Which train do they choose in the end?
f What is the advantage of taking this particular train?

Listen/read once more.

g Do they need to reserve their return tickets now?
h What does Sarah decide to do?

Un vieux monsieur et une vieille dame sont juste devant Sarah au guichet.

Vieille dame	Nous allons à Poitiers, ça prend combien de temps avec le TGV?
Employée de la SNCF	Voyons, une heure trois quarts environ madame. Vous voulez réserver?
Vieux monsieur	Deux billets s'il vous plaît.
Employée	Deux billets simples ou deux aller-retours?
Vieille dame	Deux billets aller-retours, s'il vous plaît.
Employée	Quel jour désirez-vous voyager?
Vieille dame	Lucien, nous partons demain n'est-ce pas?
Vieux monsieur	Mais non Simone nous allons à Poitiers jeudi, c'est-à-dire après demain.
Employée	Jeudi? Vous prendrez le train de quelle heure?
Vieille dame	À quelle heure y-a-t-il un train dans la matinée?

Employée	Alors jeudi ... il y a un train qui part de Bordeaux à 08.26 et qui arrive à Poitiers à 10.09. Le suivant est à 10.37 et il arrive à 12.32, et finalement il y a un TGV à 11.59 qui arrive à Poitiers à 13.50.
Vieille dame	Dans ce cas nous prendrons celui de 10.37 et nous arriverons chez ma fille pour le déjeuner...
Employée	Et pour le retour?
Vieux monsieur	C'est-à-dire ... nous ne savons pas encore.
Employée	Ce n'est pas nécessaire de réserver votre retour maintenant, vous pourrez le faire plus tard. Vous avez votre carte Senior?
Vieux monsieur	Simone, c'est toi qui a les cartes Senior?
Vieille dame	Je ne sais pas où je les ai mises ... attendez, il faut que je réfléchisse.
Sarah à Dominique	Tu avais raison, je vais réserver mon billet à la billetterie automatique.

le suivant	*the next one* (verb **suivre** *to follow*)
la carte Senior	*SNCF concession card for old-age pensioners*
réfléchir	*to reflect/to think back*
la billetterie automatique	*the ticket machine*

Les réservations

Link the following English phrases to the equivalent French expressions:

1 Would you like to make a reservation?
2 Which day would you like to travel?
3 We are leaving tomorrow, aren't we?
4 We'll get to my daughter in time for lunch.
5 We don't know yet.
6 Wait, I have to think.
7 I don't know where I put them.
8 You were right.

a Nous ne savons pas encore.
b Nous partons demain, n'est-ce-pas?
c Attendez, il faut que je réfléchisse.
d Vous voulez réserver?
e Quel jour désirez-vous voyager?
f Je ne sais pas où je les ai mises.
g Tu avais raison.
h Nous arriverons chez ma fille pour le déjeuner.

▶ Exercise 3 À vous de réserver un billet

Arcachon → Bordeaux → Paris/Île de France

TGV vert: toutes les réductions (minimum 15%) sont calculées sur le prix normal de niveau

Pour connaître le prix de votre billet, consultez
– Si vous voyagez en 1ère classe la page 46
– Si vous voyagez en 2e classe la page 47

TGV ne circulant pas ce jour-là

N° du TGV		8402	8404	8410	8412	7850	8414	7860(11)	8518	8420	8420	8526	8528
Restauration										(4)			
Arcachon	D				a	b	b	b	b			b	b
Facture	D				a	b	b	b	b			b	b
Bordeaux	D	4.59	6.01	6.08	6.42	6.46	7.05	7.59	8.22		8.26	10.37	10.44
Libourne	D	5.18		6.27		7.26							
Angoulême	D	6.03		7.10			8.11	8.58		9.25	9.25	11.44	
Ruffec	D			e				c		c	e	e	
Poitiers	D	6.47	7.55	7.55		8.28	8.56	9.43		10.09	10.09	12.32	
Châtellerault	D	7.04	8.12	8.12									
Saint-Pierre-des-Corps	D					9.08	9.37	10.23		10.25	10.25		
Massy TGV	D					9.58		11.13		10.54	10.54		
Marne la Vallée Chessy	D					10.34		11.53					
Aéroport Ch.de Gaulle TGV	D					10.49		12.06					
Paris-Montparnasse 1-2	D	8.20	9.00	9.30	9.40		10.35		11.25	11.50	11.50	14.05	13.50

You are at the ticket office in Bordeaux station. You are travelling tomorrow. You want to reserve a single ticket on the TGV. You want to get to Paris by 11 a.m. Look at the train timetable and decide which train you need to catch.

Listen to the recording and respond to the employee's questions.

a Vous   *Say you would like to reserve a ticket to Paris, please.*
   Employée Vous voyagez aujourd'hui?
b Vous   *Say no, you are travelling tomorrow.*
   Employée Vous prenez le train de quelle heure?
c Vous   *Say the time of your train.*
   Employée Vous prenez un billet aller-retour?
d Vous   *Say no, you would like a single. Ask the price of the ticket.*

▶ Grammar

There are two words for each of the following parts of the day and also for the year:

un jour	une journée	*a day*
un matin	une matinée	*a morning*
un soir	une soirée	*an evening*
un an	une année	*a year*

There is only a slight difference in meaning between the two forms and indeed that difference is not translatable in English. **Un jour, un matin, un soir, un an** are more likely to describe a portion of time defined by the calendar or the clock (objective connotation). **Une journée, une matinée, une soirée, une année** have a social connotation and are more likely to express the time experienced by individuals (more subjective):

Nous partirons dans trois jours.	*We'll leave in three days time.*
Nous avons passé une excellente journée au bord de la mer.	*We spent an excellent day at the seaside.*
Il passe un an à Paris.	*He is spending one year in Paris.*
Bonne année tout le monde!	*Have a good year everyone!*

It is important to understand the subtle difference between the two sets of words but in some cases either word can be used according to the emphasis given by the speaker.

Exercise 4 Choisissez le bon mot

For each sentence choose one of the two words in brackets to fill the gaps.

a Nous avons passé _____ magnifique chez nos amis. (un soir/une soirée)
b Dans trois _____ il aura cinquante ans. (ans/années)
c Il y a sept _____ dans une semaine. (jours/journées)
d Mon frère a onze _____ de moins que moi. (ans/années)

3 Les points de vente et les billetteries automatiques
Sales points and automatic ticket machines

Read the information on the next page about buying tickets.

Vrai ou faux? Having read the information on where to buy tickets and how to use automatic ticket machines say whether the following statements are true or false (**vrai** ou **faux**):

a You cannot buy your tickets more than two months in advance at the ticket office.

b All stations have a special ticket office for advance booking.

c At the ticket machine you can only buy your ticket 61 days in advance of travelling.

d If you use the ticket machine you can use up to 15 € in coins.

e You won't get any change.

f You can use your credit card for any journey.

g You can get your meal reservation from the machine too.

Surfez sur le web

• Trouvez la carte du TGV sur internet (www.res.ch/cartedu.htm) ainsi vous pourrez découvrir les nouvelles destinations du TGV en France et en Belgique.

• Si vous êtes passionné du train visitez le site de La Vie du Rail www.laviedurail.com. Pour entendre "siffler le train" cliquez sur "La vie du Rail" puis sur "Trésor du Rail". Sélectionnez "Ambiances sonores."

Web extension exercise

Voici ce que vous pouvez lire dans ce magazine hebdomadaire:

L'édition magazine

La Vie du Rail Magazine est n°1 dans le domaine du rail et des transports dans le monde. Hebdomadaire historique des cheminots, il comptabilise 600 000 lecteurs. Chaque semaine, découvrez toute l'actualité des transports, retrouvez les équipements, les technologies et les personnalités qui comptent, lisez les analyses et les partis pris des décideurs du secteur, sans oublier les loisirs, des astuces* et des conseils pour être bien dans la vie.

* tips

Cliquez ici pour

vous abonner

Ou téléphonez au 0 811 02 12 12

N° Azur, prox d'un appel local

Répondez aux questions

1 What rank does La Vie du Rail occupy amongst rail buffs' magazines?
2 How often is it published?
3 What type of issues would you expect to read about?
4 Name two ways of subscribing to La Vie du Rail.

Accueil Grandes Lignes

Guide du voyageur

Les points de vente HABITUELS

LES POINTS DE VENTE

Tous les billets sont vendus dans les gares, les boutiques SNCF et les agences de voyages.

Achetez-les à l'avance, ils sont valables 2 mois.

Que vous prépariez votre voyage ou soyez en instance de départ, tous les guichets délivrent, en principe, l'ensemble des prestations.

Certaines grandes gares disposent de guichets vous permettant de préparer votre voyage à l'écart des flux de départs immédiats.

LES BILLETTERIES AUTOMATIQUES

Ce sont des guichets en libre service qui vous permettent d'acheter un billet pour un trajet en France ou à destination de l'étranger (principales relations):

• de 61 jours à quelques minutes avant votre départ (sauf train autre que TGV avec réservation)
• avec ou sans réservation
• avec supplément éventuellement.

Vous pouvez également y réserver vos titres repas ou y retirer vos commandes passées par téléphone.

Comme moyen de paiement, la billetterie automatique accepte à partir de 2 € les cartes Bleues, Visa françaises ou étrangères, Eurocard/Mastercard, American Express et Diner's Club International.

La billetterie automatique accepte les pièces jusqu'à un montant total de 15 € et rend la monnaie.

> La billetterie automatique vous permet d'éviter les files d'attentes aux guichets.

[www.sncf.com]

Mots cachés

Find twenty words or expressions hidden in the grid. They all relate to train journeys and buying and booking tickets.

```
A R R I V E E S A R T Y U C V B M B T A
Z E F G H N M K L O S E R S T A Z C V L
D S I M P L E F S D F G H O R A I   R E L
R E W A S V B G N M J D E P A R T S V E
G R A N D E S L I G N E S D I A S W B R
T V S A F T E D D T Y U I N G S A N -
F A A W E G A H F E S V O Y A G E G D R
V T S S D G U J I U Y T R D G F A O F E
B I L L E T E R I E S F F R D X N G T
C O F F G U O K L Y F D F G A S C R T O
V N D U W R M D G T R R M I N I T E L U
N E E J E G A R E S F F F U D B F S Y R
G U I C H E T F Z A G F G K E J G T U A
M F D H A B I L L E T D U Y V K H A E E
O G F N S S Q H G L N S I T I U J U A I
P B H F S A U K E R K G K F T T H R D O
V A L A B L E L K L H U U D E R T A F U
N P O I N T S D E V E N T E S D S N C F
F H W E T G G U I T H U T D S E F T G Y
G S D M O N T P A R N A S S E S R S E A
```

Hidden words in translation

arrivals, departures, name for French railway company, high-speed train, ticket machines, ticket office, Minitel, main lines, timetable, single, return, ticket, stations, name of a Paris station, buffet car, valid, travel, booking, sales outlet, automatic.

19

à l'hôpital
at the hospital

In this unit you will learn
- more about public transport
- what to say at the hospital if you have to go in for a minor injury
- indirect object pronouns
- more about the subjunctive

1 Sarah téléphone à sa sœur
Sarah telephones her sister

Read this short passage and the SNCF leaflet **L'horaire garanti** opposite.

Le train de Bordeaux arrive à Montparnasse à dix-neuf heures quinze, avec dix minutes de retard. Sarah descend, mais ne voit pas sa sœur sur le quai. Elle attend quelques moments puis elle décide de téléphoner chez sa sœur. Elle a son téléphone portable dans son sac.

Did you understand? Then answer these questions!

a At what time does Sarah's train arrive in Paris?
b What was the scheduled arrival time? Will Sarah get any compensation? (see below: **L'horaire garanti**)
c Can she see her sister on the platform?
d What does she decide to do after a few moments?
e What has she got in her bag?

---

son téléphone portable   *her mobile phone*
un portable/un mobile   *are both used*

If you are using Pay as you Go, you can buy **une carte recharge** if you have run out of credit.

La SNCF s'engage...

ET TOUJOURS : L'HORAIRE GARANTI

Depuis le 1ᵉʳ septembre 1996, la SNCF s'engage à offrir une compensation **dès qu'un train Grandes Lignes est en retard d'au moins 30 minutes.**
Cette compensation représente :
– 25% du prix du billet du trajet concerné lorsque votre retard à destination est de 30 minutes à 1 heure,

– 50% du prix du trajet si le retard est supérieur à 1 heure.
Elle est réalisée sous forme de bons d'achat trains ("bons Voyage"). Pour en bénéficier, il est nécessaire d'avoir acquitté et effectué un parcours d'au moins 100 kilomètres en train Grandes Lignes.

▶2 Allô! *Hello!*

Sarah parle au téléphone à son beau-frère, Guillaume.

You may need to look at the words in the vocabulary box before you answer the questions.

Listen to / read the dialogue and answer the questions.

a What does Sarah think she has lost?
b What is the telephone number that Sarah has just dialled?

Listen/read again.

c Where is Marie-Claire?
d How did she cut herself?
e Does Guillaume think it is serious?

Listen/read one more time.

f Who are Ariane and Pierre?
g What does Guillaume suggest Sarah should do?
h Is it because Sarah does not know her way round the métro?

emmener	*to take someone/something somewhere*
rejoindre	*to rejoin/to meet someone somewhere*
un point de suture	*a stitch (medical)*
une piqûre	*an injection/insect bite*
J'ai perdu	*I have lost*
Ouf!	*Phew! (sigh of relief)*

Sarah	Zut! J'ai perdu mon portable! Ouf! le voilà! Alors ... zéro un, quarante-huit, zéro cinq, trente-neuf, seize. Bon ça sonne! Allô!
Guillaume	Allô oui?
Sarah	Guillaume, ici Sarah. Tu sais où est...
Guillaume	Ah Sarah! Encore heureux que tu aies téléphoné! J'étais inquiet...
Sarah	Qu'est-ce qu'il se passe?
Guillaume	Marie-Claire a eu un petit accident, elle est aux urgences à l'hôpital.
Sarah	Quoi? Qu'est-ce qu'il lui est arrivé?
Guillaume	Rien de grave ... elle s'est coupée en ouvrant une boîte pour le chat. La voisine l'a emmenée à l'hôpital.
Sarah	Tu veux que j'aille la rejoindre à l'hôpital?
Guillaume	Non, non elle ne devrait pas être longtemps ... juste quelques points de suture et une piqûre anti-tétanique, c'est tout!

Sarah	Et les enfants? Où sont Ariane et Pierre?
Guillaume	Ici, avec moi. Ecoute … je suis désolé … prends un taxi.
Sarah	Non! Je connais bien le trajet en métro: je vais jusqu'à Châtelet, je change et je prends la direction Château de Vincennes et je descends à Nation.
Guillaume	Oui, c'est cela mais si tu as beaucoup de bagages un taxi sera plus pratique.
Sarah	Bon d'accord, j'arrive!

Link the following English phrases to the equivalent French expressions.

1 I was worried.
2 What is happening?
3 What happened to her?
4 nothing serious
5 She cut herself.
6 The neighbour has taken her to hospital.
7 She should not be long.
8 I get out at Nation.

a Elle ne devrait pas être longtemps.
b Elle s'est coupée.
c La voisine l'a emmenée à l'hôpital.
d J'étais inquiet.
e Qu'est-ce qu'il lui est arrivé?
f Je descends à Nation.
g Qu'est-ce qu'il se passe?
h rien de grave

Grammar

1 Indirect object pronouns

You have already come across the whole range of pronouns but there are still some complexities which need to be explained. In the dialogue Sarah says:

Qu'est-ce qu'il **lui** est arrivé?

What has happened to her/him?

The model for the structure in this particular example is:

Il est arrivé quelque chose à quelqu'un.
Qu'est-ce qu'il est arrivé à Marie-Claire?

Something has happened to someone.
What has happened to Marie-Claire?

When the object (here **Marie-Claire**) is linked to the verb by a preposition (here à), this object is called an indirect object. When a personal pronoun (here **lui**) is used to replace the indirect object it is referred to as an indirect object pronoun. The plural form of **lui** is **leur**. The other object pronouns (**me, te, nous, vous**) are the same whether the object is direct or indirect.

This can be more easily demonstrated in simpler examples, using the present tense:

Je donne les fleurs **à ma mère**.	*I give the flowers **to my mother**.*
Je donne les chocolats **à mes parents**.	*I give the chocolates **to my parents**.*

In both examples there are two objects after **donne** and it is possible to use two pronouns side by side to replace them but, taking one thing at a time, **à ma mère** is replaced by **lui** and **à mes parents** is replaced by **leur**:

Je **lui** donne les fleurs.	*I give **her** the flowers.*
Je **leur** donne les chocolats.	*I give **them** the chocolates.*

Other examples:

J'ai réservé une place **pour ma mère**.	*I've reserved a place for my mother.*
Je **lui** ai reservé une place.	*I've reserved **her** a place.*
Tu as écrit **à tes parents**?	*Have you written to your parents?*
Non, je ne **leur** ai pas écrit.	*No, I haven't written **to them**.*

2 Emphatic pronouns

These are generally used after a preposition: **à** *at*, **avec** *with*, **de** *from/of*, **dans** *in*, **chez** *at*, **pour** *for / in order to*, **sans** *without*, **sous** *under*, **sur** *on / on top of*:

Il est parti sans **moi**.	*He left without **me**.*

(sans **moi**, sans **toi**, sans **lui**, sans **elle**, sans **nous**, sans **vous**, sans **elles**, sans **eux**)

3 More examples of the subjunctive

There are two examples in the dialogue. Did you find them?

Tu veux que j'**aille** la rejoindre à l'hôpital?	*Would you like me to meet her at the hospital?* (The verb is **aller**.)
Encore heureux que tu **aies** téléphoné!	*Just as well you phoned!*

In the second example the verb is in the past subjunctive, formed with **avoir** in the present subjunctive and the past participle of **téléphoner**.

Three essential verbs in the present subjunctive

	ALLER	**AVOIR**	**ETRE**
Il faut que	j'aille	j'aie	je sois
Il faut que	tu ailles	tu aies	tu sois
Il faut que	elle aille	elle ait	elle soit
Il faut que	nous allions	nous ayons	nous soyons
Il faut que	vous alliez	vous ayez	vous soyez
Il faut que	ils aillent	ils aient	ils soient

▶ Exercise 1 Vous passez beaucoup trop de temps au téléphone!

You have been telephoning all the people named in the box on the same day. Listen to the recording and fill in the grid. Say at what time you phoned them all. Remember to use the correct pronoun. A written example is provided for you (first line of the grid).

Names	**Questions on the recording**	**Your answer**
a Nadine (11.30)	A quelle heure avez-vous téléphoné à Nadine?	Je **lui** ai téléphoné à onze heures trente.
b Mathieu (12.00)		
c Chantal et Marc (17.15)		
d Votre sœur (18.45)		
e Vos parents (20.10)		
f Votre fiancé(e) (22.45)		

▶ Pronunciation

la, là, l'a, l'as: all four sound the same *la, la, la, la* but they all mean something different.

- **la** Definite article: **la** voisine *the neighbour*

- **là** An adverb: Marie-Claire n'est pas **là** (means *there* but frequently used to mean *here*)

- **l'a** Pronoun **le** or **la** in front of verb **avoir**: La voisine **l'a** emmenée à l'hôpital. *The neighbour took her to the hospital.*

- **l'as** Same as above but with **avoir** in the second person singular: Tu **l'as** vue? *Have you seen her?*

3 À l'hôpital *At the hospital*

C'est le mois d'août. A l'Hôpital d'Arcachon il y a beaucoup de personnes avec des maux et blessures en tous genres qui attendent de voir un docteur.

Look at the pictures and the words in the vocabulary box opposite to find out more about parts of the body and what aches and injuries people have.

Il s'est cassé la jambe en jouant au football

LES PARTIES DU CORPS

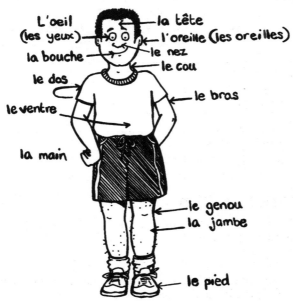

J'ai mal à la tête	*I have a headache*	
J'ai mal au ventre	*I have a stomach ache*	
Je me suis coupé	*I cut myself*	
Je me suis brûlé	*I burnt myself*	
Je suis blessé	*I am injured*	
J'ai une insolation	*I have a sun stroke*	
J'ai pris un coup de soleil	*I have got sunburnt*	
J'ai de la fièvre	*I have got a high temperature*	
J'ai du mal à respirer	*I can't breathe properly*	

▶ **Exercise 2 Les maux et blessures** *Aches and injuries*

Listen on the recording to the eight young people at the hospital casualty department. They speak in the order listed in the grid, but what's wrong has got mixed up. Link their names to what they say is wrong with them. You may need to stop the recording after each person speaks and listen to it several times. Try to write just a word or two in French in the first column next to the name of each patient to say what's wrong with them.

Qu'est-ce qui ne va pas?	Noms	What's wrong?
	1 Marie-José	**a** infected mosquito bites
	2 Alain	**b** toothache
	3 Adrienne	**c** a hand burnt with an iron
	4 Benoît	**d** headache
	5 Elise	**e** hurt knees
	6 Julien	**f** probably a broken arm
	7 Cécile	**g** a backache
	8 Didier	**h** a foot cut walking on a broken bottle

▶ **4 J'ai mal au ventre**
I have a tummy ache

Still at Arcachon hospital, a doctor is now seeing to a little girl called Magalie Dumas.

Listen to / read the dialogue and answer these questions:

a Is Magalie still crying?
b Where does it hurt?
c What is her temperature? Is it very high?

Listen/read again.

d What is Magalie's mother worried about?
e What did she have for lunch?

Listen/read once more.

f What meal did she last eat?
g When was she sick?
h What does the doctor say should happen tonight?

pleurer	to cry	vomir	to vomit
montrer	to show	garder	to keep

Dr Lebrun	C'est bien Magalie, tu ne pleures plus, tu es une grande fille. Alors montre-moi où ça fait mal.
Magalie	Là. Oh! Oh! J'ai mal au ventre.
Dr Lebrun	Ça fait mal quand je touche ici?
Magalie	Non. Aïe! Ici ça fait très mal!
Dr Lebrun	Elle a un peu de température, 38°2.
Madame Dumas	Vous croyez que c'est une crise d'appendicite Docteur?
Dr Lebrun	Non, je ne pense pas. Est-ce qu'elle a mangé ce midi?
Madame Dumas	Non, elle n'a rien mangé depuis le petit déjeuner. Elle a vomi vers dix heures ce matin.
Dr Lebrun	Nous allons la garder en observation cette nuit. Si tout va bien elle pourra sortir demain matin.

Now link the following English phrases to the equivalent French expressions.

1 You are not crying any more.
2 Show me where it hurts.
3 She has a bit of a temperature.
4 She has eaten nothing since breakfast.
5 We are going to keep her tonight for observation.
6 She was sick at about 10 a.m.

a Montre-moi où ça fait mal?
b Elle a vomi vers dix heures.
c Tu ne pleures plus.
d Elle a un peu de température.
e Elle n'a rien mangé depuis le petit déjeuner.
f Nous allons la garder en observation cette nuit.

ⓘ La pharmacie

For many French people **la pharmacie** is the first port of call in case of a minor injury or illness. **La Sécurité Sociale**, which is the equivalent of the National Health Service, is organized differently in France. When you go to your doctor you pay the full price of the visit, and at the chemist you pay the full price of the medicine, **les**

médicaments, and then you fill in a form to claim re-imbursement. There are many people who cannot afford to pay up front for treatment and medicine and go to the pharmacist instead.

Pharmacists are mostly helpful and advise people to go to their doctor if there is any doubt. Apart from advising people on minor ailments they also offer help with checking wild mushrooms, especially in small country towns.

Before travelling in Europe, European citizens are advised to apply for their European Health Insurance Card, which is a certificate of entitlement to health benefits during a stay in a member state (for UK citizens go to www.dh.gov.uk/travellers).

Exercise 3 Tout savoir sur le mal de dos

Look at the poster below and answer the questions.

C.H.U. (Centre Hospitalo-Universitaire) means *Hospital*.

PLONEOUR-LANVERN
LE MAL DE DOS
RÉUNION - DÉBAT
Animée par le Docteur FRIAT, Médecin
Service de rééducation fonctionnelle du C.H.U. de BREST

MERCREDI 21 MARS 2007, à 20H30
Salle Polyvalente, Plonéour-Lanvern
CAMPAGNE DE PRÉVENTION MENÉE PAR:

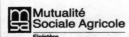 

Mutualité Sociale Agricole Finistère — GROUPAMA BRETAGNE — Le Télégramme

a When is there a meeting at Plonéour-Lanvern?
b Who is leading the debate?
c What is the debate about?

d Where is the meeting taking place?

e Where does Dr Friat normally work?

▶ **Exercise 4 À vous de jouer à "Jacques a dit"**

This is a game similar to "Simon Says" – you only do what Jacques says if Jacques' name appears before the command. You need to recognize the following commands, and others may be used:

- Levez (raise)
- Baissez (lower)
- Grattez (scratch)
- Touchez (touch)
- Frappez (hit)

Listen to the recording and write down how you responded to each of the commands.

Surfez sur le web

- Si vous avez mal au dos consultez le site www.undospourlavie.org (un dos pour la vie = literally *a back for life*). Vous trouverez des photos montrant des bonnes postures à adopter.
- Pour en savoir plus sur le jeu de "Jacques a dit" visitez le site http://www.tibooparc.com/anniversaire/jeu12.htm qui donne tous les détails sur ce jeu pour les enfants.

Web extension

Jeu de "Jacques a dit"

- Jeu calme (à partir de 5 ans)
- Intérieur

Règle du jeu:

Un enfant est désigné comme étant "Jacques". Les autres sont en cercle autour de lui. "Jacques" donne des consignes à ses petits camarades.

Quand la consigne est précédée des mots magiques : "Jacques a dit", les enfants doivent exécuter l'ordre donné (ex: "Jacques a dit levez les bras", tous les enfants doivent alors lever les bras).

Si la consigne n'est pas précédée des mots magiques, les enfants ne doivent pas bouger (ex : L'enfant dit juste "Levez les bras", les autres ne doivent pas lever les bras).

Si un enfant se trompe il est éliminé. Le dernier restant devient "Jacques" à son tour.

Un jeu parfait pour commencer la fête.

Web extension exercise

1 How old should children be to play this game?
2 What are the magic words?
3 What happens if a child makes a mistake?
4 What happens to the winner?

20

on prend le métro

catching the métro

In this unit you will learn
- what to say if you need to apologize
- everything you need to know about the Paris métro
- more on the perfect tense

▶ 1 Je te prie de m'excuser
Please excuse me

C'est mercredi matin. Marie-Claire est en congé de maladie. Elle bavarde avec sa sœur. Les enfants sont toujours en vacances. Sarah leur a promis de les emmener au zoo du Bois de Boulogne.

Listen to the recording several times, and then fill in the boxes. You'll need to pause the recording several times when you hear the information required to fill in the boxes: what is Sarah doing or what will she be doing at each point in time? All this information is hidden in the chatting (**bavardage**) between the two sisters.

Calendar of events		What is Sarah doing / planning to do? Who with?
a	Wednesday a.m.	
b	Wednesday p.m.	
c	Saturday p.m.	
d	Sunday lunch time	
e	Sunday 6.00 p.m.	
f	Sunday 6.22 p.m.	
g	Monday a.m.	

bouger	*to move*	**se débrouiller**	*to manage*
s'inquiéter	*to worry*	**être bête**	*to be silly*
prévenir	*to inform/to warn*		

Now read the dialogue.

Sarah	Bonjour grande sœur, ça va mieux?
Marie-Claire	Oh écoute, je te prie de m'excuser pour hier soir!
Sarah	Mais tu n'y pouvais rien! Ce n'est pas de ta faute!
Marie-Claire	Non mais tout de même, je suis désolée!
Sarah	Ce que tu es bête! Ne t'inquiète pas pour cela! De toute façon je me suis bien débrouillée! Tu ne m'as pas dit si tu allais mieux.
Marie-Claire	Oui, ça va un peu mieux. On m'a fait six points de suture mais ça me fait encore mal quand je bouge la main. Je vais prendre trois jours de congé maladie et

	je reprendrai le travail lundi matin. Au fait, tu restes jusqu'à quand?
Sarah	Jusqu'à dimanche soir. Il faudra que je sois à Paris-Nord à dix-huit heures pour enregistrer mon billet pour l'Eurostar de dix-huit heures vingt-deux. Moi aussi je reprends le travail lundi matin. Au fait Tante Eliane sait que je suis à Paris?
Marie-Claire	Oui, je l'ai prévenue. Elle nous invite tous à déjeuner dimanche midi. Je regrette mais je n'ai pas pu faire autrement.
Sarah	Non, cela ne fait rien, au contraire, je ne l'ai pas vue depuis Noël l'année dernière, ça me fera plaisir de la revoir.
Ariane	Maman, Tante Sarah a promis de nous emmener au zoo cet après-midi.
Pierre	Et puis aussi on va faire une grande balade dans le Bois de Boulogne et si on a le temps on s'arrêtera à Châtelet et on ira sur les quais voir les magasins d'animaux.
Marie-Claire	Eh bien dites-donc, vous en avez de la chance! Eh bien samedi soir on ira tous au cinéma.

Now link the following English phrases to the equivalent French expressions.

1 How silly you are!
2 In any case I managed!
3 I am feeling a bit better.
4 I am going to take three days of sick leave
5 to register my ticket for Eurostar
6 She is inviting us all for lunch.
7 I shall be pleased to see her again.
8 We are going to go for a long walk.

a Elle nous invite tous à déjeuner.
b pour enregistrer mon billet pour l'Eurostar
c Ce que tu es bête!
d Ça me fera plaisir de la revoir.
e De toute façon je me suis bien débrouillée!
f On va faire une grande balade.
g Ça va un peu mieux.
h Je vais prendre trois jours de congé de maladie.

Grammar

1 How to apologize and how to respond to an apology

Most of the expressions used here are from the dialogue above so that you can see how they fit in context.

Excuses: *Apologies*

Je vous prie de m'excuser.
(a bit formal but not unusual in polite conversations) *Please excuse me.*

Excuse-moi/Excusez-moi.
Excuse me. (more matter of fact)

Je suis désolé(e)/Désolé(e)!
I am sorry/Sorry!

Je regrette mais…
I am sorry but…

Je n'ai pas pu faire autrement.
I could not do anything different.

Je vous demande pardon.
Please forgive me.
(e.g. asking forgiveness when walking in front of someone)

Vous pardonnez!/Pardonnez!
'scuse! (matter of fact, bordering on rude – much is in the tone)

Réponses/Réactions: *Responses*

Most of the responses apply to any of the apologies listed on the left.

Ne t'inquiète pas! *Don't worry about it!*

Ne vous inquiétez pas! *Don't worry about it!*

Ce n'est pas grave! *Nothing serious!*

Cela/ça ne fait rien!
Ça n'a pas d'importance!
Peu importe!
} *It doesn't matter!*

N'y pense/pensez plus! *Forget it!*

Ce n'est pas de ta/votre faute.
It's not your fault.

Ne vous en faites pas. *Don't worry.*

Il n'y a pas de mal! *There is no harm done!*

Je vous en prie. *Go ahead / don't mind me.*

Exercise 1 Répondre aux excuses

Say how you would respond to the following. There is more than one answer in each situation.

a Someone bumps into you in the tube and says: **Oh excusez-moi!**
Vous:

b Someone breaks a vase in your house (not a collection item): **Oh je suis désolé, j'ai cassé le vase!**
Vous:

c Someone phoning you on their mobile phone (**un portable**) to let you know they are late: **Je regrette, je vais être en retard d'une heure. Je vous fais attendre...**
Vous:

d Someone saying why they were late (a problem at home): **Je n'ai pas pu faire autrement, il y avait un problème à la maison, alors...**
Vous:

Grammar

Note that if you are more interested in learning spoken French or background information about France you need not spend too much time on this section.

The perfect tense and agreement with the direct object

As usual there are several examples of the perfect tense in the dialogue:

dire *to say*:
   Tu ne m'as pas dit   *You did not tell me*

promettre *to promise*:
   Tante Sarah nous a **promis**.   *Aunt Sarah promised us.*

prévenir *to inform*:
   Je l'ai **prévenue**.   *I have informed her (Tante Eliane).*

Have you noticed the difference between the two spellings of the past participle **prévenu**?

You might need to go back to page 167 to remind yourself about the difference between verbs with **être** with the perfect tense and those with **avoir**.

With **être** (including reflexive verbs) the number and the gender of the subject affect the ending of the past participle:

   Marie-Claire est **allée** à l'hôpital. (**allé** gains an -e because Marie-Claire is feminine).

   Les Dupont sont **partis** en Espagne. (**parti** gains an -s because there is more than one Dupont in the family).

With verbs with **avoir** in the perfect tense there is no agreement between the subject and the past participle of the verb. If the subject is feminine or plural it does not affect the ending of the past participle:

Elle a **vu** sa tante à Noël.   *She saw her aunt at Christmas.*

But:

Elle l'a vue.   *She saw her.*

When a direct object (**sa tante/l'**) is placed before the verb, however, the past participle must 'agree' with the object i.e. it gains an -e if the object is feminine, an -s if it is plural and -es if it is feminine plural.

In the last example, a direct object pronoun (**l'**) is used instead of the direct object (**sa tante**).

In the example, the direct object pronoun precedes the past participle which consequently gains an -e in agreement (**vue**).

In this next example, as **Marie-Claire** (the direct object of the sentence) follows the verbs, there is no agreement between the object and the verb:

La voisine a **emmené**   *The neighbour took*
Marie-Claire à l'hôpital.   *Marie-Claire to the hospital.*

But in the following example, the object does agree with the verb because as a direct object pronoun it precedes the past participle. Thus **emmené** gains an -e to agree with **l'** (standing for **Marie-Claire**):

La voisine l'a emmenée.   *The neighbour took her.*

The explanation above is only important for those learners who wish to understand the spelling of the language and learn to write French correctly. Orally, of course, there is no difference at all between **emmené** and **emmenée** or **prévenu** and **prévenue**.

However, in some cases agreement of the past participle does make a difference to the sound of a verb:

J'ai **mis la carte postale** dans   *I put the postcard in the post*
la boîte à lettres.   *box.*
Je l'ai **mise** dans la boîte à   *I put it in the post box.*
lettres.
Nous avons **pris les clefs**   *We took the car keys.*
de la voiture.
Nous **les** avons **prises**.   *We took them.*

Mis sounds [*mi*] and **mise** sounds [*miz*]; **pris** sounds [*pri*] and **prises** sounds [*priz*].

Try to identify other examples in the next dialogue and the next units.

◗ Les quais de la Seine

In the dialogue Sarah has promised Ariane and Pierre that if they have time they will stop **sur les quais** to go and have a look at pet shops. **Les quais de la Seine**, the river banks throughout the centre of Paris, are amongst the city's most interesting places, with hundreds of little wooden boxes which open as stalls where people sell old books, maps, stamps postcards, etc. One of the most interesting **quais** is on the right bank of the **Seine** between **Châtelet** and **Pont-Neuf**. On one side there are **les bouquinistes** with their bookstalls and on the side of the buildings there is a multitude of pet shops with wonderful birds, cats, dogs and more exotic animals, next to flowers and seed shops selling a large variety of bulbs and seeds of all sorts. In recent years in the summer a section of the embankment has been transformed into a riverside resort.

Web Extension

Visitez le site http://marais.evous.fr/actualites/calendrier/paris-plage.html pour voir le programme de Paris plage 2007.

Voyez aussi Wikipedia: http://fr.wikipedia.org/wiki/Paris-Plage

Voici ce que vous pouvez lire:

Paris-Plage est aujourd'hui une opération **estivale** menée par la Mairie de Paris depuis **2002**. Chaque année, entre juillet et août, pendant environ 4 à 5 semaines, sur 3,5 km, la voie sur berge **rive droite** de la **Seine** et la **place de l'Hôtel-de-Ville** accueillent des activités ludiques et **sportives**, ainsi que des **plages** de sable et d'herbe, des **palmiers**,... La circulation automobile est interrompue sur cette portion de la voie rapide Georges-Pompidou pendant la durée de l'opération, de son installation à son démontage.

Web extension exercise

1 When did the Mayor of Paris launch this new institution?
2 When exactly does it take place?
3 Where exactly is it situated?
4 What activity is temporarily suspended because of it?

▶2 Acheter des tickets *Buying tickets*

Sarah, Ariane et Pierre sont en route pour leur promenade. Ils sont à la station de métro Nation. Ils se dirigent vers le guichet.

Listen to / read the dialogue and answer these questions.

a Does Sarah need to get tickets for the children?
b What kind of tickets have they got?
c Who says that Sarah is a child?

Listen / read again.

d Why does Sarah say to the children she wants to think for a minute?
e What does she get in the end?

Listen / read once more.

f Which **direction** will they take to go back?
g Why do the children choose les Sablons as the station where they want to get off?

demi-tarif	*half-fare*
un carnet de tickets	*a book of tickets (10)*
une station de métro	*a tube station*
une gare R.E.R./une gare S.N.C.F.	*an RER or SNCF strain station*
un changement	*connection (on métro or railway line)*

Sarah	Attendez les gamins! Il faut que j'achète des tickets.
Ariane	On en a, nous, des tickets.
Sarah	Ah oui? Bon très bien mais ce sont des tickets demi-tarifs pour les enfants et moi je ne suis plus une enfant!
Ariane	Si, tu es une enfant!
Sarah	Eh bien voilà! Je vous remercie les petits! Sérieusement, est-ce que je prends une carte ou un carnet? Laissez-moi réfléchir une minute.
	...
Sarah	Pardon madame, c'est combien la carte Mobilis, Zone 1 et 2?
Employée	Cela dépend où vous allez et combien de voyages differents vous allez faire...
Sarah	Ah oui, je vois. Je vais prendre un carnet de tickets s'il vous plaît.

Ariane	Moi, je sais quelle ligne il faut prendre, c'est la ligne 1, en direction de la Grande Arche de La Défense. C'est facile, il n'y a même pas de changements.
Pierre	Et pour rentrer c'est la direction Château de Vincennes. A quelle station on descend?
Sarah	On a le choix entre la Porte Maillot et les Sablons. C'est plus ou moins la même distance pour le zoo. Si on descend aux Sablons on peut prendre le petit train du Bois de Boulogne.
Ariane et Pierre	Les Sablons!

Link the following English phrases to the French equivalent expressions.

1 Kids, wait!
2 I am no longer a child.
3 Do I get a travel card or a book of tickets?
4 I know which line we have to take.
5 At which station do we get off?
6 It's more or less the same distance to the zoo.

a A quelle station on descend?
b Moi, je sais quelle ligne il faut prendre.
c Attendez les gamins!
d C'est plus ou moins la même distance pour le zoo.
e Je ne suis plus une enfant.
f Est-ce que j'achète une carte ou un carnet?

❻ Les transports parisiens

La Grande Arche de la Défense is a métro station named after the monument it leads to. **La Grande Arche** is President Mitterand's legacy to Paris. It is a tall futuristic building built under Mitterand between 1983 and 1989. It is spectacular in itself for its view over Paris and l'Ile-de-France but also because of its location which symbolically lines it up with l'Avenue de la Grande Armée and les Champs-Elysées and therefore with L'Arc de Triomphe and L'Obélisque de Louxor, Place de la Concorde.

Travelling around Paris you can use the bus or the métro which are run by **la R.A.T.P. (Réseau Autonome des Transports Parisiens)** and **le R.E.R. (Réseau Express Régional)**, a train service which serves the Parisian suburbs of l'Ile-de-France.

Les titres de transports is the official name for tickets. In normal usage there are two separate words for ticket in French: **un billet (de train)** and **un ticket de bus / de métro**. Paris commuters have a range of season tickets which they can use but for visitors there are three options: the individual ticket (not economical unless you only have one journey to make), **un carnet de tickets** with ten tickets and finally **la carte Mobilis** which is a day travel card with options for all zones. Within Paris you can use just one ticket for any journey, whether you have two stops or twenty on your journey; the cost is the same. You can also use one of your tickets for the cablecar in Montmartre, **le Funiculaire de Montmartre**.

Exercise 2 Vous vous déplacez de temps en temps
Look at the leaflet and answer the questions.

Et pour les touristes

A   Paris Visite:
C'est la carte idéale pour voyager à volonté sur tous les réseaux de transports urbains d'Ile-de-France dans la limite des zones choisies pendant 1, 2, 3 ou 5 jours.
Une carte pour voyager malin : pas de perte de temps, les enfants de 4 à moins de 12 ans paient moitié prix, accès à la 1re classe en RER et sur les trains Ile-de-France.
Elle n'a que des avantages : 14 partenaires proposent réductions, offres exceptionnelles, en exclusivité.

En vente également

B   Carte Musées et Monuments
Un laissez-passer de 1, 3 ou 5 jours pour visiter 70 musées et monuments de la région Ile-de-France.

C   Passeport Disneyland® Paris
En même temps que votre titre de transport, vous pouvez acheter votre passeport Disneyland Paris dans toutes les gares RER de la RATP (sauf Marne-la-Vallée/Chessy), les principales stations de métro, les Agences Commerciales RATP, les terminus bus de la Gare de Lyon et de la Place d'Italie, le Carrousel du Louvre et les points RATP de l'aéroport Roissy Charles-de-Gaulle.

---

a   Which of the three cards advertised is only a travel card?
b   What do these three cards entitle tourists to do?
c   Where can you buy your Passport for Disneyland Paris?
d   Where can't you buy one?
e   Which card has a half-fare tariff for children aged between 4 and 12?
f   Can you buy a Carte Musées et Monuments for one day? For six days?

Points de vente et mode de paiement

Now look at the second leaflet, below, and answer these questions.

g Make a list of all the places where you can buy Mobilis, Tickets, Ticket jeunes.

h How much do you need to spend before you can pay your fare with a credit card?

Vous vous déplacez de temps en temps

Mobilis: un seul ticket pour toute une journée.

Pendant une journée entière, Mobilis vous ouvre l'accès aux réseaux RATP, SNCF Ile-de-France, APTR et ADATRIF (à l'exception des dessertes aéroportuaires).

Muni de votre carte nominative et d'un coupon valable pour une journée, vous pouvez, à votre gré, combiner les trajets et vous déplacer dans les zones géographiques que vous avez choisies. Economique, Mobilis propose un tarif forfaitaire en fonction des zones sélectionnées.

Zones de validité	Tarifs Mobilis
Zones 1–2	5,50 €
Zones 1–3	7,30 €
Zones 1–4	9,15 €
Zones 1–5	12,30 €
Zones 1–6	15,60 €
Zones 1–7	17,20 €
Zones 1–8	18,70 €

Ticket Jeunes se déplacer partout le samedi, le dimanche ou un jour férié.

Pour tous les titulaires de la Carte Jeunes (française ou étrangère), le Ticket Jeunes permet de se déplacer partout pendant toute une journée, le samedi, le dimanche ou un jour férié. Le Ticket Jeunes est nominatif et permet de circuler en 2e classe sur les réseaux RATP (sauf Orlyval), SNCF Ile-de-France, APTR et ADATRIF dans la limite des zones choisies.

Zones de validité	Tarifs Ticket Jeunes
Zones 1–3	3,20 €
Zones 1–5	3,40 €
Zones 1–8	9,60 €
Création Zones 3–8	4,85 €

Points de vente Mobilis, Tickets, Ticket Jeunes:

■ Toutes les stations de métro, gares RER.
■ Terminus des lignes de bus.
■ Commerces et bureaux de tabac signalés par le visuel RATP.
■ Distributeurs automatiques pour les tickets.

Vous vous déplacez de temps en temps

Ticket ou Carnet pour un ou plusieurs déplacements dans Paris et Ile-de-France.

Un ticket pour un seul voyage, c'est idéal pour un déplacement occasionnel. Il peut être vendu soit en carnet.

Dans le métro, et dans le RER à l'intérieur de Paris, un seul ticket suffit quelles que soient les correspondances effectuées et la longueur de votre parcours.

Dans le RER en banlieue, le tarif varie selon la longueur de votre parcours.

Dans le bus à l'intérieur de Paris, un ticket permet un seul trajet, sans correspondance, quelle que soit la longueur du parcours (sauf sur les lignes PC, Balabus et Noctambus).

Pour les Noctambus, une tarification spéciale est appliquée.

Dans le bus et le tram, en banlieue et pour tout trajet incluant un parcours hors des limites de Paris, un ou plusieurs tickets sont nécessaires selon le nombre de sections parcourues.

Dans le Funiculaire de Montmartre, un ticket permet d'effectuer un seul trajet (montée ou descente), sans correspondance possible avec le métro ou le bus.

Tickets	Plein tarif	Demi-tarif
A l'unité	1,50 €	
Carnet de 10 tickets	10,90 €	5,45 €

Surfez sur le web

• Visitez le site de la RATP et découvrez des tas d'informations utiles: http://www.ratp.fr/. Vous y trouverez aussi un plan interactif des transports parisiens.

Cité Futée   *Clever City*

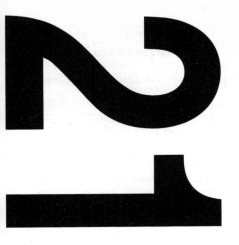

21

si on gagnait le gros lot...

if we won the jackpot....

In this unit you will learn
- about some places to visit in Paris
- how to discuss where to go and what to visit
- how to express what you would like to do if you had more time and money (the conditional tense)

▶ 1 On pourrait sortir *We could go out*

C'est vendredi matin. Marie-Claire est toujours en congé de maladie mais elle se sent beaucoup mieux. Sarah et Marie-Claire font des projets pour la journée. Les deux sœurs s'entendent très bien.

Listen to / read the dialogue. Sarah and her sister are chatting about places they might be going to and about what they might do when they get there. Tick only what they have agreed to do.

a to go to the Louvre
b to go to the Musée d'Orsay
c to go and see the Impressionist paintings
d to go to the Bazar de l'Hôtel de Ville
e to go to the Samaritaine
f to go for a cup of tea

Listen/read again and answer these questions.

g Considering that Marie-Claire is still on sick leave, why do the two young women decide to go out?
h What does Marie-Claire wish for?

Sarah	Toi ça va mieux, cela se voit! Tu es de meilleure humeur ce matin! Si tu allais mieux on pourrait peut-être sortir.
Marie-Claire	Oui je me sens beaucoup mieux et puis les gosses sont chez la mère de Guillaume jusqu'à ce soir, le mari au travail ... À nous la liberté!
Sarah	Tu veux venir avec moi, je pensais faire une balade dans Paris?
Marie-Claire	Mais pourquoi pas? Ma main est encore douloureuse mais je ferai bien attention. Tu n'aurais pas envie d'aller au Louvre?
Sarah	Le Louvre ... non, ça ne me dit rien et puis nous n'aurions pas assez de temps, il y a toujours une telle queue!
Marie-Claire	Oui, je sais, si j'avais le temps ... et l'argent ... je sortirais beaucoup plus souvent.
Sarah	Écoute, si on allait au Musée d'Orsay on pourrait juste aller voir les Impressionnistes, non? Et après si on voulait, on aurait assez de temps pour faire les grands magasins: le Bazar de l'Hôtel de Ville ou je ne sais pas moi...ou bien alors on pourrait aller à L'Orangerie qui vient d'être rénovée.
Marie-Claire	Génial! J'adore Monet et je n'ai pas encore vu la nouvelle salle aux Nymphéas...mais au lieu du Bazar de L'Hôtel de Ville on pourrait aller à la Samaritaine

...mais non! Que je suis bête! La Samaritaine est fermée pour rénovations.	
Sarah	Ah oui c'est vrai! C'est dommage! Mais ça ne fait rien, on ira prendre une tasse de thé à la terrasse du BHV.

être de bonne humeur	*to be in a good mood*
de meilleure humeur	*in a better mood*
se sentir mieux	*to feel better*
douloureux/se	*painful*
Cela ne me dit rien (colloquial).	*I don't fancy it.*
au lieu de	*instead of*
une telle queue	*such a queue*
les gosses	*kids* (similar to **les gamins** but slightly pejorative)
Que je suis bête!	*How silly of me!*

Link the following English phrases to the French.

1 It shows!
2 The kids are at Guillaume's mother's.
3 Do you fancy going to the Louvre?
4 We would not have enough time.
5 We would have time to go to the department stores.
6 We'll go for a cup of tea at the terrace at the top.

a Nous n'aurions pas assez de temps.
b Cela se voit.
c On ira prendre une tasse de thé tout en haut à la terrasse.
d Les gosses sont chez la mère de Guillaume.
e Tu as envie d'aller au Louvre?
f On aurait assez de temps pour faire les grands magasins.

Grammar

1 Faire

Faire can mean a lot more than *to make* or *to do*.

faire les grands magasins *to go window-shopping*, Lit. *to do the shops*
faire du lèche-vitrine *to go window-shopping*, Lit. *to do window licking*

Faire is also used to express that someone has done it all:

> Il a fait la Chine, l'Afrique, l'Amérique du Sud... *He's done China, Africa, South America...*

> Ça ne fait rien, *It does not matter,* Lit. *It does nothing*

2 The conditional and the imperfect

You have already met and used the conditional tense (see Unit 7, page 69). It conveys the notion that if conditions were fulfilled something would happen. It is used frequently in conversational French, especially with a few verbs which you are now familiar with:

Aller	Finir	Ending pattern for all verbs in the conditional		
j'irais	je finirais	je	_____	rais
tu irais	tu finirais	tu	_____	rais
elle irait	elle finirait	elle	_____	rait
nous irions	nous finirions	nous	_____	rions
vous iriez	vous finiriez	vous	_____	riez
ils iraient	ils finiraient	ils	_____	raient

Je voudrais faire une balade	*I would like to...* (**vouloir**)
Je devrais rentrer chez moi	*I ought to...* (**devoir**)
On pourrait aller au cinéma	*We could...* (**pouvoir**)
Il faudrait partir avant la nuit	*We should...* (**falloir**)

Here are two verbs in the conditional and the conditional verb ending pattern:

You have noticed before that within one short conversation people use many different tenses. The imperfect tense and the conditional are often used together in the same sentence to convey the notion that if the condition was (imperfect) right something would (conditional) happen.

Look at the examples in the dialogue on page 228. First of all note that **si** *if* together with a verb in the imperfect is often used with the conditional:

Si ça allait mieux on pourrait peut-être sortir.	*If you were better we could go out.*
Si j'avais le temps et l'argent je sortirais beaucoup plus souvent.	*If I had more time and money I would go out more often.*

| Si on allait au Musée d'Orsay on pourrait aller voir... | *If we went to the Musée d'Orsay we could go and see...* |

The emerging pattern here is therefore:

- **si** + verb in the imperfect + verb in the conditional

or

- verb in the conditional + **si** + verb in the imperfect

It is also possible to have the conditional on its own with the condition unspoken but present in the mind of the speaker and understood by the listener:

| Nous n'aurions pas assez de temps. | *We would not have enough time.* |

Note that when the doubt is lifted or when the condition is fulfilled the future tense is used instead of the conditional:

| On ira prendre une tasse de thé... | *We'll go for a cup of tea...* |

It has been agreed by the sisters that this is exactly what they will do rather than what they would like to do.

Reminder: The ending pattern for the future tense is as follows:

je	——**rai**	nous	——**rons**
tu	——**ras**	vous	——**rez**
elle	——**ra**	ils	——**ront**

(See also page 101.)

Exercise 1 Faites des phrases

Find the ending for each of the sentences in the left-hand column.

1 Si je savais son numéro de téléphone je...	**a** réussirait à ses examens.
2 Si j'étais riche je ...	**b** iraient à l'hôpital.
3 Si Corinne travaillait mieux elle ...	**c** n'aurait pas d'accidents.
4 Si vous aviez le temps qu'est-ce que vous ...	**d** ferais un voyage autour du Monde.
5 S'il conduisait moins vite il ...	**e** saurais ce qui se passe. (**savoir**, *to know*)
6 Si tu lisais le journal tu ...	**f** nous changerait les idées.
7 S'ils étaient malades ils ...	**g** lui téléphonerais.
8 Si on allait au cinéma, ça ...	**h** feriez?

ℹ️ Paris

The following Paris landmarks are mentioned in the dialogue:

- **Le Louvre** is a vast art gallery and museum on the right bank of the Seine which used to be the residence of French kings before they moved to Versailles. In 1989 a large glass pyramid was added to it which in fact operates as a large dome for the underground reception area.

- **Le Musée d'Orsay** is an old main line station which stopped being used for main-line purposes as long ago as 1939. Since 1986 it has been an art museum and a cultural centre which houses many works of the Impressionists.

- **Le Bazar de l'Hôtel de Ville** (www.bhv.fr) is the oldest department store in Paris. Its old rival, **La Samaritaine**, also on the right bank of the Seine, immediately opposite **Le Pont-Neuf** (despite its name, the oldest bridge in Paris), closed down in March 2006, for renovation. Its terrace was one of the best vantage points in Paris. Both places are within close walking distance from the Métro station **Châtelet**. From **Châtelet** you can also walk to **Le Centre Pompidou**, a contemporary art museum and one of the best venue to see street theatre and entertainment. It was built in the 1970s on the site of **Les Halles de Paris**, which used to be the central market for the capital. Nearby, **Le Forum des Halles**, is a vast underground shopping centre which includes shops, a swimming pool, a multiplex cinema, and a FNAC (**Fédération Nationale d'AChats**), a vast book, DVD and music shop and ticket office for shows.

- **L'Orangerie**, situated in **Le Jardin des Tuileries** (between **la Place de La Concorde** and **Le Louvre**) was chosen by Claude Monet as a permanent exhibition hall for his water lily paintings. It reopened in 2006 after major renovation works.

▶2 Qu'est-ce que tu ferais?
What would you do?

Sarah et Marie-Claire sont assises à la terrasse de la Samaritaine. Elles se relaxent un peu en jouant un jeu.

Listen to / read the dialogue, and answer the questions.

a What game are they playing?
b What would she have if it happened and why?

Listen / read again.

c Why would she live in Paris?
d Would she carry on working?

Listen / read once more.

e When would she swim?
f What would she do in Paris? (try to list everything mentioned, but if not, find at least three)
g Who would be with her in her paradise?
h Write a caption for the picture, taking account of what Marie-Claire says she would do if she had time and money.

Sarah	Dis-moi Marie-Claire, honnêtement et sans tricher, ce que tu ferais vraiment si tu gagnais le gros lot au Loto?
Marie-Claire	Alors d'accord ... euh ... Eh bien j'aurais un grand appartement à Paris, parce que j'adore vivre à Paris, et une maison sur la Côte d'Azur parce que j'aime bien le soleil.
Sarah	Tu continuerais à travailler?
Marie-Claire	Euh, non! Comme cela j'aurais plus de temps pour moi.
Sarah	Et qu'est-ce que tu ferais avec tout ce temps?
Marie-Claire	J'irais à la piscine tous les jours, je lirais tous les livres que je voudrais, j'irais au cinéma, au théâtre, à l'Opéra, dans de très bons restaurants. Et puis de temps en temps je ferais des petits voyages quelque part, aux sports d'hiver par exemple. C'est dingue tout ce qu'on pourrait faire!
Sarah	Tu serais toute seule dans ton paradis?
Marie-Claire	Non, je serais avec toute ma famille, toi y compris!
Sarah	Merci, ma chère, c'est très aimable à toi!

sans tricher	*no cheating*
c'est dingue	*it's crazy* (colloquial expression)
also **dingo: il est dingo**	*he is mad*

▶ Exercise 2 Qu'est-ce que vous feriez?

You are asked: 'Qu'est-ce que vous feriez si vous gagniez le gros lot au Loto?'

a Work out how you would say that you would have a big house in Brittany, that you would have a boat, that you would go fishing and watch TV in the evening.
b How would you say that you would take a trip round the world?
c Listen to the recording and check your answers.

Exercise 3 Les jeux instantanés (scratch cards)

Vous avez acheté une carte jeu. Vous l'avez grattée (gratter *to scratch*). Est-ce que vous avez gagné?

©Tous droits réservés à la Française des Jeux.

Look at the scratch card and answer these three questions.

a What is the rule of the game?
b What is the cost of this scratch card?
c What happens if you find 3 ☆ on your card?

*Gagner, cela
n'arrive pas
qu'aux autres*®

(Lit. *Winning does not happen only to others.*)

Exercise 4 Avez-vous gagné au Loto?

Look at the following grid. There are two days of the week when the Loto is drawn and on each of these days there are two draws within a few minutes of one another.

a On which days is the lottery drawn each week?
b How much would you pay if you opted for eight numbers on only one of the two days?
c How much would you pay if you opted for eight numbers on both days?
d How many numbers would you be able to tick for 252 €?
e Up to how many weeks could you have a subscription for?
f How much would you pay for four weeks, having ticked eight numbers for both days?

©Tous droits réservés à la Française des Jeux.

▶ Exercise 5 Vous avez coché?

Tick eight numbers on the Loto card above. In order to win anything you need to get between three and six numbers correct.

Écoutez et voyez si vous avez gagné! Ne trichez pas!

Pas de chance? Mais si vous aviez choisi les bon numéros, vous auriez gagné le gros lot...

3 Un peu de littérature
A little bit of literature

Here is an extract from *Dora Bruder*, a novel by the contemporary French writer Patrick Modiano.

> *Elle allait certainement le dimanche retrouver ses parents qui occupaient encore la chambre du 41 boulevard Ornano. Je regarde le plan du métro et j'essaye d'imaginer le trajet qu'elle suivait. Pour éviter de trop nombreux changements de lignes, le plus simple était de prendre le métro à Nation, qui était assez proche du pensionnat. Direction Pont de Sèvres. Changement à Strasbourg-St-Denis. Direction Porte de Clignancourt. Elle descendait à Simplon, juste en face du cinéma et de l'hôtel.*

(Editions Gallimard 1997, page 46)

And here's what the Larousse dictionary says about Patrick Modiano:

> **MODIANO** (Patrick), écrivain français né à Boulogne-Billancourt en 1945. Ses romans forment une quête de l'identité à travers un passé douloureux et énigmatique.

Did you understand it all? Now answer these questions.

a What did Dora most certainly do on Sunday?
b Where did her parents live?
c What is the author imagining?
d At which station would she catch the métro? Where would she get out?
e How many changes did she have to make?
f What was there next to the hotel?
g What is Modiano's date of birth?
h What are his novels mainly about?

trajet	*route*	**roman**	*novel (book)*
éviter	*avoid*	**quête**	*enquiry*
pensionnat	*boarding school*	**à travers**	*through*
écrivain	*writer*	**douloureux**	*painful*

Surfez sur le web

Les promenades dans Paris: il y a beaucoup de choses à voir à Paris, par exemple les promenades à pied ne coûtent rien. Découvrez **le Canal St Martin, la Promenade Plantée** ou **le parc des Buttes Chaumont.** Pour en savoir plus visitez http://www.a-paris.net/A-paris-balade-paris.htm. C'est le site internet le plus utile sur la capitale, malgré les fautes d'orthographe!

Si vous aimez lire des romans historiques et que vous avez lu le roman de Tracy Chevalier *The Lady and the Unicorn* profitez d'une visite à Paris pour visiter le Musée du Moyen Age pour voir de près la du tapisserie de la Dame à la Licorne. En attendant visitez le site http://www.musee-moyenage.fr/. Cliquez sur "information" pour trouver l'adresse du musée puis sur "plan du site" → les collections → les tapisseries pour avoir un aperçu des collections.

Web extension exercise

Did you find the six tapestries? Five of them represent the senses. Find the French words for sight, hearing, touch, smell and taste.

22

strikes **les grèves**

In this unit you will learn
- about the French media
- about possessive adjectives and pronouns
- about strikes and French trade unions

▶1 C'est le mien! *It's mine!*

C'est vendredi soir. Les enfants sont tous les deux dans la chambre d'Ariane. Soudain on entend des cris: ils se disputent. Leur père va voir ce qu'il se passe.

Listen to / read the dialogue, and answer the questions.

a Why are they fighting?
b Where is Pierre's game?
c Whose game has he got now?

Listen/read again.

d Who shouted?
e What does Pierre claim he can prove?
f What does Guillaume tell them to do?

Listen/read once more.

g Why does Pierre call Ariane a liar?
h How does she retaliate?
i What does Guillaume tell them to do?

Ariane donne un coup de pied à Pierre

Ariane	Donne-moi ça! C'est à moi!
Pierre	Non, c'est le mien!
Ariane	Mais non, tu as laissé le tien chez Bonne Maman et tu le sais bien!
Guillaume	Qu'est-ce que c'est que tout ce bruit? Qui a crié?
Ariane	C'est Pierre, il a pris mon jeu et il dit que c'est le sien!
Pierre	Mais elle est complèment dingue! C'est le mien, je peux te le prouver!
Ariane	Je te dis que ce n'est pas le tien!
Guillaume	Bon, ça suffit! Vous allez venir vous asseoir avec nous dans la salle de séjour et vous allez regarder la télé tranquillement. Il y a un programme très intéressant sur les animaux.
Ariane	J'aime pas les animaux!
Pierre	Menteuse! Aïe!! Elle m'a donné un coup de pied dans la jambe!
Guillaume	Bon, c'est terminé pour ce soir. Ni jeux, ni télé mais le lit! Immédiatement!

un cri*	a shout
crier	to shout
un coup de pied	a kick
menteuse/menteur	liar
ni … ni…	neither … nor…
Ça suffit!	That's enough!

Cri is another **faux-ami**; *to cry* is **pleurer**.

Link the following English phrases to the equivalent French expressions.

1 Give me that!
2 You left yours at Grandma's.
3 What's all this noise?
4 It's mine and I can prove it to you!
5 That's enough!
6 She kicked me in the leg.
7 You are going to come and sit with us.
8 No games, no TV but bed!

a Ça suffit!
b Elle m'a donné un coup de pied dans la jambe.
c Vous allez venir vous asseoir avec nous.
d Donne-moi ça!
e Ni jeux, ni télé mais le lit!
f Tu as laissé le tien chez Bonne Maman.
g Qu'est-ce que c'est que tout ce bruit?
h C'est le mien, je peux te le prouver!

Grammar

1 Possessive adjectives and pronouns

Possessive adjectives and pronouns are used to say that something belongs to someone. The following examples show three different ways of saying something belongs to 'me':

C'est **à moi**
C'est **mon jeu** / C'est **le mien**
C'est **ma chambre** / C'est **la mienne**
Ce sont **mes chaussures** / Ce sont **les miennes**
Ce sont **mes crayons** / Ce sont **les miens**

To express possession you can choose between:

1 an emphatic pronoun: **c'est à moi**, when you are talking about something you can point to;

2 a possessive adjective before a noun: **mon jeu, mes chaussures**. Remember, the adjective agrees with the gender and number of the noun it accompanies;

3 A possessive pronoun which replaces the noun altogether: **le mien, les miennes**. Here the form of the pronoun depends on the number and gender of the noun it replaces.

Study the following table which shows the whole range of possessive adjectives and pronouns and also the use of the emphatic pronoun, following a preposition (in this case **à**).

Emphatic pronouns	Possessive adjectives	Possessive pronouns
C'est **à moi**	C'est **mon/ma**... Ce sont **mes**...	C'est **le mien / la mienne** Ce sont **les miens / les miennes**
C'est **à toi**	C'est **ton/ta**... Ce sont **tes**...	C'est **le tien / la tienne** Ce sont **les tiens / les tiennes**
C'est **à lui/ à elle**	C'est **son/sa**... Ce sont **ses**...	C'est **le sien / la sienne** Ce sont **les siens / les siennes**
C'est **à nous**	C'est **notre**... Ce sont **nos**...	C'est **le nôtre / la nôtre** Ce sont **les nôtres**
C'est **à vous**	C'est **votre**... Ce sont **vos**...	C'est **le vôtre / la vôtre** Ce sont **les vôtres**
C'est **à elles/ à eux**	C'est **leur**... Ce sont **leurs**...	C'est **le leur / la leur** Ce sont **les leurs**

Exercise 1 Au bureau des objets trouvés

Maintenant vous êtes au bureau des objets trouvés (*lost property office* but literally *found property*). You report that you have lost seven items in the following order: umbrella, roller skates, reading glasses, wallet, keys, bag and watch. Work through the grid below, item by item, and say if the object shown to you is yours or not. (The gender of the article is indicated.)

Exemple:

Vous	J'ai perdu mes lunettes de soleil (*sunglasses*).
Employée	Ce sont les vôtres?
Vous	Non, ce ne sont pas les miennes.

Employée du bureau des objects trouvés		Vous
a C'est votre parapluie?	(masc.)	Non, ce n'est pas...
b Ce sont vos patins à roulettes?	(masc.)	Oui, ce sont...
c Ce sont vos lunettes?	(fem.)	Oui...
d C'est votre portefeuille?	(masc.)	Non...
e Ce sont vos clefs?	(fem.)	Oui...
f C'est votre sac?	(masc.)	Oui...
g C'est votre montre?	(fem.)	Non...

▶ Exercise 2 Oui, c'est le mien

This time the items are yours (four of the above but not in the same order). Listen to the recording and claim your property.

Exemple:

Employée   Ce sont vos lunettes de soleil?
Vous   Oui, ce sont les miennes.

Bonne continuation!

◆ 2 On regarde la télé
Watching television

Les enfants sont couchés. Marie-Claire regarde le programme de télévision.

Look at the TV listings for this evening, listen to the recording, and answer the questions below.

a Guillaume has heard on the news that lorry drivers might go on strike. When is the strike likely to start?
b Why is he telling Sarah?
c What is Sarah's first reaction?

Listen again.

d What has already started on Canal+?
e Which programme would Guillaume like to watch after the film?
f Why should it interest Sarah?

TELEVISION

TF1   F2   F3   C+   5e ARTE   M6 ^   Câble et satellite

TF1 — 20.45

LA BELLE VIE
Téléfilm humoristique français de Gérard Marx (2/2) (1997). 120 min. VF. Avec : Jean Yanne (Julius), Danièle Evenou (Linda), Paulette Dubost (Mamé), Vanessa Devraine (Fanny), Christian Rauth (Gaspard). Une famille d'origine modeste devient milliardaire et rachète un château pour y habiter.

22.55
LE DROIT DE SAVOIR
Magazine présenté par Charles Villeneuve. «Un enfant à tout prix». Un reportage réalisé par Cathelyne Hemery, David Gosset et Philippe Véron en 1997. L'adoption d'enfants à l'étranger, en particulier au Viêt-nam et en Russie.

F2 — 20.55

URGENCES
Série médicale américaine. Deux épisodes : Se voiler la face. – Boomerang. VF. 90 min.

22.35
MOTS CROISÉS
Magazine présenté par Arlette Chabot et Alain Duhamel. «Quelle école pour nos enfants ?» Invités : Claude Allègre, Alain Madelin
23.50 En fin de compte.
23.55 Journal

MOTS CROISÉS
le magazine politique mensuel de la rédaction
présenté par
Arlette CHABOT Alain DUHAMEL
ce soir
22h35

F3 — 20.50

LES CONQUÉRANTS DE CARSON CITY
Film américain d'André De Toth (1952). Western. 84 min. VF. Avec : Randolph Scott (Jeff Kincaid), Lucille Norman (Susan Mitchell), Raymond Massey (Big Jack Davis). Un ingénieur se bat pour l'ouverture d'une ligne de chemin de fer.
22.20 La dernière séance. Au sommaire : Actualités. - Tex Avery.
22.50 Soir 3.

23.15
TERREUR A L'OUEST
Film américain d'André De Toth (1954). Western. 80 min. VO. Avec : Randolph Scott (Jim Kipp), Marie Windsor (Alice Williams), Dolorès Dorn (Julie). Un justicier solitaire poursuit trois criminels dont il ignore encore le signalement.
0.35 La dernière séance. Tex Avery.

C+ — 20.35

RIDICULE
Film français de Patrice Leconte (1996). Comédie. 102 min. VF. En 16/9. Redif le 30. Avec : Charles Berling, Fanny Ardant. Un jeune noble naïf et passionné découvre les artifices et les dangers de la cour de Versailles.
22.15 Flash infos.

22.20
PARTY
Film franco-portugais de Manoel de Oliveira (1996). 90 min. VF. 1ère diff. Redif le 28. Avec : Michel Piccoli, Irène Papas. Un séducteur impénitent s'efforce de charmer sa jeune hôtesse, lors d'une garden-party.
23.55 Caméléone. Film de Benoît Cohen (1996). Policier. 92 min. VF. En 16/9. Dern. diff.

5e ARTE — 20.45

LA LEÇON DE PIANO
Film de Jane Campion (1992). 125 min. VO. En 16/9. Avec : Holly Hunter (Ada), Harvey Keitel (Baines). Une jeune pianiste muette entre deux hommes, en Nouvelle-Zélande.
22.40 Kinorama.

22.55
L'ARGENT
Film de Robert Bresson (1983). 85 min. VF. Avec : Christian Patey (Yvon), Sylvie van den Elsen.
0.15 Court circuit - Bon voyage. Court-métrage d'A. Hitchcock.
0.45 La rate. Téléfilm de Martin Buchhorn.
2.15 Tracks.

M6 — 20.45

D.A.R.Y.L.
Film américain de Simon Wincer (1985). Science-fiction. 100 min. VF. Avec : Barret Oliver (Daryl), Mary Beth Hurt (Joyce Richardson), Kathryn Walker (Ellen Lamb). Un robot rêve de devenir un humain.

22.40
COUPS POUR COUPS
Film américain de Deran Sarafian (1990). Policier. 90 min. VF. Avec : Jean-Claude Van Damme (Louis Burke), Robert Guillaume (Naylor). Pour enquêter sur une série de meurtres inexpliqués dans un pénitencier, un inspecteur de police endosse l'identité d'un gangster.

Câble et satellite — 20.30

M. HIRE
Film français de Patrice Leconte (1989). Drama. 90'. En 16/9. **21.50** La main gauche du seigneur. Film américain d'Edward Dmytryk (1955). Aventures. VO. 85'. En 16/9. **23.20** Le femme secrète. Film français de Sébastien Grall (1986). Comédie dramatique. 90'. En 16/9. **0.55** Secret mortel. Film américain de Michael Scott (1995). Policier. 88'.

CINÉ CINÉFIL
20.30 Arsène Lupin. Film américain de Jack Conway (1932). Policier. NB. VO. 86'. **22.00** Fanny Elssler. Film allemand de Paul Martin (1937). Romanesque. NB. VO. **23.25** Fabiola. Film italien d'Alessandro Blasetti (2/2) (1949). Aventures. NB. 90'. **0.45** L'empereur de Californie. Film allemand de Luis Trenker (1936). Western. NB. VO. 90'.

Now read the dialogue.

Guillaume   Sarah, je viens d'écouter le journal de dix-neuf heures sur France Inter, les routiers menacent de se mettre en grève à partir de dimanche, ça pourrait affecter ton voyage de retour!

Sarah   Super! Comme cela je resterai à Paris! Sérieusement parlant, je ne pense pas que l'Eurostar soit affecté par le blocage des routes mais on ne sait jamais. On verra bien!

Marie-Claire	Au fait il y a *Ridicule* qui passe à Canal+. Ça fait presque une demi-heure que cela a commencé.
Sarah	Parce que vous avez Canal+ maintenant?
Marie-Claire	Oui, c'est surtout pour les nouveaux films puisque nous ne sortons presque pas.
Sarah	Eh bien c'est bien! Alors on regarde le film?
Guillaume	Oui mais je voulais voir *Mots Croisés* après.
Marie-Claire	Ah oui, c'est vrai. Toi qui aimes la politique, Sarah, ça t'intéressera sûrement.

| **le journal (d'information)/les informations/les infos** | *the news* |

France Inter is part of **Radio France**, the French national radio organization. **Radio France** broadcasts many other radio stations such as **France Musique**, **France Culture**, **France Info**. You can use Podcasts to listen to their programmes.

| **les routiers** (short for **chauffeurs routiers**) | *lorry drivers* |
| **mots-croisés** | *crosswords* |

Here, on France 2, it is the name of a televised political debate between politicians (the title plays on the expression **mots croisés**)

Link the following English phrases to the equivalent French expressions.

1 I have just listened to the news.
2 It could affect your return journey.
3 We'll see.
4 You can never tell.
5 The lorry drivers are threatening to go on strike.
6 Since we hardly ever go out.

a On ne sait jamais.
b Les routiers menacent de se mettre en grève.
c Puisque nous ne sortons presque jamais.
d On verra.
e Ça pourrait affecter ton voyage de retour.
f Je viens d'écouter le journal.

À vous de choisir

Look at the TV listing opposite above and answer the questions below (there may be more than one answer for some of the questions).

| **VF: Version Française** | *dubbed* |
| **VO: Version Originale** | *with subtitles* |

Which channel would you watch and at what time...

a ...if you wanted to watch a film in English?
b ...if you wanted to watch a medical comedy?
c ...if you wished to see the late night news?
d ...if you wanted to watch a political debate?
e ...if you wanted to watch a programme on the adoption of children from other countries?
f ...if you fancied watching a science-fiction film?
g ...if you wanted to see *Monsieur Hire*, a film you have been meaning to see for a long time?
h On which condition would you be able to watch it?
i Look at the small ad for *Mots Croisés*. Can you find the word which indicates that it is a monthly programme?
j What is the theme of this month's debate?

2 On regarde beaucoup les jeux à la télé en France

French people have always been keen on television games. Now many are hooked by games such as **Le Maillon Faible** (*The Weakest Link*) – an exact replica of the English and American versions presented by Laurence Boccolini, who acts and dresses like Ann Robinson. There is also the most popular: **Qui Veut Gagner Des Millions?** With a maximum prize of one million euros, which is not as much as in the English version of the programme, **Loft Story**, one of the **Télé Réalité** games which was very successful for a few years is no longer on French TV but seems to have taken by storm the province of Québec (see the Canadian website www.loftstory.tqs.ca for updates on the latest show).

3 Loft Story
La version Canadienne

Si possible visitez le site de la version canadienne de Loft Story dont l'adresse est indiquée au paragraphe précédent.

Les six gars et les sept filles qui participent à LOFT STORY circulent dans des locaux d'une superficie de 7000 pieds carrés sur deux étages. En plus des pièces comme les chambres, la salle à manger et le salon, les lofteurs et les lofteuses pourront se tenir en forme dans une salle de conditionnement physique ultramoderne.

Le confessionnal, cette pièce où les participants peuvent s'isoler pour s'adresser en privé aux téléspectateurs, sera situé au deuxième étage du loft, au-dessus des chambres. Dans chacune des pièces, on retrouvera des fenêtres-miroirs, permettant aux caméramans de filmer les allées et venues des lofteurs et des lofteuses.

Vingt-deux caméras robotisées seront installées un peu partout afin de ne rien manquer des échanges entre les gars et les filles... Cinquante-cinq microphones seront dissimulés dans chaque pièce afin de bien comprendre ce qui se dira et se tramera entre les participants.

Dans ce loft d'une dizaine de pièces, les six gars et les sept filles disposeront de tout l'espace nécessaire pour nous faire partager leurs états d'âme et s'adonner à de nombreuses activités.

a How many participants are there?
b Make a list of all the rooms in the house.
c What is the most private room in the house?
d Where is it situated? What is its use ?
e List the different pieces of equipment used to record the participants' every utterance and action.
f What can the participants do to keep in good shape?
g What is the use of the two-way mirrors?
h In square feet, what is the size of the Loft?

ⓘ Les grèves et les syndicats

Only 10% of French workers belong to a trade union but when serious issues are raised there is usually a spontaneous response from the vast majority of people within a profession or an industry. Workers join in if a strike is called whether they are members of a trade union or not. All categories of workers go on strike at one time or other and take to the streets. Doctors, nurses, dentists, teachers and even lawyers (see headlines below) go on strike when they need to put pressure on the government.

In the spring of 2006, following social unrest in the Paris suburbs, the Government tried to introduce a new formula for young people's first work contracts. This was strongly objected to by thousands of workers and students who demonstrated and went on strikes for several weeks. In the end the government relented and changed its plans. This movement was the follow-up of a first period of unrest that took place in the autumn of 2005 in **"les cités"**, the social housing estates, often deprived and run down situated in **"les banlieues"** (the suburbs) of Paris and other French towns. See the website for Libération http://www.liberation.fr/dossiers/banlieues/actualite/210864.FR.php

Menace de grève des avocats

Les bâtonniers protestent contre le manque de moyens.

Les bâtonniers is a term sometimes used to refer to barristers. They are threatening to go on strike because of insufficient funding.

There are two main trade unions in France: both cover all trades and professions and have within them groupings for the various categories of workers. The difference between them is now a historical division which no longer applies but still marks each one's tendencies:

- **La CGT** (**C**onfédération **G**énérale du **T**ravail) was traditionally affiliated to the French Communist Party. It has not significantly declined since the demise of communism.
- **La CFDT** (**C**onfédération **F**rançaise **D**émocratique du **T**ravail) is more aligned with the French Socialist Party.

There are also two much smaller trade union organizations:

- **FO** (**F**orce **O**uvrière – the name means *workers' power*) is of a moderate and reformist tendency.
- **La CFTC** (**C**onfédération **F**rançaise des **T**ravailleurs **C**hrétiens) is a Christian trade unionists' organization.

Quote from a lorry driver interviewed on France Inter: **'Ce que nous n'obtiendrons* pas par la négociation, nous l'obtiendrons par la rue.'** For this reason strikes by some categories of workers such as **les routiers** *lorry drivers* have a wide impact!

* future of **obtenir**, *to obtain*

4 Que disent les journaux?
What do the newspapers say?

Read the following newspaper article and answer the questions.

La grève dans les écoles de la Seine–Saint-Denis va-t-elle faire boule de neige?

Les syndicats d'enseignants de quinze établissements scolaires de la région de Créteil ont appelé à la grève pour protester contre «les graves insuffisances pour faire face aux besoins et lutter contre l'échec scolaire». Le ministre de l'Education Nationale avait proposé des réformes scolaires «pour donner aux élèves le goût d'apprendre et de se cultiver tout au long de la vie avec des itinéraires de découvertes». Les enseignants disent que «ces itinéraires prétendent résoudre l'échec scolaire. Or pour leur faire place dans l'emploi du temps on a été obligé de diminuer les horaires de français, mathématiques et histoire-géographie de deux heures par semaines.» Les professeurs réclament aussi la création de 6000 postes supplémentaires dans le 93*.

*93 is the number for the area of La Seine–Saint-Denis. In France each 'département' has a number which is linked to its alphabetical order, except for those for Paris suburbs which all have numbers in the 90s. These numbers also appear as the last number on car number plates.

les enseignants	teachers
établissements scolaires	schools
l'échec scolaire	school failure
une boule de neige	snowball
lutter	to fight
résoudre	to resolve

1 What question is raised in the title of the above article?
2 How many schools are facing strike action?
3 Where are these schools?
4 What new initiatives does the Minister wish to introduce?
5 What are teachers protesting against? Why?
6 What else do teachers want for this particular area?

Un entretien avec Jean-Marc Four

Gaëlle Graham	Jean-Marc, vous êtes journaliste, que faites-vous en Angleterre?
Jean-Marc Four	Je suis le correspondant de Radio France
Gaëlle Graham	Vous aimez votre travail?
Jean-Marc Four	Oui, il faut aimer ce travail pour l'exercer.
Gaëlle Graham	Est-ce que c'est difficile?
Jean-Marc Four	Ni facile, ni difficile, c'est une question de formation et de curiosité.
Gaëlle Graham	Du point de vue professionnel, quel est le meilleur moment de la journée?
Jean-Marc Four	Le moment où l'on parle en direct à la radio.
Gaëlle Graham	Cela fait combien de temps que vous travaillez à Londres?
Jean-Marc Four	Quatre ans.
Gaëlle Graham	Vous aimez Londres?
Jean-Marc Four	Beaucoup, Londres est une ville passionnante pour un journaliste.
Gaëlle Graham	Vous pensez y rester encore quelques années?
Jean-Marc Four	Non, je m'apprête à partir car les contrats de correspondants étrangers durent quatre ans.
Gaëlle Graham	Ah c'est dommage! Vous êtes content de rentrer à Paris ou est-ce que vous regretterez Londres?
Jean-Marc Four	Les deux. J'aime Londres mais c'est agréable aussi de rentrer dans son pays.
Gaëlle Graham	Alors bon retour en France et bonne chance!
Jean-Marc Four	Merci et bonne chance à vous également!

Jean-Marc Four now works at **La Maison de la Radio** in Paris where he presents a daily news and cultural programme about world issues.

Web extension exercise

Du lundi au vendredi écoutez l'émission de Jean-Marc Four "**Et pourtant elle tourne**". The title refers to the rotation of the earth. It can be literally, translated as *And yet it moves*
http://www.radiofrance.fr/franceinter/em/etpourtantelletourne/

23

la vie de famille
family life

In this unit you will learn
- about the cinema
- about sport in France
- one more past tense: the pluperfect

▶ 1 Moi, j'en ai ras-le-bol! *I'm fed up!*

C'est samedi matin et Marie-Claire est débordée!

Listen to / read the dialogue. You need to concentrate on what the various people in the family are planning to do. Complete the empty boxes according to what each person is doing in the morning, afternoon and evening.

Saturday	Marie-Claire	Guillaume	Sarah	Ariane	Pierre
Morning	Housework Shopping				
Afternoon		Football match	Cinema		
Evening	Cinema			At home	

débordée	*snowed under*	**aider**	*to help*
le ménage	*housework*	**en avoir**	*to be fed up*
la rentrée	*start of the new school year*	**ras-le-bol**	*(lit. up to the brim)*
ranger	*to tidy up*		

Ariane Maman, c'est aujourd'hui que tu nous emmènes au cinéma? Tu avais dit qu'on irait voir *Azur et Asmar...*

Marie-Claire Oui ma chérie, mais nous n'avons pas encore décidé ce que nous allons faire aujourd'hui.

Pierre Tu nous avais promis!

Marie-Claire Oui je sais mais c'est un peu compliqué...

Guillaume Marie-Claire, je t'avais prévenue qu'aujourd'hui c'est le sport toute la journée ... Je pars dans cinq minutes, là...

Marie-Claire Quoi? Mais où vas-tu?

Guillaume Mais je te l'ai dit avant-hier! Ce matin je vais à Bercy faire une partie de tennis avec les copains du bureau et cet après-midi je vais au foot avec Lionel. On va voir Paris-Saint Germain. C'est le premier match de la saison, on ne peut pas rater ça!

Marie-Claire Il est possible que tu me l'aies dit mais j'avais complètement oublié. Moi j'en ai ras-le-bol! Je comptais sur toi pour m'aider à faire le ménage et les courses pour la semaine prochaine. Tu as sans doute oublié que c'est mardi, la rentrée!

Sarah   Bien, moi je vous propose une solution: Guillaume tu vas à Bercy et à ton match de foot, les enfants, ce matin on va tous aider Marie-Claire avec le ménage et les courses et si vous avez bien travaillé, je vous emmènerai voir *Azur et Asmar* cet après midi. Maman profitera du calme pour se reposer.

Ariane   Super! Je vais ranger ma chambre. Tu viens Pierre?

Guillaume Et moi, ce soir je garderai les enfants et vous deux vous pourrez aller au cinéma si vous en avez envie.

Link the following English phrases to the equivalent French expressions.

1 You had said we would go and see.
2 I was counting on you to help with the shopping.
3 I told you the day before yesterday.
4 I shall look after the children.
5 We are all going to help.
6 We can't miss that!

a On va tous aider.
b On ne peut pas rater ça!
c Je garderai les enfants.
d Tu avais dit qu'on irait voir.
e Je te l'ai dit avant-hier.
f Je comptais sur toi pour les courses.

Grammar

1 The pluperfect

This is another past tense, used for an action which took place prior to something else happening:

Tu avais dit qu'on irait voir *Azur et Asmar*.
You had said that we would go and see Azur et Asnar.

Ariane is reminding her mother what had been said prior to today.

There is very little difference between the structures of the pluperfect and the perfect tense.

- Perfect: **avoir** or **être** in the present tense + past participle
- Pluperfect: **avoir** or **être** in the imperfect tense + past participle

J'**ai** dit	*I have said*	Elle **est** partie	*She has left*
J'**avais** dit	*I had said*	Elle **était** partie	*She had left*

Other examples in the dialogue:

Tu nous avais promis.   *You had promised.*
Je t'avais prévenue.   *I had warned you.*
J'avais oublié.   *I had forgotten.*

Note that in many cases the pluperfect and the perfect are used in the same sentence, for example when:

- Something was planned, said or done but more recent events altered the situation:

Michael Schumacher, deux fois champion du monde, **avait voulu** gagner mais à Jerez il **a** tout **perdu** dans un accrochage avec Jacques Villeneuve.

Michael Schumacher, twice world champion, had wanted to win but at Jerez he lost everything in a collision with Jacques Villeneuve.

This example is from a 1997 newspaper article. The old affinity between France and Canada meant that, at the peak of his career, francophone Jacques Villeneuve received support and full media attention in France.

Et Schumacher? En tout il a été sept fois champion du monde. Jacques Villeneuve ne l'a été qu'une seule fois, en 1997!

- something is done as a consequence of a prior state of things:

Le garçon **a volé** des pommes parce qu'il **n'avait** pas **mangé** depuis deux jours.

The boy stole some apples because he hadn't eaten for two days.

Check that you know your past participles:

prendre	pris
pouvoir	pu
devoir	dû
boire	bu
pleuvoir	plu
perdre	perdu
avoir	eu

Exercise 1 Terminez les phrases

Find a suitable end for each of the sentences.

1 Sylvie avait beaucoup travaillé
2 Les Durand avaient gagné le gros lot;
3 J'avais pris mon parapluie;
4 Loïc avait dit qu'il viendrait à Paris
5 Les jeunes avaient trop bu
6 Laurent était allé en Angleterre pour les vacances
7 Il a appelé la police
8 Le voleur est entré sans effort;

a mais malheureusement il n'a pas pu.
b pour déclarer qu'on lui avait volé sa voiture.
c on avait dû laisser la porte ouverte.
d et elle a réussi son examen.
e et il a décidé d'y rester.
f malheureusement ils ont tout perdu.
g alors il n'a pas plu.
h et ils ont eu un accident.

ℹ Les Français et le sport

Lots of people are keen to watch sports on TV but not so keen to participate. The attitude to sport has been changing slowly though. In the 80s and 90s most French towns started to build well-equipped sports centres. If you want one, look for a sign saying: **Salle omnisports**. The biggest sports centre in France is **Le Palais Omnisports de Paris-Bercy** – a vast centre built mainly for indoor games and also for international competitions, with a capacity for 17,000 spectators. French people are also getting away from lazy beach holidays and spending more time walking, cycling through the countryside on their **VTT (Vélos Tous Terrains,** *mountain bikes***)**, surfing and wind surfing, skiing, swimming and sailing. And when you hear some French people say: **Je fais du footing**, what they mean is that they go jogging. **Jogging** is also used.

But spectator sports are as popular as ever with **Le Tour de France Cycliste** (watched by millions from the roadsides) at the top of the list and **le foot** close second, and third, horse racing, **la course de chevaux/hippique**. In the dialogue, Guillaume is going to **Le Parc des Princes** to see his team **Paris-Saint Germain**. **Paris-SG** or **le PSG** is the only first-division club in Paris.

Les clubs français

These are some of the major teams:

Lyon: **Olympique de Lyon**
Auxerre: **Association Jeunesse Auxerroise**
Bordeaux: **Les Girondins de Bordeaux**
Guingamp: **En avant Guingamp** (*Forward Guinguamp* – from a tiny Brittany town)
Marseille: **Olympique de Marseille**
Lens: **Racing Club de Lens**
Monaco: **Association Sportive de Monaco**
Nantes: **Football Club Nantes Atlantique**

Many sporting events take place or finish in Paris every year. Look at the table below:

Calendrier annuel des évènements sportifs à Paris

DATES ET ÉVÈNEMENTS SPORTIFS	LIEUX: OÙ DANS PARIS
Premier janvier Départ du Rallye de Paris-Dakar	Esplanade de Vincennes
Dernier dimanche de janvier Prix d'Amérique (*course de chevaux*)	Hippodrome de Vincennes
Février – mars Tournoi des Cinq Nations (rugby)	Parc des Princes
Avril Marathon de Paris; Festival d'Arts Martiaux	À travers Paris; Palais Omnisports de Bercy
Première quinzaine d'avril (un dimanche) Prix du Président de la République	Hippodrome d'Auteuil
Fin mai / début juin Internationaux de France de Tennis	Stade Roland-Garros
Juin Finale de la coupe de France de Football; Course des serveuses et garçons de café	Parc des Princes; Des Champs-Elysées à la Bastille
Troisième dimanche de juin Grand Steeple-Chase	Hippodrome d'Auteuil
Dernier dimanche de juin Grand Prix de Paris	Hippodrome de Longchamp
Mi-juillet Arrivée du Tour de France Cycliste	Champs-Elysées (départ et arrivée)
Mi-septembre (un samedi) Prix d'été	Hippodrome de Vincennes
Premier dimanche d'octobre Prix de L'Arc de Triomphe	Hippodrome de Longchamp
Octobre Les Vingt Kilomètres de Paris (course à pied)	Tour Eiffel
Deuxième dimanche d'octobre Course de côte de voitures anciennes (*uphill race*)	Rue Lepic (Montmartre)
Fin octobre Tennis: Le Tournoi de Paris (*Paris Open*)	Paris-Bercy

Exercise 2 Les évènements sportifs

Look again at the table of sporting events in Paris, and answer these questions.

a How many types of sporting events are listed?
b What are they?
c When is the barmen and women's race?
d Where does it take place?
e When is the Prix du Président de la République?
f What race starts and finishes at the Eiffel Tower?

Exercise 3 Est-ce que vous connaissez bien les deux meilleurs footballeurs français?

L'un est toujours la personnalité préférée des français, malgré son expulsion pour avoir donné un coup de tête volontaire dans la poitrine de Marco Materazzi, au cours de la Coupe du Monde 2006, l'autre joue pour l'équipe anglaise d'Arsenal et est le chouchou des foules.

Using the information listed below fill in the gaps in the grid

Marseille, française, Zidane, 1,88m, 92, Arsenal FC, Paris, Real Madrid, 23 juin 1972, 108, milieu de terrain, Zinédine, 1,85m, attaquant, française, 39, 17 août 1977, Henry, 31.

1. Prénom:	1. Prénom: Thierry
2. Nom:	2. Nom:
3. Nationalité:	3. Nationalité:
4. Date de naissance:	4. Date de naissance:
5. Lieu de naissance:	5. Lieu de naissance:
6. Taille:	6. Taille:
7. Poste:	7. Poste:
8. Club avant la coupe du Monde:	8. Club avant la coupe du Monde:
9. Nombres de sélections:	9. Nombres de sélections:
10. Nombres de buts:	11. Nombres de buts (jusqu à 2006):

Surfez sur le web

Si vous êtes sportif ou sportive visitez les sites suivantes:
• Pour le football visitez www.maxifoot.com
• Pour tout savoir sur les derniers transferts et sur les clubs français et étrangers visitez www.football365.fr

- Pour tous les résultats du monde du basket trouvez www.basketzone.com
- Pour les amateurs de rugby allez voir www.totalrugby.com et www.rugbyrama.com
- Google Olympique Lyonnais or go to www.olweb.fr (site officiel) or www.olympiquelyonnais.com

▶ 2 Aller au cinéma *Going to the cinema*

*Sarah et Marie-Claire ont finalement décidé d'aller au cinéma. Elles ont acheté **L'Officiel des Spectacles*** et cherchent des films qu'elles aimeraient voir.*

*A very comprehensive weekly guide of What's on in Paris, including visits of monuments, children entertainment, markets, restaurants, conferences etc…

Listen to the recording and look at the list of films below selected by Sarah and Marie-Claire then answer the questions:

a Why does Sarah say she will let Marie-Claire choose the film?
b What does Marie-Claire say about *Paris je t'aime*?
c Which film do they choose to see?

La liste de Sarah et Marie-Claire (par order alphabétique)

Arthur et les Minimoys (2006 1h35) Aventure et animation de Luc Besson: comme tous les enfants de son âge Arthur est fasciné par les histoires que lui raconte sa grand-mère pour l'endormir. Mais..si ces histoires étaient vraies?

Azur et Asmar (2004 1h39) Animation de Michel Ocelot: il y a bien longtemps, deux enfants étaient bercés par la même femme. Elevés comme deux frères, les enfants sont séparés brutalement …

Hors de Prix (2006 1h43) Comédie de Pierre Salvadori avec Audrey Tautou et Gad Elmaleh. Jean, serveur timide d'un grand hôtel, passe pour un milliardaire aux yeux d'Irène, une aventurière intéressée. Quand elle découvre qui il est réellement elle le fuit aussitôt. Mais Jean, amoureux, se lance à sa poursuite et la retrouve sur la Côte d'Azur.

Les Infiltrés (VO) (2006 2h30) Film américain de Martin Scorsese avec Leonardo de Caprio, Matt Damon et Jack Nicholson:

le "parrain", Lou Costello règne en maître sur Boston. Pour le démasquer la police locale charge un jeune flic, Billy Costigan, d'infiltrer le gang du vieux malfaiteur..

Marie-Antoinette (2005 2h03) Film américain de Sofia Coppola. Drame historique où la jeune Marie-Antoinette découvre un monde hostile et codifié, un univers frivole où chacun observe et juge l'autre…

Paris je t'aime (2006 1h50) Film à sketches collectifs: voyages dans différents arrondissements de Paris à travers une série d'anecdotes amoureuses. Avec Fanny Ardant, Juliette Binoche, Steve Buscemi, Sergio Castellitto, Willem Dafœ, Gérard Depardieu, Marianne Faithfull, Ben Gazzara, Bob Hoskins, Nick Nolte, Natalie Portman, Gena Rowlands et Ludivine Sagnier.

Sarah	Je te laisse choisir parce que je sors beaucoup plus souvent que toi quand je suis à Londres. De toutes façons j'aimerais certainement ton choix.
Marie-Claire	J'ai coché *Azur et Asmar* mais en fait tu l'as vu samedi avec les enfants. Je les emmènerai sans doute voir *Arthur et les Minimoys* samedi prochain.
Sarah	*Les Infiltrés* c'est la version originale sous-titrée en français je crois. Le titre anglais est *The Departed*. J'aime bien les films de Scorsese mais je le verrai certainement à Londres.
Marie-Claire	*Paris Je t'aime* vient de sortir en DVD, je te l'offre pour ton anniversaire si tu veux. C'est formidable, c'est plein d'acteurs connus et ce sont des histoires qui se passent dans chaque arrondissement de Paris.
Sarah	Bon eh bien il nous reste le choix entre *Marie-Antoinette* et *Hors de Prix*. Qu'est ce que tu préfères?
Marie-Claire	Moi j'adore Audrey Tautou, tu as vu *Amélie*?
Sarah	Bien sûr, j'ai adoré, bon alors c'est décidé on va voir *Hors de Prix*! Je suis sûre que nous ne serons pas déçues.

je te laisse choisir	*I let you choose*
la version sous-titrée	*subtitled version*
de toutes façons	*in any case*
déçues/déçu/e	*disappointed*

a Say you would like to see Paris je t'aime because you love Paris.
b Say you would like to see Arthur et les Minimoys because you love films directed by Luc Besson.
c Say you would like to see Marie-Antoinette because it is interesting to see an American film about French history.
d Say you would like to see Azur et Asmar because the story, the animation and the music are beautiful.

Exercise 4 Abonnez-vous
Et si vous aimez vraiment le cinéma abonnez-vous!

The form below is for a year's subscription to *Les Cahiers du Cinéma*, the oldest and most famous cinema magazine which, from its early days, has been influential on French cinema.

Fill in the form (as an exercise!) and answer these questions.

a What was the special offer?
b How many issues would you receive for that price?
c How can you pay?

OFFRE D'ABONNEMENT DÉCOUVERTE

BULLETIN D'ABONNEMENT
A retourner avec le règlement aux Cahiers du Cinéma
Service abonnement - B 1202 - 60732 Ste Geneviève Cedex
ou abonnez-vous en ligne sur www.cahiersducinema.com

OUI, je souhaite profiter de cette offre spéciale, pour m'abonner pour 5 numéros aux *Cahiers du Cinéma* au tarif de **17€** au lieu de 29,50€, soit une réduction de plus de **40%**.

Je joins mes coordonnées : ▢ Mme ▢ M. ▢ Melle

Nom ....

Prénom ....

Adresse ....

Code postal └─┴─┴─┴─┴─┘ Ville ....

Pays ....

E-mail ....

Je joins mon règlement par :

▢ Chèque bancaire ou postal à l'ordre des *Cahiers du Cinéma*
▢ Carte bancaire

N° └─┴─┴─┴─┴─┴─┴─┴─┴─┴─┴─┴─┴─┴─┴─┴─┘

Date de validité └─┴─┴─┴─┘ Signature :

Notez les 3 derniers chiffres du numéro
inscrit au dos de votre carte près de la signature └─┴─┴─┘

▢ Je souhaite recevoir une facture acquittée

CAHIERS CINEMA
Tarif DOM-TOM et étranger, nous consulter au (33) 03 44 31 80 48
Conformément à la Loi Informatique et Liberté, vous disposez d'un droit d'accès et rectification aux informations vous concernant.

www.cahiersducinema.com

Surfez sur le web

Pour les amateurs de cinéma surfez sur le web pour trouver des informations sur les derniers films et tous les grands classiques du cinéma.

- www.cahiersducinema.com.
  If you are a real film buff this is the site for you.
- www.MK2.com
  Depuis 1974, mk2 distribution a distribué plus de 300 films de plus de 30 nationalités différentes.
- www.cinemathequefrancaise.fr
  La Cinémathèque Française has moved its premises to Parc de Bercy. See website for special events.
- http://www.azuretasmar-lefilm.com/demo.html (this is a good example of a trailer available on the web)

24

un repas familial
a family meal

In this unit you will learn
- about French meals
- recipe vocabulary
- how to talk about the family
- how to talk about travelling
- **qui** and **que** (relative pronouns)

▶1 Mettre le couvert *To lay the table*

La famille se retrouve chez tante Eliane, Rue du Docteur Blanche, à Passy dans le seizième arrondissement de Paris. Bruno, un de ses fils, est enseignant à Lyon mais en ce moment il est en vacances chez sa mère. Son autre fils, Daniel, travaille à l'étranger.

Listen to the recording and answer the questions.

a What does aunt Eliane ask the children to do?

b What does she ask them to be careful with?

c What does she give them to take to Bruno?

d What will they drink with the meal?

Listen again, several times if necessary.

e And now write down Tante Eliane's menu in French and say what it means.

> *Menu de*
> *Tante Eliane*
>
> *Dimanche 31 août*

Tante Eliane	Vous venez avec moi dans la salle à manger les petits, vous allez m'aider à mettre le couvert.
Ariane	Moi, je sais mettre le couvert.
Pierre	Et moi aussi je sais.
Tante	Alors faites bien attention à ma vaisselle, surtout les verres. Alors vous faites comme cela. La petite assiette sur la grande assiette, la fourchette à gauche, le couteau à droite et la cuillère à dessert devant le verre. Voilà, c'est bien!
Pierre	On a fini!
Tante	Bon, tu veux demander à Bruno de m'ouvrir la bouteille de vin blanc qui est au frigo? Tiens, donne-lui le tire-bouchon.
Ariane	Qu'est-ce qu'on mange? J'ai faim!
Tante	Ah! J'aime bien que les enfants aient de l'appétit! Je vous ai préparé un très bon menu. Alors comme entrée on a du bon melon et après je vais vous servir une truite au champagne et raisins avec des pommes de terre sautées.
Pierre	Et pour le dessert?

| Tante | Ah mais avant le dessert il y a de la salade et du bon fromage et pour le dessert ... une tarte aux pommes! |
| Pierre et Ariane | Miam-miam! |

Le couvert

In the dialogue can you find the French for the following items of crockery, cutlery, etc.?

a a glass
b a plate
c a knife
d a fork

e a spoon
f crockery/dishes
g a corkscrew

Link the following English phrases to the equivalent French expressions.

1 You are going to help to lay the table.
2 Mind my dishes.
3 Do you mind asking Bruno to open the bottle of wine for me?
4 Give him the corkscrew.
5 I like it when children have an appetite.
6 And for dessert ... an apple tart.

a Donne-lui le tire-bouchon.
b Et pour le dessert ... une tarte aux pommes.
c J'aime que les enfants aient de l'appétit.
d Vous allez m'aider à mettre le couvert.
e Faites attention à ma vaisselle.
f Tu veux demander à Bruno de m'ouvrir la bouteille de vin?

⒤ La cuisine et la nourriture *Cooking and food*

French home cooking has been very traditional for a long time but now people are starting to experiment. There is also the influence of North-African cooking such as couscous-based dishes which are integrated into what people eat at home.

There is a slight attempt to eat things other than meat for the main course. However, the pattern of serving the lettuce after the main course, followed by the cheese followed by dessert is absolutely standard.

An important family meal on a special occasion such as a wedding, a communion or a christening (**un baptême**) would probably have either a seafood dish to start with or **un plateau de charcuterie** with various cooked meats. There would be a fish course followed by a meat dish. Traditionally only one vegetable is served, often a potato dish. Big family reunions often take place around the table and often last for hours. Lots of wine tends to be served.

Everyday cooking can be more sober but even when people are on their own they take pleasure in cooking something nice: **se mijoter un bon petit plat**. **Mijoter** means *to stew*, but in terms of French cooking, **mijoter** means cooking slowly, with care and attention, just the correct proportion of ingredients, making sure that the sauce is just right.

2 Une bonne recette: La grande truite au champagne et aux raisins frais
A good recipe: trout in champagne with fresh grapes

Before you can read this recipe you need a few items of vocabulary which are new to you. Some can be guessed but others need to be learnt. The vocabulary can be divided into three categories: nouns of ingredients, adjectives describing the condition of the ingredients, and instructions (here verbs in the infinitive). Once you can read this recipe you can tackle others.

In each of the three boxes below match the equivalent French and English expressions. Some have already been done for you.

Qu'est-ce qu'il faut?

Les ingrédients

1	échalotes	a	*mushrooms*
2	beurre	b	*salt and pepper*
3	champignons	c	*shallots*
4	jaunes d'œufs	d	*fresh dill leaves*
5	feuilles d'aneth fraîches	e	*butter*
6	sel et poivre	f	*egg yolks*

Les procédés (*processes*) et les ustensiles de cuisine

7	le temps de cuisson	g	*boiling point*
8	ébullition	h	*cooking time*
9	la lèchefrite ⟶	i	*cooking pan (in oven)*
10	le four ⟶	j	*the oven*

Comment sont nos ingrédients?

11	épluché(e)(s) ──────────►	k	*peeled*
12	lavé(e)(s)	l	*heated*
13	vidé(e)(s) ──────────►	m	*gutted (emptied)*
14	hâché(e)(s) ──────────►	n	chopped
15	chauffé(e)(s)	o	washed

Maintenant que faut-il faire?

16	parsemer ──────────►	p	to sprinkle
17	faire cuire	q	to remove (the skin)
18	arroser ──────────►	r	to water
19	mouiller ──────────►	s	to wet, dampen
20	ajouter	t	to season
21	mélanger	u	to cook
22	ôter (la peau)	v	to add
23	épaissir ──────────►	w	to thicken
24	verser ──────────►	x	to pour
25	assaisonner	y	to mix
26	napper ──────────►	z	to cover with a sauce

Et voilà! La cuisine de A à Z!

Vous pouvez maintenant suivre n'importe quelle recette française!

Lisez la recette! Now read carefully the recipe for trout in champagne overleaf, and answer the questions which follow.

a This recipe is for how many persons?
b How long will it take to cook?
c How much champagne is used?
d What must be done to the champagne before pouring it on the trout?
e When do you need to add the champagne?
f What needs to be done to the trout's tail and head?

TRUITE FRANCE

UNE ENVIE DE VRAI

*à découvrir la truite de France
et ses recettes
mode et tradition*

AU FOUR,
EN FETE, LA GRANDE TRUITE
AU CHAMPAGNE ET RAISINS FRAIS

Ingrédients

- 1 grande truite d'env. 2,5 kg
- 3 échalotes
- 100 g de beurre
- 125 g de champignons de Paris
- 1/2 bout. de champagne
- 10 grains de raisin noir frais épluchés
- 10 grains de raisin blanc frais épluchés
- Asperges
- 125 g de crème fraîche
- 2 ou 3 jaunes d'oeufs
- Baies de poivre rose
- Feuilles d'aneth fraîches
- Sel et poivre

Temps de cuisson
Environ 45 minutes.

Préparation pour 6/8 personnes.

La truite étant vidée et lavée, saler et poivrer l'intérieur. Garnir le fond d'une léchefrite d'une feuille d'aluminium, la parsemer d'échalotes hâchées et de champignons, y déposer la truite, après avoir enveloppé la tête et la queue de papier d'aluminium. Saler, poivrer, mouiller avec la moitié du champagne, couvrir le plat d'aluminium.

Faire cuire à 200°C (thermostat 6) pendant 45 minutes environ. Une ou deux fois en cours de cuisson, arroser la truite de champagne chauffé en soulevant la feuille d'aluminium.

Sortir la truite et ôter la peau des deux côtés. Dresser sur un plat de service. Pour la sauce, à ébullition, verser le jus de cuisson dans une casserole, ajouter la crème mélangée aux jaunes d'œufs. Assaisonner, faire épaissir, ajouter grains de raisins et baies de poivre rose et napper la truite.

Exercise 1 Un peu de diététique

Avez-vous un bon équilibre alimentaire? Pour le savoir, testez-vous.

Cochez les cases qui correspondent à vos habitudes alimentaires.

VOS HABITUDES ALIMENTAIRES	Toujours	Parfois	Jamais
1 Vous buvez de l'eau tout au long de la journée?			
2 Vous optez pour les fruits et légumes?			
3 Vous restez raisonnable avec le gras et le sucre?			
4 Vous consommez des fibres?			
5 Vous préférez le poisson et les volailles?			
6 Vous consommez des céréales?			
7 Vous utilisez des huiles végétales?			
8 Vous déjeunez copieusement et dînez légèrement?			
9 Vous limitez votre consommation d'alcool?			
10 Vous mangez avec plaisir et en bonne compagnie?			

le gras	fat
la volaille	poultry
parfois	sometimes

La solution:

Pour chaque question où vous avez coché la première colonne: accordez-vous 1 point; la deuxième colonne: 2 points; et la troisième: 3 points.

Et le verdict:

De 1 à 12 points: C'est bien! Vous avez un régime équilibré.

De 13 à 23 points: Encore un petit effort! Vous pouvez mieux faire et vous faire du bien.

De 24 à 30 points: C'est le désastre! Vous allez à la catastrophe à moins de faire quelque chose immédiatement.

Surfez sur le web

- Si vous aimez les bonnes recettes faciles à comprendre avec beaucoup d'illustrations allez demander conseils chez www.supertoinette.com. Vous y trouverez des centaines de recettes super.
- Si vous êtes au régime (*on a diet*) allez voir au bas de la page d'accueil: dans la rubrique recettes minceur, vous trouverez des dizaines de recettes avec le nombre de calories pour chaque plat.
- Choisissez "**Les pommes de terre farcies à la ricotta**" Vous m'en donnerez des nouvelles!

Web extension

Recette pommes de terre farcies à la ricotta	**Ingrédients	2P| 1h15**
• 420 g de grosses pommes de terre (2) • 130 g de ricotta • 9 g d'ail • Quelques brins de ciboulette (*chives*) • Sel	• Poivre du moulin • 5 g de vinaigre de Xérès • 8 feuilles de basilic • 2 pincées de cannelle (*cinnamon*)

Web extension exercise

Vrai ou Faux Dans la recette des pommes de terre farcies à la ricotta.

1 The potatoes are stuffed with camembert
2 Use 9 grams of shallots
3 Use a teaspoon of cinnamon
4 This is a recipe for one person
5 The potatoes should be cooked in the oven – not in the microwave (justify your answer)

▶3 Des nouvelles de la famille
Family news

Tout le monde est encore à table, la truite au champagne est délicieuse, le vin est bon et on échange des nouvelles de la famille.

Listen to the recording and answer the questions.

a Where is Daniel now?
b When is he coming back to France?
c Does he like it?
d Is he married?

Listen again.

e Who is Tante Eliane going to Canada with?
f Why is she going with her?

Listen once more.

g When are they leaving? From where?
h When are they returning?

un ordinateur	*a computer*
célibataire	*single* (applies to men or women)
ma belle-sœur	*my sister-in-law*
à cause de	*because of*

Sarah	Au fait, comment va Daniel?
Tante Eliane	Il va bien, il voyage beaucoup … Euh … en ce moment il est au Japon mais il rentrera en France à Noël.
Sarah	Ah bon! Ça fait combien de temps qu'il est là-bas?
Tante	Oh, à peu près trois mois. Il travaille pour une firme qui fabrique des ordinateurs et en ce moment il passe trois mois en France et trois mois au Japon.
Sarah	Ça lui plaît?
Tante	Ah oui, énormément. Et puis tant qu'il est célibataire il n'y a pas de problèmes. Oh mais je ne vous ai pas dit? Cette fois-ci c'est moi qui pars en voyage!
Marie-Claire	Ah bon! Et où vas-tu?
Tante	Au Canada! J'y vais avec ma belle-sœur qui habite à Nantes. C'est un voyage organisé. Ils avaient acheté les billets et maintenant son mari ne peut pas y aller à cause de son travail alors j'y vais à sa place.

Guillaume	Et quand est-ce que tu pars?
Tante	Eh bien le départ de Nantes est le 12 octobre et nous rentrons le 21.
Marie-Claire	Bon, alors on te souhaite un bon voyage et n'oublie pas de nous envoyer une carte postale, hein!

Link the following English phrases to the equivalent French expressions.

1 How long has he been there?
2 He works for a firm which manufactures computers.
3 as long as he is single...
4 I am going with my sister-in-law.
5 Don't forget to send a postcard.
6 It's a package tour.

a C'est un voyage organisé.
b tant qu'il est célibataire...
c N'oublie pas de nous envoyer une carte postale.
d Ça fait combien de temps qu'il est là-bas?
e J'y vais avec ma belle-sœur.
f Il travaille pour une firme qui fabrique des ordinateurs.

Grammar

1 *Qui* or *que*?

These are relative pronouns. Although similar, they have two different functions:

- **Qui** *who, which, that* represents people or objects. It acts as the subject of the verb:

  une firme qui fabrique des ordinateurs
  c'est **moi qui** pars

In the two examples above **qui** represents the noun which precedes it and which is the subject of the sentence. **Qui** links two sentences, making one longer and more elegant sentence:

C'est ma belle sœur. Elle habite à Nantes. Becomes **C'est ma belle sœur qui habite à Nantes.**

- **Que/qu'** *which, that, whom* also links two sentences, but it represents the direct object of the sentence. It represents people or objects.

Le voyage que je vais faire est un voyage organisé.

In this type of sentence **que** is placed immediately before the subject. This should be more obvious in the next two examples:

Regarde, c'est **le type que** j'ai vu hier.

Look, it's the guy I saw yesterday.

Here **que** represents **le type** (the object). **Que** precedes **j'** (the subject) who did the action of seeing the man (the object).

Regarde, c'est **le type qui** a vu l'accident.

Look, it's the guy who saw the accident.

In this sentence **qui** represents **le type** (here the subject) who saw the accident (the object).

Qui is always followed by a verb, sometimes preceded by an indirect pronoun:

C'est toi **qui** lui as donné les clefs!

It's you who gave her the keys!

In the above example, **qui** represents the subject **toi**. In the following sentence **que** represents the object **les clefs** and precedes the subject **tu**. Note that as the object **les clefs** precedes the verb, the past participle agrees with the number and gender of the object (donn**ées**):

Voici les clefs **que** tu lui as données.

Here are the keys you gave him.

Exercise 2 Remplissez les blancs

In each of the sentences fill the gap(s) with **qui, que** or **qu'**.

a Ce _____ j'aime ce sont les enfants _____ sont polis!
b La recette _____ je préfère c'est celle de la truite aux amandes.
c Le film _____ je voulais voir passe à la télé ce soir.
d Ce sont les années _____ j'ai passées en Angleterre à apprendre l'anglais _____ me seront les plus utiles.
e C'est toi _____ as les clefs?
f Pourquoi est-ce que ce sont toujours les mêmes _____ décident?

1400 €

Départ de Nantes

PROGRAMME

JOUR 5
MONTRÉAL-QUÉBEC
Petit déjeuner à l'hôtel. Départ pour la visite guidée, métropole cosmopolite, Montréal présente mille et un visages, mille et un éclats. Vous découvrirez le centre-ville et ses gratte-ciel, le Vieux Montréal et ses rues recouvertes de gros pavés, le Vieux Port qui offre une fenêtre sur St-Laurent, l'Eglise Notre-Dame, le Mont-Royal, l'Ile Ste-Hélène, le Jardin Botanique et le Stade Olympique. Départ pour Québec. Déjeuner à la Cabane à Sucre Chez Pierre. Dîner de homard au restaurant le Monte Carlo. 5e nuit Hôtel LE COTTAGE ou similaire.

JOUR 6
QUÉBEC
Petit déjeuner à l'hôtel. Départ de l'hôtel pour la visite guidée de la ville Québec, berceau de la civilisation française en Amérique du Nord. La seule ville fortifiée au Nord du Mexique. Vous verrez le Vieux-Québec, le Château Frontenac, la Place Royale, la Colline Parlementaire et la Citadelle. Déjeuner et temps "libre" dans le Vieux Québec pour découvrir ses boutiques et musées à pied. Dîner au restaurant La Cage aux Sports. 6e nuit Hôtel LE COTTAGE ou similaire.

JOUR 7
QUÉBEC-CHARLEVOIX
Petit déjeuner à l'hôtel. Départ pour la région de Charlevoix, nous ferons quelques arrêts, premier arrêt aux Chutes Montmorency (1 fois et-demi la hauteur des Chutes du Niagara). Déjeuner à Tadoussac, suivi de temps libre pour visiter ce très beau petit village ou faire l'excursion des baleines (en option); pour les autres nous ferons la visite du Manoir Richelieu. Dîner à votre hôtel. 8e nuit au MANOIR CHARLEVOIX.

Exercise 3 Un peu de lecture

Tante Eliane shows her family what she is going to see in Canada.

Look at the schedule for Days 5, 6 and 7.

| les gratte-ciel | skyscrapers | un homard | a lobster |
| des pavés | cobblestones | des baleines | whales |

Vrai ou faux?

Say whether the following statements based on the schedule are true or false.

a They will see skyscrapers in Tadoussac.
b Québec is one of two fortified towns north of Mexico.
c There is a lobster dinner at the end of day 7.
d The excursion to see the whales is optional.
e There will be some free time to see old Quebec.
f Mont-Royal offers a window on the St Laurent.
g Montmorency Falls are one and a half times higher than Niagara Falls.
h There is a guided tour of Tadoussac.
i Québec is the cradle of French civilization in North America.
j L'Ile Ste Hélène is a church.

Cherchez l'erreur

Attention: dans le texte pour le Jour 7 il y a **une petite erreur d'imprimerie** (*a small printing error*). L'avez-vous découverte?

Surfez sur le web

Au Québec

Tante Eliane visitera le village historique de Tadoussac, le mieux connu des Français et pour cause! C'est le berceau (*lit. cot*) de la Nouvelle France. En 1535, Jacques Cartier jette l'ancre à Tadoussac, suivi quelques années plus tard par Pierre de Chauvin, qui y débarque en 1599. En 1600, on y érige le premier poste officiel de traite des fourrures (*fur trade*) en Nouvelle-France, ce qui en fait le plus vieux village en Amérique du Nord, plus vieux même que Québec. Pour en savoir plus visitez le sites des plus beaux villages du Québec: www.beauxvillages.qc.ca.

Vive le Québec libre! Comme vous pouvez le constater la France et le Québec sont très liés et des personnages politiques français l'ont souvent exprimé en ces termes, comme par exemple le général De Gaulle en juillet 1967 et Ségolène Royal, alors candidate à la présidence de la République, en janvier 2007.

Mais ce n'est pas tout! En 2008 Québec fête son 400e anniversaire.

De juin à septembre 2008, vous pourrez y vivre une expérience mémorable du 400e anniversaire de Québec en découvrant la ville et son histoire sous un jour nouveau. Pour en savoir d'avantage sur Espace 400e, consultez les sites suivant www.monquebec 2008.com/fr/ espace 400e.phy ainsi que www.bonjourquebec.com.

Si vous avez envie de visiter d'autres pays francophones visitez www.francegazette.com et cliquez sur **Planetantilles** ou bien lisez les articles **Francophonie**. Si vous ne pouvez pas voyager, visitez-les virtuellement!

Web extension exercise

1 What is the name of the best known village of the province of Québec?
2 What is happening in 2008 in Québec?

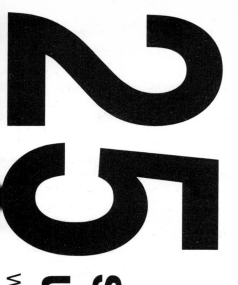

25

si on achetait une maison?

what if we bought a house?

In this unit you will learn
- how to express sadness and feeling depressed
- the order of pronouns
- about planning to buy a house in France
- some legal requirements when buying a property

▶ 1 Avant le départ *Before the departure*

Toute la famille accompagne Sarah à la gare du Nord d'où elle doit repartir pour Londres.

Listen to the recording once, and answer these questions.

a Why is Sarah feeling a bit low?
b How does Ariane feel about Sarah's departure?
c Is Sarah looking forward to going back to work?

Listen again.

d Who is Marie-Claire going to 'phone tonight?
e Why tonight?

Listen once more.

f What is Mrs Burgess planning to do? (two things)
g What does Guillaume suggest?
h Does Marie-Claire think it is a good idea?

Now read the dialogue.

J'ai le cafard.

> *Feeling depressed:*
> **Il a le cafard**
> **Il est déprimé**
> **Il n'a pas la pêche** (colloquial)
> **Il n'a pas le moral**

Sarah	Ah la la, je n'ai pas envie de rentrer!
Guillaume	Eh bien reste!
Sarah	Non … je ne peux pas, seulement j'ai toujours un peu le cafard quand je quitte la France.
Ariane	Moi non plus je ne veux pas que tu partes. On est triste quand tu t'en vas!
Marie-Claire	Tu regrettes de ne pas avoir accepté l'offre d'emploi chez Gallimard?
Sarah	Non, pas du tout, je n'y pensais même plus. Non, ce n'est pas grave, je suis un peu déprimée mais ce n'est tout de même pas la grosse dépression! C'est tout simplement que je n'ai pas la pêche quand il s'agit de reprendre le travail!
Marie-Claire	En fait de déprime il ne faut pas que j'oublie de téléphoner à Maman ce soir. C'est la rentrée pour elle

Sarah	aussi demain et, en général, elle non plus elle n'a pas le moral avant de reprendre les cours.
Sarah	Alors fais bien attention. Elle va sûrement te faire part de ses projets: elle voudrait prendre sa retraite à cinquante-cinq ans et s'acheter une petite maison dans le Midi.
Marie-Claire	Oui je sais, elle m'en a déjà parlé. Elle dit que cette idée, c'est toi qui la lui as donnée!
Guillaume	Et si on achetait une maison entre nous tous! On pourrait peut-être trouver quelque chose de pas trop cher à rénover ...
Marie-Claire	Ah oui! Dis, Guillaume, et qui est-ce qui les ferait, ces rénovations?

triste	*sad*
faire part de	*to inform about*
un faire-part de naissance/	*announcement of birth/*
mariage/décès	*wedding/death*
Gallimard	*one of the most important French publishing companies*

Link the following English phrases to the equivalent French expressions.

1 Do you regret turning down Gallimard's job offer?
2 I was no longer thinking about it.
3 before going back to school.
4 She has already spoken to me about it.
5 She would like to retire at 55.

a Elle m'en a déjà parlé.
b Elle voudrait prendre sa retraite à 55 ans.
c Je n'y pensais même plus.
d avant de reprendre les cours.
e Tu regrettes de ne pas avoir accepté l'offre d'emploi chez Gallimard?

Grammar

1 Order of pronouns: *le, la, les* and *lui*

In the following sequence, the nouns in the sentence are replaced by pronouns:

Tu as donné **cette idée à Maman.**
Tu **lui** as donné cette idée. (**lui** represents **à Maman**)

Tu l'as donnée à Maman. (**la/l'** represents **cette idée**)
Tu **la lui** as donnée.

Word order, especially the order of pronouns may appear difficult but there is a simple principle which can help: **le, la** and **les** are weaker pronouns, in terms of sound, than **lui** and **leur**. They are always placed before **lui** or **leur**:

J'ai donné **mon billet au contrôleur**: Je **le lui** ai donné.

J'ai donné **mon permis de conduire aux gendarmes**: Je **le leur** ai donné.

In a negative sentence there are even more words to line up. The same principle applies:

Je ne le lui ai pas donné.
Je ne le leur ai pas donné.

In more slovenly speech there is a tendency to rush all the pronouns together and to drop **ne** (which is weaker than **pas**) and also **le**:

J'lui ai pas donné.

and in the affirmative too there is a tendency to drop **le**:

J'lui ai donné.

The two examples above are not what you are advised to say but you will hear them frequently.

2 Moi aussi *me too* / moi non plus *me neither*

These two expressions are frequently used. They are strictly direct responses, agreeing with something someone else has said:

Je n'aime pas les départs!   Response: **Non, moi non plus.**
Elle adore les voyages!   Response: **Oui, moi aussi.**

▶ Exercise 1 Vous êtes d'accord

Listen to the recording and react to what is being said. You agree with everything said:

Exemples:
Statements   **Responses**
Je n'ai jamais aimé le football.   Moi non plus!
Nous avons souvent visité la   Moi aussi! /nous aussi!
   Bretagne.

▶2 Chez le notaire *At the notary's*

Depuis plusieurs mois déjà, Dominique et son copain Gildas ont décidé d'acheter une petite maison dans le Finistère. Ils en ont trouvé une qu'ils aiment beaucoup mais avant de faire les démarches nécessaires ils ont décidé de s'adresser à Maître Le Corre, leur notaire.

À VENDRE

S'ADRESSER À

Me le Corre
Notaire à Lanvec
Tel: 02 98 7154

Listen to or read the dialogue below and answer these questions.

a Why are Gildas and Dominique consulting a lawyer?
b What would they like to find out?

Listen to or read the dialogue again.

c How did they find the house?
d Have they contacted the owner?
e Have they seen the house?
f What would they like the lawyer to do?

Listen or read once more.

g Who would check the present owner's civic status?
h What are Gildas and Dominique going to do?

un notaire	notary, a lawyer who deals specifically with property and family transactions such as wills, donations, etc.
Maître *(abbreviation **Me**)*	a **notaire**'s title
l'état civil	civic status
l'urbanisme	town planning department
recueillir des renseignements	to gather information/to do a search
le compromis de vente: l'avant-contrat	the pre-contract

Gildas	Nous avons trouvé une petite maison que nous aimerions acheter. Nous avons pensé qu'il serait peut-être préférable de nous adresser à vous d'abord.
Me Le Corre	Vous avez eu tout à fait raison. Il vaut toujours mieux s'adresser à un notaire puisque c'est obligatoirement le notaire qui se chargera de rédiger l'acte de vente.
Dominique	Comment pouvons-nous être certains qu'il n'y a aucun problème avec la propriété et les propriétaires actuels?
Me Le Corre	C'est le rôle du notaire de le découvrir. Mais comment avez-vous trouvé la maison en question?
Dominique	Nous avons vu une petite annonce dans le journal, tout simplement.
Gildas	Oui, nous sommes allés voir la maison et nous pensons que c'est exactement ce que nous cherchions. Jusqu'ici c'est tout.
Me Le Corre	Et vous n'avez pas pris contact avec les propriétaires?
Gildas	Non, pas encore. Nous avons préféré venir en discuter avec vous d'abord.
Dominique	Vous pourriez organiser une visite de la maison parce que pour le moment nous ne l'avons vue que de l'extérieur?
Me Le Corre	Oui bien sûr mais la mission du notaire va beaucoup plus loin que ça: si vous me chargez de l'affaire, je vous informe, je vous conseille, je vérifie l'état civil du vendeur, je peux aussi recueillir des renseignements d'urbanisme ...
Gildas	Pour vérifier s'il n'y a pas d'autoroute ou autres constructions en projet?
Me Le Corre	Exactement. Je vous préparerais le compromis de vente, c'est-à-dire un avant-contrat, et ensuite le contrat si tout va bien.
Gildas	Eh bien nous allons réfléchir mais de toute façon nous reviendrons vous voir.

Link the following English phrases to the equivalent French expressions.

1 It would be preferable to consult you first.
2 You were absolutely right.
3 The lawyer will take care of drawing up the deeds of sale.

a Vous avez eu tout à fait raison.
b si vous me chargez de l'affaire

4 We've only seen it from
   the outside.
5 if you ask me to take care
   of the business
6 We are going to think
   about it.

c Nous ne l'avons vue que de
   l'extérieur.
d Nous allons réfléchir.
e Il serait peut-être préférable
   de nous adresser à vous
   d'abord.
f Le notaire se chargera de
   rédiger l'acte de vente.

Vrai ou faux?

Say which of the following statements are true or false.

a Dominique and Gildas have visited the house and they like it.
b They saw the advert in a newspaper.
c They have been in contact with the vendor.
d They have found exactly what they were looking for.
e They have asked the lawyer to start the search as soon as
  possible.
f She can get information from the planning department.
g By law the deed of sale has to be prepared by a lawyer.
h The notary's mission is to inform and to advise.

🔟 Acheter une maison

If you decide to buy a house in France it is wise to go through a
notaire. If you don't know a **notaire** you may know someone who
does or you can find one by looking out for a prominent oval brass
sign with the symbol of justice embossed on it. You may find that you
need a **notaire** who speaks English so that he can explain the details
of the transaction to you. You might like to find a helpful **notaire**
before you have a property in mind.

If you have found a house you would like to buy, you have to be
absolutely sure that you want it and that you won't change your
mind, because, once you have signed a pre-contract, **compromis
de vente** or **avant-contrat,** there is no going back unless the search
has revealed elements which would render the pre-contract null and
void, such as the fact that the property is threatened by some
planning development or that the vendor is not solvent.

On signing **le compromis de vente** you engage yourself to buy the
property by paying a deposit, **le dépôt de garantie,** a sum of money
between 5% and 10% of the value of the property.

Following the signing of **le compromis de vente** there is a
mandatory delay for the lawyer to carry out the necessary checks

and to prepare the deed of sale. Your financial position and the availability of a mortgage will also be checked. If the search reveals something untoward, the sale will be stopped and you will receive your deposit back. If all the conditions are fulfilled then the sale must go ahead. If for some external reasons you then breach the pre-contract, you lose your deposit to the vendor. On the other hand, if the vendor is no longer willing to sign the contract, **signer le contrat**, then the sale is dealt with by a tribunal. This means that **le compromis de vente** is a solid guarantee both for vendor and buyer. There is no gazumping in France. Specifically when buying an apartment you may see a notice saying **conforme à la Loi Carrez**. By law the seller is under obligation to declare the surface which is for sale – not including shared areas. Failure to do so accurately could mean that the buyer can declare the sale null and void even after the deed of sale has been signed.

Exercise 2 Acheter ou vendre dans les meilleures conditions

In the leaflet below read carefully the desirable and necessary stages which apply if you sell or buy a property. Some are the same for both parties.

conseil/avis	*advice*
conseils patrimoniaux	*advice on the property*
mise au point	*preparation*
les frais	*expenses*
le bien	*the property*
l'achat/l'acquisition	*the purchase*
la vente	*the sale*

On the leaflet the first nine points can be referred to as **A** (**acquisition**) and the next nine **V** (**vente**).

Indicate which stage of the proceedings the following statements refer to.

Exemple:

Advice on opportunity to buy: **1A**
Advice on sale opportunity: **1V**

a Advice on the price of the property
b Cost evaluation (including legal cost)
c Advertising the offer
d Property evaluation
e Organization of the visit to the property
f Preparation of the pre-contract

g Preparation of the deed of sale
h Search for suitable property in the area

ACHETER OU VENDRE DANS LES MEILLEURES CONDITIONS

La transaction immobilière notariale s'adresse à tous les particuliers, acquéreur ou vendeur d'un bien immobilier. En neuf étapes, le notaire vous assure un service rigoureux et professionnel, dans les meilleures conditions financières et de délai.

L'acquisition en 9 étapes

1. Conseils sur l'opportunité de l'achat.
2. Recherche des biens à vendre dans la région.
3. Organisation de la visite du bien.
4. Avis sur le prix et conseil personnalisé.
5. Evaluation des frais.
6. Information sur les meilleures conditions de crédit.
7. Mise au point de l'avant-contrat.
8. Elaboration et signature de l'acte authentique de vente.
9. Conseils patrimoniaux.

La vente en 9 étapes

1. Conseils sur l'opportunité de la vente.
2. Evaluation proposée du bien.
3. Examen des conditions de la vente.
4. Signature d'un mandat avec ou sans exclusivité.
5. Publicité de l'offre.
6. Accueil des acquéreurs potentiels et organisation de la visite du bien.
7. Mise au point de l'avant-contrat.
8. Elaboration et signature de l'acte authentique de vente.
9. Conseils patrimoniaux.

Exercise 3 La maison de votre choix

You too have decided to buy a small house in Brittany, so you have been looking at the small ads. Today's newspaper offers 13 properties for sale. Look at the adverts, reproduced below.

à aménager/aménageable	*to modernize/convertion*
agrandissement	*extension*
une grange	*a barn*
démolir	*to pull down*
un grenier	*an attic/loft*
de la pierre	*stone*
jardin clos	*enclosed garden/secluded*

Say which property would suit you if you were looking for the following:

(More than one advert may apply)

a a small house by the sea
b a four-bedroom house
c ruins to renovate
d a secluded garden
e preferably a stone house in the centre of a small town or a village
f a house with potential for extension
g vacant property
h reduced legal cost

VENTES MAISONS

1) Vends **GRANGE à démolir**, petite et grande portes + escalier en pierre de taille. Tél. 02.98.66.39.41

2) **PONT-DE-BUIS**, maison pierres, **2 niveaux**, terrain permis agrandissement, **meublée**. 102.200 € Libre. Tél. 02.98.77.31.66.

3) Particulier vend **GUISCRIFF**, maison, cuisine, chambre, sanitaires, grenier aménageable, terrain, dépendances. 60.500 € à débattre. Bon état. Tél. 02.97.44.61.37

4) **PONT-CROIX** place de l'Eglise, maison pierre **4 chambres**, grenier aménageable, jardinet, dépendances à rénover, possibilité commerce. 187.000 € à débattre. Tél. 02.98.71.39.81

5) Vends maison **SAINT-MARTIN-DES-CHAMPS**, quartier calme, jardin clos, cave, garage extérieur, **6 CHAMBRES**, chauffage gaz. 194.400 € Tél. 01.60.66.31.71.

VENTES MAISONS

6) Idéal pour loisirs et retraite, **MOËLAN-SUR-MER**, aur cœur d'un village proche plage, commerce et port, maison traditionnelle, jardin et parking privés, **3 chambres**, séjour, kitchenette équipée, belles prestations, frais notaires réduit. 130.000 € Tél. 02.98.37.69.75

7) A saisir entre mer et campagne, dans un cadre exceptionnel, 200 m plage, entre **CONCARNEAU ET LA POINTE DE TRÉVIGNON**, maison plus terrain, chambres, séjour, cuisine, belle prestation, frais de notaire réduit, 180.000 € Tél. 02.98.27.69.39.

8) **FOREST-LANDERNEAU**, maison **T5**, 5 chambres, salon, séjour, cuisine, cheminée, grand sous-sol, jardin 1.300 m², chauffage électrique. Tél. 02.98.77.66.33.

9) Vends maison **CHATEAULIN, 4 chambres**, salon, séjour, cuisine, cheminée, grand sous-sol, 1er étage à aménager, terrain arboré. 199.500 € Tél. 02.98.96.66.71

10) **LESCONIL**, sur plage, grande maison, standing, confortable, toute l'année, jardin clos, dépendances, 378.500 € Particulier. Tél. 02.98.44.65.66.

11) Vends maison **CHATEAULIN, 3 CHAMBRES**, salon-séjour, cuisine, grand sous-sol, 1er étage à aménager, terrain arboré, 210.000 € Tél. 02.98.74.75.45

12) Vends région **PRIZIAC, 2 maisons ruines superbes**, encadrements fenêtres, portes, terrain à proximité. Tél. 02.98.75.63.20.

13) **PONT-L'ABBÉ centre-ville**, vends maison pierre, jardin clos, calme, 205.500 € accès direct jardin public. Tél. 02.98.78.91.49 (heures repas).

▶ **Exercise 4 Le notaire vous pose des questions**

You are four different customers. Using the adverts above for guidance, answer Me Le Corre's question (she asks everyone the same thing):

Me Le Corre: **Qu'est-ce que vous recherchez exactement?**

Client(e) 1 *You are looking for a small stone house close to the coast.*

Client(e) 2 *You are looking for a five-bedroom house with a cellar.*

Client(e) 3 *You are looking for a small house with a secluded garden.*

Client(e) 4 *You are looking for a small house with a convertible loft.*

Exercise 5 Trouvez les intrus *Find the odd ones out*

a In the ads above there is one property for sale which is never going to be liveable in. Which one is it?
b Which is the only one mentioning a fireplace?
c Which property has direct access to the park?

d Which property could be developed for commercial purposes?
e Which is the only one which already has building permission for an extension?

Surfez sur le web

Vous pouvez consulter le web pour trouver des maisons à acheter dans toutes les régions de France.

- www.seloger.com
  Ce site est facile à utiliser si vous savez exactement ce que vous voulez
- Si vous voulez construire votre maison ou bien en rénover une vieille, allez voir www.vivremamaison.com

---

Web extension

Les Sans Domiciles Fixes (SDF) en France

Malheureusement tout le monde ne peut pas acheter ou louer une maison. Dans la plupart des villes de France il y a de nombreux sans abris ou SDF (*people without a roof over their heads*). En novembre 2006 une nouvelle association, **Les Enfants de Don Quichotte**, a été fondée pour faire pression sur le gouvernement. A Paris par exemple 200 tentes ont été distribuées pour abriter des SDFs parisiens et ont été installées le long du canal St Martin.

Voir http://fr.wikipedia.org/wiki/Les_Enfants_de_Don_Quichotte pour plus de détails.

Congratulations on completing *Teach Yourself French*!

I hope you have enjoyed working your way through the course. I am always keen to receive feedback from people who have used the course, so why not contact me and let me know your reactions? I'll be particularly please to receive your praise, but I should also like to know if things could be improved. I always welcome comments and suggestions, and do my best to incorporate constructive suggestions into later editions.

You can contact me through the publishers at: Teach Yourself Books, Hodder Headline Ltd, 338 Euston Road, London NW1 3BH, UK.

Bonne chance!
Gaëlle Graham

1 Profils *Profiles*

▶ Listen to the recording several times. You will hear information which should allow you to complete these profiles of two friends. Fill them in in French. You may need to revise what you have learnt so far.

1	2
Nom:	Nom:
Prénom:	Prénom:
Âge:	Âge:
Adresse:	Adresse:
Numéro de téléphone:	Numéro de téléphone:
Nationalité:	Nationalité:
Nationalité du père:	Nationalité du père:
Nationalité de la mère:	Nationalité de la mère:
Profession:	Profession:
Lieu de travail:	Lieu de travail:
Aime:	Aime:
N'aime pas:	N'aime pas:

(Unités 1 à 5)

2 Une promenade à Saint Malo
A walk in St Malo

Follow the directions on the map and say what your starting
point is and where you are going.

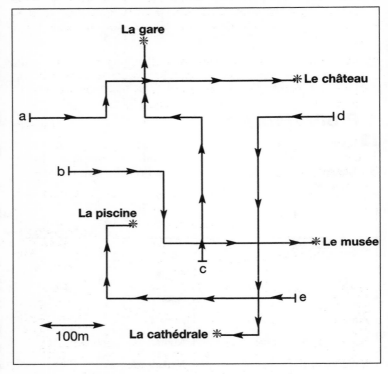

Exemple: Alors pour aller au musée vous allez vers la droite.
Après cent cinquante mètres vous tournez à droite. Continuez
sur cent mètres et vous tournez à gauche et le musée est à deux
cents mètres.

Réponse: From **b** to the museum

1 Pour aller à la gare vous allez tout droit. Après deux cents
mètres vous tournez à gauche. Vous continuez encore sur cent
mètres, puis vous tournez à droite et la gare est à cent mètres
environ.

2 Pour aller à la piscine vous allez vers la gauche, vous allez tout droit sur deux cent cinquante mètres. Vous tournez à droite. Vous continuez sur cent mètres et vous tournez encore à droite. La piscine est à cinquante mètres.

3 Pour aller à la cathédrale? Vous allez vers la gauche. Vous tournez à gauche après cent mètres. Vous continuez sur trois cents mètres et vous tournez à droite. La cathédrale est à cinquante mètres.

4 Alors, pour aller au château vous allez vers la droite. Après cent mètres vous tournez à gauche. Vous tournez à droite après cinquante mètres et vous continuez sur deux cent cinquante mètres pour arriver au château.

(Unité 5)

3 Numbers

Read the card and say what spelling rule applies for 20 and 100.

(Unités 4 et 5)

4 Grand jeu-concours

At 45 you are the managing director of a company from Rennes (Ille-et-Vilaine). You are representing your firm at an annual four-day conference in St Malo. Your firm has always favoured St Malo as a venue for this conference because of the excellent facilities and the range of activities available. You enjoy going to the swimming pool and going on your own around museums in your free time. You are staying in the conference centre hotel.

YOUR TASK:

Fill in the questionnaire on the next two pages as if you were the person described above and win the main prize in the competition.

1 What is the main prize?
2 What is the deadline for entering the competition?
3 Who are the organizers of the competition?

Grand JEU-CONCOURS

Jusqu'au 14 septembre

Bienvenue
à SAINT-MALO

Vous êtes de passage ou en vacances à SAINT-MALO, nous souhaitons mieux vous connaître, recueillir vos attentes et vos appréciations. C'est pourquoi **LA VILLE et L'OFFICE DU TOURISME** vous proposent de remplir ce questionnaire pour participer au **JEU-CONCOURS**.

Chaque semaine, **GAGNEZ UN ALLER-RETOUR** pour l'Angleterre pour 2 personnes et de nombreux autres lots.
VOIR AU DOS

❶ – COMMENT AVEZ-VOUS CONNU SAINT-MALO?

☐ Bouche à oreille
☐ Foires ou salons
☐ Reportages TV ou presse
☐ Guides touristiques ou Agences de voyage
☐ Office du Tourisme
☐ Excursions précédentes
☐ Déplacements professionnels

❷ – FIDÉLISATION

☐ Premier séjour à Saint-Malo
☐ Visites occasionnelles à Saint-Malo
☐ Visites régulières à Saint-Malo

❸ – ACTIVITÉS PRATIQUÉES
   (*Plusieurs réponses possibles*)

☐ Culturelles   ☐ Autres : préciser
☐ Découvertes   ----------------------------
☐ Nautiques
☐ Sportives
☐ Animations gratuites
☐ Thermalisme
☐ Déplacements professionnels et congrès

❹ – SATISFACTION :
   Êtes-vous satisfait de votre séjour à Saint-Malo ?
☐ Pas du tout   Justifier votre réponse_____
☐ Plutôt pas   _____
☐ Plutôt satisfait   _____
☐ Très satisfait

❺ – DURÉE DU SÉJOUR :

☐ La journée   ☐ 2 à 3 jours   ☐ 4 à 8 jours
☐ 9 à 15 jours   ☐ 16 jours et plus

❻ – MODE D'HÉBERGEMENT

☐ Hôtel   ☐ Camping-car   ☐ Camping
☐ Location meublé   ☐ Résidence secondaire ☐ Bateau
☐ Amis – Famille –   ☐ Gîtes – chambres   ☐ Famille
  Parents   d'hôtes   d'accueil

❼ – ÂGE

☐ - de 25 ans   ☐ 25/34 ans   ☐ 35/44 ans
☐ 45/54 ans   ☐ 55/65 ans   ☐ + de 65 ans

8 – ACCOMPAGNEMENT
(*Êtes-vous venu à Saint-Malo…?*)

☐ Seul   ☐ En couple
☐ En famille   ☐ Avec des amis

9 – CATÉGORIE SOCIO-PROFESSIONNELLE

☐ Agriculteur   ☐ Chef d'entreprise,
☐ Cadre et profession libérale   commerçant, artisan
☐ Employé   ☐ Cadre moyen
☐ Retraité   ☐ Ouvrier
☐ Autres   ☐ Scolaire et étudiant

10 – ORIGINE GÉOGRAPHIQUE

☐ Ille-et-Vilaine
☐ Autre département : |___|___| (n° du département)
☐ Étranger (Préciser la nationalité et la région) _____

Pour participer au JEU CONCOURS,
n'oubliez pas d'indiquer vos coordonnées ci-dessous :

NOM:............................PRÉNOM:..............

Adresse ....

Lieu d'hébergement à Saint-Malo ....

Tél. : ....

ATTENTION!

Toutes les rubriques du questionnaire doivent être remplies
pour valider votre participation au JEU CONCOURS.

DÉPOSEZ VOS BULLETINS DANS L'URNE

NB:
Les renseignements font l'objet d'un traitement automatisé.
Conformément aux prescriptions de la loi nous vous informons que:
• les informations recueillies sont destinées à l'Office du Tourisme et au service économique de la Ville de Saint-Malo.
• l'intéressé a la possibilité de consulter sa fiche informatisée auprès du service concerné.

(Unités 6 à 9)

5 Quelle attitude!

In **Unit 9** the boy and the girl express their wishes differently:

Jeune garçon   Moi je veux........
Jeune fille   Je voudrais....

1 What verbs and tenses do they use to express their respective wishes?
2 What do you think the difference indicates?
3 A boy asks for an ice cream. He might say a) Je veux une glace or b) je voudrais une glace. To which request are you more likely to reply Mais oui bien sûr!

6 Aujourd'hui c'est samedi

Cochez les cases – tick the boxes

Go back to unit 9 and read the dialogue entitled **C'est samedi matin** once more. Tick the correct boxes below, to make a meaningful sentence, in accordance with the dialogue.

Dimanche matin ☐ Lundi matin ☐ Aujourd'hui ☐ les parents et les trois enfants ☐ les parents ☐ toute la famille ☐ vont ☐ va ☐ au Mont Saint Michel ☐ à la plage ☐ au barrage de la Rance ☐

Now write down your complete sentence.

7 La voiture idéale

Neuf personnes (ou couples) avec des goûts bien individuels

Look at the cars below. In the second column of the grid indicate which car is most likely to belong to each of the nine people described. The third and fourth columns are jumbled. Choose where these people are mostly likely to live and what is likely to be their favourite eating place.

Une voiture safari pour aller partout et vivre l'aventure. 1

Une voiture sérieuse pour le confort et la sécurité. 2

Une voiture éclatante, agressive, qui ne passe pas inaperçue. 3

Une petite voiture nerveuse et maniable, pour se faufiler partout. 4

Une voiture-bus, pour transporter la famille, les amis. 5

Une voiture sport pour le plaisir de piloter et de conduire vite. 6

Une camionnette, pour l'utilité et l'économie. 7

Une voiture gag pour s'amuser et aller partout librement. 8

Une voiture futuriste conduite par ordinateur. 9

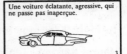

Neuf caractères très différents	La voiture de leurs rêves	Où habitent-ils?	Où mangent-ils?/ qu'est-ce qu'ils aiment?
1 André Morin a trente-cinq ans, célibataire. Il vient d'être nommé Directeur d'une grande banque parisienne. Il aime la vitesse, les avions, le ski, le ski nautique, etc. Quelle est la voiture de ses rêves?		**a** À Lyon dans une grande maison avec une piscine et un grand jardin.	**j** Ils adorent les pique-niques à la campagne.
2 Gérard Duigou a tout juste dix-huit ans. Il aime la mer, la plage et s'amuser avec ses copains. Quelle sera sa première voiture?		**b** Une petite maison dans la campagne pas loin de Toulouse	**k** Elle aime surtout les bons couscous de sa mère.
3 M. et Mme Dumas ont cinq enfants. Ils vont souvent chez leurs parents dans le Midi. Quelle voiture viennent-ils d'acheter?		**c** Dans une grande propriété à Deauville.	**l** À la cantine universitaire.
4 Jean-Yves et Florence Beaumont habitent à Toulouse où ils sont tous les deux enseignants dans un collège. Ils adorent passer leurs week-ends à explorer les Pyrénées. Leur rêve est d'aller en Afrique. Quelle est leur voiture?		**d** Dans un élégant appartement du seizième arrondissement de Paris.	**m** Chez Maxime ou à la Tour d'Argent, les deux restaurants les plus chers de Paris.

5 Etienne Vaillant a habité à Grenoble toute sa vie. Il est maintenant chercheur à l'université de Grenoble où il travaille sur un prototype de voiture futuristique.		**e** Dans un studio avec vue sur le vieux port.	**n** À MacDonald's aussi souvent que possible!
6 Bernard Fargeon est fermier. Il a une ferme d'élevage de poulets dans le Finistère. Il y a cinq ans il a acheté un véhicule pratique pour transporter la nourriture pour la volaille et aussi pour transporter sa mère qui est Bigoudène.		**f** Il partage un appartement avec des copains.	**o** Chez Maxime ou à la Tour d'Argent, les deux restaurants les plus chers de Paris.
7 Olivier Dubois est le PDG (Président Directeur Général) d'une chaîne d'hypermarchés. Il aime le confort, le luxe et tout ce qui est solide. Quelle voiture a-t-il choisi?		**g** Il habite toujours chez ses parents. Sa chambre a un décor de science-fiction.	**p** Dans les restaurants chics du quartier de l'Opéra Garnier.
8 Laurent Dubois, le fils de M. Dubois, ne travaille pas mais avec l'argent de son père il s'est acheté une vieille Cadillac rouge, remise à neuf.		**h** Une ferme dans un village sur la Baie d'Audierne.	**q** Une soupe bien chaude après une longue promenade en montagne.
9 Adidja Ahmed est docteur à Marseille. Elle a choisi une petite voiture rapide et pratique pour aller visiter ses patients. Quelle est sa voiture?		**i** Il habite à Paris avec son amie qui est chanteuse à l'Opéra.	**r** Il aime un bon poulet rôti cuit à la ferme.

(Unités 10 à 16)

8 Les jeunes et l'emploi

Read carefully this short newspaper article about three young students.

1 Étudiantes stagiaires

VIE QUOTIDIENNE
«Il ne suffit pas de cocher des cases»
Étudiants stagiaires

Que faisiez-vous du 28 août au 25 octobre ? Et bien, pendant que certains profitaient encore de leurs dernières semaines de vacances, Jenny, Maria et Nathalie bossaient. Etudiantes en maîtrise A.G.E. (traduisez Administration et Gestion d'Entreprise), elles ont effectué durant huit semaines un stage non rémunéré à la Caisse d'Allocations Familiales (CAF) de Brest. Premier contact avec le monde du travail.

elles bossaient	*they worked*
bosser	*to work (slang)*
cocher des cases	*to tick boxes* (as in multiple choice questions)

Now answer these questions.

a What did the three students do from 28 August to 25 October?
b What is their area of study?
c Were they paid for their work?
d Was the work experience carried out in term time?
e What did this type of work do for them in terms of experience?

2 La chasse aux jobs

Read the article below about the search for a part-time job. Then turn to the grid opposite and fill in the jobs in the order in which they appear in the article. The contents of the grid are jumbled so match each list of points with the correct job category and the correct heading. (Don't worry if you can't understand it all – just try to get the gist of the article.)

La chasse aux jobs

Maigres bourses ou parents compréhensifs ne suffisent plus à subvenir à vos besoins ? La chasse aux jobs est ouverte toute l'année. La concurrence est rude et mieux vaut se pointer devant votre employeur avec une bonne dose de motivation et une idée précise de ce que vous voulez. Conseils et idées en vrac.

Fast-foods et cafétérias

C'est payé tout juste le SMIC et les pourboires sont interdits. Cadences infernales, patrons omniprésents et cuisines aseptisées. Les grandes chaînes recrutent également assez régulièrement et le rythme y est légèrement plus supportable. Pour postuler, présentez-vous directement dans chaque restaurant (mais pas au moment du rush) ou envoyez lettre de candidature et CV avec photo. Un conseil : écumez les centres commerciaux. Il est rare qu'ils ne contiennent pas un ou deux points de restauration. Pour les emplois de serveur(se), les jobs sont mieux payés en général, pourboires aidant.

Télémarketing et sondages

Les horaires sont très modulables. Il vous suffit de faire preuve d'amabilité au téléphone et de ne pas être allergique à la répétition. Les sociétés de télémarketing préfèrent que le premier contact s'établisse par téléphone. Un excellent moyen pour elles de mesurer vos capacités et d'opérer une première sélection.

Distribution de prospectus

Lisez les journaux gratuits pour trouver une annonce. Avoir le pied solide et posséder une voiture sont deux atouts. L'étudiant est payé au nombre de journaux ou tracts distribués.

Pensez aussi aux grandes surfaces, parkings, gardiennages, livraisons à domicile...

3 main job categories (List them in the order they appear in the article)	Requirements to secure a job	Advantages (if any)	Inconveniences (if any)
1)	**a** • Flexitime	**b** • Large fast food firms recruit regularly • Serving jobs are better paid • Tips allowed	**c** • Go and introduce yourself directly • Send a letter of application + CV • Check all the shopping centres
2)	**d** • Only paid minimum wage • Tips are not allowed • Fast rhythm of work • Bosses always present	**e** • Paid according to number of newspapers or leaflets distributed	**f** • Good if you have two assets: solid feet and a car
3)	**g** • Selection over the telephone • Need a good telephone manner	**h** • Read the free press for job adverts	**i** • Very repetitive job

(Unités 17 à 20)

▶ 9 Paris et le tourisme

Vrai ou faux?Ecoutez le débat à la radio et dites si les phrases suivantes sont vraies ou fausses:

1 On a besoin d'un seul billet pour tout déplacement.
2 Il n'y a pas de transport la nuit.
3 Les enfants de dix ans doivent payer plein tarif.
4 On peut voyager jusqu'à Disneyland.
5 On peut choisir un seul billet pour la zone 1 à 6.
6 Il ne faut pas de photo d'identité.
7 La carte Paris-Visite n'est pas valable pour le funiculaire de Montmartre.
8 On peut acheter un billet valable 4 jours.

(Unité 20)

10 Les loisirs et vous: sondage d'opinion *Leisure activities and you: opinion poll*

This is a real French opinion poll. For part A pretend you are Stéphane Jacquelin:

- You like science-fiction films and psychological drama
- You enjoy TV programmes on classical music, religion and philosophy. You also like TV games shows
- You regularly read history magazines

Put a circle around **1** (**oui**) for all the activities mentioned above and circle **2** (**non**) for all the others.

A. Aimez-vous?

Une réponse par ligne. Entourez le 1 ou le 2.

	oui	non
a Les films d'arts martiaux (karaté, kung fu …).	1	2
b Les films de science-fiction.	1	2
c Les films musicaux, disco, rock…	1	2
e La musique pop, le rock.	1	2

f Les variétés, les chansons.

| 1 | 2 |

g Les livres érotiques ou suggestifs.

| 1 | 2 |

h Je suis intéressé(e) par les émissions TV et les magazines sur la musique classique.

| 1 | 2 |

i Je suis intéressé(e) par les émissions TV sur la religion, la philosophie.

| 1 | 2 |

j J'aime les journaux sur la santé, les informations médicales.

| 1 | 2 |

k J'aime les émissions de jeux à la télévision.

| 1 | 2 |

l Je lis régulièrement un ou des magazines (revues) d'histoire.

| 1 | 2 |

B Les sports

For part B circle as many answers as you like to find out if you are sporty, or a TV sports fan.

Parmi les sports suivants, lesquels pratiquez-vous et lesquels aimez-vous regarder? Répondez à chaque colonne. Autant de réponses que vous voulez.

	Je pratique	Je regarde
Tennis, autres sports à raquettes.	1	2
Cyclisme.	1	2
Courses de voiture et de motos.	1	2
Jogging ou athlétisme.	1	2

• Vous totalisez entre 7 et 8 points: vous êtes un fanatique du sport!

(Unités 21 à 25)

11 Encore une bonne recette, simple et rapide à réaliser *Another good recipe: simple and quick to make*

en dés	*diced*
des pignons de pin	*pine kernels*
un brin de menthe	*a leaf of mint*
un four à micro-ondes	*microwave oven*

Read the recipe and answer the questions.

COUSCOUS PILAF

PRÉPARATION: 20 minutes
CUISSON: 5 minutes
POUR 2 PERSONNES

- ○ 1 petite pomme évidée, épluchée et coupée en dés
- ○ 50 g de céleri blanc en petits morceaux
- ○ 50 g de jeunes oignons en fines rondelles
- ○ 1 cuillère à soupe de raisins secs blancs
- ○ 2 moitiés d'abricot sec en petits morceaux
- ○ 30 g de pignons de pin grillés
- ○ 2 cuillères à café de margarine, 175 ml d'eau
- ○ 75 ml de nectar d'abricots ou de poires
- ○ ½ cuillère à café de curry en poudre
- ○ 40 g de couscous

Pour la garniture: un brin de menthe

RÉALISATION

Mettez la pomme, le céleri, les oignons, les raisins, les abricots, les pignons de pin et la margarine dans le plat et mélangez. Placez le plat à couvert au four à micro-ondes pendant 2 minutes. Ajoutez l'eau, le nectar et le curry au mélange et remettez le plat, à couvert, 3 minutes au four. Incorporez le couscous au mélange aux fruits, couvrez le plat et laissez gonfler le couscous pendant 5 minutes. Disposez le couscous pilaf sur un plat et garnissez avec la menthe.

---

a How long does it take to prepare from beginning to end?
b How much liquid is required in all?
c How do you prepare the onions?
d How much curry powder is needed?
e What can you use if you don't have apricot juice?
f How many raisins do you need?
g What is the mint for?
h What do you add the water and juice to?
i At what stage do you add the couscous?
j How long does the dish need to rest before serving?

(Unités 21 à 25)

transcripts

Only the scripts of listening comprehensions or other listening exercises which are not already printed in the units are to be found in this section.

Unit 2

Exercise 1: D'où êtes-vous?

Lucien	Bonjour, je m'appelle Lucien. Et vous comment vous appelez-vous?
Vous	Je m'appelle Françoise.
Lucien	Enchanté de faire votre connaissance. D'où êtes-vous?
Vous	Je suis de Boulogne. Et vous?
Lucien	Je suis de Bruxelles

Exercise 2: Le Loto

Et maintenant voici le tirage du loto. Les numéros gagants sont le 21, le 45, le 53, le 65, le 9, le 50, le 11, le 24 et le 37.

Exercise 3: Quel âge avez-vous?

1 J'ai 21 ans. 2 Il a 38 ans. 3 Elle a 69 ans. 4 Il a 40 ans.

Unit 4

Exercise 3: C'est combien?

Dominique	C'est combien les cigarettes?
Sarah	Euh… c'est 48 € les dix paquets.
Dominique	Et le whisky?
Sarah	C'est 22 €.
Dominique	Et le gin?
Sarah	C'est 16 €.
Dominique	Et le Cognac?
Sarah	C'est 27 €.

Unit 5

Exercise 4: Répondez aux touristes

a Pour aller à la piscine s'il vous plaît? C'est à droite.
b Le musée s'il vous plaît? C'est à 200 m.
c La cathédrale, c'est loin? Non, c'est tout près.
d Pour aller à l'office de tourisme s'il vous plaît? C'est tout droit.
e Pour aller au château? C'est à gauche.

Unit 6

3 À l'heure française

Femme	En général je me lève à sept heures et demie. Je déjeune à midi et demi et je me couche à onze heures. Le dimanche je me lève entre dix heures et dix heures et demie.
Homme	Je me lève à sept heures. Je prends mon déjeuner entre une heure et une heure et demie. Je me couche vers minuit.
Fille	Alors je me lève à sept heures et quart. Je déjeune à midi et je me couche à vingt-deux heures.
Garçon	Je me lève à six heures quarante-cinq. Je prends mon déjeuner à midi et demi et je me couche à neuf heures. Quelquefois le week-end je me couche à minuit.

Exercise 2: Quelle heure est-il?

a Il est dix-sept heures cinq. b Il est midi et demi. c Il est huit heures cinquante-six. d Il est sept heures moins le quart. e Il est une heure vingt. f Il est trois heures. g Il est onze heures quinze. h Il est minuit moins le quart.

Exercise 3: Matin ou après-midi?

Jean-Pierre	Allô oui?
Martine	Salut Jean-Pierre, c'est Martine.
Jean-Pierre	Tu sais quelle heure il est? Il est quatre heures du matin ici!
Martine	Oh pardon! Il est deux heures de l'aprés-midi ici en Australie!

Unit 8

Exercise 5: Écoutez et écrivez

1 **Sylvie Lécaille** Je m'appelle Mademoiselle Sylvie Lécaille. Lécaille ça s'épelle L-é-c-a-i-l-l-e.
2 **Gaétan Leberre** Alors mon nom c'est Gaétan Leberre. Gaétan ça s'épelle G-a-é-t-a-n et Leberre L-e-b-e-r-r-e.

3 **Yannick Tanguy** Je m'appelle Yannick Tanguy. Yannick ça s'épelle Y-a-n-n-i-c-k et Tanguy T-a-n-g-u-y.

Unit 9

Exercise 3: J'ai besoin de ... / Je voudrais ...

1 Je voudrais du jambon et du pâté.
Vous: Allez à la charcuterie!

2 J'ai besoin de médicaments
Vous: Allez à la pharmacie!

3 Je voudrais acheter des journaux
Vous: Allez à la Maison de la Presse!

4 J'ai besoin de timbres poste
Vous: Allez à la poste!

5 Je voudrais du pain et des gâteaux
Vous: Allez à la boulangerie-pâtisserie!

6 J'ai besoin d'un plan de la ville
Vous: Allez à l'Office de Tourisme!

Unit 10

Exercise 1: La cuisine française

Pierre Je crois que la cuisine française est la meilleure du monde.
Lionel Oui, moi je suis tout à fait d'accord avec vous. Nous avons les meilleurs chefs et les meilleurs restaurants.
Pierre Vous avez raison et la preuve c'est que nos chefs sont demandés partout dans le monde.
Pascale Eh bien moi je ne suis pas d'accord avec vous. Je crois qu'il y a de la bonne cuisine partout dans le monde. Qu'est-ce que vous pensez de la cuisine chinoise ou de la cuisine italienne par example? Moi je pense que c'est une question de goût, c'est tout!

Exercise 3: Le souper marin

Michel C'est quel jour le souper marin?
Vous Le 15 août.
Michel C'est à quelle heure?
Vous C'est à partir de 19h30.
Michel Qu'est-ce qu'il y a au menu?
Vous Soupe de poissons, moules, frites et dessert.
Michel C'est combien?
Vous 10 €.

Unit 11

Exercise 2: Où sont-ils en vacances?

1 Bonjour, je m'appelle Fabienne. Dans la ville où je suis le temps est couvert et les températures sont entre 15 et 21 degrés.
2 Bonjour, je m'appelle Jérôme. Dans la ville où je suis il fait de l'orage et les températures sont entre 21 et 29 degrés.
3 Bonjour, je m'appelle Stéphanie. Dans la ville où je suis il fait de l'orage et les températures sont entre 7 et 12 degrés.
4 Bonjour, je m'appelle Alexandre. Dans la ville où je suis il fait de l'orage et les températures sont entre 12 et 23 degrés.

Unit 12

Exercise 3: Bon appétit!

Serveuse Monsieur-dame, qu'est-ce que vous avez choisi?
Florence Moi j'adore les fruits de mer. Je prends le menu à 45 €.
Serveuse Excellent! Et pour Monsieur?
Luc Alors moi je vais prendre le menu à 20 €.
Serveuse Oui … et qu'est-ce que vous prendrez comme entrées?
Luc Alors, comme entrée je prends la Coquille St Jacques à la Bretonne et puis comme plat principal je prends la Brochette de joues de Lotte à la Diable avec salade de saison.
Serveuse Très bien. Vous prendrez le plateau de fromage ou un dessert?
Luc Je vais prendre un dessert … une glace si vous en avez.
Serveuse Certainement Monsieur.
Une autre table … vous, un autre client
Serveuse Vous avez choisi? Qu'est-ce que vous allez prendre?
Vous Je vais prendre le menu à 25 €.
Serveuse Et qu'allez-vous prendre comme entrée?
Vous Je vais prendre les six huîtres chaudes avec cocktail d'algues.
Serveuse Oui, et comme plat principal?
Vous Je vais prendre la Brochette de St Jacques au beurre blanc.
Serveuse Et après le plateau de fromage vous prendrez un dessert?
Vous Oui, une glace à la fraise, s'il vous plaît.

Unit 13

Exercise 3: À la station service

Marc Le plein de gazole pour la camionnette SVP.

Sandrine	Mettez vingt litres de super dans ma vieille voiture de sport SVP.
Martine	Trente litres d'essence sans plomb SVP.

3 Les informations: un weekend meurtrier sur les routes françaises

"Le weekend du quinze août a été marqué par de nombreux accidents de la route. L'accident le plus grave s'est produit sur la route nationale dix lorsqu'un car portugais a percuté un camion débouchant d'une route privée. Sur les 42 passagers huit ont été tués et 24 autres ont été blessés.

À St Nazaire un cycliste a été tué dans une collision avec une voiture et sur la D 940 entre Calais et Boulogne huit personnes ont été blessées dans un accident impliquant quatre voitures."

Unit 14

Exercise 2: Un coup de téléphone

Propriétaire	Allô, j'écoute!
1 Vous	J'ai vu une annonce pour un studio dans Libé. C'est bien ici?
Propriétaire	Oui, c'est bien cela.
2 Vous	C'est à quel étage?
Propriétaire	C'est au sixième.
3 Vous	Il y a un ascenseur?
Propriétaire	Euh, non mais monter et descendre les escaliers est excellent pour la santé!
4 Vous	Il y a le chauffage central?
Propriétaire	Non, le chauffage est électrique.
5 Vous	Il y a une cuisine?
Propriétaire	Oui il y a une cuisine moderne toute équipée.
6 Vous	C'est bien 400 € toutes charges comprises?
Propriétaire	C'est bien cela. Vous pouvez visiter aujourd'hui?
7 Vous	Je viendrais cet après-midi si vous êtes disponible.

Unit 16

Exercise 2: À votre tour de poser des questions

a Vous	Vous êtes allée au Maroc avec le groupe?
Adidja	Oui, j'y suis allée.
b Vous	Combien de jeunes sont allés au Maroc?
Adidja	Dix-huit. Huit filles et dix garçons.
c Vous	Vous êtes restés combien de temps?
Adidja	Nous sommes restés trois semaines.

d Vous Ils ont rencontré des jeunes marocains?
Adidja Oui, beaucoup. C'était formidable.

Unit 17

Exercise 2: À l'A.N.P.E.

a Employé Quel genre de métiers vous intéresse?
Vous Je m'intéresse aux métiers de l'hôtellerie.
b Employé Qu'est-ce qui vous intéresse?
Vous Je m'intéresse aux métiers de la photographie.
c Employé Qu'est-ce qui vous intéresse?
Vous Je m'intéresse aux métiers de la restauration.
d Employé Quel genre de métiers vous intéresse?
Vous Je m'intéresse aux métiers de la santé.
e Employé A quoi vous intéressez-vous?
Vous Je m'intéresse aux métiers de l'habillement.

Unit 18

Exercise 2: Ça prend combien de temps…?

Exemple:

Question Ça prend combien de temps pour aller de Paris à Marseille
par le TGV?

Vous Ça prend deux heures cinquante-cinq.

a Ça prend combien de temps pour aller à Nantes?
Ça prend deux heures.
b Ça prend combien de temps pour aller à Toulouse?
Ça prend cinq heures.
c Ça prend combien de temps pour aller à Lyon?
Ça prend une heure cinquante-cinq.
d Ça prend combien de temps pour aller à Lille?
Ça prend exactement une heure.

Exercise 3: À vous de réserver un billet

a Vous Je voudrais réserver un billet pour Paris SVP.
Employée Vous voyagez aujourd'hui?
b Vous Non, je voyage demain.
Employée Vous prenez le train de quelle heure?
c Vous Je prends le train de 7h 05.
Employée Vous prenez un billet aller-retour?
d Vous Non, je prends un billet simple. C'est combien?

Unit 19

Exercise 1: Vous passez beaucoup trop de temps au téléphone!

a À quelle heure avez-vous téléphoné à Nadine?
Je lui ai téléphoné à onze heures trente.
b À quelle heure avez-vous téléphoné à Mathieu?
Je lui ai téléphoné à midi.
c À quelle heure avez-vous téléphoné à Chantal et à Marc?
Je leur ai téléphoné à 17h15.
d À quelle heure avez-vous téléphoné à votre sœur?
Je lui ai téléphoné à 18h45.
e À quelle heure avez-vous téléphoné à vos parents?
Je leur ai téléphoné à 20h10.
f À quelle heure avez-vous téléphoné à votre fiancé(e)?
Je lui ai téléphoné à 22h45.

Exercise 2: Les maux et blessures

Marie-José J'ai mal au dos.
Alain Je suis blessé aux genoux.
Adrienne J'ai mal à la tête.
Benoît J'ai mal aux dents.
Elise Je crois que je me suis cassé le bras.
Julien Je me suis brûlé la main avec le fer à repasser.
Cécile Je me suis coupé le pied en marchant sur une bouteille cassée.
Didier J'ai des piqûres de moustiques infectées.

Exercise 4: Jacques a dit…

1 Jacques a dit 'levez le bras droit'
2 Baissez le bras
3 Grattez la tête
4 Jacques a dit 'touchez la bouche avec la main gauche'
5 Jacques a dit 'baissez le bras droit'
6 Levez le pied droit
7 Frappez le nez
8 Dansez
9 Jacques a dit 'chantez'
10 Jacques a dit 'touchez le pied gauche'
11 Jacques a dit 'levez la main droite'
12 Asseyez-vous

Unit 21

Exercise 2: Qu'est-ce que vous feriez?

a   Qu'est-ce que vous feriez si vous gagniez le gros lot au Loto?
    J'aurais une grande maison en Bretagne, j'aurais un bateau, j'irais à
    la pêche et le soir je regarderais la télé.
b   Est-ce que vous feriez des voyages?
    Je ferais un voyage autour du monde.

Exercise 5: Vous avez coché?

Et voici les numéros gagnants pour le deuxiéme tirage du Loto: le 35,
le 8, le 15, le 28, le 13, le 45, le 11, le 25, et le 12 est le numéro
complémentaire.

Unit 22

Exercise 2: Oui, c'est le mien

1   Ce sac, c'est à vous?
    Oui, c'est le mien.
2   Ce sont vos clefs?
    Oui, ce sont les miennes.
3   C'est votre montre?
    Oui, c'est la mienne.
4   Ce sont vos patins à roulettes?
    Oui, ce sont les miens.

Unit 25

Exercise 1: Vous êtes d'accord

1   J'adore la cuisine française.
    Moi aussi.
2   Je n'aime pas les voyages organisés.
    Moi non plus.
3   Nous aimons beaucoup la Bretagne.
    Moi aussi.
4   Je n'aime pas la rentrée.
    Moi non plus.
5   Je déteste prendre l'avion.
    Moi aussi.
6   Je préfère rester chez moi.
    Moi aussi.

Exercise 4: Le notaire vous pose des questions

| Me Le Corre | Qu'est-ce que vous recherchez exactement? |
| 1 | Je cherche une petite maison de pierre près de la côte. |

2   Je cherche une maison de cinq chambres avec cave.

3   Je cherche une petite maison avec un jardin clos.

4   Je cherche une petite maison avec un grenier aménageable.

Unité de révision

1 Profils

1 Je m'appelle Sarah Burgess. J'ai 28 ans. J'habite 12 Stella Avenue, Londres SW2. Mon numéro de téléphone est le 020 8476 5656. Je suis de nationalité britannique, mon père est de nationalité britannique, ma mère est de nationalité française. Je suis éditrice chez Hodder & Stoughton. J'aime les voyages, le cinéma, la lecture. Je n'aime pas le sport à la télévision. **2** Je m'appelle Dominique Périer. J'ai 36 ans. J'habite 5 Avenue de la Vieille Ville à St Nazaire en France. Mon numéro de téléphone est le 02 40 45 18 11. Je suis de nationalité française, mon père et ma mère sont de nationalité française. Je suis professeur de philosophie au lycée de St Nazaire. J'aime beaucoup les chats, l'opéra et les musées d'art. Je n'aime pas la télévision. Je n'aime pas les voitures.

9 Paris et le tourisme

Présentateur du programme	Et vous pensez que Paris est accessible à tous nos visiteurs?
Représentante de la RATP	Mais certainement avec Paris-Visite les touristes peuvent allez partout dans Paris et la région parisienne.
Présentateur	C'est quoi Paris-Visite ?
Représentante	Eh bien c'est un seul et unique billet qui permet de voyager à volonté sur tous les modes de transport : métro, bus, tram, funiculaire de Montmartre, Noctambus pour voyager la nuit…
Présentateur	Ça c'est bien mais pour ce qui est de la banlieue qu'est-ce que vous leur proposez aux touristes?
Représentante	Eh bien toujours avec ce même billet ils peuvent prendre les trains de banlieue, suivant les zones qu'ils ont choisis soit zone 1 à 3 ou bien la zone 1 à 8. Ils peuvent se rendre avec le même billet jusqu'à Disneyland, Versailles et jusqu'aux aéroports parisiens.
Présentateur	Il faut acheter un nouveau billet tous les jours ?
Représentante	Non, pour une visite de cinq jours ont peut acheter un billet qui sera valable cinq jours, en

	fait il y a quatre possibilités : un billet pour un jour, deux, trois ou cinq jours.
Présentateur	Il y a des réductions pour les enfants ?
Représentante	Bien sûr, il y a un tarif réduit pour les enfants de 4 à 11 ans.
Présentateur	Et cela est compliqué comme démarche ? Ça prend beaucoup de temps ?
Représentante	Pas du tout ! Vous voyagez sans perdre de temps, un seul achat et pas besoin de photo !
Présentateur	Alors j'espère que les touristes seront nombreux dans la capitale !
Représentante	Merci !

key to the exercises

Unit 1

Exercise 1 a Bonjour Madame Corre! **b** Au revoir Marie-Claire. **c** Bonne nuit Paul! **d** Bon après-midi Mademoiselle! **e** À tout à l'heure / à bientôt Monsieur Jarre. **Comment ça va?** Monsieur Blanchard is feeling fine; Madame Lebrun is feeling so so. **Exercise 2 1c 2a 3e 4f 5d 6b Exercise 3 Dialogue 1: c** New Year **Dialogue 2: b** Françoise's birthday **Dialogue 3: a** Estelle and Paul's wedding **Exercise 4 D1c D2b D3c 5 a** un kilo de pommes **b** cinq euros **c** un sandwich au fromage **d** une bière **e** la gare **5 Dans la rue a** the post office **b** the tourist office **c** the supermarket **d** the Citroën garage **Web exercise: 1** Mariage **2** Bonne Fête **3** Fêtes → Fêtes Nationales

Unit 2

1 Enchanté de faire votre connaissance a Alain **b** Claire **c** Paris **d** Marseille **e** Je suis de Paris. **f** Enchanté de faire votre connaissance. **Exercise 1 a** Je m'appelle Françoise. **b** Je suis de Boulogne. Et vous? **Exercise 2 a** Between 2 and 10 **b** Twenty numbers for each draw **c** 3 € for two draws and 1,5 € for one **d** The winning numbers are: 21, 45, 53, 65, 9, 50, 11, 13, 24, 37. (Winning numbers in our grid are in bold type) **2 Je suis la mère d'Isabelle a** Isabelle's mother **b** David's **c** no – she's French **d** Mark Thompson **e** in England **f** J'habite en Angleterre. **g** La tante de David. **h** Je vous présente Madame ... **i** Mon fils. **j** Ma fille. **3 Tu as quel âge? a** J'ai douze ans. **b** Mon frère, il a quatorze ans. **c** Je n'ai pas de frère. **d** Moi aussi! **e** Tu as quel âge? **Exercise 3 a** J'ai vingt et un ans. **b** Il a trente-huit ans. **c** Elle a soixante-neuf ans. **d** Il a quarante ans. **4 Vous parlez français? a** French and English **b** Both **c** French **d** Il est professeur de français. **e** Cela dépend. **f** Je parle français ou anglais. **g** Je parle français à la maison. **h** Les enfants parlent couramment les deux langues. **i** Il parle bien le français. **Exercise 4 1c 2e 3d 4a 5b Exercise 5 a** Grand-mother **b** Father **c** Aunt **d** Cousin **e** Brother **Exercise 6 5** is the odd one out – **mon oncle** is the only male.

Unit 3

2 Natalie a 36 **b** yes **c** two **d** Yes **e** Cinema, travelling, reading, photography **f** Je suis professeur d'histoire. **g** J'aime voyager. **h** J'habite à Vannes en Bretagne. **i** J'aime aller au cinéma. **j** Je n'aime pas faire le ménage. **3 Antoine a** 29 **b** Paris **c** German **d** Watching films and sports on TV, photography and travelling **e** Je demeure à Paris. **f** J'aime bien regarder des films à la télé. **g** J'ai horreur des voitures. **h** Je vais au travail à vélo. **Grammar Alors** moi: *so*; **Alors** je vais au travail à vélo: *therefore* **4 Monique a** 45 **b** Her husband **c** At the post office **d** A little **e** She hates it **f** Je travaille à la poste. **g** Je parle un peu l'anglais. **h** Je n'ai pas d'enfants. **i** J'apprends le vietnamien. **j** il est au chômage. **5 Pierre a** 52 **b** Monique **c** At Renault **d** In Dijon **e** Ma mère est veuve. **f** Je travaille chez Renault. **g** Elle habite chez nous. **h** J'adore les voyages et la lecture. **i** Je n'aime pas la télé sauf les documentaires. **j** Je comprends un peu l'anglais. **Exercise 1** Je m'appelle Anne-Marie Pélerin. J'ai quarante-cinq ans. J'habite à Boulogne. Je suis dentiste. Je parle français, anglais et allemand. J'adore le football et la photographie. **Exercise 2:**

	NAMES	QUESTIONS ANSWERS
Natalie		Je m'appelle Natalie
Antoine		J'ai vingt-neuf ans
Natalie	Quelle est votre profession?	
Monique		Je travaille à la poste
Pierre	Où habitez-vous?	
Antoine	Quelles langues parlez-vous?	
Monique	Vous aimez le sport?	
Pierre		Oui, je suis marié avec Monique

Exercise 3 a Faux **b** Faux **c** Vrai **d** Vrai **e** Vrai **f** Faux **Exercise 4 f**

Unit 4

1 Au pont cinq a five **b** eight **c** Information desk. Deck 7 **d** It's in the evening (they say **bonsoir**) **e** 017 Linked phrases: **1d 2e 3a 4b 5c Exercise 1 1d 2f 4g 6b 7c 11a 12h 13j 15e 17i Exercise 2 a** C'est au pont sept. **b** C'est au pont neuf. **c** C'est au pont neuf. **d** C'est au pont neuf. **e** C'est au pont sept. **2 Est-ce qu'il y a un cinéma? a** Yes, there are two **b** No **c** *Le Come-back* **d** 23.00 **e** 10 € **Linked phrases: 1c, 2d, 3a, 4b Exercise 3 a** 27 € **b** 22 € **c** 15 € for 10 packets **d** 16 €

Unit 5

1 Pour aller à… a2 b2 c3 Linked phrases: 1e 2c 3a 4f 5d 6b 2 Vous tournez à gauche a Dominique **b** A passer-by **c** 500 metres **d** Not at all **Linked phrases: 1f 2g 3a 4b 5c 6d 7e Exercise 1 a** Et toi tu **connais**?

b Vous allez/vous tournez **Exercise 2 1c 2a 3c Exercise 3** Q1: Le petit aquarium SVP? Q2: La cathédrale SVP? Q3: Le Musée SVP? **Exercise 4 a** C'est à droite. **b** C'est à 200 m. **c** Non, c'est tout près. **d** C'est tout droit. **e** C'est à gauche.

Unit 6

1 Où stationner? 1 2 hours **2** There a special tariff for residents. **3** Your receipt **2 Tu as de la monnaie? 1a 2** 3 to 4 hours **3** 1€ x 1 2€ x 1 50c x 1 **Web extension exercise** 1. 7 2. 4 3. 3 4. 2 **4** With the following coins: **a** 50c x 1, **b** 1 € x 1 **d** 20c x 2 **e** 10c x 1 **Linked phrases: 1e 2d 3f 4a 5c 6b Exercise 1 a** monnaie **b** me repose **c** reste **d** argent **e** argent **3 À l'heure française a** votre déjeuner, **ton** déjeuner

b	Q1	Q2	Q3
Femme		12.30	11.00
Homme	7.00		about midnight
Fille	7.15		10.00
Garçon		12.30	9.00

c The woman **d** Midnight **Exercise 2 1e 2h 3a 4b 5c 6g 7f 8d Exercise 3 a** 4 a.m. **b** 2 p.m. **Exercise 4 a** 5th channel **b** Saturday 9 August at 2.30 p.m. and Wednesday 13 August at 12.30 p.m. **c** At what altitude do giant pandas live? **Exercise 5 a** 1 July to 31 August **b** No, there are no guided tours at the weekend between 1 September and 30 June **c** 10 a.m. to 11.30 and 2.30 to 6 p.m. **d** From 10 a.m. to 3 p.m. **e** School parties and groups of 10+ if they pre-book **f** It's free **g** Musée ouvert **toute** l'année, **Tous** les jours du 1er juillet au 31 août **h** In French, unless names for the days of the week and the months of the year are at the beginning of a sentence, they are spelt without capital letters.

Unit 7

1 Choisir un hôtel 1c 2e 3f 4b 5a 6d Symbols 1h 2j 3k 4m 5b 6c 7n 8a 9i 10d 11e 12g 13f 14l 2 Quelques renseignements 1 One room for two people for one night, in a 3 star hotel with sea view **2** A hotel where he/she can take a small dog **3** One room for one person in a not too expensive hotel with restaurant and swimming pool **4** A large room for three people in a hotel with a lift (disabled daughter in wheelchair) **Exercise 1 a** Je voudrais une chambre pour une personne avec vue sur la mer. **b** Je voudrais une chambre double dans un hôtel. **c** Nous cherchons un hôtel avec piscine. **d** On voudrait une chambre d'hôtel pour le week-end **Chambre d'hôtes a** Chez des agriculteurs **b** Pour une ou plusieurs nuits **c** Un petit déjeuner campagnard **d** Vos hôtes vous serviront **Services "plus" a** dentifrice **b** chauffe biberon **c** sèche-cheveux **d** brosse à dents **e** crème à raser **f** télécopie **4 Un petit hotel a** Yes **b** No, there are plenty of restaurants in St Malo. **c** Yes **d** No but

they can phone to check availability. **e** Cela devrait être possible.
f Pouvez-vous nous renseigner? **g** Vous vous chargez des réservations?
h Non, je suis désolé madame! **i** Nous passons quelques jours dans la
région. **Exercise 2 a** (inside the old town) **b** 18 **c** Yes, they have
English TV channels **d** A lift **e** Between 35 € and 50 €

Unit 8

1 Quel hôtel choisir? a Station Hotel **b** It's convenient, easy with
luggage and it's the cheapest. **c** Near the station **d** Madame Olivier
e More comfortable **Linked phrases: 1c 2a 3f 4e 5b 6h 7d Exercise
1 a** Faux **b** Vrai **c** Faux **Exercise 2 a** Café des Amis **b** Café du Port
c Café de la Vieille Ville **d** Café de l'Europe

Exercise 3

```
C Q A D H B G T I C R V
H A P D E O U Y T N H I
S Q F X G L T W T T Y E
H O T E L D U P O R T I
R E G T D F M E D A W L
T G H W A E F P F M F L
A N G L A I S V I L L E
A M G L B I S Q C R U P
B C V N F T H W A Q S F
```

2 À l'hôtel de la Plage a yes **b** two nights **c** third floor
d 25 **e** from 8 to 10 a.m. **f** at 11 p.m. **Linked phrases: 1e 2d 3a 4f 5g
6c 7b Exercise 4 1** Lécaille **2** Gaétan Leberre **3** Yannick Tanguy
Exercise 5 a Je prends/peux, Tu peux/prends, Il/elle/on prend/peut,
Nous prenons, Vous prenez, Ils/elles peuvent/prennent **b** Vous **prendrez**
... Oui nous le **prendrons c** Where there is a will there is is a way.
Un entretien avec ... 1 dogs, cats and rabbits **2** She has a diploma
3 When a dog owner collects his/her dog and leaves the salon proud of
the dog.

Unit 9

1 C'est à côté du... a Try to find a post office **b** Yes (PTT) **c** A tour of
the ramparts **d** 2 An hour's time **Linked phrases: 1e 2a 3f 4h 5g 6c 7d
8b Vrai ou faux? a** Faux **b** Vrai **c** Faux **d** Faux **e** Faux

Exercise 1

	A	B	C	D
1	M & Mme Olivier	vont	choisir	des cartes postales
2	Tu	vas	téléphoner	à ton frère
3	Sarah Burgess	va	prendre	le petit déjeuner au lit
4	Vous	allez	visiter	la vieille ville
5	Je	vais	rester	à St Malo
6	On	va	chercher	du travail
7	Les enfants	vont	faire	une promenade
8	Nous	allons	voir	le dernier film de Spielberg

2 Une si jolie petite ville! 4f 7a 8d 10c 15b 16e 17g Directions from Pl. de la République Passant: camping municipal Vous: camping … charcuterie Passant: mairie Vous: bibliothèque **3 Qu'est-ce qu'on va faire? a** Mum **b** The girl **c** Take the little train in St Malo **d** Dad **e** What they will do tomorrow **Linked phrases 1d 2e 3a 4b 5f 6c Exercise 2 a** The intra-muros (the old town) and places around St Malo **b** It is the starting place and the end of the train ride **c** No, only in July and August **Exercise 3 1** Allez à la charcuterie! **2** Allez à la pharmacie! **3** Allez à la Maison de la Presse! **4** Allez à la Poste! **5** Allez à la boulangerie-pâtisserie! **6** Allez à l'Office de Tourisme! **Web extension** Porte St Vincent is in St Malo, at the feet of the ramparts, 50m away from the tourist office, 10km from Dinard, 32 Km from Dinan, 15km from Cancale, 56 km from Mont St Michel and roughly an hour away from Jersey and Guernsey.

Unit 10

1 Où est-ce qu'on mange? a A picnic **b** The other side of the street **c** 8,50 € all included **Linked phrases: 1g 2e 3a 4f 5b 6h 7d 8c Exercise 1 a** Chauvinism **b** When it is a question of cuisine/cookery **c** two **d** The chefs and French restaurants **e** China and Italy **f** one **2 Les repas… a** Fine food and good meals **b** Christening, communion or confirmation, a wedding, an exam result, a birthday, Christmas and the New Year. **c** 7 to 8 p.m. **d** Children **e** Souper is later than dîner and it is also a lighter meal. **f** At the canteen, cafeteria, restaurant or at home if they live close to their work place. **Exercise 2 a 4** and 6, **b 1** and 5, **c** 4, **d 2** and 3, **e** 7, **f** 4, **g** 7, **h** 3, **i** 5, **j** 6 **4 Le goûter à la ferme a** Orchards and cider making **b** Apple juice or cider **c** jams or preserves **d** Every afternoon from 1 May to 15 September **e** You need to book **Exercise 3 a** Le 15 août **b** A partir de 19h30 **c** Soupe de poissons, moules, frites et dessert **d** dix euros **Moules-frites** Les Belges sont amateurs de moules-frites qu'ils mangent dans des restaurants ou des brasseries. Le chanteur et poète Jacques Brel a célébré cette coutume nationale dans ses chansons.

Unit 11

1 Il va faire de l'orage a This afternoon **b** To listen to the weather forecast **c** The Pyrenees, the Alps and Corsica **d**3 **e**4 **f**2 **g**2 **h** 2 and 3

Un peu de géographie 1 Bretagne, Caen **2** Lille **3** Strasbourg, Nord-est **4** Poitou-Charentes, Limousin **5** Bordeaux **6** Auvergne, Lyon **7** Marseille, Nice, Corse **Exercise 1 a** Poitou-Charentes, Centre, Limousin, Aquitaine, Midi-Pyrénées, Auvergne, Rhône-Alpes **b** Bretagne, Pays de la Loire, Normandie, Nord-Picardie, Ile-de-France, Nord-Est, Bourgogne, Franche-Comté **c** The same as the areas with thunderstorms **d** & **e** Nord-Picardie, Ile de France **f** Pourtour méditerranéen, Corse **g** Nord-Est, Bourgogne, Franche-Comté **h** Bretagne, Pays de la Loire, Normandie **Exercise 2 a 1** à Dublin **2** à Athènes **3** à Moscou **4** à Oslo **b 1** A Varsovie le temps est ensoleillé **2** Il fait de l'orage **Web extension exercise 1** heat waves **2** coup de soleil **3** rhume des foins

Unit 12

1 Un peu de lecture 1b **2**c **3**a **4**c **5**b **Exercise 1 1** Je viens d'arriver à Paris. **2** Tu viens de finir tes examens. **3** Jean-Paul vient de gagner le gros lot au Loto. **4** Nous venons de visiter St Malo. **5** Vous venez de choisir un menu. **6** Elles viennent de voir un bon film. **Exercise 2 1** J'ai écouté les infos à la radio. **2** Tu as fini ton travail. **3** On a mangé des moules-frites. **4** Nous avons choisi un hôtel pas trop cher. **5** Vous avez posté vos cartes postales. **6** S & D ont réservé une cabine. **2 Au café de la Baie a** No Sarah orders a draft beer and Dominique a shandy **b** Ice cream **c** No, she is on a diet **d** Sarah **e** Dominique. Sarah paid last time **f** 9,50 € Yes 50c **g** Je vous apporte la carte **h** Prends un sorbet; il y a moins de calories **i** Une glace à la fraise et un sorbet au citron **j** Tu as payé la dernière fois **k** Quelques minutes plus tard **l** Un peu plus tard **Perfect tense:** Vous avez choisi, tu as payé; **Present tense:** je vous sers, je conduis, je vous apporte, tu prends, je suis, il y a, paie, c'est, fait; **Immediate future:** je vais prendre, nous allons prendre. **3 Au restaurant a** A table by the window **b** No, they ask for the menu **c** A children's menu **d** Yes **e** It's only available at lunch time **f** Two menus at 20 €, two children's menus and a bottle of Muscadet **Web extension exercise:** Vrai – especially if you chose *une brasserie*

Exercise 3

	Menus (prix)	First course	Second course	Cheese	Dessert
Luc	20 €	Scallops	Monkfish	No	Ice cream
Florence	45 €	Sea food platter	Lobster	Cheese	Choice of dessert
Vous	25 €	6 huîtres chaudes avec cocktail d'algues	brochette de St Jaques au beurre blanc	fromage	glace à la fraise

Unit 13

1 Il y a une déviation a There is a diversion in 500 m **b** 50 km/hour **c** Service station **d** On the right Linked phrases: **1e 2h 3g 4b 5f 6a 7c 8d Exercise 1 1 a** or **c 2e 3d 4b 5f 6 a** or **c Exercise 2 3** Vérifier la pression des pneus **Exercise 3 1 C, 2 A, 3 B, 4** a full tank of diesel, 20 litres of leaded 4 star petrol, 30 litres of unleaded petrol **Exercise 4 a** A16 **b** N43 **c** D940 **2 Les panneaux a** The end of the area where the signs apply **b** Blue **c** Red **d** A blue square Checklist **1 3 4 6 7 9 10**

3 Les informations...

Accidents	Type of vehicle involved in the accident	Place where accident occurred	No. of people killed	No. of people injured
1	Portuguese coach and lorry	RN10	8	24
2	Bicycle and a car	St Nazaire	1	–
3	Four cars	D940 Calais–Boulogne	0	8

Exercise 5 1f 2g 3a 4d 5e 6c 7b

Unit 14

1 L'appart de Dominique a Fourth floor **b** No **c** Yes, the view is great, it's cheap and the neighbours are quiet **d** There is no lift **e** Going up and down stairs **f** Dominique and her boyfriend **g** The sea Linked phrases: **1h 2e 3g 4k 5b 6c 7d 8f 9j 10a 11i** Grammar **1** je le loue; si, les voilà; l'à décoré; tu la vois? **2** appartement; clefs; appartement; mer. **Exercise 1 2, 3, 5, 6, 7, 9, 10, 14, 16, 17, 20 2 Où loger? a** Her mother **b** A room in the university campus **c** Rent a studio flat or share a flat with one or two girl friends. **d** She is going to find a holiday job. Linked phrases: **1d 2f 3a 4e 5c 6b 3 Corinne cherche... 1 4: a, b, d** and **j 2b 3 k** and **g** (although **g** is too expensive for her) **4** 400–550 € **5a Exercise 2 1e 2g 3a 4f 5d 6c 7b**

Unit 15

1 Rien dans le frigo a Milk, cheese, yogurts, butter, bread, fish, fruit and vegetables, washing-up liquid and tins of cat food **b** Her cat **c** Her neighbour **d** Film for her camera, batteries for her torch, white wine and a cake **e** For Sarah and Dominique's evening meal **f** A pair of shoes and a pullover **g** No **h** Green **i** Fish counter Linked phrases: **1e 2f 3h 4b 5c 6a 7d 8g Dom. plaisante** Sarah has just told Dominique that red does not suit her. In reply Dominique suggests that they move on to the fish counter, saying that she hopes they don't sell goldfish. The French

word for goldfish is **poisson rouge** (lit. *red fish*). **On va a quel rayon?**
3, 12, 13, 21, 22, 23, 24, 25, 26, 28, 33, 36 and 40 **Exercise 1 1e 2f
3a 4b 5d 6c Exercise 2 a** White nectarines **b** 1 to 3 August **c** A
Sunday **d** In the town centre on Tuesday 12 and Wednesday 13 August
e Bedding **f** 4800 € **g** Wednesday 6 August **h** Furniture **2 Au rayon
charcuterie** Bayonne ham: six slices; garlic sausage: 12 slices;
farmhouse pâté: 250 g; Greek mushrooms: 200 g; scallops: 4

P	A	C	C	D	M	N	G	H	I	L	P	K
A	D	S	E	A	P	O	M	M	E	S	O	D
M	S	Q	R	D	S	A	T	E	E	G	M	H
P	E	T	I	T	S	P	O	I	S	K	M	K
L	R	G	S	F	T	Y	M	S	E	L	E	H
E	A	R	E	B	A	N	A	N	E	S	S	A
M	I	O	S	D	C	E	T	A	P	A	D	R
O	S	I	Z	A	H	R	E	T	O	L	E	I
U	I	R	C	V	O	B	S	M	I	A	T	C
S	N	E	R	H	U	S	G	D	R	D	E	O
S	C	A	R	O	T	T	E	S	E	E	R	T
E	T	U	Y	U	H	N	F	D	S	V	R	S
S	F	X	J	V	B	C	A	S	W	R	E	M

Unit 16

1 Je suis animateur **1b 2c 3** Sports, photography, music and travel
4 Morocco **5** three weeks **6** 18 young people and 3 adults **7** With their
families **8** Young Moroccans **Linked phrases 1h 2f 3e 4g 5a 6b 7d 8c
Exercise 1 1c** Djamel is the youth worker who organized the journey.
2e Sarah and Dominique arrived at Gildas's. **3f** I went up the Eiffel
Tower. **4a** The young people went to Morocco. **5b** You went away with
a group of young people? **6d** The group stayed three weeks in
Morocco. **Exercise 2 a** Vous aussi, vous êtes allée au Maroc avec le
groupe? **b** Combien de jeunes y sont allés/sont allés au Maroc? **c** Vous
êtes restés combien de temps? **d** Vous avez rencontré des jeunes
marocains? **2 Je suis né en France a** If it was the first time he had been
to Morocco **b** In France **c** His parents and sisters **d** About ten times
e Arabic **f** Three: Arabic, French and English **Exercise 3 1c 2e 3a 4b
5d Exercise 4 a** 50%: cinquante pour cent **b** 48%: quarante-huit pour
cent **c** 65%: soixante-cinq pour cent **d** 32%: trente-deux pour cent
Web extension exercise: 1 French footballer **2** Paris suburbs
3 Because they are negative towards young people of the « banlieues ».
4 Interior Minister **5** Thuram has not lived there for many years.

Unit 17

1 Mon père était professeur a It's very good **b** Sarah is bilingual **c** Her mother and her father **d** He died **e** Five years ago **f** Fine **g** Because he is tiring Sarah out with his questions **h** Her room **i** Two years ago

Noms	profession/métier	profession/job
Dominique ✓	Prof de Philo	Philosophy teacher
Sarah ✓	Editrice	Editor
Mme Périer	Pharmacienne	Pharmacist
M. Périer	Viticulteur	Wine grower
Mr. Burgess	Professeur d'allemand	German teacher
Mrs. Burgess ✓	Professeur de français	French teacher

Exercise 1 a Je dansais **b** Je skiais/je faisais du ski **c** Je faisais du basket **d** J'allais à la pêche **e** Je faisais de la planche à roulettes **f** Je jouais du piano **2 À l'ANPE a** He does not know **b** He was a baker's apprentice **c** He works full-time as a baker **d** Go out to clubs in the evening **e** 5 a.m. **f** In a pharmacy **Linked phrases: 1d 2f 3a 4c 5b 6e 3 Le contrat 1** Between 16 and 26 **2** two years **3** It can be extended to three and reduced to one **4** Two months **5** The contract can be broken **6** Five weeks **7** Six weeks before the date of birth and ten afterwards **8 a** four days **b** three days **9** General and technical **10** Between one and two weeks per month **Exercise 2 a** Je m'intéresse aux métiers de la restauration. **b** Je m'intéresse à la photographie. **c** Je m'intéresse aux métiers de la bouche. **d** Je m'intéresse aux métiers de la santé. **e** Je m'intéresse aux métiers de l'habillement. **Exercise 3 a** Job offers **b** You can look up all adverts for the last fortnight **c** You can send your CV immediately via the Internet **d** Sales assistants, doorman, confectioner, waitresses, apprentice (in a delicatessen), home helps **e** Secretarial jobs or accountancy, sales, electrician **f** At least 26 **g** You must be dynamic, motivated and interested in information technology **h** Maths, physics, chemistry, economics or management

Unit 18

1 Vous prenez le TGV? a She has to go back to work **b** Bordeaux, les Landes and the local wine **c** She likes it a lot **d** To Paris **e** By train (TGV) **f** 3 hours **g** 12 hours **h** To make her train reservation **i** Between 3 and 4 p.m. **j** Her sister **Linked phrases: 1d 2f 3a 4g 5b 6c 7h 8e Exercise 1 1b 2c 3d 4a 5f 6e Exercise 2 a** Ça prend deux heures **b** Ça prend cinq heures **c** Ça prend une heure cinquante-cinq **d** Ça prend exactement une heure **2 Au guichet de la gare a** 1h45 **b** return tickets **c** on Thursday **d** 10.09 **e** 10.37 **f** It arrives at Poitiers just in time for lunch **g** No **h** Book her ticket at the ticket machine **Linked phrases: 1d 2e 3b 4h 5a 6c 7f 8g Exercise 3 a** Je voudrais réserver un billet pour Paris SVP. **b** Non, je voyage demain. **c** Je prends le train de sept heures cinq. **d** Non, je prends un billet simple. C'est combien? **Exercise 4 a** une soirée **b** ans **c** jours **d** ans **3 Les points de vente… a** Vrai **b** Faux **c** Vrai **d** Vrai **e** Faux **f** Faux **g** Vrai

A	R	R	I	V	E	E	S	A	R	T	Y	U	C	V	B	M	B	T	A
Z	E	F	G	H	N	M	K	L	O	S	E	R	A	T	A	Z	C	V	L
D	S	I	M	P	L	E	F	S	D	F	G	H	O	R	A	I	R	E	L
R	E	W	A	S	V	B	G	N	M	J	D	E	P	A	R	T	S	V	E
O	R	A	N	D	E	L	I	G	N	E	S	D	I	A	S	W	B	R	
T	V	S	A	F	T	F	E	D	D	T	Y	U	I	N	G	S	A	N	
F	A	A	W	E	G	A	H	F	E	S	V	O	Y	A	G	E	G	D	R
V	T	S	S	D	G	U	J	I	U	Y	T	R	D	G	F	A	O	F	E
B	I	L	L	E	T	T	E	R	I	E	C	F	F	R	D	X	N	G	T
C	O	F	F	G	I	O	K	L	Y	F	D	F	G	A	S	C	R	T	O
V	N	D	U	W	R	M	D	G	T	R	R	M	I	N	I	T	E	L	U
N	E	E	J	E	G	A	R	E	S	F	F	F	U	D	B	F	S	Y	R
G	U	I	C	H	E	T	F	Z	A	G	F	G	K	E	J	G	T	U	A
M	F	D	H	A	B	I	L	L	E	T	D	U	Y	V	K	H	A	E	E
O	G	F	N	S	S	O	H	G	L	N	S	I	T	I	U	J	U	A	I
P	B	H	F	S	A	U	K	E	R	K	G	K	F	T	T	H	R	D	O
V	A	L	A	B	L	E	L	K	L	H	U	U	D	E	R	T	A	F	U
N	P	O	I	N	T	S	D	E	V	E	N	T	E	O	D	S	N	C	F
F	H	W	E	T	G	G	U	I	T	H	U	T	D	S	E	F	T	G	Y
G	S	D	M	O	N	T	P	A	R	N	A	S	S	E	S	R	S	E	A

Web extension exercise: 1 No **1 2** weekly **3** all rail news (equipment, technology and people who matter) **4** On the internet – click on Vous Abonner or by telephone

Unit 19

1 Sarah téléphone à sa sœur **a** 19.15 **b** 19.05 She will not get compensation (her train was less than 30 minutes, late) **c** No **d** To telephone her sister **e** a mobile phone **2 Allô! a** her mobile phone **b** 01–48 05 39 16 **c** At the hospital **d** Opening a tin of cat food **e** Not really **f** Marie-Claire's children **g** Get a taxi **h** No, she knows her way very well **Linked phrases: 1d 2g 3e 4h 5b 6c 7a 8f**

Exercise 1

Names	Questions on the recording	Your answer
Nadine	A quelle heure avez-vous téléphoné à Nadine?	Je lui ai téléphoné à onze heures trente
Mathieu	… à Mathieu?	Je lui ai téléphoné à midi
Chantal et Marc	… à Chantal et Marc?	Je leur ai téléphoné à dix-sept heures quinze
Votre sœur	… à votre sœur?	Je lui ai téléphoné à dix-huit heures quarante-cinq
Vos parents	… à vos parents?	Je leur ai téléphoné à vingt heures dix
Votre fiancé/e	… à votre fiancée?	Je lui ai téléphoné à vingt-deux heures quarante-cinq

Exercise 2 1g mal au dos **2e** blessé aux genoux **3d** mal à la tête **4b** mal aux dents **5f** bras cassé **6c** main brûlée avec un fer **7h** coupé le pied en marchant sur une bouteille cassée **8a** piqûres de moustiques infectées **4 J'ai mal au ventre a** No **b** Stomach **c** 38.2 degrees (it's slightly high) **d** appendicitis **e** Nothing at all **f** Breakfast **g** 10 a.m. **h** She should be kept at the hospital for observation **Linked phrases: 1c 2a 3d 4e 5f 6b**
Exercise 3 a Wednesday 21 March 2007 at 8.30 p.m. **b** Dr Friat **c** Backache **d** Salle polyvalente (*village hall*) **e** C.H.U. of Brest
Exercise 4 1 lift right arm **2** nothing **3** nothing **4** touch mouth with left hand **5** lower right arm **6** nothing **7** nothing **8** nothing **9** sang **10** touch left foot **11** lift right hand **12** nothing **Web extension exercise:** Jacques a dit: **1** from age 5. **2** Jacques a dit **3** he/she is no longer in the game **4** the winner becomes Jacques

Unit 20

1 Je te prie… Calendar of events a Chatting to her sister **b** Will take the children out to the Bois de Boulogne zoo and go for a walk **c** All go to the cinema **d** Lunch at Tante Eliane **e** Gare du Nord: register train ticket **f** Takes Eurostar back to London **g** Starts work in London **Linked phrases: 1c 2e 3g 4h 5b 6a 7d 8f Exercise 1 a** Il n'y a pas de mal **b** Ce n'est pas grave **c** Ne vous inquiétez pas **d** Cela ne fait rien **2 Acheter des tickets a** No they have got some **b** Half-fare **c** Children **d** She needs to think which kind of ticket she needs to buy **e** A carnet of tickets **f** Direction Porte de Vincennes **g** Because they may be able to have a ride on the little train at the Bois de Boulogne **Linked phrases: 1c 2e 3f 4b 5a 6d Exercise 2 a** Card A **b** B is for museums and monuments, C is for Disneyland **c** In all RER and RATP stations **d** Marne-la-Vallée/Chessy (Disneyland station) **e** Card A **f** For 1, 3 or 5 days **g** All metro and RER stations, bus terminals, shops and tobacconists with the RATP sign, ticket machines **h** 6,50 € **Web extension exercise 1** Since 2002 **2** four to five weeks in July and August **3** On the right bank of the Seine **4** The traffic

Unit 21

On pourrait sortir b c d f g Marie-Claire is feeling much better and she will be careful **h** More time and money **Linked phrases: 1b 2d 3e 4a 5f 6c Exercise 1 1g 2d 3a 4h 5c 6e 7b 8f 2** Qu'est-ce que tu ferais? **a** Marie-Claire is imagining what she would do if she won the jackpot. **b** A large appartment in Paris and a house on the Mediterranean. **c** Because she loves Paris. **d** No, she would have all the time to herself. **e** Every morning. **f** She would go to the cinema, theatre, opera, fine restaurants. **g** All her family including Sarah **Exercise 2 1** J'aurais une grande maison en Bretagne, j'aurais un bateau, j'irais à la pêche et le soir je regarderais la télé. **2** Je ferais un voyage autour du monde. **Exercise 3 a** Three identical sums of money on the card and you win that amount **b** 2 € **c** you win 20 000–1 000 000 € on the wheel **Exercise 4 a** Wednesdays and Saturdays **b** 16,8 € **c** 33,6 € **d** 10 **e** 5 **f** 134,4 € **Exercise 5** Winning numbers: 35, 8, 15, 28, 13, 45, 11, 25; bonus number is 12 **3 Un peu de littérature a** She would go and meet her parents **b** In a hotel room at 41 Boulevard Ornano **c** Her journey **d** Nation. Simplon **e** One **f** A cinema **g** 1945 **h** A quest for the identity of people and their painful and enigmatic past **Web extension exercise:** la vue, l'ouïe, le toucher, l'odorat et le goût.

Unit 22

1 C'est le mien a Over a game **b** He left it at his grandmother's **c** Ariane's **d** Pierre **e** That it is his game **f** To go and sit down in the living-room and watch TV **g** Because she says she does not like animals **h** She kicks Pierre **i** Go to bed **Linked phrases: 1d 2f 3g 4h 5a 6b 7c 8e Exercise 1 a** Non ce n'est pas le mien. **b** Oui ce sont les miens. **c** Oui ce sont les miennes. **d** Non ce n'est pas le mien. **e** Oui ce sont les miennes. **f** Oui c'est le mien. **g** Non ce n'est pas la mienne. **Exercise 2** Q1: Ce sac est à vous? R1: Oui c'est le mien. Q2: Ce sont vos clefs? R2: Oui ce sont les miennes. Q3: C'est votre montre? R3: Oui c'est la mienne. Q4: Ce sont vos patins à roulettes? R4: Oui ce sont les miens. **2 On regarde la télé a** From Sunday **b** It might affect her return journey **c** Good, she can stay in Paris! **d** A film called *Ridicule* **e** *Mots-Croisés* **f** Because she is interested in politics **Linked phrases: 1f 2e 3d 4a 5b 6c**

À vous de choisir **a** Channel 5 (ARTE) at 20.45 **b** F2 at 20.55 **c** F2: 23.55/F3: 22.50/C+: 22.15 **d** F2: 22.35 **e** TF1: 22.55 **f** M6: 20.45 **g** Cable TV: 20.30 **h** If you had cable TV **i** *Mensuel* **j** 'Which school for our children?' **3 Le retour de Loft Story a** 13 **b** Bedrooms, dining rooms, sitting room, a gym and the « confessional » **c** the confessional **d** it is on the second floor and is used for individuals to address TV audience **e** 22 cameras and 55 microphones **f** use the gym **g** the filming of the competitors **h** 7000 **4 Que disent les journaux? 1** Will this strike snowball to the other towns in France? **2** 15 **3** in La Seine-Saint-Denis **4** Personal itineraries/programmes to motivate pupils and give a taste for life-long learning **5** The new initiatives, because changes have had to be made to the timetable. They object to French, Maths, History and Geography having to be cut by two hours a week. **6** They want an extra 6000 teachers for La Seine–Saint-Denis.

Unit 23
1 Moi, j'en ai ras-le-bol!

Saturday	Marie-Claire	Guillaume	Sarah	Ariane	Pierre
Morning	Housework Shopping	**Bercy Sports centre, playing tennis with his office friends**	**Housework and shopping**	**Housework and shopping**	**Housework and shopping**
Afternoon	**Having a rest at home**	Football match	Cinema	**Cinema**	**Cinema**
Evening	Cinema	**At home looking after the children**	**Cinema**	At home	**At home**

Linked phrases: 1d 2f 3e 4c 5a 6b Exercise 1 1d 2f 3g 4a 5h 6e 7b 8c Exercise 2 a Around 10 **b** Car rally, horse racing, rugby, running (marathon and 20 km), martial arts, tennis, football, waiters' races, cycling: Tour de France, vintage cars race **c** In June **d** From the Champs-Elysées to Bastille **e** On a Sunday during first two weeks of April **f** A 20 km run

Exercise 3 Est-ce que vous connaissez bien les deux meilleurs footballeurs français?

1. Prénom: Zinédine	1. Prénom: Thierry
2. Nom: Zidane	2. Nom: Henry
3. Nationalité: française	3. Nationalité: française
4. Date de naissance: 23 juin 1972	4. Date de naissance: 17 août 1977
5. Lieu de naissance: Marseille	5. Lieu de naissance: Paris
6. Taille: 1,85 m	6. Taille:1,88m
7. Poste: milieu de terrain	7. Poste: attaquant
8. Club avant la coupe du Monde: Real Madrid	8. Club avant la coupe du Monde: Arsenal FC
9. Nombres de selections: 108	9. Nombres de selections: 92
10. Nombres de buts: 31	10. Nombres de buts: 39 up to 2006

2 Aller au cinéma a when she is in London she gets more opportunities to go to the cinema than M-C. **b** *Paris je t'aime* has just come out on DVD and M-C will give a copy to Sarah for her birthday **c** *Hors de Prix* **Exercise 4 a** a Je voudrais voir *Paris je t'aime* parce que j'adore Paris. **b** j'aime beaucoup les films de Luc Besson. **c** c'est intéressant de voir un fil américains sur l'histoire de France **d** l'histoire, l'animation et la musique sont très belles. **Exercise 5 a** 40% discount **b** 5 issues for 17€ **c** cheque, postal order or credit card

Unit 24

1 Mettre le couvert a To help her lay the table **b** Her crockery and her glasses **c** The corkscrew **d** White wine **e Menu de Tante Eliane:** Melon, *Melon*, Truite au champagne et raisins, *Trout in Champagne with grapes*, Pommes de terre sautés, *Sauté potatoes*, Salade, *Salad*, Fromage, *Cheese*, Tarte aux pommes, *Apple Tart* Le **couvert a** un verre **b** une assiette **c** un couteau **d** une fourchette **e** une cuillère **f** la vaisselle **g** un tire-bouchon Linked phrases: **1d 2e 3f 4a 5c 6b 2 Une bonne recette** Ingredients: **1c 2e 3a 4f 5d 6b** Utensils: **7h 8g 9i 10j** Preparation of ingredients: **11k 12o 13m 14n 15l** What to do: **16p 17u 18r 19s 20v 21y 22q 23w 24x 25t 26z** Lisez la recette! **a** 6 to 8 **b** 45 minutes **c** Half a bottle **d** Heated **e** Once or twice during the cooking time **f** They need to be wrapped in aluminium paper **3 Des nouvelles de la famille a** In Japan **b** For Xmas **c** Yes **d** No, he is single **e** Her sister-in-law **f** Because her brother-in-law cannot go **g** 12 October, from Nantes **h** 21 October Linked phrases: **1d 2f 3b 4e 5c 6a Exercise 2 a** que, qui **b** que **c** que **d** que, qui **e** qui **f** qui **Exercise 3 a** Faux **b** Faux **c** Faux **d** Vrai **e** Vrai **f** Faux **g** Vrai **h** Faux **i** Vrai **j** Faux **Printing error:**

In the last sentence for Day 7 of the visit it refers to la **8e nuit** instead of **7e**. **Web extension exercises** – Recette pommes de terre farcies à la ricotta **1** Faux (ricotta) **2** F (9g of garlic) **3** F (2 pinches) **4** F (2 people) **5** Vrai (1h15 minutes of cooking) **Au Québec 1** Tadoussac **2** 4th centenary of Québec

Unit 25

1 Avant le départ a Because she is leaving **b** sad **c** No **d** Their mother **e** Because she too is going back to work tomorrow **f** Retire at 55 and buy a small house in the South of France **g** All buy a house together and renovate it **h** Not really **Linked phrases: 1e 2c 3d 4a 5b Exercise 1 1** S: J'adore la cuisine française R: Moi aussi **2** S: Je n'aime pas les voyages organisés R: Moi non plus **3** S: Nous aimons beaucoup la Bretagne R: Nous/moi aussi **4** S: Je n'aime pas la rentrée R: Moi non plus **5** S: Je déteste prendre l'avion R: Moi aussi **6** S: Je préfère rester chez moi R: Moi aussi **2 Chez le notaire a** Because they intend to buy a house **b** Whether there are any problems **c** An advert in a newspaper **d** No, not yet **e** Yes **f** Arrange a visit **g** The lawyer **h** Think about it **Linked phrases: 1e 2a 3f 4c 5b 6d Vrai ou faux? a** Vrai **b** Vrai **c** Faux **d** Vrai **e** Faux **f** Vrai **g** Vrai **h** Vrai **Exercise 2 a** 4A **b** 5A **c** 5V **d** 2V **e** 3A **f** 7A **g** 8A and 8V **h** 2A **Exercise 3 a** 6 and 7 **b** 8 **c** 12 **d** 5 10 13 **e** 2, 4, 13 **f** 2 (also 3, 9), **g** 2, **h** 6 **Exercise 4** C1: Je cherche une petite maison de pierres près de la côte. C2: Je cherche une maison de cinq chambres avec cave. C3: Je cherche une petite maison avec un jardin clos. C4: Je cherche une petite maison avec grenier aménageable **Exercise 5 a** 1 **b** 8 **c** 13 **d** 4 **e** 2

Unité de révision

1 Profiles 1 Nom: Burgess; Prénom: Sarah; Âge: 28 ans; Adresse: 12 Stella Avenue, Londres SW2; Numéro de téléphone: 020 8476 5656; Nationalité: britannique; Nationalité du père: britannique; Nationalité de la mère: française; Profession: éditrice, Lieu de travail: Hodder & Stoughton, Londres, Aime: les voyages, le cinéma, la lecture; N'aime pas: le sport à la télévision **2** Nom: Périer; Prénom: Dominique; Âge: 36 ans; Adresse: 5 Avenue de la Vieille Ville; St Nazaire; France; Numéro de téléphone: 02 40 45 1811; Nationalité: française, Nationalité du père: française; Nationalité de la mère: française; Profession: professeur de philosophie; Lieu de travail: lycée de St Nazaire; Aime: les chats, l'opéra, les musées d'art; N'aime pas: la télévision, les voitures

2 Une promenade à St Malo (1) from **c** to the station, (2) from **e** to the swimming pool, (3) from **d** to the cathedral, (4) from **a** to the castle

3 Orthographe des nombres vingt and cent only have **s** in the plural if they come at the end of the number e.g. deux cent**s,** quatre vingts, but deux cent trois, quatre-vingt-cinq

4 Grand jeu-concours 1 A trip to England for two **2** 14 September **3** The town and the tourist office.

5 Quelle attitude ! 1 They both use the verb vouloir *je veux* is the present tense and *je voudrais* is the conditional. **2** The difference shows 2 different attitudes *je veux* is likely to be perceived as impolite **3** To a)

6 Aujourd'hui c'est samedi Aujourd'hui les parents et les trois enfants vont au barrage de la Rance/Aujourd'hui toute la famille va au barrage de la Rance

7 La voiture idéale 1 6-d-m/o **2** 8-f-n **3** 5-a-j **4** 1-b-q **5** 9-g-l **6** 7-h-r **7** 2-c-m/o **8** 3-i-p **9** 4-e-k

8 Les jeunes et l'emploi 1 a Work experience **b** Administration and management **c** No **d** It was eight weeks of their holidays **e** It gave them their first contact with the world of work **2 1** Fast food and cafeteria: **c b d 2** Telephone marketing and opinion polls: **g a i 3** Leaflet distribution: **h f e**

9 Paris et le tourisme 1 V **2** F there is a night bus, **3** F children of 4 to 11 pay a reduced rate, **4** V **5** F the zones are 1 to 3 and 1 to 8 **6** V **7** F **8** F tickets are for 1, 2, 3 or 5 days

10 Les loisirs et vous 1A Oui: **b d h i k l** Non: **a c e f g j**

11 Encore une bonne recette a 25 minutes **b** 175 cl of water + 75 cl of juice **c** Thin slices **d** Half a teaspoon **e** Pear juice **f** One soup spoon **g** Garnish **h** The mixture **i** After the fruit mixture is cooked **j** Five minutes

Adjectives

Adjectives are used to provide more information about nouns. In English they can appear in front of a noun or they can stand on their own after a verb such as *to be/to look/to seem*:

The *new* school opens today.   It looks *good*.

In French, adjectives have the same function but their spelling is affected by the noun they are linked with. Also they stand either before or after the nouns and in some cases the meaning of the adjective changes slightly according to where it is placed. The two factors which affect the spelling of adjectives are the gender and number of the noun:

un **joli petit** village	*a **pretty little** village*
une **jolie petite** ville	*a **pretty little** town*

In French, *village* is masculine and *town* feminine. -e indicates the feminine form except if the adjective finishes with an -e in its generic form:

un quartier **tranquille**	*a **quiet** district*
une région **tranquille**	*a **quiet** area*

Adjectives linked to plural nouns tend to take an -s but in some cases (as for the feminine) there are more drastic changes. If there is already an -s at the end of the adjective, it does not change in the plural form:

J'aime un **bon** verre de cidre **frais** avec des moules bien **fraîches**.	*I like a **good** glass of fresh cider with very **fresh** mussels.*
J'aime une **bonne** bière bien **fraîche** avec des fruits de mer bien **frais**.	*I like a **good cool** beer with very **fresh** seafood.*

Examples of a few adjectives which change more drastically:

Quel beau château!	*What a **beautiful** castle!*
Quelle belle journée!	*What a **beautiful** day!*

Quels **beaux** enfants!	*What **beautiful** children!*
C'est le tarif **normal**.	*It's the **normal** price.*
Ce sont des gens **normaux**.	*They are **normal** people.*
Ils mènent une vie **normale**.	*They lead a **normal** life.*
Ce sont des attitudes tout à fait **normales**.	*These are perfectly **normal** attitudes.*

Possessive adjectives: For the full list of words such as **mon, ma, mes** *my,* **son, sa, ses,** *her/his,* **votre** *your,* see page 241.

Adverbs

Just as adjectives provide more information about nouns, so adverbs tend to provide more information about verbs or adjectives:

Il marche **vite**.	*He walks **fast**.*
Le voyage s'est **bien** passé.	*The journey went **well**.*
Ils ne sont **nullement** fatigués.	*They are **not at all** tired.*

For easy recognition of a large number of French adverbs you need to note the following pattern: adjective in feminine form + -**ment** (equivalent of -**ly** in English):

| **Heureusement** qu'il fait beau. | ***Luckily** the weather is good.* |
| Les gendarmes sont arrivés **rapidement**. | *The policemen arrived **rapidly**.* |

An adverb can also provide information about another adverb:

| Ils conduisent **trop vite**. | *They drive **too fast**.* |

Articles

The definite article

This term is given to *the* in English and to **la, le, l'** and **les** in French. **Le** is used in front of masculine nouns, **la** with feminine nouns, **l'** if a noun starts with a vowel or a mute **h; les** is used in front of nouns in the plural form:

À la naissance d'un enfant il faut déclarer **la** date, **le** lieu de naissance, **le** nom et **les** prénoms de l'enfant et **les** noms des parents.
*When a child is born you have to declare **the** date, **the** place of birth, **the** surname and first names of **the** child and **the** names of **the** parents.*

Auxiliary verbs

Auxiliary verbs are used as a support to the main verb, for example, I *am* working, you *are* working. Here *am* and *are* are used to support the verb *work*. By its very nature an auxiliary verb does not normally stand on its own, because it is the main verb which carries the meaning. *Working* gives us the information as to what activity is going on. **Avoir** *to have* and **être** *to be* are the main auxiliary verbs in the two languages and are mainly used to form past tenses. Others are **pouvoir** *can*, **venir de ...** *to have just ...*, also *to do* in English.

Est-ce que vous travaillez le samedi?	*Do you work on Saturdays?*
Je **viens de** voir un très bon film.	*I **have just** seen a very good film.*
J'**ai** perdu ma montre.	*I **have** lost my watch.*
Pourriez-vous m'indiquer la bonne route?	***Could** you show me the right way?*
Ils **sont** partis de bonne heure.	*They left early / They **have** left early.*

The indefinite article

This is the term given to the words *a* and *an* in English and to **un**, **une**, **des** in French:

Il y a **des** jours où **un** rien me donne **un** mal de tête ou **une** migraine.
*There are **some** days when nothing much can give me **a** headache or **a** migraine.*

Comparatives

When we make comparisons, we need the comparative form of the adjective. In English this usually means adding *-er* to the adjective or putting *more*, *less* or *as* in front of it. In French you add **plus**, **moins** or **aussi** in front of adjectives:

Tu es **plus** fort que moi.	*You are stronger than me.*

Il est **plus** intelligent que son frère et beaucoup **moins** beau. Mais ils ont **aussi** mauvais caractère.
*He is **more** intelligent than his brother and **less** good-looking but they are **just** as bad tempered.*

Conjunctions

Conjunctions are words such as *and* and *although*. They link words, or clauses or sentences:

Nous sommes allés à Paris **mais** nous n'avons pas vu la tour Eiffel.
*We went to Paris **but** we did not see the Eiffel Tower.*
Nous avons fait une promenade **bien qu'il** pleuve.
*We went for a walk **although** it was raining.*
Je vous téléphonerai plus tard **si** vous voulez.
*I'll call you later **if** you want.*

Gender

In English, grammatical gender is only used for male and female persons or animals, so for example we refer to a man as *he* and a woman as *she*. Objects of indeterminate sex are referred to as having *neuter* gender. So a table is referred to as *it*. In French all nouns have a gender which is either masculine or feminine and although the gender of the word is linked to the sex of the person or the animal in most cases, there are very few guide lines to help you guess whether other nouns are feminine or masculine.

Le vélo de Paul et la bicyclette de Pierre: both words mean *bike* although one is masculine and the other feminine. In this case it is likely that **bicyclette** is feminine because it ends with -ette and words ending with -ette are usually feminine words e.g **une fillette** *a little girl*. It is not normally so easy to rationalize the reason for the gender of words. It is important to remember that it is the word which is feminine or masculine, not the object it refers to.

Imperative

The imperative is the form of the verb used to give orders, commands or advice:

Viens ici!	***Come** here!* (order)
Roulez à droite.	***Drive** on the right.* (command)
Faites attention en traversant la rue.	***Be** careful when you cross the road.* (advice)
Écoutons les informations.	***Let's listen** to the news.*
Regarde la télé.	***Watch** TV.*
N'attrape pas froid!	***Don't catch** a cold!*

The imperative is used for notices everywhere to direct or guide our actions:

Poussez! *Push!*	**Tirez!** *Pull!*
Cochez les cases. *Tick the boxes.*	**Ralentissez!** *Slow down!*

Infinitive

The infinitive is the basic form of the verb. This is the form that you will find in the dictionary. In English the infinitive is usually accompanied by the word *to*, e.g. *to go, to play*.

In French the infinitive form of a verb is noticeable by its ending. There are three major groups of verbs: -er verbs (ending in -er: **chercher, regarder, manger**), -ir verbs (ending in -ir: **choisir, finir**) and -re and -oir verbs (ending in -re: **prendre, attendre** or -oir: **vouloir, pouvoir**).

Verbs are used in the infinitive in two particular types of circumstances:

> Je vais **acheter** du fromage.   I *am going* **to buy** some cheese.

A second verb is always in the infinitive, except when the first verb is **avoir** or **être**. A verb following a preposition such as **à, de, sans,** etc is always in the infinitive form.

> J'ai passé toute la journée   I *spent the whole day* **tidying**
>   **à ranger** mes placards   **up** *my cupboards.*

Nouns

Nouns are words like **maison** *house*, **pain** *bread*, **beauté** *beauty*. A useful test of a noun is whether you can put **le, la** or **les** *the* in front of it.

Object

The term object expresses the 'receiving end' relationship of a noun and a verb. So, for instance, **le facteur** *the postman* is said to be the object at the receiving end of the biting in the sentence:

> Le chien a mordu **le facteur.**   *The dog bit* **the postman.**
> J'ai donné **des fleurs à ma mère.** *I gave* **flowers** *to* **my mother.**

In this particular example **des fleurs** is referred to as the direct object because there is nothing between it and the verb, and **ma mère** is referred to as the indirect object because it is linked to the verb with a preposition (**à, de,** etc).

It is important to know whether a noun is a direct or indirect object when it comes to using a pronoun to replace the noun.

Some verbs don't need an object:

> Le chien a aboyé.   *The dog barked.*

Past participle

This is the name for the part of the verb which follows the auxiliary verbs **avoir** and **être** in the perfect and pluperfect tenses. Verbs ending with -**er** in the infinitive tend to have a past participle ending with -**é**. Other endings for past participles are -**i** for most -**ir** verbs, -**u** for most -**oir** verbs and -**is** for most -**re** verbs:

> J'ai **regardé** la télé. (**regarder**, *to watch*)
> Yannick a **fini** son travail. (**finir**, *to finish*)
> Les garçons ont **voulu** partir en Angleterre. (**vouloir**, *to want*)
> Ariane a **mis** le couvert. (**mettre**, *to put / to set the table*)

Prepositions

Words like **à** *at*, **avec** *with*, **de** *of the*, **dans** *in*, **chez** *at someone's house*, **pour** *for*, **sans** *without*, **sous** *under*, **sur** *on* are called prepositions. Prepositions often tell us about positions or relationships. They are normally followed by a noun or pronoun:

Ton livre est **sur** la table.	*Your book is **on** the table.*
Il a laissé son parapluie **dans** le train.	*He left his umbrella **in** the train.*
Voici un cadeau **pour** toi.	*This present is **for** you.*
Elle est sortie **avec** son copain.	*She went out **with** her boyfriend.*

Present participle

The part of a French verb which is often equivalent to *-ing* in English:

Ils sifflent en **travaillant**.	*They whistle while **working**.*
En **réfléchissant** bien…	***Thinking** about it…*
La chance **aidant** il a réussi son examen.	*With **the help of** luck he has passed his exam.*

Pronouns

Pronouns fulfil a similar function to nouns and often stand in the place of nouns which have already been mentioned:

La **maison** a plus de 200 ans.	*The **house** is over 200 years old.*
Elle est très belle.	***It** is very beautiful.*

(*House* is the noun and *it* is the pronoun.)

TABLE OF PRONOUNS

Subject pronouns	Reflexive pronouns	Direct object pronouns	Indirect object pronouns	Emphatic pronouns
je	me/m'	me/m'	me/m'	moi
tu	te/t'	te/t'	te/t'	toi
il	se/s'	le/l'	lui	lui
elle	se/s'	la/l'	lui	elle
on	se/s'			soi
nous	nous	nous	nous	nous
vous	vous	vous	vous	vous
ils	se/s'	les	leur	eux
elles	se/s'	les	leur	elles

For more explanations of pronouns, please refer to the following sections of the book: Unit 12 page 117 (emphatic pronouns), Unit 19 page 206 (indirect object pronouns), Unit 22 page 240 (possessive pronouns) and Unit 25 pages 277–8 (order of pronouns). For relative pronouns see **relative clauses**.

Reflexive verbs

When the subject and the object of a verb are one and the same, the verb is said to be reflexive:

Jean **se lève** à 6 heures.	*John **gets** (**himself**) **up** at 6 a.m.*
Je **me lave** bien.	*I wash **myself** thoroughly.*
Florence **s'est blessée**.	*Florence **hurt herself**.*

In French nearly all verbs can be reflexive if they are preceded by a reflexive pronoun:

Il a lavé sa chemise.	*He has washed his shirt.*
Il **s'est lavé** les mains.	*He **has washed his** (**own**) *hands.*
Je regarde la télé.	*I watch TV.*
Je **me regarde** dans le mirroir.	*I **look at myself** in the mirror.*

When reflexive verbs are used in the perfect tense, they are always used with **être**. But when the same verb is not in its reflexive form, it takes **avoir** in the perfect tense.

Hélène **a coupé** du bois.	*Helen cut some wood.*
Hélène **s'est coupé** la main avec la scie.	*Helen cut her hand with the saw.*
J'**ai vu** la télé.	*I saw the TV.*
Je **me suis vue** à la télé.	*I saw myself on TV.*

Relative clauses and relative pronouns

A relative pronoun such as **que** *which/that* or **qui** *who* can be used to provide more information about a noun which has just been mentioned. The resulting clause is called a relative clause:

Je connais la personne **qui habite** à côté de chez toi.
*I know the person **who lives next door to you**.*
La voiture **que je conduis** a presque dix ans.
*The car (**which**) **I drive** is nearly ten years old.*

(In French it is not possible to omit the relative pronoun **que**.) See page 259 for more about relative pronouns.

Subject

The term 'subject' expresses a relationship between a noun and a verb. The subject is the person or thing doing the action, as here for instance:

Le **chien** a mordu le facteur.   *The dog bit the postman.*

Because it is the dog that does the biting, the dog is said to be the subject of the verb **mordre** *to bite.*

Superlatives

The superlative is used for the most extreme version of a comparison:

Ce magasin est **le moins cher** de tous.
*This shop is **the cheapest** of all.*
C'est **la plus belle** femme du monde.
*She is **the most beautiful** woman in the world.*
Le champion du monde de Formule Un, c'est **le meilleur** pilote du monde.
*The Formula One champion is **the best** driver in the world.*

Tense

Most languages use changes in the verb form to indicate an aspect of time. These changes in the verb are referred to as 'tense', and the tense may be present, past or future. Tenses are often reinforced with expressions of time:

Past: Hier je suis allé à Londres. *Yesterday I went to London.*
Present: Aujourd'hui je reste à la maison. *Today I am staying at home.*
Future: Demain je prendrai l'avion pour Berlin. *Tomorrow I'll be flying to Berlin.*

The course introduces verbs in the present tense. This includes the subjunctive (see pages 190 and 207) – a verbal form referred to as a 'mood', mostly used in the present to express regrets, doubts and uncertainties. Several past tenses are used throughout the course: the perfect tense (pages 114, 168 and 219), the imperfect (page 177) and the pluperfect (page 242). The future tense also features in the course (page 101).

The conditional tense (pages 69 and 230) is used to indicate that if certain conditions were fulfilled something else would happen.

Verbs

Verbs often communicate actions, states and sensations. So, for instance, the verb **jouer** *to play* expresses an action, the verb **exister** *to exist* expresses a state and the verb **voir** *to see* expresses a sensation. A verb may also be defined by its role in the sentence or clause. It usually has a subject:

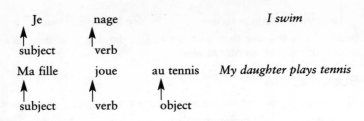

Irregular verbs

Life would be easier if all verbs behaved in a regular fashion. Unfortunately, all European languages have verbs which do not follow a set pattern and which are therefore commonly referred to as irregular verbs

There are 30 useful verbs in the verb table which follows. Most are irregular but, all the same, most can be used as a pattern for a few other verbs.

verb tables

Trente verbes utiles (*Thirty useful verbs*)

1 Four regular verbs (with subject pronouns: je, tu, il, elle, on, nous, vous, ils, elles)

Present indicative Présent de l'indicatif	Perfect Passé composé	Imperfect Imparfait	Conditional Conditionnel	Future Futur	Present subjunctive Présent du subjonctif	Imperative Impératif

Parler *to speak, to talk* Past participle: parlé Present participle: parlant

je parle	j'ai parlé	je parlais	je parlerais	je parlerai	(que) je parle	
tu parles	tu as parlé	tu parlais	tu parlerais	tu parleras	tu parles	parle
il/elle parle	il a parlé	il parlait	il parlerait	il parlera	il parle	
nous parlons	nous avons parlé	nous parlions	nous parlerions	nous parlerons	nous parlions	parlons
vous parlez	vous avez parlé	vous parliez	vous parleriez	vous parlerez	vous parliez	parlez
ils/elles parlent	ils ont parlé	ils parlaient	ils parleraient	ils parleront	ils parlent	

Remplir *to fill* Past participle: rempli Present participle: remplissant

je remplis	j'ai rempli	je remplissais	je remplirais	je remplirai	(que) je remplisse	
tu remplis	tu as rempli	tu remplissais	tu remplirais	tu rempliras	tu remplisses	remplis
il/elle remplit	il a rempli	il remplissait	il remplirait	il remplira	il remplisse	
nous remplissons	nous avons rempli	nous remplissions	nous remplirions	nous remplirons	nous remplissions	remplissions
vous remplissez	vous avez rempli	vous remplissiez	vous rempliriez	vous remplirez	vous remplissiez	remplissez
ils/elles remplissent	ils ont rempli	ils remplissaient	ils rempliraient	ils rempliront	ils remplissent	

Present indicative	Perfect	Imperfect	Conditional	Future	Present subjunctive	Imperative

Vendre *to sell* Past participle: **vendu** Present participle: **vendant**

Present indicative	Perfect	Imperfect	Conditional	Future	Present subjunctive	Imperative
je vends	j'ai vendu	je vendais	je vendrais	je vendrai	(que) je vende	
tu vends	tu as vendu	tu vendais	tu vendrais	tu vendras	tu vendes	vends
il/elle vend	il a vendu	il vendait	il vendrait	il vendra	il vende	
nous vendons	nous avons vendu	nous vendions	nous vendrions	nous vendrons	nous vendions	vendons
vous vendez	vous avez vendu	vous vendiez	vous vendriez	vous vendrez	vous vendiez	vendez
ils/elles vendent	ils ont vendu	ils vendaient	ils vendraient	ils vendront	ils vendent	

Se lever *to get up* Past participle: **levé** Present participle: **levant**. Note that there is an accent on the first e of **lever** when the following syllable has a neutral sound, e.g. je me **lève**, je me **lève**, je me **lèverai**

Present indicative	Perfect	Imperfect	Conditional	Future	Present subjunctive	Imperative
je me lève	je me suis levé(e)	je me levais	je me lèverais	je me lèverai	(que) je me lève	
tu te lèves	tu t'es levé(e)	tu te levais	tu te lèverais	tu te lèveras	tu te lèves	lève-toi
il/elle se lève	il(elle) s'est levé(e)	il se levait	il se lèverait	il se lèvera	il se lève	
nous nous levons	nous nous sommes levés(es)	nous nous levions	nous nous lèverions	nous nous lèverons	nous nous levions	levons-nous
vous vous levez	vous vous êtes levé(s)(es)(e)	vous vous leviez	vous vous lèveriez	vous vous lèverez	vous vous leviez	levez-vous
ils/elles se lèvent	ils se sont levés	ils se levaient	ils se lèveraient	ils se lèveront	ils se lèvent	
		elles se sont levées				

2 Twenty-six irregular verbs

Present indicative	Perfect	Imperfect	Conditional	Future	Present subjunctive	Imperative

Aller *to go* Past participle: **allé** Present participle: **allant**

Present indicative	Perfect	Imperfect	Conditional	Future	Present subjunctive	Imperative
je vais	suis allé(e)	allais	irais	irai	aille	
tu vas	es allé(e)	allais	irais	iras	ailles	va
il/elle va	est allé(e)	allait	irait	ira	aille	
nous allons	sommes allés(e)	allions	irions	irons	allions	allons
vous allez	êtes allé(e)(s) (es)	alliez	iriez	irez	alliez	allez
ils/elles vont	sont allés(es)	allaient	iraient	iront	aillent	

S'asseoir *to sit* assis – asseyant

Present indicative	Perfect	Imperfect	Conditional	Future	Present subjunctive	Imperative
je m'assieds	me suis assis(e)	m'asseyais	m'assiérais	m'assiérai	m'asseye	
tu t'assieds	t'es assis(e)	t'asseyais	t'assiérais	t'assiéras	t'asseyes	assieds-toi
il/elle s'assied	s'est assis(e)	s'asseyait	s'assiérait	s'assiéra	s'asseye	
nous nous asseyons	nous sommes assis(es)	nous asseyions	nous assiérions	nous assiérons	nous asseyions	asseyons-nous
vous vous asseyez	vous êtes assis (e)(es)	vous asseyiez	vous assiériez	vous assiérez	vous asseyiez	asseyez-vous
ils/elles s'asseyent	se sont assis(es)	s'asseyaient	s'assiéraient	s'assiéront	s'asseyent	

Present indicative	Perfect	Imperfect	Conditional	Future	Present subjunctive	Imperative

Avoir *to have*: eu – ayant

Present indicative	Perfect	Imperfect	Conditional	Future	Present subjunctive	Imperative
j'ai	ai eu	avais	aurais	aurai	aie	
tu as	as eu	avais	aurais	auras	aies	aie
il/elle a	a eu	avait	aurait	aura	ait	
nous avons	avons eu	avions	aurions	aurons	ayons	ayons
vous avez	avez eu	aviez	auriez	aurez	ayez	ayez
ils/elles ont	ont eu	avaient	auraient	auront	aient	

Boire *to drink*: bu – buvant

Present indicative	Perfect	Imperfect	Conditional	Future	Present subjunctive	Imperative
je bois	ai bu	buvais	boirais	boirai	boive	
tu bois	as bu	buvais	boirais	boiras	boives	bois
il/elle boit	a bu	buvait	boirait	boira	boive	
nous buvons	avons bu	buvions	boirions	boirons	buvions	buvons
vous buvez	avez bu	buviez	boiriez	boirez	buviez	buvez
ils/elles boivent	ont bu	buvaient	boiraient	boiront	boivent	

Commencer *to begin*: commencé – commençant (ç is necessary to keep the sound /s/ before a, o or u)

Present indicative	Perfect	Imperfect	Conditional	Future	Present subjunctive	Imperative
je commence	ai commencé	commençais	commencerais	commencerai	commence	
tu commences	as commencé	commençais	commencerais	commenceras	commences	commence
il/elle commence	a commencé	commençait	commencerait	commencera	commence	
nous commençons	avons commencé	commencions	commencerions	commencerons	commencions	commençons
vous commencez	avez commencé	commenciez	commenceriez	commencerez	commenciez	commencez
ils/elles commencent	ont commencé	commençaient	commenceraient	commenceront	commencent	

Conduire *to drive*: conduit – conduisant

Present indicative	Perfect	Imperfect	Conditional	Future	Present subjunctive	Imperative
je conduis	ai conduit	conduisais	conduirais	conduirai	conduise	
tu conduis	as conduit	conduisais	conduirais	conduiras	conduises	conduis
il/elle conduit	a conduit	conduisait	conduirait	conduira	conduise	
nous conduisons	avons conduit	conduisions	conduirions	conduirons	conduisions	conduisons
vous conduisez	avez conduit	conduisiez	conduiriez	conduirez	conduisiez	conduisez
ils/elles conduisent	ont conduit	conduisaient	conduiraient	conduiront	conduisent	

Present indicative	Perfect	Imperfect	Conditional	Future	Present subjunctive	Imperative

Connaître *to know:* connu – connaissant

je connais	ai connu	connaissais	connaîtrais	connaîtrai	connaisse	
tu connais	as connu	connaissais	connaîtrais	connaîtras	connaisses	connais
il/elle connaît	a connu	connaissait	connaîtrait	connaîtra	connaisse	
nous connaissons	avons connu	connaissions	connaîtrions	connaîtrons	connaissions	connaissons
vous connaissez	avez connu	connaissiez	connaîtriez	connaîtrez	connaissiez	connaissez
ils/elles connaissent	ont connu	connaissaient	connaîtraient	connaîtront	connaissent	

Croire *to believe:* cru – croyant

je crois	ai cru	croyais	croirais	croirai	croie	
tu crois	as cru	croyais	croirais	croiras	croies	crois
il/elle croit	a cru	croyait	croirait	croira	croie	
nous croyons	avons cru	croyions	croirions	croirons	croyions	croyons
vous croyez	avez cru	croyiez	croiriez	croirez	croyiez	croyez
ils/elles croient	ont cru	croyaient	croiraient	croiront	croient	

Devoir *to have to (I must):* dû – devant

je dois	ai dû	devais	devrais	devrai	doive	
tu dois	as dû	devais	devrais	devras	doives	dois
il/elle doit	a dû	devait	devrait	devra	doive	
nous devons	avons dû	devions	devrions	devrons	devions	devons
vous devez	avez dû	deviez	devriez	devrez	deviez	devez
ils/elles doivent	ont dû	devaient	devraient	devront	doivent	

Dire *to say:* dit – disant

je dis	ai dit	disais	dirais	dirai	dise	
tu dis	as dit	disais	dirais	diras	dises	dis
il/elle dit	a dit	disait	dirait	dira	dise	
nous disons	avons dit	disions	dirions	dirons	disions	disons
vous dites	avez dit	disiez	diriez	direz	disiez	dites
ils/elles disent	ont dit	disaient	diraient	diront	disent	

Entendre *to hear*: entendu – entendant

j'entends	ai entendu	entendais	entendrai	entendrais	entende	
tu entends	as entendu	entendais	entendras	entendrais	entendes	entends
il/elle entend	a entendu	entendait	entendra	entendrait	entende	
nous entendons	avons entendu	entendions	entendrons	entendrions	entendions	entendons
vous entendez	avez entendu	entendiez	entendrez	entendriez	entendiez	entendez
ils/elles entendent	ont entendu	entendaient	entendront	entendraient	entendent	

Envoyer *to send*: envoyé – envoyant

j'envoie	ai envoyé	envoyais	enverrai	enverrais	envoie	
tu envoies	as envoyé	envoyais	enverras	enverrais	envoies	envoie
il/elle envoie	a envoyé	envoyait	enverra	enverrait	envoie	
nous envoyons	avons envoyé	envoyions	enverrons	enverrions	envoyions	envoyons
vous envoyez	avez envoyé	envoyiez	enverrez	enverriez	envoyiez	envoyez
ils/elles envoient	ont envoyé	envoyaient	enverront	enverraient	envoient	

Être *to be*: été – étant

je suis	ai été	étais	serai	serais	sois	
tu es	as été	étais	seras	serais	sois	sois
il/elle est	a été	était	sera	serait	soit	
nous sommes	avons été	étions	serons	serions	soyons	soyons
vous êtes	avez été	étiez	serez	seriez	soyez	soyez
ils/elles sont	ont été	étaient	seront	seraient	soient	

Faire *to do, to make*: fait – faisant

je fais	ai fait	faisais	ferai	ferais	fasse	
tu fais	as fait	faisais	feras	ferais	fasses	fais
il/elle fait	a fait	faisait	fera	ferait	fasse	
nous faisons	avons fait	faisions	ferons	ferions	fassions	faisons
vous faites	avez fait	faisiez	ferez	feriez	fassiez	faites
ils/elles font	ont fait	faisaient	feront	feraient	fassent	

Falloir *to be necessary (impersonal only):* Past participle: **fallu** No present participle

Present indicative	Perfect	Imperfect	Conditional	Future	Present subjunctive	Imperative
il faut	il a fallu	il fallait	il faudrait	il faudra	(qu'il faille)	

Manger *to eat:* **mangé – mangeant** (e is added after the g in order to keep the soft sound before a, o and u)

Present indicative	Perfect	Imperfect	Conditional	Future	Present subjunctive	Imperative
je mange	ai mangé	mangeais	mangerais	mangerai	mange	
tu manges	as mangé	mangeais	mangerais	mangeras	manges	mange
il/elle mange	a mangé	mangeait	mangerait	mangera	mange	
nous mangeons	avons mangé	mangions	mangerions	mangerons	mangions	mangeons
vous mangez	avez mangé	mangiez	mangeriez	mangerez	mangiez	mangez
ils/elles mangent	ont mangé	mangeaient	mangeraient	mangeront	mangent	

Mettre *to put:* **mis – mettant**

Present indicative	Perfect	Imperfect	Conditional	Future	Present subjunctive	Imperative
je mets	ai mis	mettais	mettrais	mettrai	mette	
tu mets	as mis	mettais	mettrais	mettras	mettes	mets
il/elle met	a mis	mettait	mettrait	mettra	mette	
nous mettons	avons mis	mettions	mettrions	mettrons	mettions	mettons
vous mettez	avez mis	mettiez	mettriez	mettrez	mettiez	mettez
ils/elles mettent	ont mis	mettaient	mettraient	mettront	mettent	

Ouvrir *to open:* **ouvert – ouvrant**

Present indicative	Perfect	Imperfect	Conditional	Future	Present subjunctive	Imperative
j'ouvre	ai ouvert	ouvrais	ouvrirais	ouvrirai	ouvre	
tu ouvres	as ouvert	ouvrais	ouvrirais	ouvriras	ouvres	ouvre
il/elle ouvre	a ouvert	ouvrait	ouvrirait	ouvrira	ouvre	
nous ouvrons	avons ouvert	ouvrions	ouvririons	ouvrirons	ouvrions	ouvrons
vous ouvrez	avez ouvert	ouvriez	ouvririez	ouvrirez	ouvriez	ouvrez
ils/elles ouvrent	ont ouvert	ouvraient	ouvriraient	ouvriront	ouvrent	

Pleuvoir *to rain (impersonal only):* **plu – pleuvant**

il pleut	il a plu	il pleuvait	il pleuvrait	il pleuvra	(qu'il pleuve	

Pouvoir *to be able to (I can):* **pu – pouvant**

je peux	ai pu	pouvais	pourrais	pourrai	puisse	
tu peux	as pu	pouvais	pourrais	pourras	puisses	
il/elle peut	a pu	pouvait	pourrait	pourra	puisse	
nous pouvons	avons pu	pouvions	pourrions	pourrons	puissions	
vous pouvez	avez pu	pouviez	pourriez	pourrez	puissiez	
ils/elles peuvent	ont pu	pouvaient	pourraient	pourront	puissent	

Prendre *to take:* **pris – prenant**

je prends	ai pris	prenais	prendrais	prendrai	prenne	
tu prends	as pris	prenais	prendrais	prendras	prennes	prends
il/elle prend	a pris	prenait	prendrait	prendra	prenne	
nous prenons	avons pris	prenions	prendrions	prendrons	prenions	prenons
vous prenez	avez pris	preniez	prendriez	prendrez	preniez	prenez
ils/elles prennent	ont pris	prenaient	prendraient	prendront	prennent	

Savoir *to know:* **su – sachant**

je sais	ai su	savais	saurais	saurai	sache	
tu sais	as su	savais	saurais	sauras	saches	sache
il/elle sait	a su	savait	saurait	saura	sache	
nous savons	avons su	savions	saurions	saurons	sachions	sachons
vous savez	avez su	saviez	sauriez	saurez	sachiez	sachez
ils/elles savent	ont su	savaient	sauraient	sauront	sachent	

Present indicative	Perfect	Imperfect	Conditional	Future	Present subjunctive	Imperative

Sortir *to go out*: sorti – sortant

Present indicative	Perfect	Imperfect	Conditional	Future	Present subjunctive	Imperative
je sors	suis sorti(e)	sortais	sortirais	sortirai	sorte	
tu sors	es sorti(e)	sortais	sortirais	sortiras	sortes	sors
il/elle sort	est sorti(e)	sortait	sortirait	sortira	sorte	
nous sortons	sommes sortis(es)	sortions	sortirions	sortirons	sortions	sortons
vous sortez	êtes sorti(e)(s) (es)	sortiez	sortiriez	sortirez	sortiez	sortez
ils/elles sortent	sont sortis(es)	sortaient	sortiraient	sortiront	sortent	

Venir *to come*: venu – venant

Present indicative	Perfect	Imperfect	Conditional	Future	Present subjunctive	Imperative
je viens	suis venu(e)	venais	viendrais	viendrai	vienne	
tu viens	es venu(e)	venais	viendrais	viendras	viennes	viens
il/elle vient	est venu(e)	venait	viendrait	viendra	vienne	
nous venons	sommes venus(es)	venions	viendrions	viendrons	venions	venons
vous venez	êtes venu(e)(s) (es)	veniez	viendriez	viendrez	veniez	venez
ils/elles viennent	sont venus(es)	venaient	viendraient	viendront	viennent	

Voir *to see*: vu – voyant

Present indicative	Perfect	Imperfect	Conditional	Future	Present subjunctive	Imperative
je vois	ai vu	voyais	verrais	verrai	voie	
tu vois	as vu	voyais	verrais	verras	voies	voie
il/elle voit	a vu	voyait	verrait	verra	voie	
nous voyons	avons vu	voyions	verrions	verrons	voyions	voyons
vous voyez	avez vu	voyiez	verriez	verrez	voyiez	voyez
ils/elles voient	ont vu	voyaient	verraient	verront	voient	

Vouloir *to want*: voulu – voulant

Present indicative	Perfect	Imperfect	Conditional	Future	Present subjunctive	Imperative
je veux	ai voulu	voulais	voudrais	voudrai	veuille	
tu veux	as voulu	voulais	voudrais	voudras	veuilles	veuille
il/elle veut	a voulu	voulait	voudrait	voudra	veuille	
nous voulons	avons voulu	voulions	voudrions	voudrons	voulions	veuillons
vous voulez	avez voulu	vouliez	voudriez	voudrez	vouliez	veuillez
ils/elles veulent	ont voulu	voulaient	voudraient	voudront	veuillent	

French–English vocabulary

adj *adjective*
adv *adverb*
aux *auxiliary*
conj *conjunction*
dem pron *demonstrative pronoun*
excl *exclamation*
f *feminine*
gen *generally*
impers *impersonal*
inv *invariable*
m *masculine*
n *noun*
nf *feminine noun*
nm *masculine noun*
nmf *masculine and feminine noun*

phr *phrase*
pl *plural*
pp *past participle*
prep *preposition*
pron *pronoun*
qch *quelque chose* (something)
qn *quelqu'un* (somebody)
rel *relative*
sb *somebody*
sth *something*
usu *usually*
vi *intransitive verb*
vtr *transitive verb*
v refl *reflexive verb*
(v être) *takes être in perfect tense*

à *prep to; at; with*

abonné *nmf subscriber; season ticket holder*

abonnement *nm subscription; season ticket*

d'abord *phr first*

absolument *adv absolutely*

accident *nm accident; hitch; mishap*

accompagner *vtr to accompany, to go with*

accord *nm agreement;* **je suis d'~** *I agree*

accueil *nm welcome, reception; reception desk*

accueil *adj* **page d' –** *home page* (computer)

accueillant, -e *adj hospitable, welcoming*

accueillir *vtr to welcome; to receive; to greet*

acheter *vtr to buy*

acheteur, -euse *nmf buyer, purchaser*

acquéreur *nm buyer, purchaser*

acquérir *vtr to acquire; to purchase*

acquisition *nf purchase*

acteur, -trice *nmf actor/actress*

actif, -ive *adj active;* **la vie active** *working life*

activité *nf activity*

actuel, -elle *adj present, current*

addition *nf bill*

adieu *goodbye, farewell*

adorer *vtr to adore*

adresse *nf address*

s'adresser a qn *v refl (+ v être) to speak to sb*

aéroport *nm airport*

affiche *nf poster*

agaçant, -e *adj annoying, irritating*

âge *nm age*

agence *nf agency;* **~ immobilière** *estate agents*

agglomération *nf town; (smaller) village*

agir *to act;* **s'agir de** *v impers* de quoi s'agit-il? *what is it about?; what's the matter?*

agréable *adj nice, pleasant*

aider *vtr to help*

ail, *pl* ~s *or* **aulx** *nm garlic*

ailleurs *adv elsewhere* **d'ailleurs** *phr besides*

aimable *adj pleasant; kind; polite*

aimer *vtr to love; to like, to be fond of*

ainsi *adv thus*

ajouter *vtr to add (à to)*

alcool *nm alcohol*

alentour *adv* la ville et la région ~ *the town and surrounding area*

alimentation *food;* magasin d' ~ *food shop, grocery store*

Allemagne *nf Germany*

allemand, ~e *adj German; nm (lang) German*

aller *v aux* je vais apprendre l'italien *I'm going to learn Italian vi* comment ça va? *how are you? to go;* **s'en aller** *v refl (+ v être) to go, to leave*

allumer *vtr to light*

alors *adv then*

améliorer *vtr* **s'améliorer** *refl (+ v être) to improve*

aménagement *nm development*

aménager *vtr to convert; to do up [house, attic]*

amener *vtr to accompany, to bring sb*

américain *adj American*

ami, -e *nmf friend*

amitié *nf friendship*

amusant, ~ e *adj entertaining; funny*

amuser *vtr to entertain;* **s'amuser** *v refl (+ v être) to have fun, to play;* pour s'~ *for fun*

an *nm year*

ancien, -ienne *adj old*

anglais, ~e *adj English*

Anglais, ~e *nmf Englishman/Englishwoman*

Angleterre *nf England*

animal, ~e, *mpl* -aux *animal*

animateur, -trice *coordinator*

animer *vtr to lead*

année *nf year*

anniversaire *nm birthday*

ANPE *nf (abbr =* **Agence nationale**

pour l'emploi) *French national employment agency*

août *nm August*

apercevoir *vtr to make out; to catch sight of*

apéritif *nm drink*

à-peu-près *nm inv approximation*

appareil *nm appliance; telephone;* ~ photo *camera*

appartement *nm flat*

appeler *vtr to call*

s'appeler *v refl (+ v être)* comment t'appelles-tu? *what's your name?*

appétit *nm appetite*

apprendre *vtr to learn*

apprenti ~e *nmf apprentice*

apprentissage *nm apprenticeship*

après *adv afterward(s), after; later*

après-midi *nm/nf inv afternoon*

argent *nm money; silver*

arrêter *vtr to stop*

arrière *adj inv back*

arriver *(+ v être) vi to arrive*

arrondissement *nm administrative division*

s'asseoir *v refl (+ v être) to sit down*

assez *adv enough*

attendre *vtr to wait for*

au *prep (=* à le) *see* à

auberge *nf inn;* ~ de jeunesse *youth hostel*

aujourd'hui *adv today*

aussi *adv too, as well, also*

aussitôt *adv immediately*

auteur *nm author*

autocar *nm coach*

automne *nm autumn*

autoroute *nf motorway*

autour de *phr around*

autre *other*

avant *adv before*

avant-hier *adv the day before yesterday*

avec *prep with*

avenir *nm future*

averse *nf shower (rain)*

avion *nm plane*

avis *nm inv opinion*

avocat *nm lawyer*

avoir *vtr to have*

avril *nm April*

bagage *nm piece of luggage*

baguette *nf French stick*

bain *nm bath*

balcon *nm balcony*
banlieue *nf suburbs*
bar-tabac *nm café (selling stamps and cigarettes)*
bas, basse *adj low*
bateau *nm boat, ship*
bâtonnier *nm president of the Bar*
bavarder *vi to talk to, to chatter*
beau, belle *adj beautiful; handsome; good; fine*
beaucoup *adv a lot*
beau-frère *nm brother-in-law*
Belgique *nf Belgium*
belle-mère *nf mother-in-law*
belle-soeur *nf sister-in-law*
besoin *nm need* avoir ~ de *to need*
bête *adj stupid, silly*
beur *nmf second-generation North African (living in France) (slang)*
beurre *nm butter*
bibliothèque *nf library*
bicyclette *nf bicycle*
bien *adj inv good; adv well*
bien que *phr although*
bière *nf beer*
bijou *nm piece of jewellery*
bilan *nm outcome, result*
bilingue *adj bilingual*
blanc, blanché *adj white*
blessé, ~e *nmf injured or wounded man/woman*
blessure *nf injury*
bleu ~e *adj blue*
bois *nm inv wood*
boisson *nf drink*
boîte *nf box; tin*
bon, bonne *adj good*
bonne-maman *nf grandma*
bord *nm* le ~ de la mer *the seaside*
bouche *nf mouth*
bouche-à-oreille *nm inv* le ~ *word of mouth*
boucher, -ère *nmf butcher*
boucherie *nf butcher's shop*
bouchon *nm cork*
bouillir *vi to boil*
boulanger, -ère *nmf baker*
boulangerie *nf bakery*
bout *nm end; tip*
briser *vtr to break*
brouillard *nm fog*
bruit *nm noise*
brûler *vtr to burn*
bureau *nm office*

ça *that; this*
caisse *nf cash desk*
carrefour *nm crossroads*
carte *nf card;* ~ à puce *smart card*
en tout cas *phr in any case*
case *nf box (on form)*
casserole *nf saucepan, pan*
cave *nf cellar*
céder *vtr* ~ le passage *to give way*
celui / celle / ceux / celles *pron the one(s)*
celui-ci / celle-ci / ceux-ci / celles-ci *this one; these*
celui-là *pron that one*
cent *adj a hundred*
chacun, -e *each*
chambre *nf bedroom; room*
champignon *nm mushroom*
change *nm exchange rate*
chaque *each, every*
charcuterie *nf pork butcher's*
se charger *v refl (+ v être)* se ~ de *to take responsibility for*
chat *nm cat*
château *nm castle*
chaud *adj hot*
chaussure *nf shoe*
chauvin ~e *adj chauvinistic*
cher, chère *adj dear*
chercher *vtr to look for*
cheveu *nm hair*
chèvre *nm goat('s cheese)*
chez *prep* ~ qn *at sb's place*
chien *nm dog*
chiffre *nm figure*
chinois, ~e *adj Chinese*
chômage *nm unemployment*
chose *nf thing*
chou *nm cabbage*
ciel *nm sky*
clos *adj closed*
cocher *tr to tick*
coffre *nm (of car) boot*
coin *nm corner*
collège *nm secondary school*
combien de *how many, how much*
comme *conj as*
comment *adv how*
comprendre *vtr to understand*
compter *vtr to count*
concours *nm inv competition*
conduire *vtr to drive*
conduite *nf (of vehicle) driving*
confiture *nf jam*
connaître *vtr to know*

conseil *nm advice*
contre *prep against*
convenu, -e *adj agreed*
copain, copine *nmf friend; boyfriend/girlfriend*
corps *nm inv body*
à côte *phr nearby*
se coucher *v refl (+ v être) to go to bed*
coup *blow;* donner un ~ de pied *to kick*
couper *vtr to cut;* se couper *to cut oneself*
couramment *adv fluently*
courir *vi to run*
courriel *nf e-mail*
court ~e *adj short*
couteau *nm knife*
coûter *vtr to cost*
couvert *adj [sky] overcast;* mettre le ~ *to lay the table*
crêpe *nf pancake*
crever *vtr puncture*
croire *vtr to believe*
cuillère *nf spoon*
cuillerée *nf spoonful*
cuire *vtr to cook*
cuisine *nf kitchen; cooking*

dans *prep in*
déboucher *vtr to uncork*
début *nm beginning; start*
découvrir *vtr to discover*
défense *nf '~ de fumer' 'no smoking'*
défi *nm challenge*
dehors *adv outside*
déjà *adv already*
déjeuner *vi to have lunch; nm lunch*
demain *adv tomorrow*
demander *vtr to ask for*
déménagement *nm moving house*
déménager *vtr to move (furniture)*
demeurer *to reside, to live*
demi, ~e *nmf half*
demi-heure *nf half an hour*
demi-tarif *adv half-price*
dent *nf tooth*
dentifrice *nm toothpaste*
dépanner *vtr to fix [car, machine]*
départ *nm departure*
déprimer *vtr to depress; vi to be depressed*
depuis *adv since*

dernier, -ière *adj last*
derrière *prep behind*
dès que *phr as soon as*
descendre *vtr (+ v avoir) to go down, to come down sth; vi to go down (+ v être)*
désolé *pp adj sorry*
dessous *adv underneath;* en dessous *phr underneath*
dessus *adv on top*
devant *prep in front of*
devenir *vi (+ v être) to become*
deviner *vtr to guess*
devoir *vaux to have to*
diététique *adj dietary; nf dietetics*
dingue *adj (person) crazy (slang)*
dire *vtr to say*
doigt *nm finger*
donc *conj so, therefore*
donner *vtr to give*
dormir *vi to sleep*
dos *nm inv back;* mal de ~ *backache*
douche *nf shower*
droit, -e *adj straight*
droite *nf right;* tourner à ~ *to turn right*
dur, -e *adj hard*
durée *nf length*

eau *nf water*
ébullition *nf boiling*
école *nf school*
écrire *vtr to write*
éditeur, -trice *nmf editor, publisher*
en effet *phr indeed*
église *nf church*
embouteillage *nm traffic jam*
embrasser *vtr to kiss*
embrumé, ~e *adj misty*
emmener *vtr to take*
emploi *nm job; employment*
employé, ~e *nmf employee*
emporter *vtr to take [object];* pizzas à *takeaway pizzas*
en *prep in; into*
encore *adv still; again*
endroit *nm place*
enfant *nmf child*
enfin *adv finally*
ennuyeux, -euse *adj boring*
enregistrer *vtr to check in (baggage)*
enseignant, -e *nmf teacher*
enseigner *vtr to teach*
ensoleillé *adj sunny*

ensuite *adv* then
entendre *vtr* to hear
entier, -ière *adj* whole
entre *prep* between
entrée *nf* entrance; starter
entrer *vi* to come in
envie *nf* avoir ~ de qch to feel like sth
envoyer *vtr* to send
épais, épaisse *adj* thick
épicerie *nf* grocer's (shop)
éplucher *vtr* to peel
époux *nm inv* husband
équilibre *nm* balance
équipage *nm* crew
équipe *nf* team
escalier *nm* staircase; stairs
Espagne *nf* Spain
espagnol, -e *adj* Spanish *nm* l' Spanish
espérer *vtr* to hope
essayer *vtr* to try
essence *nf* petrol
essuie-glace *nm* windscreen wiper
étage *nm* floor
été *nm* summer
étre *vi* (+ v avoir) to be
étudiant, -e *nmf* student
extrait *nm* (from book, film) extract

fabriquer *vtr* to make
en face de *phr* en ~ de l'église opposite the church, across from the church
facile *adj* easy
façon *nf* way; de toute ~ anyway
faim *nf* hunger avoir ~ to be hungry
faire *vtr* to make
faire-part *nm inv* announcement
faisable *adj* c'est ~ it can be done
au fait *phr* by the way
falloir *v impers* il faut qch/qn we need sth/sb
familial, -e *adj* (meal, life, firm) family
famille *nf* family
fatigant, ~e *adj* tiring
fatiguer *vtr* to make [sb/sth] tired
fauteuil *nm* armchair; roulant wheelchair
faux, fausse *adj* wrong
féliciter *vtr* to congratulate
femme *nf* woman

fenêtre *nf* window
fer *nm* iron; ~ à repasser iron
ferme *nf* farm, farmhouse
fermer *vtr* to close
fête *nf* public holiday; name-day
feu *nm* fire
février *nm* February
fille *nf* daughter; girl
fillette *nf* little girl
fils *nm inv* son
fin, fine *adj* fine; [slice, layer] thin
finir *vtr* to finish
fois *nf inv* (with numerals) une ~ once; deux ~ twice
fort, ~e *adj* strong
fou, folle *adj* mad
four *nm* oven
fourchette *nf* fork
frais, fraîche *adj* cool; cold; fresh
fraise *nf* strawberry
framboise *nf* raspberry
frère *nm* brother
frigo *nm* fridge
froid, -e *adj* cold
fromage *nm* cheese

gagner *vtr* to win
galette *nf* pancake
Galles *nf pl* le pays de ~ Wales
gamin, -e *nmf* kid
garçon *nm* boy
gâteau, pl -x *nm* cake
gauche *nf* left
genou, pl -x *nm* knee
genre *nm* sort, kind, type
gens *nm pl* people
gestion *nf* management
gîte *nm* shelter; ~ rural self-catering cottage
gonflé, -e *adj* inflated
gonfler *vtr* to inflate [tyre]
goût *nm* taste; palate
goûter *nm* snack
grand, -e *adj* [person, tree, tower] tall
grand-mère *nf* grandmother
grand-père *nm* grandfather
gras, grasse *adj* [substance] fatty
gratter *vtr* to scratch
gratuit, -e *adj* free
grave *adj* [problem, injury] serious
gris, -e *adj* grey
gros, grosse *adj* big, large; thick

habiller *vtr to dress;* **s'habiller** *v refl (+ v être) to get dressed*
habitation *nf house*
halle *nf covered market*
haricot *nm bean;* ~ **vert** *French bean*
haut, -e *adj high; tall*
hébergement *nm accommodation*
héberger *vtr to put [sb] up*
heure *nf hour;* l'~ **d'arrivée** *the arrival time;* ~**s d'ouverture** *opening times*
hier *adv yesterday*
histoire *nf history*
hiver *nm winter*
homme *nm man*
hors-d'oeuvre *nm inv starter*
humide *adj damp*

ici *adv here*
immatriculation *nf registration*
immeuble *nm building*
immobilier *nm* l'~ *property*
imprimerie *printing*
incendie *nm fire*
infirmier *nm male nurse*
infirmière *nf nurse*
information *nf* écouter les ~s *to listen to the news*
inquiet, -iète *adj anxious; worried.* **s'inquiéter** *v refl (+ v être) to worry*
interdit, -e *pp adj prohibited, forbidden*
intéresser *vtr to interest* ça ne m'intéresse pas *I'm not interested*
irlandais, -e *adj Irish nm Irish*
italien, -ienne *adj Italian nm Italian*

jamais *adv never*
jambe *nf leg*
jambon *nm ham*
jardin *nm garden*
jaune *adj yellow*
je (j' *before vowel or mute h*) *I*
jeu, *pl* -x *nm game*
jeu-concours *nm competition*
jeudi *nm Thursday*
jeune *adj young*
jeunesse *nf youth*
joli -e *adj (gen) nice; [face] pretty*
jouer *vtr to play*
jour *nm day*
journal, *pl* -aux *nm newspaper*
journée *nf day*

juillet *nm July*
jus *nm inv juice*
jusque-là *adv until then, up to here*
juste *adv right, just*
justement *adv precisely*

là *adv there; here*
là-bas *adv over there*
laisser *vtr to leave*
lait *nm milk*
lancer *vtr to throw*
large *adj broad; wide*
lavabo *nm washbasin, washbowl*
laver *vtr to wash* se laver *v refl (+ v être) to wash;* se ~ les mains *to wash one's hands*
le, la (l' *before vowel or mute h*), *pl* **les** *the*
lecture *nf reading*
léger, -ère *adj light*
lent, -e *adj slow*
lequel / laquelle / lesquels / lesquelles *adj who; which*
se lever *v refl (+ v être) to get up*
liaison *nf link*
librairie *nf bookshop*
libre-service *adj inv self-service*
lieu *nm place;* au lieu de *phr instead of*
lire *vtr to read*
livre *nm book*
locataire *nmf tenant*
location *nf renting*
logement *nm accommodation*
loin *adv a long way,* c'est trop ~ *it's too far*
loisir *nm spare time; leisure*
Londres *n London*
longtemps *adv a long time*
louer *vtr [owner, landlord] to let; to rent out*
lourd, -e *adj heavy*
lumière *nf light*
lundi *nm Monday*
lune *nf moon*
lunettes *nf pl glasses;* ~ de soleil *sunglasses*
lycée *nm secondary school (school preparing students aged 15-18 for the Baccalauréat)*

madame, *pl* **mesdames** *Mrs; a woman whose name you do not know*

mademoiselle, *pl* **mesdemoiselles**
*Miss; a woman whose name you
do not know*

magnétophone *nm tape recorder*

magnétoscope *nm video recorder,
VCR*

maigre *adj* [person] *thin;* [cheese]
low-fat

main *nf hand*

mairie *nf town council*

mais *conj but*

maison *nf house; home*

mal *nm mpl* **maux** *adj inv wrong;
pain;* **avoir ~ partout** *to ache all
over;* **avoir ~ à la tête** *to have a
headache*

malade *adj* [person] *ill, sick*

malgré *prep in spite of, despite*

malheureusement *adv unfortunately*

Manche *nf the Channel;* **le tunnel
sous la ~** *the Channel tunnel*

manger *vtr to eat;* **il n'y a rien à ~
dans la maison** *there's no food in
the house*

manière *nf way;* **d'une ~ ou d'une
autre** *in one way or another*

manoir *nm manor (house)*

manquer *vtr to miss*

manquer de *v + prep to lack;* **on ne
manque de rien** *we don't want for
anything*

manteau, *pl* **-x** *nm coat*

marcher *vi to walk; to work;* **ma
radio marche mal** *my radio
doesn't work properly*

mardi *nm Tuesday*

marée *nf tide;* **à ~ haute/basse** *at
high/low tide*

marémoteur, -trice *adj tidal;* **usine
marémotrice** *tidal power station*

mari *nm husband*

marié, -e *pp adj married*

se marier *v refl* (+ *v* **être**) *to get
married* (**avec qn** *to sb*)

mars *nm inv March*

matin *nm morning*

mauvais, -e *adj bad*

mécanicien, -ienne *nmf mechanic*

Méditerranée *nf* **la (mer) ~** *the
Mediterranean*

meilleur, -e *adj better; best;* **le ~ des
deux** *the better of the two*

mélanger *vtr to mix*

même *adj same; adv even; phr* **agir**
or **faire de ~** *to do the same*

ménage *nm household; housework;*
faire le ~ *to do the cleaning*

mensuel, -elle *adj monthly; nm
monthly magazine*

menteur, -euse *nmf liar*

mentir *vi to lie, to tell lies*

mer *nf sea*

merci *nm thank you*

mercredi *nm Wednesday*

mère *nf mother*

météo *nf weather forecast*

métier *nm job; profession*

métro *nm underground*

mettre *vtr to put*

meuble *nm* **des ~s** *furniture*

meublé *nm furnished flat*

meubler *vtr to furnish*

miam-miam *excl yum-yum!*

micro-ondes *nm inv microwave*

midi *nm twelve o'clock, midday,
noon; lunchtime;* **le Midi** *the
South of France*

miel *nm honey*

**le mien, la mienne, les miens, les
miennes** *mine*

mieux *adj inv better;* **le ~, la ~, les
~** *the best*

milieu *nm middle;* **au ~ da la nuit**
in the middle of the night

mille *adj inv a thousand, one
thousand*

milliard *nm billion*

mince [person, leg] *slim, slender*

Minitel® *nm Minitel (terminal
linking phone users to a database)*

minuit *nm midnight*

mi-temps *nm inv part-time job;* **elle
travaille à ~** *she works part-time*

mobilier, -ière *adj* **biens ~s** *movable
property*

mobylette® *nf moped*

moi *I, me;* **c'est ~** *it's me*

moi-même *myself*

moins *minus;* **il est huit heures ~
dix** *it's ten (minutes) to eight; adv
(comparative) less*

à moins de *phr unless*

au moins *phr at least*

mois *nm inv month*

moitié *nf half;* **à ~ vide** *half empty*

môme *kid; brat (slang)*

mon, ma *pl* **mes** *my*

monde *nm world; people;* **tout le ~**
everybody

moniteur, -trice *nmf group leader*

monnaie *nf* currency; change
monsieur, *pl* **messieurs** *nm* Mr
montagne *nf* mountain
monter *vtr* (+ *v avoir*) to go up sth;
vi (+ *être*); tu es monté à pied? *did
you walk up?*
montrer *vtr* to show
mordre *vtr* to bite
morsure *nf* bite
mort *nf* death
mort, -e *adj* dead; je suis ~ de froid
I'm freezing to death
mot *nm* word
moule *nf* mussel
mourir *vi* (+ *v être*) to die
moyen, -enne *adj* [height, size]
medium; medium sized; [price]
moderate
municipal, ~e *adj* [council] local,
town
mur *nm* wall
musée *nm* museum; art gallery

nager *vtr* to swim
nageur, -euse *nmf* swimmer
naissance *nf* birth
naître *vi* (+ *v être*) to be born; elle
est née le 5 juin *she was born on
5 June*
naturellement *adv* naturally
né, -e *pp* see **naître**
nécessaire *adj* necessary
neige *nf* snow
neiger *v impers* to snow; il neige
it's snowing
n'est-ce pas *adv* c'est joli, ~? *it's
pretty, isn't it?*
net, nette *adj* [price, weight] net
nettoyage *nm* cleanup
neuf *nine*
neuf, neuve *adj* new
neveu, *pl* **-x** *nm* nephew
nez *nm* nose
ni *conj* nor, or
Noël *nm* Christmas; 'Joyeux ~'
Merry Christmas
noir *adj* black
nom *nm* name; ~ et prénom *full
name*
nombre *nm* number
nombreux, -euse *adj* numerous,
many
non *adv* no
nord *adj inv* north; northern
nord-africain, -e *adj* North African

nord-ouest *adj inv* northwest
notaire *nm* notary public
notre, *pl* **nos** *our*
nourriture *nf* food
nous *(subject)* we; *(object)* us
nous-même, *pl* **nous-mêmes**
ourselves
nouveau (**nouvel** *before vowel or
mute h*), **nouvelle** *adj* new
nouveau-né *adj* newborn
nuage *nm* cloud
nuageux, -euse *adj* [sky] cloudy
nuit *nf* night
nulle part *phr* nowhere
nullement *adv* not at all
numéro *nm* number ~ de téléphone
telephone number ~ d'abonné
customer's number; ~ d'appel
gratuit *freefone number*

obligatoire *compulsory; inevitable*
occupant, -e *occupant*
occupé, ~e [person, life] busy; [seat]
taken; [phone] engaged
s'occuper *v refl* (+ *v être*) s'~ de *to
see to, to take care of* [dinner,
tickets]
oeil, *pl* **yeux** *nm* eye
offre *nf* offer; répondre à une ~
d'emploi *to reply to a job
advertisement*
oignon *nm* onion
oiseau, *pl* **-x** *nm* bird
oncle *nm* uncle
onze *eleven*
orage *nm* storm
orageux, -euse *stormy; thundery*
ordinaire *adj* ordinary
ordinateur *nm* computer
oreille *nf* ear
oreiller *nm* pillow
organisateur, -trice *nmf* organizer
orthographe *nf* spelling
os *nm inv* bone
ou *conj* or
où *adv* where
oublier *vtr* to forget [name, date,
fact]
ouf *phew!*
oui *yes*
outil *nm* tool
ouvert, -e *adj* open
ouvrable *adj* [day] working; [hours]
business
ouvre-boîtes *nm inv* tin-opener

ouvrier, -ière *nmf worker; workman*

ouvrir *vtr to open*

paiement *nm payment*

pain *nm bread*

pancarte *nf notice*

panier *nm basket*

panneau *nm sign;* ~ **indicateur** *signpost*

pantalon *nm trousers*

papeterie *nf stationer's (shop), stationery shop*

papier *nm paper*

Pâques *nm, nf pl Easter*

par *prop* **elle est arrivée** ~ **la droite** *she came from the right;* **régler** *or* **payer** ~ **carte de crédit** *to pay by credit card*

paradis *nm inv heaven; paradise*

paraître *vi to appear, to seem, to look*

parapluie *nm umbrella*

parc *nm park*

parce que *phr because*

pardon *nm forgiveness; pardon;* **je te demande** ~ *I'm sorry* ~ ! *sorry!*

pare-chocs *nm inv bumper*

pareil, -eille *adj similar*

paresse *nf laziness*

paresseux, -euse *adj lazy*

parfait, -e *adj perfect*

parfaitement *adv perfectly*

parfois *adv sometimes*

parier *vtr to bet*

parisien, -ienne *adj Parisian*

parler *vtr to speak*

parmi *prep among, amongst*

part *nf (of food) slice, helping*

partager *vtr to share*

partir *vi (+ v être) to leave*

partout *adv everywhere*

pas *adv* **je ne prends** ~ **de sucre** *I don't take sugar*

passager, -ère *nmf passenger*

passant, -e *nmf passer-by*

passer *vtr to cross; to go through*

patin *nm skate;* ~ **à roulettes** *roller skate*

pâtissier, -ière *nmf confectioner, pastry cook*

patron, -onne *nmf boss*

pauvre *adj poor*

payer *vtr to pay for*

pays *nm country*

péage *nm toll*

peau *nf skin*

pêche *nm peach;* **avoir la** ~ *to be feeling great*

pêcher *vtr to go fishing for*

peine *nf sorrow, grief;* **avoir de la** ~ *to feel sad or upset*

pellicule *nf film*

se pencher *v refl (+ v être) to lean*

pendant *prep for;* **je t'ai attendu** ~ **des heures** *I waited for you for hours*

penser *vtr to think*

Pentecôte *nf Whitsun*

perdre *vtr to lose*

père *nm father*

permettre *vtr* ~ **à qn de faire** *to allow sb to do*

permis *nm* ~ **de conduire** *driver's licence*

petit, -e *adj small, little; short*

petite-fille *nf granddaughter*

petit-fils *nm grandson*

petits-enfants *nm pl grandchildren*

peu *adv not much*

peut-être *adv perhaps, maybe*

phare *nm headlight*

pharmacie *nm chemist's (shop)*

pharmacien, -ienne *nmf (dispensing) chemist*

pièce *nf room*

pied *nm foot*

pierre *nf stone*

piéton, -onne *adj pedestrianized; nmf pedestrian*

piqûre *nf injection, shot; sting; bite*

placard *nm cupboard*

plage *nf beach*

plaisanter *vi to joke*

plan, *nm map; (in building) plan, map*

planche *nf* ~ **à voile** *windsurfing board*

plateau, *pl* -x *tray (de of)*

plein, -e *adj full*

pleurer *vi to cry*

pleuvoir *v impers to rain;* **il pleut** *it's raining*

pluie *nf rain*

la plupart *nf inv most*

plus *adv more;* **le** ~ *the most;* **de plus** *phr furthermore;* **une fois de** ~ *once more, once again*

plusieurs *adj several*

plutôt *adv rather; fairly*

pluvieux, -ieuse *adj wet, rainy*
pneu *nm tyre*
poids *nm inv weight*
poignée *nf ~ de main handshake*
point *nm ~ de suture (Med) stitch;
~ de vue point of view*
pointure *nf shoe size*
poire *nf pear*
pois *nm petit ~ (garden) pea*
poisson *nm fish*
poivre *nm pepper*
poivrer *vtr to add pepper to [sauce]*
poli, -e *adj polite*
pomme *nf apple; ~ de terre potato;
~s frites chips*
pompe *nf ~ à essence petrol pump*
pompier, -ière *nm fireman*
pont *nm bridge; deck*
populaire *adj working-class*
portail *nm gateway, portal
(computer)*
portefeuille *nm wallet*
porter *vtr to carry*
portugais *adj Portuguese nm
Portuguese*
poulet *nm chicken*
pour *prep to; ~ faire to do; in order
to do; for; le train ~ Paris the
train for Paris*
pourquoi *why*
pourtant *adv though*
pousser *vtr to push*
pouvoir *v aux to be able to; peux-
tu soulever cette boîte? can you
lift this box?*
pratique *adj practical; convenient*
pratiquer *vtr to play [tennis]; to
practise*
préavis *nm inv notice; déposer un
~ de grève to give notice of strike
action*
premier, -ière *adj; first*
prendre *vtr to take; je vais ~ du
poisson I'll have fish; aller ~ une
bière to go for a beer*
prénom *nm first name, forename*
près *adv close; à peu ~ vide phr
practically empty*
presque *adv almost, nearly*
prêt, -e *adj ready*
preuve *nf proof*
prévenir *vtr to tell; to warn*
prévision *nf forecasting; ~s
météorologiques weather forecast*

printemps *nm inv spring*
prix *nm inv price*
prochain, ~e *adj next*
proche *adj nearby*
produit *nm product*
professeur *nm (in school) teacher*
profil *nm profile*
se promener *v refl (+ v être) to go
for a walk/drive/ride*
promettre *vtr ~ qch à qn to
promise sb sth*
prononcer *vtr to pronounce*
propos *nm inv à ~, je... by the way,
I...*
propre *adj clean*
prouver *vtr to prove*
PTT *nf pl (abbr = Administration
des postes et télécommunications
et de la télédiffusion) French
postal and telecommunications
service*
puis *adv then*

quai *nm quay; of river bank*
quand *conj when*
quart *nm quarter*
quartier *nm area; district*
Québécois, -e *nmf Quebecois,
Quebecker*
quel, quelle *who; what; which*
quelque *some; a few; any;*
quelquefois *adv sometimes*
quelqu'un *someone, somebody;
anyone, anybody*
qui *who; whom*
quitter *vtr to leave [place, person,
road]*
quoi *what; à ~ penses-tu? what are
you thinking about?*
quotidien, -ienne *adj daily; nm
daily (paper)*

raccrocher *vtr to hang [sth] back
up ~ le combiné to put the
telephone down.*
raisin *nm grape*
raison *nf reason; ~ d'agir reason
for action*
ralentir *vtr, vi to slow down*
rallye *nm (car) rally*
ranger *vtr to put away; to tidy*
rapide *adj quick, rapid*
rapidement *adv quickly; fast*
se raser *v refl (+ v être) to shave*

rasoir nm ~ électrique *electric shaver*

rater vtr *to miss*

rayon nm *department*

recette nf ~ (de cuisine) *recipe*

recevoir vtr *to receive, to get*

reconnaître vtr *to recognize; to identify*

réfléchir à vtr + prep *to think about*

réfrigérateur nm *refrigerator*

regarder vtr *to look at [person, scene, landscape]*

régime nm *diet;* être au ~ *to be on a diet*

région nf *region; area;* le vin de la ~ *the local wine*

regretter vtr *o be sorry about, to regret*

rejoindre vtr *to meet up with*

remarquer vtr *to point out*

remercier *to thank* (de qch *for sth*)

remplir vtr *to fill (up) [container]; to fill in or out [form]*

rencontre nf *meeting; encounter*

rencontrer vtr *to meet [person]*

rendez-vous nm inv *appointment*

renseignement nm *information*

renseigner vtr ~ qn *to give information to sb*

rentrée nf *(general) return to work (after the slack period of the summer break, in France)*

réparer vtr *to repair, to mend, to fix*

repasser vtr *to iron*

répétitif, -ive adj *repetitive*

répondre vtr *to answer, to reply*

réponse vtr *answer, reply*

repos vtr *rest*

reposer vtr *to rest;* se reposer v refl (+ v être) *to have a rest, to rest*

réserver vtr *to reserve, to book [seat, ticket]*

respirer vtr *to breathe in [air];* vi *to breathe*

rester vi (+ v être) *to stay, to remain*

résultat nm *result*

retard nm *lateness;* un ~ de dix minutes *a ten-minute delay;* avoir de ~ *to be late*

retour nm *return;* (billet de) ~ *return ticket*

retraite nf *retirement*

se retrouver v refl (+ v être) *to meet (again);* on s'est retrouvé en famille *the family got together*

réunion nf *meeting*

réussir vtr *to achieve* ~ à un examen *to pass an exam*

rêve nm *dreaming; dream*

se réveiller v refl (+ v être) *to wake up*

revoir vtr *to see again*

au revoir phr *goodbye, bye*

rien *nothing;* se disputer pour un ~ *to quarrel over nothing*

rire vi *to laugh*

rond, -e adj *[object, table, hole] round*

rond-point nm *roundabout*

roue nf *wheel*

rouge adj *red*

route nf *road, highway*

routier nm *lorry driver*

sage adj *wise, sensible; good, well-behaved*

saison nf *season*

salade nf *lettuce; salad;* ~ verte *green salad*

salaire nm *salary; wages*

salle nf *room; hall;* ~ d'attente *waiting room;* ~ de bains *bathroom;* ~ de jeu(x) *(for children) playroom* ~ à manger *dining room;* ~ de séjour *living room*

sans adv *without*

santé nf *health;* à votre ~! *cheers!*

saucisse nf *sausage*

saucisson nm ~ à l'ail *garlic sausage*

sauf prep *except, but*

savoir vtr *to know [truth, answer]*

sécurité nf *security;* en toute ~ *in complete safety*

selon prep *according to*

semaine nf *week*

sens nm inv *direction, way*

sentinelle nf *sentry*

sentir vtr *to smell*

serveur, -euse nmf *waiter/waitress*

servir vtr *to serve;* qu'est-ce que je vous sers (à boire)? *what would you like to drink?*

se servir v refl (+ v être) *(at table) to help oneself*

seul, -e adj *alone, on one's own*

seulement adv *only*

si nm inv *if;* adv *yes; so* c'est un homme ~ agréable *he's such a pleasant man*

siffler *vtr to whistle [tune]*
sinon *otherwise, or else*
skier *vi to ski*
sœur *nf sister*
soif *nf thirst;* avoir ~ *to be thirsty*
soir *nm evening; night*
soirée *nf evening;* dans *or* pendant la ~ *in the evening*
en solde *phr* acheter une veste en ~ *to buy a jacket in a sale*
soldes *nm pl sales; sale*
sommaire *nm contents*
sommeil *nm sleep;* avoir ~ *to be or feel sleepy*
son, sa, *pl* **ses** *his/her/its*
sondage d'opinion *nm opinion poll*
sortir *vi (+ v* être*) to go out; to come out;* être sorti *to be out*
sous *prep under, underneath*
souvent *adv often*
stage *nm professional training; work experience*
studio *nm studio flat*
sud *adj inv south*
suffire *vi to be enough;* ça suffit (comme ça)! *that's enough!*
suivant, ~e *adj following; next;* le ~ *the following one; the next one*
sur *prep on;* ~ la table *on the table*
sympathique *adj nice; pleasant*
syndicat *nm trade union*

tabac *nm tobacco*
taille *nf size*
tant *adv (so) much*
tante *nf aunt*
tard *adv late;* plus ~ *later*
tarif *nm rate*
tarte *nf (food) tart;* ~ aux fraises *strawberry tart*
tasse *nf cup;* ~ à thé *teacup;* ~ de thé *cup of tea*
tel, telle *adj such;* je n'ai jamais rien vu de ~ *I've never seen anything like it*
télécopieur *nm fax machine, fax*
tellement *adv so*
temps *nm inv weather; time*
tenir *vtr to hold*
terrain *nm ground*
terrasse *nf terrace;* s'installer à la ~ d'un café *to sit at a table outside a café*
tête *nf head*
tien, tienne, le tien, la tienne, les

tiens, les tiennes *yours*
timbre *nm stamp*
tirer *vtr to pull*
toi *pron you*
toile *nm fabric, web (computer)* – d'araignée *spider's web*
tomber *vi (+ v* être*) to fall*
tonnerre *nm thunder*
tort *nm* avoir ~ *to be wrong*
tôt *adv [start] early*
toujours *adv always*
tourner *vtr to turn*
tout ~e *mpl* tous *fpl* toutes *everything; all; anything*
trafic *nm traffic*
tranquille *adj [person, life, street, day] quiet*
tranquillement *adv quietly*
travail *nm work;* chercher du/ un ~ *to look for work/a job*
travailler *vtr to work*
traverser *vtr to cross*
très *adv very*
triste *adj sad*
trop *adv too; too much*
trouver *vtr to find*
tutoyer *vtr to address [sb] using the 'tu' form*

université *nf university*
urgence *nf urgency;* le service des ~s, les ~s *the casualty department*
utile *adj useful*
utiliser *vtr to use*

vacances *nf pl holiday*
vache *adj mean, nasty (slang) nf cow*
vachement *adv really;* il a ~ maigri *he's lost a hell of a lot of weight*
valise *nf suitcase*
véhicule *nm vehicle*
vélo *nm bike;* ~ tout terrain, VTT *mountain bike*
vendeur, -euse *nmf shop assistant*
vendre *vtr to sell*
vendredi *nm Friday*
venir *v aux* venir de faire *to have just done;* elle vient de partir *she's just left; vi (+ v* être*) to come*
vent *nm wind*
vente *nf sale*
ventre *nm stomach;* avoir mal au ~ *to have stomach ache*
vérifier *vtr to check*
verre *nm glass*

vers *prep toward(s)*
vert, ~e *adj green*
vêtement *nm piece of clothing*
veuf, veuve *adj widowed*
viande *nf meat*
vide *adj empty*
vie *nf life*
vieux, vieille *adj old*
ville *nf town; city*
vin *nm wine*
virage *nm bend*
vite *adv quickly;* ~! *quick!*
vitesse *nf speed*
vivre *vi to live*
voici *prep here is, this is; here are*
voilà *prep here is, this is; here are*
voir *vtr to see*
voisin, ~e *nmf neighbour*
volant *nm steering wheel*
vomir *vtr to vomit*
votre, pl vos *your*
vôtre: mes biens sont ~s *all I have is yours*

vouloir *vtr to want*
vous *you*
vous-même *yourself*
vouvoyer *vtr to address [sb] using the 'vous' form*
voyage *nm trip; journey*
voyager *vi to travel*
voyageur, -euse *nmf passenger*
vrai, ~e *true; real, genuine*

y *it;* il ~ a *there is/are;* il ~ a du vin? il n'~ en a plus *wine? there's none left;* il n'~ a qu'à téléphoner *just phone*
yaourt *nm yoghurt*
yeux *nm pl see* oeil

zéro *nm zero, nought*
zone *nf zone, area;* ~ d'activités *business park*
zut *damn!*

a *adjective*
adv *adverb*
aux *auxiliary*
conj *conjunction*
excl *exclamation*
f *feminine*
i *intransitive*
m *masculine*
n *noun*

phr *phrase*
pl *plural*
prep *preposition*
pron *pronoun*
qch *quelque chose* (something)
rel *relative*
tr *transitive*
v *verb*

---

a, an *un, une;* **a man,** *un homme;*
an apple, *une pomme*
able *a. capable, compétent,*
habile
aboard *adv. à bord;* **to go a.,**
monter à bord
about *adv. & prep. autour (de);*
au sujet de; **while you are a. it,**
pendant que vous y êtes
above *adv. & prep. au dessus*
(de)
abroad *adv. à l'étranger*
accelerate *v.tr. accélérer*
accompany *v.tr. accompagner*
account *n. compte;* **my bank a.,**
mon compte en banque
accurate *a. exact, juste, précis*
ache *n. mal m, douleur f*
acquire *v.tr. acquérir*
across *adv. & prep. en travers*
(de), **to walk a. (a street),**
traverser (une rue)
acute *a.* 1. *aigu.* 2. *(douleur)*
aiguë
add *v.tr. ajouter*
address *n. adresse f*

adequate *a. suffisant*
admit *v.tr. admettre*
adventure *n. aventure f*
advice *n. conseil(s) m*
advise *v.tr. conseiller*
aerial *n. antenne f*
afford *v.tr. (usu. with can) avoir*
les moyens
afraid *a. effrayé;* **to be a.,** *avoir*
peur
Africa *l'Afrique f*
African *a. & n. africain, -aine*
after *adv. après;* **the day a.**
tomorrow, *après-demain*
again *de nouveau, encore;* **once**
a., *encore une fois*
against *prep. contre*
agenda *programme m (d'une*
réunion)
ago *adv.* **ten years a.,** *il y a dix*
ans
agree *v.i. & tr. consentir*
alas *excl. hélas!*
alcohol *n. alcool m*
alike *a. semblable, pareil*
alive *adj. vivant*

all *a., pron., & adv.* tout; **a. day,** (pendant) toute la journée; **a. men,** tous les hommes

allow (permit) permettre

alone *a.* seul

along *prep.* le long de; **to go a. a street,** suivre une rue

aloud *adv.* à haute voix

already *adv.* déjà

also *adv.* aussi

altogether *adv.* (wholly) entièrement, tout à fait; **how much a.?** combien en tout?

always *adv.* toujours

America l'Amérique f; **North, South, A.,** l'Amérique du Nord, du Sud

American *a. & n.* américain, -aine

amiable *a.* aimable

amid(st) *prep.* au milieu de; parmi

among(st) *prep.* parmi, entre

and *conj.* et

anger *n.* colère f

angry *a.* fâché, en colère

animator *n.* animateur, -trice (d'un groupe, d'un club)

anniversary *n.* anniversaire m

another *a. & pron.* encore; **a. cup of tea,** encore une tasse de thé; (a similar) une(e) autre, un(e) second(e)

answer *n.* 1. réponse; 2. solution f (d'un problème)

anxious *adj.* inquiet

anything *pron. & n.* quelque chose

anyway *adv. & conj.* en tout cas, de toute façon

anywhere *adv.* n'importe où

apartment appartement m

apple *n.* pomme f

apprentice *n.* apprenti, -ie

apricot *n.* abricot m

April *n.* avril m

area *n.* région f

arm *n.* bras m; **armchair,** *n.* fauteuil

around *adv.* autour, à l'entour

artichoke *n.* artichaut m

as *adv.* aussi, si; **you're as tall as I am,** as me, vous êtes aussi grand que moi

ash *n.* cendre(s); **ashtray** *n.* cendrier m

ask *v.tr. & i.* demander

asleep *adv. & a.* endormi

assault *v.tr.* attaquer; **to be assaulted,** être victime d'une agression

assist *v.tr.* aider

astonish *v.tr.* étonner

at **at table, at school,** à table, à l'école

attend **to a. a meeting** assister à une réunion

August *n.* août m

aunt *n.* tante f

autumn *n.* automne m

average *n.* moyenne f

avoid *v.tr.* éviter

awake *v.i.* s'éveiller, se réveiller

away *adv.* loin; au loin

back *n.* dos m

bad *a.* mauvais

bag *n.* sac m

baggage *n.* bagages mpl

bake *v.tr.* cuire, faire cuire (qch.)

ball *n.* balle f

bank *n.* banque f

bargain *n.* affaire f

barrister *n.* avocat m

basket *n.* panier m

be *v.i.* être

beach *n.* plage f

bean *n.* haricot m

beautiful *a.* beau, belle; magnifique

because *conj.* parce que

become *v.i.* devenir

bed *n.* lit m; **twin beds,** lits jumeaux; **double b.,** grand lit

bee *n.* abeille f

beef *n.* bœuf m

beer *n.* bière f

beetroot *n.* betterave f

before *adv.* avant; devant

begin *v.tr. & i.* commencer

behind *adv.* derrière

Belgian *a. & n.* belge (mf)

Belgium la Belgique

believe *v.tr.* croire

bell *n.* cloche f

belly *n.* ventre m

belong *v.i.* appartenir

below *adv.* en bas, (au-)dessous

belt *n.* ceinture f

bench *n.* banc m

bend   *n. (of road) virage m;* **bends for 3 miles,** *virages sur 5 kilomètres*
beneath   *adv. dessous, au-dessous, en bas*
best   *a. & n. (le) meilleur, (la) meilleure; le mieux*
better   *adj. meilleur*
between   *prep. entre*
beverage   *n. boisson f*
big   *a. (large) grand; (bulky) gros*
bill   *n. (in restaurant) addition f*
black   *a. noir*
blood   *n. sang m*
blue   *a. bleu*
boat   *n. bateau m*
body   *n. corps m*
boil   *v.i. bouillir*
bone   *n. os m*
book   *n. livre m*
boss   *n. patron, chef m*
bottle   *n. bouteille f*
box   *n. boîte f*
boy   *n. garçon m*
brake   *n. frein m;* **hand b.,** *frein à main*
bread   *n. pain m*
break   *v.i. casser*
breakfast   *n. (petit) déjeuner m*
Britain   **Great B.,** *la Grande-Bretagne*
British   *a. britannique*
Brittany   *la Bretagne*
broken   *a. cassé*
brother   *n. frère m*
brown   *a. brun; marron*
build   *v.tr. bâtir (une maison)*
burn   *v.tr. & i. brûler*
business   *n. affaire f*
busy   *a. affairé, occupé; actif*
but   *conj. mais*
butcher   *n. boucher m*
butter   *n. beurre m*
by   *prep. (near) (au)près de, à côté de*
bye(-bye)   *au revoir!*

cake   *n. gâteau m*
call   *v.tr. appeler*
can[1]   *n. boîte f (de conserves, de bière)*
can[2]   *v. aux. pouvoir*
car   *n. auto(mobile) f, voiture f; rail: voiture, wagon m*

card   *n. carte f*
carpet   *n. tapis m*
carry   *v.tr. porter*
cat   *n. chat*
chair   *n. chaise f*
Channel   *la Manche*
cheap   *a. bon marché*
child   *n. enfant mf*
China   *la Chine*
Christmas   *n. Noël m*
church   *n. église f*
clean   *a. propre, net*
clear   *a. clair*
clock   *n. (large) horloge f; (smaller) pendule f*
close   *v.tr. fermer*
clothes   *n.pl. vêtements mpl*
cloud   *n. nuage m*
code   **the Highway C.,** *le code de la route*
coffee   *n. café m*
coin   *n. pièce f de monnaie*
cold   *a. froid*
colour   *n. couleur f*
come   *v.i. venir, arriver*
computer   *n. ordinateur nm*
construct   *v.tr. construire; bâtir*
cook   *v.tr. (faire) cuire*
cool   *a. frais, f. fraîche*
cost   *v.i. coûter*
count   *v.tr. compter*
country   *n. pays m, région f*
crash   *(car) accident m*
cross   *v.tr. traverser (la rue)*
crowd   *n. foule f*
cry   *v.tr. pleurer*
cup   *n. tasse f;* **c. of tea,** *tasse de thé*
custom   *(bureaux de la) douane*
cut   *v.tr. couper*

dairy   **d. produce,** *produits laitiers mpl*
dark   *a. sombre, obscur*
day   *n. jour m*
dead   *a. mort;* **he's d.,** *il est mort*
dear   *a. cher*
death   *n. mort f*
deep   *a. profond*
Denmark   *le Danemark*
depart   *v.i. s'en aller, partir*
depth   *n. profondeur f*
die   *v.i. mourir*
dinner   *n. dîner m*

discover *v.tr.* découvrir, trouver
do *v. aux., v.i., v.tr.* faire
dog *n.* chien *m*
door *n.* porte *f*
down *adv.* en bas; **to go d.,** descendre
dozen *n.* douzaine *f*
dream *n.* rêve *m*
dress *n.* robe *f*
drive *n.* left-hand d., *conduite f à gauche; v.tr.* conduire (une auto)
drunk *a.* ivre
dry *a.* sec, *f.* sèche
duck *n.* canard *m*
duty *n.* devoir *m*

each *a.* chaque; **e. day,** chaque jour; tous les jours
ear *n.* oreille *f*
early *a.* de bonne heure
earth *n.* terre *f*; monde *m*
Easter *n.* Pâques *m*; **E. Day,** le jour de Pâques
easy *a.* facile
eat *v.tr.* manger
egg *n.* œuf *m*; boiled e., œuf à la coque
eight *huit (m)*; **to be e. (years old),** avoir huit ans
elbow *n.* coude *m*
eleven *onze (m)*
e-mail *n.* courriel *nm*
emergency *n.* cas urgent *m*
end *n.* fin *f*
engine *n.* moteur *m*
England *l'Angleterre f*; **in E.,** en Angleterre
English *a. & n.* anglais, -aise
enjoy *v.tr.* aimer, **to e. oneself,** s'amuser
enough *a.* assez
enter *v.i.* entrer
entrance *n.* entrée *f*
envelop *n.* enveloppe *f*
eve *n.* veille *f*; **Christmas E.,** la veille de Noël
even *adv.* même
evening *n.* soir *m*; soirée *f*
event *n.* événement *m*
ever *adv.* jamais
every *a.* chaque
except *prep.* excepté; sauf
exhaust e. pipe, *tuyau m d'échappement*
exit *n.* sortie *f*

expense *n.* dépense *f*; **expensive,** *a.* coûteux, cher; **to be e.,** coûter cher
explain *v.tr.* expliquer
eye *n.* œil *m*, *pl.* yeux; **to have blue eyes,** avoir les yeux bleus

fall *v.i.* tomber
false *a.* faux
family *n.* famille *f*
famous *a.* célèbre, renommé
far *adv.* (of place) loin
fare *n.* prix *m* du voyage, de la place
fast *a.* rapide; **vite,** not so f.! *pas si vite!* doucement
fasten *v.tr.* attacher
fat *a.* gros; gras
father *n.* père *m*
fault *n.* défaut *m*; imperfection *f*
fear *n.* peur *f*
February *n.* février *m*
feel *v.tr.* toucher
fetch *v.tr.* aller chercher
few *a.* peu de; **he has f. friends,** *il a peu d'amis*
field *n.* champ *m*
fill *v.tr.* remplir
find *v.tr.* trouver, rencontrer, découvrir
finger *n.* doigt *m*
finish *v.tr.* finir, terminer
fire *n.* feu *m*
first *a.* premier; **the f. of April,** le premier avril
fish *n.* poisson *m*
five *cinq (m)*
flag *n.* drapeau *m*
flat *a.* plat; horizontal; **f. roof,** *toit plat*
flight *n.* vol *m*
flower *n.* fleur *f*
flu *n.* grippe *f*
fly *v.i.* voler
fog *n.* brouillard *m*
follow *v.tr.* suivre
food *n.* nourriture *f*; aliments *mpl*
foot *n.* pied *m*
for *prep.* pour
forbid *v.tr.* défendre, interdire; **smoking forbidden,** *défense de fumer*
forget *v.tr.* oublier
fork *n.* fourchette *f*
fortnight *n.* quinzaine *f*; quinze jours *m*

forty *quarante (m)*
forward *adv. en avant*
four *quatre (m)*
free *a. & adv. libre;* is this table f.? *est-ce que cette table est libre?; gratuit*
French *a. français*
Friday *n. vendredi m*
fridge *n. réfrigérateur m*
friend *n. ami, f amie*
from *prep. de*
full *a. plein, rempli*
fun *n. amusement m*
furniture *n. meubles mpl*
further *davantage plus;* **furthermore** *adv. de plus*

gale *n. coup m de vent;* it's blowing a g., *le vent souffle en tempête*
game *n. jeu m*
garden *n. jardin m*
garlic *n. ail m*
gas *n. gaz m;* g. cooker, *cuisinière f à gaz*
gate *n. porte f (de ville); portail m*
genuine *a. authentique, véritable*
Germany *l'Allemagne*
get *v.tr. obtenir;* if I g. the time, *si j'ai le temps;* to g. dressed, *s'habiller*
gift *n. cadeau m*
girl *n.f. jeune fille;* little g., *petite fille*
give *v.tr. donner*
glad *a. heureux, content*
glass *n. verre m*
go *v.i. aller;* come and go, *aller et venir*
gold *n. or m*
good *a. bon*
grape *n. raisin m;* bunch of grapes, *grappe f de raisin*
grass *n. herbe f*
great *a. grand*
green *a. vert*
grey *adj. gris (m)*
grow *v.i. (of plant) pousser; (of pers.) grandir*
guess *v.tr. deviner*
guest *n. invité*

habit *n. habitude f,* to be in the h. of doing..., *avoir l'habitude de faire...*

hair *n. (of head) cheveu m;* to do one's h., *se coiffer*
half *n. moitié f*
ham *n. jambon m;* h. and eggs, *œufs au jambon*
hand *n. main f*
happen *v.i. arriver; se passer*
happy *a. heureux*
hat *n. chapeau m*
have *v.tr. avoir, posséder;* he has no friends, *il n'a pas d'amis*
he *pron. il*
head *n. tête f;* headache, *n. mal m de tête;* headlamp *n. phare f*
hear *v.tr. entendre*
heat *n. chaleur f*
heavy *a. lourd*
height *n. hauteur f*
hello *excl. bonjour!*
help *n. aide f, assistance f, secours m;* with the h. of a friend, *avec l'aide d'un ami*
her *pron. la, lui, elle; adj. son, sa, ses*
here *adv. ici*
hers *pron. le sien, la sienne, les sien(ne)s*
herself *pron. elle-même*
hide *v.tr. cacher*
high *a. haut*
him *pron. le, lui*
himself *pron. lui-même*
hire *v.tr. louer (une voiture)*
his *a. son, sa, ses; pron. le sien, la sienne, les sien(ne)s*
hit *v.tr. frapper*
holiday *n. fête f; jour m férié;* the holidays, *les vacances;* a month's h., *un mois de vacances f;* where did you spend your h.? *où avez-vous passé vos vacances?*
home *n. chez-soi m;* at h., *à la maison, chez soi*
home page *n. accueil nm*
honey *n. miel m*
hope *v.i. espérer*
horse *n. cheval, -aux m*
hot *a. chaud*
hour *n. heure f;* an h. and a half, *une heure et demie;* half an h., *une demi-heure*
house *n. maison f*
how *adv. comment*
however *adv. toutefois, cependant, pourtant*

huge *a. énorme*
hundred *cent (m)*
hunger *n. faim f;* to be hungry, *avoir faim*
hurry *v.tr. hâter, presser*
hurt *v.tr. blesser*
husband *n. mari m*

I *pron. je*
ice *n. glace f*
idea *n. idée f*
if *conj. si*
ill *a. mauvais; malade*
impede *v.tr. empêcher*
in *prep. en, à, dans;* in Europe, *en Europe;* in Japan, *au Japon;* in Paris, *à Paris;* in the country, *à la campagne*
include *v.tr. comprendre, renfermer;* we were six including our host, *nous étions six y compris notre hôte*
income *n. revenu m*
indeed *adv. en effet; vraiment*
India *l'Inde f*
indoor *n. intérieur m*
inside *n. dedans m; intérieur m*
instance *n. exemple m, cas m;* for i., *par exemple*
instead *prep. phr. au lieu de*
interview *n. entrevue f*
into *prep. dans, en;* to go i. a house, *entrer dans une maison*
iron *n. fer m*
island *n. île f*
it *pron. il, f. elle*
Italian *a. italien*
Italy *l'Italie f*
its *adj. son, sa, ses*
itself *pron. lui-même, elle-même*

jam *n. confiture f;* strawberry j., *confiture(s) de fraises*
jaw *n. mâchoire f*
jewel *n. bijou m*
job *n. tâche f; travail m*
joke *n. plaisanterie f, farce f*
juice *n. jus m*
July *n. juillet m*
June *n. juin m*

keep *v.tr. garder*
key *n. clef f, clé f*
kind *a. bon, aimable, bienveillant;* kindness *n. bonté f*

king *n. roi m*
kitchen *n. čuisine f*
knee *n. genou m*
knife *n. couteau m*
know *v.tr. & i. connaître*

lady *n. dame f;* ladies and gentlemen! *mesdames, mesdemoiselles, messieurs!*
lager *n. bière blonde f*
lake *n. lac m*
land *n. terre f;* by l. and sea, *sur terre et sur mer*
lane *n. route f; voie f;* four l. highway, *route à quatre voies*
large *a. grand; gros; fort;* to grow l., *larger, grossir, grandir*
last *a. dernier;* she was the l. to arrive, *elle arriva la dernière;* the l. but one, *l'avant-dernier*
late *a.* I am l., *je suis en retard*
laugh *n. rire m; v.i. rire*
launderette *n. laverie f automatique*
law *n. loi f*
lawn *n. pelouse f; gazon m*
lazy *a. paresseux*
lean *a. maigre*
learn *v.tr. apprendre*
leather *n. cuir m;* l. shoes, *chaussures f en cuir*
leave *v.tr. laisser;* to l. the door open, *laisser la porte ouverte; quitter*
left *a. gauche;* on the l. bank, *sur la rive gauche; adv.* turn l., *tournez à gauche*
leg *n. jambe f*
lemon *n. citron m*
length *n. longueur f*
less *n. moins m; adv.* l. known, *moins connu;* l. and l., *de moins en moins*
life *n. vie f;* it's a matter of l. and death, *c'est une question de vie ou de mort*
light[1] *n. lumière f;* traffic lights, *feux de circulation*
light[2] *a.* it is l., *il fait jour*
like[1] *a. semblable, pareil, tel;* l. father, l. son, *tel père, tel fils*
like[2] *v.tr. aimer;* I l. him, *je l'aime bien*
lip *n. lèvre f*
listen *v.i. écouter*

little   *a. petit*
live   *a. vivant; en vie*
lock   *n. serrure f*
loft   *n. grenier m*
look   *n. regard m; v.i. & tr.
regarder; to l. out of the window,
regarder par la fenêtre*
lose   *v.tr. perdre*
lot   *beaucoup*
love   *n. amour m*
low   *a. bas, basse; l. tide, marée
basse*
luck   *n. hasard m, chance f,
fortune f; good l., bonne chance*
luggage   *n. bagage(s) m(pl)*

mad   *a. fou*
mail   *n. courrier m; la poste*
main   *a. principal; premier,
essentiel*
make   *v.tr. faire; to m. a noise,
faire du bruit*
man   *n. homme m*
manner   *n. manière f, façon f*
manor   *n. m. (house), manoir m*
map   *n. carte f*
March   *n. mars m; in M., au mois
de mars*
market   *n. marché m*
marmalade   *n. confiture f d'oranges*
may[1]   *aux. might, I m. do it with
luck, avec de la chance je peux le
faire; he m. miss the train, il se
peut qu'il manque le train; m. I?
vous permettez?*
May[2]   *n. mai m; in M., en mai; au
mois de mai*
me   *pron. me, moi*
meal   *n. repas m*
mean   *v.tr. vouloir dire; signifier*
meat   *n. viande f*
medium   *n. milieu m; a. moyen*
meet   *v.tr. rencontrer*
memory   *n. mémoire f*
middle   *a. du milieu; m. size,
grandeur moyenne; the m.
class(es), la classe moyenne*
milk   *n. lait m*
mine   *pron. le mien, la mienne, les
mien(ne)s*
mislay   *v.tr. égarer (ses clefs, etc.)*
mispronounce   *v.tr. mal prononcer*
mist   *n. brume f*
mistake   *n. erreur f; faute f*

Monday   *n. lundi m*
money   *n. monnaie f; argent m*
month   *n. mois m*
moon   *n. lune f*
more   *a. plus; m. than ten men,
plus de dix hommes; some m.
bread, encore du pain*
Morocco   *le Maroc*
most   *a. le plus*
mother   *n. mère f*
moutain   *n. montagne f*
mouth   *n. bouche f*
move   *v.tr. déplacer; bouger*
much   *a. beaucoup; with m. care,
avec beaucoup de soin*
mum   *maman f*
must   *modal aux. you m. hurry up,
il faut vous dépêcher*
my   *adj. mon, f. ma, pl. mes*
myself   *pron. moi(-même)*

name   *n. nom m; full n., nom et
prénoms*
near   *adv. près, proche*
neck   *n. cou m*
need   *n. besoin m*
never   *adv. jamais*
new   *a. nouveau, nouvelle*
news   *n. nouvelle(s) f(pl); n.
(bulletin), informations fpl*
next   *a. prochain*
no   *non*
nobody   *pron. personne m*
noise   *n. bruit m*
none   *pron. aucun*
nor   *conj. (ne, ni...) ni; he has
neither father n. mother, il n'a ni
père ni mère*
Normandy   *la Normandie*
north   *n. nord m*
nose   *n. nez m*
not   *adv. pas*
nothing   *n. or pron. rien*
noun   *n. substantif m, nom m*
November   *n. novembre m*
now   *adv. maintenant*
nowhere   *adv. nulle part*
number   *n. nombre m; numéro m*
nurse   *n. infirmière f*

obvious   *a. évident, clair, manifeste*
occur   *v.i. (of event) avoir lieu;
arriver; se produire*
October   *n. octobre m*

of *prep. de*
office *n. bureau m*
oil *n. huile f;* olive o., *huile d'olive*
old *a. vieux; âgé*
on *prep. sur*
once *adv. une fois*
one *adj. & n. un*
only *a. seul, unique;* o. son, *fils unique; adv. seulement;* if o. I knew! *si seulement je le savais!*
open *a. ouvert*
opposite *a. en face*
other *a. autre;* the o. one, *l'autre;* the o. day, *l'autre jour*
our *poss.a. notre, pl. nos*
ours *pron. le/la nôtre, les nôtres*
ourselves *pron. nous-mêmes*
out *adv. dehors;* to go o., *sortir*
outside *n. extérieur m*
outskirts *n. banlieue f*
outward the o. voyage, *l'aller m*
oven *n. four m*
owe *v.tr. devoir*
own *v.tr. posséder*
oyster *n. huître f*

paint *n. peinture f*
pan *n. casserole f*
paper *n. papier m; journal m;* weekly p., *hebdomadaire m*
partner *n. associé, -ée; partenaire mf*
pay *v.tr. payer*
pea *n. pois m;* green peas, *petits pois*
peace *n. paix f*
pen *n. stylo m*
pencil *n. crayon m*
people *n. peuple m; habitants mpl (d'une ville)*
permit *v.tr. permettre*
petrol *n. essence f*
pig *n. porc m, cochon m*
pillow *n. oreiller m;* p.-case, s. taie *f d'oreiller*
pink *adj. & n. rose (m)*
plate *n. assiette f*
platform *quai m;* departure p., *(quai de) départ m;* arrival p., *(quai d')arrivée f*
play *n. jeu; v.i. jouer*
please (if you) p., *s'il vous plaît*
plum *n. prune f*
pool *n.* swimming p., *piscine f*

poor *a. pauvre*
pork *(viande f de) porc m*
portal *n. portail nm*
poultry *n. volaille f*
prepay *v.tr. payer d'avance*
present *n. cadeau m*
pretty *a. joli; beau*
prevent *v.tr. empêcher*
previous *a. préalable*
price *n. prix m*
pronounce *v.tr. prononcer*
property *n. propriété f*
proprietor *n. propriétaire mf*
proud *a. fier, orgueilleux*
pub *n. bistro(t) m*
pull *v.i. & tr. tirer*
punish *v.tr. punir*
pupil *n. élève mf*
push *v.tr. pousser*
put *v.tr. mettre*

quarrel *n. querelle f, dispute f*
quarter *n. quart m*
query *n. question f*
quick *a. rapide*
quiet *n. tranquillité f, repos m, calme m; a. tranquille, calme, silencieux;* b. q.! *taisez-vous!*
quite *adv. tout à fait; entièrement*

rabbit *n. lapin m*
rain *n. pluie f*
rather *adv. plutôt; un peu; assez;* r. pretty, *assez joli*
read *v.tr. lire;* to teach s.o. to r., *apprendre à lire à qn*
ready *a. prêt*
real *adj. vrai*
rebate *n. rabais m*
receipt *n. reçu m, quittance f*
receive *v.tr. recevoir*
recipe *recette f*
recover to r. one's health, *v.i. guérir*
red *a. & s. rouge (m)*
reduce *v.tr. réduire*
refrigerator *n. réfrigérateur m*
remain *v.i. rester*
remember *v.tr. se souvenir; se rappeler*
rent *n. loyer m; v.tr. (a)* (let) *louer (une maison); (b)* (hire) *louer, prendre en location (une maison)*
repair *n. réparation f*

reply *n. réponse f*
report *n. rapport m*
request *s. demande f, requête f*
rescue *n. sauvetage m*
resort seaside r. *station balnéaire, plage f*
respond *v.i. répondre*
rest *n. repos m*
return *n. retour m;* the r. to school, *la rentrée (des classes)*
reward *n. récompense f*
rice *n. riz m*
ride *n. promenade f (à cheval, à vélo)*
right *à droite*
river *n. fleuve m; rivière f*
road *n. route f*
roast *v.tr. rôtir, faire rôtir*
rob *v.tr. voler*
rock *n. rocher m*
roof *n. toit m, toiture f*
rope *n. corde f*
round *a. rond, circulaire*
run *v.i. courir*
Russia *la Russie*

safe *a.* s. and sound, *sain et sauf; sans danger*
sale *n. vente f*
salt *n. sel*
same *a. & pron. (le, la) même, (les) mêmes;* he's the s. age as myself, *il a le même âge que moi*
sand *n. sable m*
Saturday *n. samedi m;* he comes on Saturdays, *il vient le samedi*
sausage *n. saucisse f*
save *v.tr. sauver*
say *v.tr. dire*
school *n. école f*
Scot *n. Écossais, -aise;* she's a S., *c'est une Écossaise*
screen *n. écran m*
sea *n. mer f*
season *n. saison f*
seat *n. siège m*
see *v.tr. voir*
seem *v.i. sembler, paraître*
sell *v.tr. vendre*
send *v.tr. envoyer*
seven *a. & s. sept (m)*
shave to have a s., *se raser; v.tr. raser*
she *pron. elle*

sheet *n. drap m (de lit); feuille f (de papier)*
shoe *n. chaussure f;* I shouldn't like to be in his shoes, *je ne voudrais pas être à sa place*
shop *n. magasin m*
short *a. court*
show *n. spectacle m (de théâtre)*
shower *n. averse f;* to take a s., *prendre une douche*
shriek *n. cri m*
shy *a. timide*
sick *a. malade;* she's still s., *elle est toujours malade*
side *n. côté m*
sight *n. vue f*
silver *n. argent m;* s. spoon, *cuiller f d'argent*
similar *a. semblable, pareil*
since *adv. depuis*
single *a. seul, unique*
sink *n. évier m (de cuisine)*
sit *v.i. s'asseoir; être assis*
site *n. emplacement m*
size *n. dimension f; taille (de vêtements); pointure f (de chaussures)*
skin *n. peau f*
skirt *n. jupe f*
sleep *n. sommeil m*
slice *n. tranche f*
slow *a. lent*
small *a. petit*
smart *a. élégant, distingué, chic*
smell *n. odeur f; parfum m*
smile *n. sourire m*
smoke *n. fumée f*
snow *n. neige f*
so *adv. si, tellement; tant, aussi*
soap *s. savon m*
soft *a. doux;* s. voice, *voix douce*
solicitor *n. notaire m*
some *a. quelque*
somebody, someone *n. or pron. quelqu'un*
something *n. or pron. quelque chose m*
sometimes *adv. quelquefois, parfois*
somewhere *adv. quelque part*
son *n. fils m*
song *n. chant m; chanson f*
soon *av. bientôt, tôt*

sore *a. douloureux;* **to be s. all over,** *avoir mal partout*

sound *n. son m, bruit m;* **s. engineer,** *ingénieur m du son*

south *a. & n. sud (m)*

space *n. espace m, intervalle m*

Spain *l'Espagne f*

Spanish *a. espagnol*

spare **s. parts,** **s. spares,** *pièces f de rechange, pièces détachées*

speak *v.i. parler*

spectacle *n. pl. lunettes f*

speed *n. vitesse f*

spend *v.tr. dépenser*

spice *n. épice f*

spinach *n. épinards mpl*

spine *n. colonne vertébrale; dos m*

spoon *n. cuiller f, cuillère f*

spring *n. printemps m;* **in (the) s.,** *au printemps*

staff *n. personnel m;* **teaching s.,** *personnel enseignant*

stamp *n. timbre m*

stand *v.i. être debout*

star *n. étoile f*

starve **I'm starving,** *je meurs de faim*

state **the United States of America,** *les États-Unis d'Amérique*

station *n.* **service s.,** *station-service f;* **(railway) s.,** *gare f*

stay *n. séjour m; visite f*

steeple *n. clocher m*

step *n. pas m*

stomach *n. estomac m;* **s. ache,** *douleurs fpl d'estomac*

stop *n. arrêt m;* **bus s.,** *arrêt d'autobus*

storey *n. étage m (d'une maison)*

storm *n. orage m*

story *n. histoire f, récit m*

straight *a. droit;* **s. line,** *ligne droite*

strawberry *n. fraise f*

street *n. rue f*

strike *n. grève f*

strong *a. fort*

subscribe **to s. to a newspaper,** *s'abonner, prendre un abonnement, à un journal*

such *a. tel, pareil, semblable*

sudden *a. soudain, subit*

sugar *n. sucre m*

sum *n. somme f*

summer *n. été m*

sun *n. soleil m*

sure *a. sûr, certain*

surgeon *n. chirurgien, -ienne*

Sweden *la Suède;* **Swede,** *n. Suédois, -oise*

swim *v.i. & tr. nager*

switch *n. interrupteur m*

take *v.tr. prendre*

talk *v.i. parler;* **to learn to t.,** *apprendre à parler*

tall *a. grand*

tap *n. robinet;* **t. water,** *eau f du robinet*

taste *n. goût m*

tax *n. impôt m;* **income t.,** *impôt sur le revenu*

tea *n. thé m;* **t. bag,** *sachet m de thé*

teach *v.tr. enseigner*

team *n. équipe f*

tell *v.tr. dire;* **to t. the truth,** *dire la vérité*

ten *a. & s. dix (m)*

term *n. trimestre m*

than *conj. que*

thank *n.pl.* **thanks,** *remerciement(s) m*

that[1] *pron., pl.* **those;** *cela; ça;* **what's t.?** *qu'est-ce que c'est que ça?*

that[2] *rel. pron. (for subject) qui; (for object) que*

that[3] *conj. que*

the *le, la*

their *a. leur, pl. leurs*

theirs *pron. le/la leur, les leurs*

them *pron. les; eux*

themselves *pron. eux-mêmes*

then *adv. alors*

there *adv. là*

they *pron. ils, elles*

thick *a. épais; (of book)*

thief *n. voleur, -euse*

thin *a. mince*

thing *n. chose f*

think *v.tr. & i. penser, réfléchir*

third *adj. troisième*

thirst *n. soif f*

thirteen *a. & n. treize (m)*

thirty *a. & n. trente (m)*

this *pron. ceci; ce*

though *conj. quoique, bien que*

thought   n. pensée; idée f
thousand   a. & s. mille (m)
three   a. & s. trois (m)
throat   n. gorge f; to have a sore t., avoir mal à la gorge
through   prep. à travers
thunder   n. tonnerre m
Thursday   n. jeudi m
tide   n. marée f; high, low, t., marée haute, basse
till   prep. jusqu'à
time   n. temps m
tip   n. pourboire m
to   prep. à
together   adv. ensemble
toll   n. péage m
tomorrow   adv. & n. demain (m); t. night, demain soir
tonight   adv. & n. cette nuit; ce soir
too   adv. trop; t. much money, trop d'argent
tooth   n. dent f; toothache, n. mal m de dents
towel   n. serviette f (de toilette)
town   n. ville f
toy   n. jouet m
traffic   n. trafic m
travel   n. voyages mpl
tree   n. arbre m
trip   n. excursion f; voyage m
trousers   n.pl. pantalon m
true   a. vrai
truth   n. vérité f
try   v.tr. essayer; to t. a dish, goûter
twelve   a. & n. douze (m); t. o'clock, midi m, minuit m
twenty   a. & n. vingt (m)
twice   adv. deux fois
twin   a. & n. jumeau, jumelle
two   a. & n. deux (m)
tyre   n. pneu m

umbrella   n. parapluie m
uncork   v.tr. déboucher (une bouteille)
under   prep. sous; au-dessous de; to swim u. water, nager sous l'eau
undo   v.tr. défaire
unfair   a. (of pers.) injuste
unhappy   a. malheureux, triste
union   n. (trade) u., syndicat m
unknown   a. inconnu
unless   conj. à moins que

unpleasant   a. désagréable
untidy   a. (of room) en désordre
until   prep. jusqu'à
up   adv. vers le haut; to go up, monter
us   pron. nous
use   n. emploi m, usage m

vacuum   n. v. cleaner, aspirateur m
van   n. camionnette
vanilla   n. vanille f
vegetable   n. légume m
vehicle   n. véhicule m, voiture f
very   adv. très
view   n. vue f
voice   n. voix f

wage   n. salaire m, paie f
wait   v.i. attendre
wake   to w. (up), se réveiller
Wales   le Pays de Galles
walk   v.i. marcher
wall   n. mur m
wallet   n. portefeuille m
want   v.i. désirer, vouloir; he knows what he wants, il sait ce qu'il veut
war   n. guerre f
warm   a. chaud
wash   v.tr. laver; to w. oneself, se laver
watch   v.tr. observer; regarder; to w. television, regarder une émission de télévision
water   n. eau f
way   n. chemin m, route f
we   pron. nous
weak   a. faible
wear   v.tr. porter (un vêtement)
weather   n. temps m; in all weathers, par tous les temps
web   n. (computer) toile nf
Wednesday   n. mercredi m
week   n. semaine f
weep   v.i. pleurer
welcome   v.tr. souhaiter la bienvenue
well   adv. bien; to work w., bien travailler
Welsh   a. & s. gallois, du Pays de Galles
west   n. ouest m
wet   a. mouillé; humide
what   a. (rel.) (ce) que, (ce) qui

wheel   *n. roue f*

when   *adv. quand?* w. will you go?
   quand partirez-vous?

where   *adv. où?* w. am I? *où suis-je?*

which   *a. quel, f. quelle, pl. quels,
   quelles*

while   *conj. pendant que, tandis
   que*

white   *a. blanc, f. blanche*

who   *pron. qui*

whole   *a. entier; complet*

whom   *pron. qui? (rel.) que*

why   *adv. pourquoi?*

wide   *a. large*

wife   *n. femme f, épouse f*

win   *v.tr. & i. gagner; a.* w.
   number, *numéro gagnant*

wind   *n. vent m*

window   *n. fenêtre f*

wine   *n. vin m*

winner   *n. gagnant, -ante*

winter   *n. hiver m*

wish   *v.i. désirer, souhaiter*

with   *prep. avec*

within   *prep. à l'intérieur de*

without   *prep. sans*

woman   *n. femme f*

wood   *n. bois m*

wool   *n. laine f*

word   *n. mot m*

work   *n. travail, -aux m*

worry   *v.i. s'inquiéter*

worse   *a. & n. pire*

worst   *a. (le) pire*

wound   *n. blessure f*

wrong   *a. mauvais; faux, f. fausse*

Xmas   *n. Noël m*

year   *n. année f*

yellow   *a. jaune*

yes   *adv. oui*

yet   *adv. déjà; jusqu'ici;* not y., *pas
   encore*

you   *pron. tu, te, toi, vous*

young   *a. jeune*

your   *adj. ton, ta, votre; pl tes, vos*

yours   *pron. le/la tien(ne), le/la
   vôtre; pl les tien(ne)s, les vôtres*

yourself, yourselves   *pron. toi-
   même, vous-même(s)*

youth   *n. jeunesse f;* y. hostel,
   auberge f de la jeunesse

zip   *z.* fastener, *fermeture f éclair*

teach yourself

improve your french
jean-claude arragon

- Is your French rusty?
- Do you want to get up to speed quickly?
- Are you looking for more than the simplest way of expressing yourself?

Improve your French is an ideal way to extend your language skills. You will build on your existing knowledge and improve your spoken and written French so that you can communicate with confidence in a range of situations.

french conversation
jean-claude arragon

- Do you want to talk with confidence?
- Are you looking for basic conversation skills?
- Do you want to understand what people say to you?

French Conversation is a three-hour, all-audio course which you can use at any time, whether you want a quick refresher before a trip or whether you are a complete beginner. The 20 dialogues on CDs 1 and 2 will teach you the French you will need to speak and understand, without getting bogged down with grammar. CD 3, uniquely, teaches skills for listening and understanding. This is the perfect accompaniment to **Beginner's French** and **French** in the **Teach Yourself** range.